8TH EDITION

Post-Licensing Education for Florida Real Estate Sales Associates

Edward J. O'Donnell

136492

Dearborn™
Real Estate Education

This publication is designed to provide accurate and authoritative information in regard to the subject matter covered. It is sold with the understanding that the publisher is not engaged in rendering legal, accounting, or other professional advice. If legal advice or other expert assistance is required, the services of a competent professional should be sought.

President: Dr. Andrew Temte
Chief Learning Officer: Dr. Tim Smaby
Vice President, Real Estate Education: Asha Alsobrooks
Development Editor: Trude Irons

POST-LICENSING EDUCATION FOR FLORIDA REAL ESTATE SALES ASSOCIATES EIGHTH EDITION
© 2011 by Kaplan, Inc.
Published by DF Institute, Inc., d/b/a Dearborn™ Real Estate Education
332 Front St. S., Suite 501
La Crosse, WI 54601
www.dearbornRE.com

Printed in the United States of America
First revision, July 2013
ISBN: 978-1-4277-2489-2 / 1-4277-2489-X
PPN: 1610-3008

CONTENTS

ACKNOWLEDGMENTS

The author is indebted to the many real estate professionals who have provided advice and the assistance necessary for the completion of this edition.

The author is indebted to other Dearborn authors identified in this book, to the publisher's professional staff, and especially to the editor of this edition, Trude Irons. Her suggestions and prodding were done in a most agreeable way and helped make this a better book.

I also would like to acknowledge those who reviewed previous editions of this book:

John Anderson, Mary Basler, Jack R. Bennett, Richard T. Fryer, John F. Phillips, Ph.D., Curtis H. Wild, Donald L. Ross, John L. Greer, James Sweetin, Mary E. Sweetin, Anthony L. Griffon, Ron Guiberson, Linda Crawford, Audrey Van Vliet, Ronald O. Boatright, Terrance M. Fitzpatrick, Lawrence D. Greer, Robert L. Hogue, Michael Rieder, Roger L. Satterfield, Donald E. Tennant, Audrey M. Conti, Valleri Crabtree, Deborah Diesing, and Andy Gray.

INTRODUCTION

Before their first license renewal, Florida real estate sales associates must complete the 45-hour post-licensing education course on subjects approved by the Florida Real Estate Commission. This book is approved by the Commission for use in meeting the post-licensing education requirement for sales associates.

This textbook will give new licensees the opportunity to build on the principles and practices learned in the prelicensing course and to present new, hands-on training in many important subject areas.

Because many licensees work in residential real estate, the topics covered in this course book focus primarily on that part of the real estate industry. Many of the principles and practices described in this book also apply to the commercial and investment sectors.

Learning objectives are listed at the beginning of each chapter to help the student focus on the most important points. Discussion questions are provided throughout each chapter to help the student acquire a more complete understanding of the material. A quiz has been included at the end of each chapter for additional review of the material.

The book is divided into five sections arranged in the logical sequence of real estate activities: law and planning, listing and marketing properties, selling real property, obtaining financing and closing the transaction, and working with investors.

Section I updates the licensee on the many complex and important laws that regulate the licensee's daily activities. A chapter on business planning helps the new licensee get organized.

Section II focuses on building a strong listing portfolio, including prospecting, pricing the property, making the listing presentation, and getting the listing agreement signed.

Section III shows the licensee how to work with buyers effectively, from the initial contact with a buyer to analyses of the buyer's needs and ability to purchase to showing the property. A detailed section on sales and option contracts is included, as well as a chapter on writing and presenting the offer.

Section IV concentrates on obtaining financing and closing the sale. The coverage starts with an evaluation of current lending practices and programs, and it continues with a step-by-step discussion of how a loan is processed after a contract is written. Another chapter gives the new practitioner a step-by-step guide to getting the contract to closing. The responsibilities of each cooperating sales associate are covered in detail. The section ends with complete coverage of closing statements.

Section V describes the economy and the process used to analyze real estate investments. The section also describes the field of property management.

We have attempted to make this text as thorough and practical as possible and included many features that we hope you find helpful.

**Forms
To Go**

A **Forms To Go** section is in Appendix B. Symbols such as the one on the left show you when a form is available there. The section has Florida Real Estate Commission (FREC) registration forms, brokerage relationship disclosures, and other forms you might find useful in your daily practice.

WEB LINK

@

Web links are indicated throughout the book with an icon like the one shown on the left, so you can use the Internet to find more resource material.

At the end of this book are six items of interest:

1. Appendix A: Resources, which lists books and articles appropriate for further study in each subject area;

2. Appendix B: Forms To Go, providing the student with useful forms for real estate practice;

3. Practice Final Exam of 100 multiple-choice questions similar to those in the end-of-course exam;

4. Glossary of key terms identified in the chapters, with definitions;

5. Index; and

6. Student Feedback Survey to be completed once the course has been taken.

While it is difficult to design one book to meet all of the needs of every real estate sales associate, it is the author's intention to provide a bridge from basic classroom knowledge to deeper understanding and practical hands-on experience in real estate.

Please complete the Student Feedback Survey with your specific reactions and suggestions once you have completed the course and submit it so that the author may continue to improve the book.

Edward J. O'Donnell

LAYING THE FOUNDATION FOR A SUCCESSFUL CAREER

Chapter 1 will familiarize licensees with the important license law changes relating to the broker's relationships with customers. It describes the disclosure forms that licensees must give to clients and customers with whom they work and lists the situations when the disclosure requirements do not apply.

State and federal laws that affect real estate are also described to help the licensee stay current on important laws such as property condition disclosure, federal income taxes, and lead-based paint disclosures.

Chapter 2 describes the important provisions of the Fair Housing Act and the Americans with Disabilities Act.

In Chapter 3, the student will learn the basics of developing a business plan, setting goals, and time management.

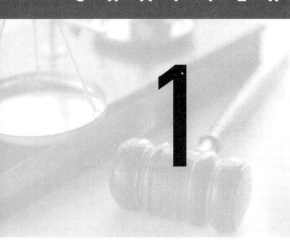

LEGAL ISSUES AND RISK MANAGEMENT

LEARNING OBJECTIVES

Upon completion of this chapter, you should be able to:

1. describe the required education for the first renewal and the required education for subsequent renewals;

2. differentiate between fraudulent misrepresentation and negligent misrepresentation;

3. list at least six questions that should be asked in a property condition disclosure form;

4. outline the differences between the duties of single agent brokers, transaction brokers, and brokers with no brokerage relationship;

5. distinguish between the terms *principal* and *customer*;

6. list the different disclosure forms a licensee must give to buyers and sellers of residential property and understand the uses of each; and

7. describe the legal requirements for including the personal name of a licensee in an advertisement.

OVERVIEW

Chapter 1 is intended to update new real estate licensees on laws and trends in the real estate industry so they can serve their customers professionally. This course must be completed before the first license renewal or before applying for a broker license. The first section of this chapter describes how to renew a real estate license. The second section is designed to help licensees avoid charges of misrepresentation. A discussion of brokerage relationships describes the duties and disclosures required of licensees in their dealings with customers. The final section of the chapter is a review and update of important laws. ■

THE REAL ESTATE LICENSE LAW

Students should be familiar with the Florida real estate license law and stay current on important changes to the law. This section covers license renewal and brokerage relationships.

RENEWING YOUR FLORIDA REAL ESTATE LICENSE

The Department of Business and Professional Regulation (DBPR) is required to send a renewal notice to the last known address of the licensee at least 60 days before the expiration date.

Licensees should send the renewal notice and a check to the Department before the renewal date or renew online with a credit card. The renewal request must be postmarked on or before the renewal date to avoid a $45 late renewal fee. The late fee does not apply to the first renewal, as the initial license will become void if not renewed by the renewal date.

> **In Practice**
>
> Licensees who do not receive a renewal notice should ensure that the Department has their current address on file. If not, they should send a change of address to the Department using Form DBPR 0080-1. Licensees may also use the Department's Web site at *www.myfloridalicense.com* to change address and to renew their license.

Required Education for Renewing the Initial License

The initial real estate license expires on the first of two dates after 18 months have elapsed following issue: March 31 or September 30.

A sales associate must successfully complete a 45-hour sales associate post-licensing course before the first renewal. A new broker must complete 60 hours of broker post-license education before the first renewal. If the licensee does not successfully complete the post-license requirement, the license becomes void. A sales associate wanting to continue in real estate would have to take the prelicense course again and pass the state exam. If a broker does not complete the required post-license course, the broker's license will become void. The broker may, however, take a 14-hour continuing education course and apply for sales associate status. If the licensee wishes to become a broker again, he must successfully complete the broker prelicense course and pass the state exam.

Students failing the post-licensing education end-of-course examination prescribed by the Florida Real Estate Commission (FREC) must wait at least 30 days from the date of the original examination and pass a different end-of-course examination. A student may retake the prescribed end-of-course examination only one time, and that exam must be taken within one year of the original end-of-course examination. Otherwise, students failing the Commission prescribed end-of-course examination must repeat the course before retaking a different form of the examination.

> **In Practice**
>
> Take your first exam more than 30 days before your renewal date. That way, if you fail, you can take the second exam before the expiration date. If you fail the exam and don't have 30 days before expiration, enroll in another course immediately. There's no limit to the number of times you can take the course. Save your license.

A licensee who has received a four-year degree in real estate from an accredited institution of higher education is exempt from the post-license education requirements.

Required Education for Subsequent Renewals

After the first renewal, the license will expire on the same date every two years. If a licensee fails to renew the license, the license will become *involuntary inactive*, and the licensee may not perform real estate services. After the first renewal, a licensee must complete an FREC-approved 14-hour continuing education course.

The DBPR will not renew a license until the required education course has been posted to the *MyFloridaLicense.com* database. Course providers must submit an electronic roster of course attendees to the department within 30 calendar days of the course completion date, within 10 business days beginning on the 30th day before the renewal deadline or prior to the renewal date, whichever occurs sooner.

AUTHORIZED BROKERAGE RELATIONSHIPS

A real estate licensee may work with potential buyers and sellers:

■ as a transaction broker (this relationship is presumed under state law unless the licensee enters into a different relationship with the customer);

■ as a single agent;

■ with no brokerage relationship; or

■ as a designated sales associate (but only in a nonresidential transaction).

Florida law prohibits **dual agency** because a licensee cannot be an advocate for both parties in a transaction.

If a single-agency relationship is established with a residential seller, all licensees in that brokerage firm have single-agent duties to that seller. It is not legal for another sales associate in the firm to represent a buyer when selling that property, nor can that sales associate be a transaction broker. It would, however, be legal for the sales associate to work with the buyer in a no-brokerage-relationship role.

If a broker has a single-agent relationship with a principal, the broker may change ("transition") to a transaction broker relationship. The licensee must make the appropriate disclosure of duties to the buyer or seller. The principal must give written consent before the change. A **customer** is not required to enter a brokerage relationship with any real estate licensee. [475.278(1)]

DISCLOSURE REQUIREMENTS FOR RESIDENTIAL PROPERTY TRANSACTIONS

A licensee in a residential sales transaction must give a brokerage relationship notice to potential buyers or sellers before or at the time of entering into a listing agreement or before the showing of property, whichever occurs first. A *residential sale* is defined as:

- property with four units or fewer,
- unimproved residential property intended for use of four units or fewer, or
- agricultural property of ten acres or fewer.

The three types of required residential brokerage notices include the following:

- No Brokerage Relationship Notice
- Single Agent Notice
- Consent to Transition to Transaction Broker Notice

Brokers must keep copies of the disclosure notices for all residential transactions that result in a written sales contract for at least five years.

Property Transactions That Do Not Require Disclosure Notices

A licensee need not give a brokerage relationship notice when:

- the licensee knows that a single agent or a transaction broker already represents the potential seller or buyer;
- an owner is selling new residential units built by the owner and the circumstances or the setting should reasonably inform the potential buyer that the owner's employee or single agent is acting on behalf of the owner, whether because of the location of the sales office or because of office signage or placards or identification badges worn by the owner's employee or single agent;
- selling nonresidential property;
- renting or leasing real property, unless the buyer has an option to purchase all or a portion of the property improved with four or fewer residential units;
- holding a bona fide open house or model home showing that does not involve eliciting confidential information, executing a contractual offer or an agreement for representation, or negotiating price, terms, or conditions of a potential sale;
- engaging in unanticipated casual conversations with a seller or buyer that do not involve eliciting confidential information, the execution of a contractual offer or agreement for representation, or negotiations concerning price, terms, or conditions of a potential sale;
- responding to general factual questions from a potential buyer or seller concerning properties that have been advertised for sale;
- the licensee's communications with a potential buyer or seller are limited to providing general factual information, oral or written, about the qualifications, background, and services of the licensee or the licensee's brokerage firm;
- auctioning, appraising, or disposing of any interest in business enterprises or business opportunities, except for property with four or fewer residential units.

TRANSACTION BROKER RELATIONSHIP

All licensees are presumed to be working as transaction brokers unless they have entered into another brokerage relationship with a customer. Because of this legal presumption, the licensee need not provide a brokerage relationship notice to the customer. A **transaction broker** provides limited representation to a buyer, a seller, or both in a real estate transaction, but does not represent either in a fiduciary capacity. The licensee "works for the contract" without being an advocate for either party. The customer is not responsible for the acts of the transaction broker.

Transaction Broker Duties

A transaction broker owes the following seven duties to the customer:

1. Dealing honestly and fairly.
2. Accounting for all funds.
3. Using skill, care, and diligence in the transaction.
4. Disclosing all known facts that materially affect the value of residential real property and are not readily observable to the buyer.
5. Presenting all offers and counteroffers in a timely manner, unless a party has previously directed the licensee otherwise in writing.
6. Limited confidentiality, unless waived in writing by a party. The transaction broker may *not* reveal to either party:
   - that the seller might accept a price less than the asking or list price,
   - that the buyer might pay a price greater than the price submitted in a written offer,
   - the motivation of any party for selling or buying property,
   - that a seller or buyer will agree to financing terms other than those offered, and
   - any other information requested by a party to remain confidential.
7. Any additional duties that are entered into by this or a separate agreement.

SINGLE AGENT RELATIONSHIP

Agency is a relationship created when one person, the **principal,** delegates to another, the **agent**, the right to act on his or her behalf in business transactions. A **single agent** represents either the buyer or seller, but not both, in a transaction. The principal relies on the single agent to give skilled and knowledgeable advice and to help negotiate the best terms in dealings with the customer. Because only single agency creates a **fiduciary relationship,** only single agents may call their customers *principals.* The principal is responsible for the acts of his single agent.

Single Agent Duties

A single agent owes the following nine specific duties to a buyer or seller:

1. Dealing honestly and fairly

2. Loyalty

3. Confidentiality

4. Obedience

5. Full disclosure

6. Accounting for all funds

7. Skill, care, and diligence in the transaction

8. Presenting all offers and counteroffers in a timely manner, unless a party has previously directed the licensee otherwise in writing

9. Disclosing all known facts that materially affect the value of residential real property and are not readily observable

Single Agent Notice

The Single Agent Notice must be given before, or at the time of, entering into a listing agreement or an agreement for representation or before the showing of property, whichever occurs first. It may be a separate and distinct disclosure document or part of another document, but it is most often made part of a listing agreement or a **buyer brokerage agreement.**

Forms To Go

The notice should be signed. If a principal who wants the single agent form of representation refuses to sign a Single Agent Notice, the licensee may still work as a single agent for that person but should note on the licensee's copy that the principal declined to sign. The Single Agent Notice is shown in Forms To Go, Appendix B.

Role of Sales Associates

Sales associates are agents of, and act for, the employing brokers. If a seller's broker has a listing, that broker and all the sales associates in that firm represent the seller.

Transitioning from Single Agent

When a single agent for one party begins working with the party on the other side of the transaction, the single agent must change to either have no brokerage relationship with the other party or transition to transaction broker. The agent may not disclose to the other party any confidential information learned while a single agent.

> **E X A M P L E :** As their single agent, Broker James listed the Smiths' house. Sally, a licensee in Broker James's office, is working as the single agent for a buyer, Mr. Farley. Mr. Farley becomes interested in the Smiths' house. Because the broker cannot represent both parties (dual agency), the broker obtains the informed written consent of both parties for him to transition to transaction broker status.

In Practice

When you're taking a listing, how do you answer a seller who wants you to remain a single agent throughout the transaction? Maybe you could explain that if you're not a transaction broker, it's unlikely that a buyer will buy the property through you and may decide to use another licensee for help. The other licensee may want to show him their listings first, and the buyer would be lost.

Consent to Transition to Transaction Broker Notice

Forms To Go

The **Consent to Transition to Transaction Broker Notice** allows a single agent to change his or her brokerage relationship to that of a transaction broker. The principal must sign this notice before the single agent becomes a transaction broker. The Consent to Transition to Transaction Broker Notice is shown in Forms To Go, Appendix B.

NO BROKERAGE RELATIONSHIP

A customer can choose not to be represented by a real estate broker. Licensees working with no brokerage relationship to the customer owe the following three duties:

1. Dealing honestly and fairly
2. Disclosing all known facts that materially affect the value of the residential real property that are not readily observable to the buyer
3. Accounting for all funds entrusted to the licensee

A single agent for one party in a transaction may decide to work with the other party as a nonrepresentative. If a broker does not have a brokerage relationship with a customer and is a single agent for the other party, the customer is at a disadvantage. It is the duty of the single agent to work diligently for his principal and to get the best price and terms for the principal.

Forms To Go

The duties of a licensee who has no brokerage relationship with a buyer or seller must be fully described and disclosed in writing to the buyer or seller. The **No Brokerage Relationship Notice** must be given to prospective buyers and sellers of residential property before showing a property. The notice need not be signed. The No Brokerage Relationship Notice is shown in Forms To Go, Appendix B.

DISCUSSION EXERCISE 1.1

Nonrepresentation. Broker Helen lists the Smiths' home as a single agent. Later, Helen shows it to Mr. Jones, a prospective buyer, and gives him a No Brokerage Relationship Notice.

While Helen is writing his offer for the property, Mr. Jones says, "I'll pay the asking price of $200,000 if I have to, but I would like to start the negotiations at $185,000."

When Helen presents the offer, she must tell the Smiths that Jones has said he will pay up to the listed price. Failure to make this disclosure would expose her to disciplinary action and civil liability for violation of her fiduciary duties.

THE DESIGNATED SALES ASSOCIATE

A broker may legally appoint one sales associate in the firm to act as the agent for the buyer (or lessee) and another sales associate in the firm to act as the agent for the seller (or lessor). This status may be used only in a nonresidential transaction. In this status, each **designated sales associate** is an advocate for the party he or she represents in the transaction and can actively help in the negotiations. The broker, however, must remain neutral. To meet the requirements of the law, buyers and sellers must have personal assets of at least $1 million, must sign disclosures that their assets meet the requirement, and must request this representation status. The licensees must give the parties a Designated Sales Associate Notice. The Designated Sales Associate Notice is shown in Forms To Go, Appendix B.

**Forms
To Go**

DISCUSSION EXERCISE 1.2

Designated Sales Associate. FatBurgers, Inc., is searching for five store locations in Pompano. It engages Mary Stevens of Pompano Commerce Realty as single agent because of her knowledge and expertise in the Pompano fast-food field. Jack Wilson, of the same firm, represents the seller of one of the potential sites.

Because FatBurgers, Inc., wants Mary to be its single agent, the broker appoints Mary as a single agent for FatBurgers, Inc., and Jack as single agent for the seller. Mary and Jack are now designated sales associates.

SELECTED LAWS REGULATING REAL ESTATE PRACTICE

In addition to Chapter 475, Florida Statutes, state and federal laws regulate the professional practices of real estate licensees, as well as the rights and duties of consumers. This section is intended to focus on those requirements. More information can be found using the Web links provided.

Florida Growth Management Act (Chapter 163 F.S.)

The Florida Growth Management Act requires that every city and county in Florida prepare a comprehensive plan of land use, together with controls that implement the plan. The comprehensive plan affects nearly every parcel of undeveloped land and many buildings that need renovation or enlargement. **Concurrency** is one of the significant requirements of the act. It requires that a minimum level of infrastructure be present before development can take place. **Infrastructure** includes such things as transportation systems, schools, and utilities.

Licensees must become knowledgeable about the comprehensive plans in their areas so that they can act competently with sellers and buyers. A licensee takes on substantial liability when representing that a site can be used for a specific purpose. Properties outside the urban services area are more difficult to subdivide, and the number of homes per acre is limited. This has affected the ability of licensees to market property for development. Most licensees, even after investigating the possible uses of an undeveloped commercial parcel, insert a land-use contingency clause into the contract for purchase. In this way, the buyer has the right to cancel the contract for property that cannot be used as represented.

Many cities and counties in Florida now require land-use disclosures before a purchaser signs a contract. These disclosures may cover items such as:

- restrictive covenants for the neighborhood;

- the buyer's responsibility to investigate whether the anticipated land use conforms to comprehensive plan, zoning, building codes, and so on; and

- whether streets and drainage are publicly maintained or are the homeowner's responsibility.

Homeowners' Association Disclosure (Chapter 689, F.S.)

Some homebuyers in Florida have been surprised shortly after the purchase when they discovered that they must pay dues to a **community association.** If owners must be members in a community association, the developers or owners of the parcel must disclose before a buyer signs a purchase contract:

- that the property owner must be a member of the community association,

- that recorded covenants govern the use and occupancy of the property,

- that the property owner is obligated to pay an assessment to the association and the failure to pay the assessment could result in a lien being placed on the property; or any land use or recreation fees and the amount of the obligation (not applicable to any condominium, cooperative, or time-share association).

Any contract or agreement for sale must refer to and incorporate the disclosure summary and shall include, in prominent language, a statement that the potential buyer should not sign the contract or agreement before having received and read the disclosure summary required by this section.

Each contract entered into for the sale of property governed by covenants subject to disclosure required by this section must contain in conspicuous type a clause that states the following:

IF THE DISCLOSURE SUMMARY REQUIRED BY SECTION 689.26, FLORIDA STATUTES, HAS NOT BEEN PROVIDED TO THE PROSPECTIVE PURCHASER BEFORE EXECUTING THIS CONTRACT FOR SALE, THIS CONTRACT IS VOIDABLE BY BUYER BY DELIVERING TO SELLER OR SELLER'S AGENT WRITTEN NOTICE OF THE BUYER'S INTENTION TO CANCEL WITHIN 3 DAYS AFTER RECEIPT OF THE DISCLOSURE SUMMARY OR PRIOR TO CLOSING, WHICHEVER OCCURS FIRST. ANY PURPORTED WAIVER OF THIS VOIDABILITY RIGHT HAS NO EFFECT. BUYER'S RIGHT TO VOID THIS CONTRACT SHALL TERMINATE AT CLOSING.

A contract that does not conform to the requirements of this subsection is voidable at the option of the purchaser within three days, or prior to closing, whichever comes first.

This section does not apply to any association regulated as Condominiums (Chapter 718), Cooperatives (Chapter 719), Vacation and Time-Sharing (Chapter 721), or Mobile Home Park Lots (Chapter 723), or to a subdivider registered under the Land Sales Act (Chapter 498). It also does not apply if disclosure regarding the association is otherwise made in connection with the requirements of those Chapters.

WEB LINK   Department of Community Affairs—Florida's Growth Management Legislation: *www.dca.state.fl.us/fdcp/ dcp/legislation/2007/sum.cfm*

Ad Valorem Tax Disclosure (Chapter 689, F.S.)

The Save Our Homes Amendment to the Florida Constitution limits the annual increases in the assessed value of a homestead property. The assessment can increase annually by 3 percent or the percentage of increase in the Consumer Price Index, whichever is less. When the property is sold, it is reassessed at full market value. Many buyers were shocked when their first tax bill was much higher than what the former owner paid.

Before the buyer signs a contract to purchase, Florida real estate licensees must give a property tax disclosure that includes the following wording:

PROPERTY TAX DISCLOSURE SUMMARY
    BUYER SHOULD NOT RELY ON THE SELLER'S CURRENT PROPERTY TAXES AS THE AMOUNT OF PROPERTY TAXES THAT THE BUYER MAY BE OBLIGATED TO PAY IN THE YEAR SUBSEQUENT TO PURCHASE. A CHANGE OF OWNERSHIP OR PROPERTY IMPROVEMENTS TRIGGERS REASSESSMENTS OF THE PROPERTY THAT COULD RESULT IN HIGHER PROPERTY TAXES. IF YOU HAVE ANY QUESTIONS CONCERNING VALUATION, CONTACT THE COUNTY PROPERTY APPRAISER'S OFFICE FOR INFORMATION.

Radon Gas Protection Act (Chapter 404.056, F.S.)

Some authorities say that **radon gas** is the second most common source of lung cancer in the United States. Radon is produced by uranium in the soil that decays and creates a gas. While radon gas is all around us, it is not usually a problem because of very low concentrations in the atmosphere. When uranium decays under a home, the gas seeps into the home through foundation cracks and plumbing lines. Improved building techniques and insulation intended to provide energy-efficient homes have the unintended side effect of trapping the gas inside the home.

Testing is the only way to learn if radon levels are a health hazard. The EPA recommends intervention if testing shows radon level at four *picocuries* per liter of air. This would be a concentration approximately ten times that of outdoor air. Exposure to radon inside the home can be reduced to an acceptable level by sealing foundation cracks and other openings.

The radon levels in a building can also be reduced by mitigation systems. Such systems use polyvinyl chloride (PVC) pipes installed through the slab with a fan that draws air from beneath the building and vents it above the roofline. Such systems may cost from $1,000 to $3,500. The electric cost for running the fan is only about five dollars per month.

The following wording must be on every sale contract and on every lease contract for more than 45 days:

RADON GAS: Radon is a naturally occurring radioactive gas that, when it has accumulated in a building in sufficient quantities, may present health risks to persons who are exposed to it over time. Levels of radon that exceed federal and state guidelines have been found in buildings in Florida. Additional information regarding radon and radon testing may be obtained from your county health department.

WEB LINK

A Citizen's Guide to Radon, 2nd ed. (U.S. EPA): *www.epa.gov/radon/pubs/citguide.html*

Federal Residential Lead-Based Paint Hazard Reduction Act

Because of the danger of neurological damage, the Residential Lead-Based Paint Hazard Reduction Act requires that disclosure be made to purchasers of residential buildings constructed before 1978. The law requires that the seller, landlord, or licensee provide the following before the contract is signed:

- A lead hazard information pamphlet
- Information about the presence of any known lead-based paint or lead-based paint hazard
- A ten-day period to conduct an inspection (does not apply to rentals)

Forms To Go

The lead warning statement shown in Forms To Go, Appendix B, must be attached to the contract.

Renovations and demolitions of properties built before 1978 can create lead dust and chips that would be harmful to children and adults. Because of this hazard, the Environmental Protection Agency (EPA) issued a rule to prevent lead contamination, effective April 22, 2010. The rule requires contractors who disturb paint in these properties to be certified and follow specific work practices. To become certified, a renovator must successfully complete an eight-hour training course offered by an accredited training provider. For more information, see the EPA's Lead Information Web site listed below.

WEB LINK

U.S. Department of Environmental Protection: National Lead Information Clearinghouse: *www.epa.gov/lead/*

U.S. Department of Housing and Urban Development: Office of Healthy Homes and Lead Hazard Control: *www.hud.gov/lea/leahome.html*

Comprehensive Environmental Response, Compensation, and Liability Act of 1980

The Comprehensive Environmental Response, Compensation, and Liability Act (CERCLA) of 1980 imposes substantial liability on owners of real property that has been contaminated with toxic or hazardous substances. The liability also extends to other parties in a transaction, such as attorneys, developers, lenders, and real estate brokers. The liability in the act is joint and several, which means that all present or former property owners may be forced to pay (joint) or only one owner may be required to pay (several).

A purchaser who wishes to avoid liability under the statute must do intensive research, usually in the form of an environmental audit. The audit is expensive and time-consuming. The statute allows the purchaser to defend against any later action by claiming **innocent purchaser status,** provided that the purchaser exercised due diligence to investigate the property. Licensees should be particularly careful when listing or selling sites such as former gas stations or dry cleaning establishments. Residential properties built on former farmland have been contaminated by pesticide use (e.g., Dioxin, DDT, etc.) or old farm gas tanks that have leaked. Other problem areas for residential licensees are old, leaking heating oil tanks buried in the ground.

WEB LINK

U.S. Environmental Protection Agency—CERCLA Overview: *www.epa.gov/superfund/*

The National Do Not Call Registry

In June 2003, the Federal Communications Commission (FCC), exercising its authority under the Telephone Consumer Protection Act (TCPA), established a National Do Not Call Registry. The registry is a list of phone numbers of consumers who do not want to be contacted by commercial telemarketers. It is managed by the Federal Trade Commission (FTC), the nation's consumer protection agency, and it is enforced by the FTC, the FCC, and state officials.

The registry now has more than 149 million phone numbers. Numbers placed on the registry remain on the list for five years. Beginning in June 2008, if they do not re-enroll, numbers for millions of people will automatically drop off.

People can register, or re-enroll their home and cell phone numbers at the Web site or by calling 1-888-382-1222.

Telemarketers must pay an annual subscription fee to access the FTC list to ensure no calls are made to protected numbers. The companies also must update their own calling lists every 31 days to ensure there are no numbers from the registry on them.

The current annual subscription fee for the list is $62 for each area code, with a maximum cost of $17,050 for access to all U.S. numbers on the list. The Florida Association of REALTORS® offers the list to its members for no charge.

From year 2003 through fiscal year 2006, telemarketers have paid more than $59 million in fees to access the database. Most of the fees are used to support the do-not-call registry program.

The rules of the do-not-call registry cover the sale of goods or services by telephone. Political organizations, charities, telephone surveyors, or companies with which a consumer has an existing business relationship are exempt from the rules of the do-not-call registry.

A company may call a consumer, even if that consumer is on the registry, for:

■ 18 months after that consumer's last purchase, delivery, or payment, even if the consumer's number is on the registry, or

■ three months after that consumer makes an inquiry or submits an application to the company.

If the consumer asks the company not to call again, the company must honor the request.

Accessing the do-not-call registry. Only sellers, telemarketers, and other service providers may have access to the registry. The do-not-call registry may not be used for any purpose other than preventing telemarketing calls to the telephone numbers on the registry. The only consumer information available from the registry is telephone numbers. The numbers are sorted and available by area code. Companies will be able to access as many area codes as desired (and paid for), by selecting, for example, all area codes within a certain state.

Telemarketers must pay for consumer data in any area code before they or their telemarketers call any consumer within that area code, even those consumers whose telephone numbers are not on the registry. The only exceptions are for sellers who call only consumers with whom they have an existing business relationship or written agreement to call and that do not access the do-not-call registry for any other purpose.

A company that is a seller or telemarketer could be liable for placing any telemarketing calls (even to numbers *not* on the do-not-call registry) unless the seller has paid the required fee for access to the registry. Violators may be subject to fines of up to $11,000 for each call placed.

If a seller or telemarketer can show that, as part of its routine business practice, it meets all the requirements of the following conditions, it will not be subject to civil penalties or sanctions for mistakenly calling a consumer who has asked for no more calls or for calling a person on the do-not-call registry. To successfully avoid penalties ("safe harbor"), the seller or telemarketer must demonstrate that it:

- has written procedures to comply with the do-not-call registry requirements;
- trains its personnel in those procedures;
- monitors and enforces compliance with these procedures;
- maintains a company-specific list of telephone numbers that it may not call;
- accesses the National Do Not Call Registry no more than three months before calling any consumer and maintains records documenting this process; and
- erred unintentionally if it did make any call in violation of the do-not-call registry rules.

The best source of information about complying with the do-not-call registry rules is the FTC's Web site. It includes business information about the registry.

WEB LINK

Federal Trade Commission: *www.ftc.gov/donotcall*

Florida's Do-Not-Call Law

The National Do Not Call Registry has not affected Florida's do-not-call law. Florida intends to continue enforcing this law and accepts new consumer telephone numbers. The national registry supersedes portions of the Florida law that are less strict. Florida telemarketers would have to consult both lists to ensure that a consumer is not on *either* list before placing a sales call. The Florida law allows licensees to contact for-sale-by-owners (FSBOs) to solicit a listing, and this is still permissible *only if the owner is not in the National Do Not Call Registry.*

In Practice

Review the list and check it twice.

Before placing a call, you should be sure that the consumer is not on any of the following three lists:

1. Federal Do Not Call Registry
2. Florida Do-Not-Call List
3. Your own in-office list

You can call a FSBO in the national registry if you have a buyer who wants to purchase the property, but you may not use the call to discuss listing the property. If the FSBO is on the Florida list but not on the national registry, you may solicit the listing if the property was advertised or has a sign in front.

WEB LINK

National Do Not Call Registry: *www.donotcall.gov*

Junk Fax Protection Act

The law requires the person who sends a fax to:

- have an "established business relationship" with the recipient or written consent from the recipient;
- have voluntarily received the recipient's fax number;
- provide the recipient the right to "opt-out" of getting more faxes; and
- remove the numbers of persons who "opt-out" within 30 days.

Federal law prohibits most unsolicited fax advertisements to any machine, either business or personal. An unsolicited advertisement is defined under the act as "any material advertising the commercial availability or quality of any property, goods, or services which is transmitted to any person without that person's prior express invitation or permission, in writing or otherwise."

An exception to the rules allows faxes to be sent to recipients with whom the sender has an "established business relationship," referred to by the acronym EBR.

What Is an Established Business Relationship?

An established business relationship (EBR) is "a prior or existing relationship formed by a voluntary two-way communication between a person or entity and a business or residential subscriber with or without an exchange of consideration (payment), on the basis of an inquiry, application, purchase, or transaction by the business or residential subscriber regarding products or services offered by such person or entity, which relationship has not been previously terminated by either party."

If the sender had an EBR with the recipient and possessed the recipient's fax number before July 9, 2005 (the date the Junk Fax Prevention Act became law), the sender may send the fax advertisements without demonstrating how the number was obtained.

Fax opt-out notice requirements. Senders of fax advertisements must provide specified notice and contact information on the fax that allows recipients to "opt-out" of any future faxes from the sender and specify the circumstances under which a request to "opt-out" complies with the Act.

The rules provide that it is unlawful to send unsolicited advertisements to any fax machine, including those at both businesses and residences, without the recipient's prior express invitation or permission. Fax advertisements, however, may be sent to recipients with whom the sender has an EBR, as long as the fax number was provided voluntarily by the recipient. Specifically, a fax advertisement may be sent to an EBR customer if the sender also:

- obtains the fax number directly from the recipient, through, for example, an application, contact information form, or membership renewal form; or

- obtains the fax number from the recipient's *own* directory, advertisement, or site on the Internet, unless the recipient has noted on such materials that it does not accept unsolicited advertisements at the fax number in question; or

- has taken reasonable steps to verify that the recipient consented to have the number listed, if obtained from a directory or other source of information compiled by a third party.

To stop unwanted fax advertisements, your "opt-out" request must:

- identify the fax number or numbers to which it relates; and

- be sent to the telephone number, fax number, Web site address, or e-mail address identified on the fax advertisement.

If you change your mind about receiving fax advertisements, you can subsequently grant express permission to receive faxes from a particular sender, orally or in writing.

Fax broadcasters. Often fax advertisements are sent in bulk on behalf of a business or entity by separate companies called fax broadcasters. Generally, the person or business on whose behalf a fax is sent or whose property, goods, or services are advertised is liable for a violation of the junk fax rules, even if the person or business did not physically send the fax. A fax broadcaster also may be liable if it has a "high degree of involvement" in the sender's fax message, such as supplying the fax numbers to which the message is sent, providing a source of fax numbers, making representations about the legality of faxing to those numbers, or advising about how to comply with the junk fax rules. Also, if a fax broadcaster is "highly involved" in the sender's fax messages, the fax broadcaster must provide its name on the fax.

WEB LINK

Federal Communications Commission: *Fax Advertising: What You Need to Know*

www.fcc.gov/cgb/consumerfacts/unwantedfaxes.html

The Controlling the Assault of Non-Solicited Pornography and Marketing Act

The Controlling the Assault of Non-Solicited Pornography and Marketing Act (CAN-SPAM Act) of 2003 establishes requirements for those who send commercial e-mail, spells out penalties for spammers and companies whose products are advertised in spam if they violate the law, and gives consumers the right to ask e-mailers to stop spamming them.

The law makes a distinction between "commercial" e-mail and "transactional or relationship" e-mail. The act covers only "commercial electronic mail messages" and regulates e-mailers whose "primary purpose" is to advertise a commercial product or service.

"Transactional or relationship" messages include situations such as e-mails informing sellers about the progress on marketing a listed property or e-mails thanking past customers and updating the relationships. As long as these e-mails don't contain false or misleading routing information, they are exempt from most provisions of the act. Informational messages, such as newsletters that don't contain advertisements are also exempt.

The law bans false or misleading header information, meaning that the "From:," " To:," and the routing information must be correct and identify the person who sent the e-mail. It requires that the e-mail give recipients an opt-out method. It also requires that commercial e-mail be identified as an advertisement and include the sender's valid physical postal address.

The new rules define the "primary purpose" of the rule as commercial if the e-mail is exclusively an advertisement for a commercial product or service, if a reasonable interpretation of the subject line would lead to the conclusion that a message is commercial, or a "transactional or relationship" message does not appear in whole or in part at the beginning of the message's body text.

The act is enforced by the Federal Trade Commission and the Department of Justice. Each violation is subject to fines up to $11,000.

WEB LINK

FTC Web site regarding CAN-SPAM Act: *www.ftc.gov/spam/*

INCOME TAX REGULATIONS AFFECTING RESIDENTIAL REAL PROPERTY

Real estate licensees are not expected to be income tax experts, but they should be knowledgeable about basic provisions of the Internal Revenue Code as they relate to real estate transactions. Licensees always should advise consumers to seek professional tax advice. An important benefit to homeowners is that interest and property taxes are deductible if the taxpayer itemizes. Additionally, all or part of the gain on sale of the property is exempt from taxes.

> **In Practice**
>
> **Be careful what you tell buyers about tax deductions.**
>
> Don't tell buyers that they can deduct property taxes and interest to get them to purchase a home. You must be certain that they have enough other deductions (e.g., combined deductions exceeding $11,400 for a married couple filing jointly in 2010) so they can take full advantage of the realty-related deductions.

A taxpayer currently may exclude up to $250,000 ($500,000 for a married couple filing jointly) of gain on the sale of a personal residence if the taxpayer owned and occupied the residence for at least two of the previous five years. If the taxpayer held the home less than two years, a prorated portion of the exclusion may apply. The number of times a homeowner may use this exclusion is unlimited, except that the exclusion can be used only once every two years. The law is advantageous to most families because it allows them to earn large profits on their residences tax free.

EXAMPLE: The Wilsons bought their home in 1992 for $50,000. In 1992, they added a deck and pool for $25,000. They lived in the home until they sold it for $300,000 in March of this year. Selling costs were $20,000. They would calculate their taxes as follows:

Selling price	$300,000
Less selling expenses	– $ 20,000
Equals amount realized	$280,000

Basis		
Original cost	$50,000	
Plus improvements	+ $25,000	
Equals adjusted basis		$75,000
Gain on sale ($280,000 − $75,000)		$205,000
Less exclusion on sale of residence		− $500,000
Taxable capital gain		**$0**

Lower Capital Gains Tax Rates on Investment Property

The rates for long-term (holding period more than 12 months) capital gains are a maximum of 15 percent.

ANTITRUST

Brokers risk their assets and careers by attempting to get other brokers to charge a standard commission. Antitrust laws prohibit any action by a party to fix prices or inhibit competition by using unfair practices. Some of the prohibited actions include:

- conspiracy to set prices,

- splitting up competitive market areas,

- conspiring to boycott cut-rate brokers or otherwise interfering with their business, and

- requiring a minimum commission before allowing listings to be circulated in any service, such as through a multiple-listing service (MLS).

DISCUSSION EXERCISE 1.3

Boycotting.   Gloria, president of Big Tree Realty, Inc., had a luncheon meeting with Samuel, president of Statewide Residential Brokers, Inc. The subject of the meeting was Southern Discount Realty and the increased market share it had achieved since it announced its new discount fee structure. Big Tree and Statewide had previously had a 47 percent market share between them, but their combined share was now 39 percent.

They agreed to tell their sales associates not to show Southern Discount Realty listings to their buyers. Also, they agreed to call several other brokers in the area to do the same.

"A broker simply cannot give good service by charging that little. It's unprofessional," Gloria said.

If you were a sales associate for Statewide Realty and your sales manager suggested that you boycott Southern Discount listings, what would your response be?

AVOIDING MISREPRESENTATION

While the legal definition is much broader, the common definition of **misrepresentation** is the act of a licensee who, either intentionally or unintentionally, fails to disclose a **material fact** or makes a **false or misleading statement** that is justifiably relied on by another, resulting in damage. Intentional misrepresentation is actionable as fraud. Unintentional misrepresentation is negligence.

Buyers sometimes claim misrepresentation by the listing brokers. All licensees, regardless of their brokerage relationship, have the duty of **disclosure,** that is, the duty to disclose material facts affecting the value of residential property. Buyers frequently ask brokers to describe a property and to make representations about the condition of the property or other facts associated with the sale. A licensee may never conceal material defects about a house.

To win a fraudulent misrepresentation case against a broker, the plaintiff must prove:

- the broker made an error in giving information, oral or written, to the buyer or failed to disclose a material fact to the buyer;
- the broker knew the statement was not accurate or the information should have been disclosed;
- the plaintiff reasonably relied on such statement; and
- the plaintiff was damaged as a result.

The buyer is entitled to relief if the representation was a material inducement to the contract. The broker's duty stems from the seller's duty not to misrepresent.

In establishing liability or in applying remedies, it does not make a difference whether the misrepresentation was fraudulent (intentional) or negligent (unintentional). The most common remedies available to the offended party include monetary damages, rescission of the contract, forfeiture of the broker's commission, and disciplinary action by the FREC.

In Practice

Don't make any of the following statements to a buyer:

- "No need to get a title search. I sold this house last year and title was fine." Chapter 475 requires that you tell buyers to get an attorney's opinion or purchase title insurance.
- "Don't worry, the seller told me by phone that I could sign the contract for her." You can't sign a contract for another person without a power of attorney.
- "I won't be able to present your offer until the seller decides what to do about the offer I submitted yesterday." Chapter 475 requires you to present all offers.
- "That roof is in great condition—I can tell just by looking at it." If it's not OK, you may get to repair it at your expense.

Practical Steps for Sales Associates

A real estate licensee can take several practical steps to decrease the risk of misrepresentation claims:

Forms To Go

1. Have the seller complete a **property condition disclosure** form, such as the one shown in Forms To Go, Appendix B, and discuss any potential problem areas.

2. Inform the seller of the legal duty to disclose material facts that affect the value of residential property and are not readily observable.

3. Find out about the following common problem areas with respect to condominiums:

   - House rules regarding children, pets, and waterbeds
   - Location of lockers and parking stalls
   - Existence of special assessments (for what and how much)
   - Maintenance fee(s) (what is included, proposed increases)
   - Planned future capital improvements
   - Existing reserves and purpose of reserves
   - Historical information as to when capital improvements were completed

4. Ask about factors external to the property that might influence its value and affect a person's decision to buy such as the following for example:

   - Abutting and nearby uses (present and proposed), such as a rock band venue next door
   - Highway expansion or rerouting of a bus line

5. Do not make statements concerning matters about which you do not have first-hand knowledge or that are not based on expert opinion or advice. Have a list of government agencies from which you can get information. Suggest that the buyer check things out, too, by giving the buyer the telephone numbers and Web site addresses of the appropriate government agency. It is best that important technical information come directly to the buyer from the government agency.

6. Do not participate with the seller in nondisclosure of required information. If the seller refuses to disclose material defects, decline the listing. Taking a listing of this nature is not worth damage claims, loss of reputation, and loss of license.

7. Avoid exaggeration. If you wish to venture a "quick" opinion about things you are not certain about, make sure the buyer understands that it is only a guess, and be certain the buyer does not rely on it in making a decision.

8. Disclose pertinent information in writing, such as in a property condition disclosure form from the sellers. The buyers should sign the disclosure indicating that they have received it. A confirmation letter would confirm earlier discussions in which you pointed out a leaky roof or the need to consult with a soil engineer, and it would affirm that neither you nor the seller makes any warranty as to the condition of the roof or the foundation. Keep copies of these documents in the transaction file.

Home Inspection

One of the most effective risk-management tools available to licensees is a home inspection. The inspection is intended to disclose defects in a building that buyers, sellers, and real estate licensees have missed. It is better to identify problems before the closing so the parties can negotiate a settlement. If a material defect is discovered after closing, the buyer may sue the licensee rather than the seller, who may now live in a distant city.

Home inspectors must be licensed by the DBPR. They must have a high school diploma, be of good character, complete a minimum of 120 hours of prescribed education, and pass a state examination.

> **In Practice**
>
> Have the buyer select his or her own inspector so there's no question about collusion. Give your buyers a list with names and phone numbers of qualified home inspectors in your area.

WEB LINK

American Society of Home Inspectors: *www.ashi.com*

Death in a Property

For years, residential licensees were unclear about what disclosures were required when a murder, suicide, or death occurred in a house. A law change in 2003 removed the duty of a seller or a licensee to disclose such incidents.

The fact that a property was, or was at any time suspected to have been, the site of a homicide, suicide, or death is not a material fact that must be disclosed in a real estate transaction. A cause of action shall not arise against an owner of real property, his or her agent, an agent of a transferee of real property, or a person licensed under Chapter 475 for the failure to disclose to the transferee that the property was or was suspected to have been the site of a homicide, suicide, or death or that an occupant of the property was infected with human immunodeficiency virus or diagnosed with acquired immune deficiency syndrome. [689.25(1)(b), F.S.]

QUICK REFERENCE CHART FOR REQUIRED DISCLOSURES

Figure 1.1 shows numerous required disclosures. It is a quick reference guide intended to help licensees understand some of the many requirements but should not be considered all-inclusive.

S U M M A R Y

When a licensee renews a license for the first time, the licensee must complete a post-license course, or the license will be void. After the first renewal, a licensee must complete 14 hours of continuing education before renewing. If a licensee fails to complete the required education, the licensee may be disciplined.

FIGURE 1.1 ■ **Florida Real Estate Disclosure Chart**

Subject	Disclosure Trigger	To	Disclosure Requirement
Ad Valorem Tax Disclosure	Contract to purchase	Buyer	Disclosure that property taxes may increase after the purchase from reassessments
Brokerage relationship disclosures	Entering into a representation agreement or showing a property	Buyer or seller	Review this chapter for detailed disclosure requirements
Condominium Act—purchase cancellation	Contract to purchase	Buyer	15-day cancellation privilege when buying from a developer; 3-day cancellation privilege when buying a resale unit
Condominium Act—recreation lease	Contract to purchase	Buyer	Whether a recreational lease exists; when membership in a recreation facilities club is required; description of the facilities and the charges
Federal Reserve's Regulation Z	When advertising financial terms on real property, a trigger item is included in ad	Readers of ads	Full disclosure of all material factors in financing, including price, down payment, monthly payment, finance costs, and annual percentage rate of interest
Florida Building Energy-Efficiency Act	Contract to purchase	Buyer	Energy-efficiency rating system description and how to get the building rated
Homeowners Association Disclosure	Contract to purchase	Buyer	Notification that the owner is required to be a member of an association; there are covenants and restrictions; there is a required assessment; there may be a land use fee
Landlord and Tenant Act	Within 30 days of signing lease	Tenant	Where deposit is being held; whether it is in an interest-bearing account and the interest rate, if any
Land use disclaimer—some jurisdictions, but not statewide	Contract to purchase	Buyer	Restrictive covenants for the neighborhood; buyer's responsibility to investigate whether the anticipated land use conforms to comprehensive plan, zoning, building codes, etc.; public or private street and drainage maintenance
Lead-based paint	Contracts for purchase or lease	Buyer or tenant	Lead hazard information pamphlet; disclosure of any known hazards; ten-day inspection and cancellation privilege
Property condition disclosure	When listing property At time of showing property	Seller Buyer	Any material defects that affect the property's value
Radon gas	Contracts for purchase or lease	Buyer or tenant	Statement as to the nature of the gas and how to get more information
Roof inspection ordinance—some jurisdictions	Closing of a real estate transaction	Buyer	Disclosure of condition of roof covering, decking, and framing, usually made within 30 days before closing

FIGURE 1.1   ▉   **Florida Real Estate Disclosure Chart (continued)**

Subject	Disclosure Trigger	To	Disclosure Requirement
Time-Share Act—purchase cancellation	Contract to purchase	Buyer	All material aspects of the property; rights and obligations of buyer and seller; ten-day cancellation privilege; notification that purchase is a leisure time activity, not an appreciating investment
Time-Share Act—unit assessments	Contract to purchase	Buyer	Annual assessment for common expenses
Wood-destroying organisms report	Closing of a real estate transaction that includes commercial or residential buildings	Buyer	Wood-destroying organisms report signed by a licensed pest inspector, made within 30 days before closing date

There are three brokerage relationships available to licensees who sell residential property:

Single agent brokers represent either the buyer or the seller, but not both, in a transaction. Only single agent brokers may call their customers *principals*. Principals are responsible for the acts of their single agent. The broker must give a Single Agent Notice before showing property or before entering a representation agreement. The notice should be signed, but if the principal declines to sign the notice, the licensee may note the fact on the form and work with the principal.

Transaction brokers provide limited representation but do not have a fiduciary relationship with the customer. The customer is not responsible for the acts of the transaction broker. Transaction brokers need not give a brokerage relationship notice to customers. A single agent may enter into a transaction broker relationship by having the principal sign a Consent to Transition to Transaction Broker Notice.

Brokers who will not represent the customer as a single agent or a transaction broker must give the customer a No Brokerage Relationship Notice before showing property. The notice need not be signed.

Brokers in nonresidential transactions may work with a customer in one of the ways shown above but need not give a brokerage relationship notice. Nonresidential brokers may appoint one sales associate in the firm to represent the seller and one sales associate to represent the buyer. As designated sales associates, they act as single agents for their principal. The broker must remain neutral. The buyer and seller must each have at least $1 million in assets and agree to the relationship. A Designated Sales Associate Notice and a Single Agent Notice must be given to each party. The law specifically forbids dual agency.

Florida regulation of real estate practices has been strengthened considerably by passage of many consumer protection laws. Licensees who fail to maintain their professional education risk violation of new laws. In some cases, the violation occurs because licensees were unaware that the law existed.

In real estate transactions, licensees must be careful to disclose fully any material facts that affect the property's value. A licensee must avoid making statements that could result in a claim of misrepresentation. The licensee must take steps, such as using a property condition disclosure statement and inspecting the property, to ensure the buyer has full knowledge of defects.

The licensee must be familiar with important federal laws including income tax regulations affecting real estate, environmental protection, and lead-based paint.

Important Florida laws and disclosure requirements that licensees must observe include comprehensive plans and concurrency, homeowners' association disclosures, energy-efficiency disclosures, and radon gas disclosures.

The professional real estate practitioner should keep a checklist of required disclosures for every type of property. By observing the law and disclosing the required information, licensees enhance their reputation for fair and honest dealing, and the consumer is informed and protected.

K E Y   T E R M S

agency
agent
buyer brokerage agreement
community association
concurrency
Consent to Transition to
    Transaction Broker Notice
customer
designated sales associate

disclosure
dual agency
false or misleading
    statement
fiduciary relationship
infrastructure
innocent purchaser status
material fact
misrepresentation

No Brokerage Relationship
    Notice
principal
property condition disclosure
radon gas
single agent
Single Agent Notice
transaction broker

P R A C T I C E   E X A M

1. A broker need NOT give a brokerage relationship disclosure when the property being shown is a
   a. triplex.
   b. single-family home valued at more than $1 million.
   c. seven-acre tract zone for agricultural use.
   d. nonresidential property.

2. A *principal* is legally represented by a
   a. single agent.
   b. dual agent.
   c. transaction broker.
   d. nonrepresentative.

3. Which statement to a prospective buyer is NOT likely to increase a licensee's liability?
   a. "The title to the property is clear; I checked the courthouse yesterday."
   b. "I used to be in construction, so I can tell you that the roof is in perfect condition."
   c. "You should be able to get information from the school board about which school your child would attend if you purchase this home."
   d. "You don't need a home inspection because the house is only five years old."

4. A licensee is legally required to disclose to a prospective homebuyer that
   a. there was a recent murder in the house.
   b. the roof occasionally leaks.
   c. the occupant of the property is infected with human immunodeficiency virus.
   d. the former owner was killed when he fell from the roof.

5. A broker may not legally work with a buyer or seller as a
   a. transaction broker.
   b. single agent.
   c. dual agent.
   d. nonrepresentative.

6. A principal is responsible for the acts of her
   a. transaction broker.
   b. dual agent.
   c. single agent.
   d. nonrepresentative.

7. A student failed her sales associate post-licensing course for the second time. What are her options if she wishes to maintain her license?
   a. She must wait 30 days and pass a different end-of-course exam.
   b. She must take the 63-hour prelicense course for sales associates and pass the course exam and the state exam.
   c. She must retake at least 45 hours of the sales associate prelicense course and pass a course exam.
   d. She must retake the course and pass a different end-of-course exam.

8. Which term is found in the Junk Fax Law?
   a. Concurrency
   b. Established business relationship
   c. Good faith estimate of settlement costs
   d. National register

9. Licensed sales associates working at the seller's single-agent brokerage firm
   a. may represent either the seller or the buyer in a transaction.
   b. are legally bound to represent the seller.
   c. may have another principal in the transaction.
   d. may be transaction brokers for the buyer to ensure limited confidentiality.

10. If Jill sells commercial property exclusively, she
    a. must give the customer a No Brokerage Relationship Notice before showing property.
    b. may be a single agent, a transaction broker, a designated sales associate, or have no brokerage relationship with the customer.
    c. must give the customer a Single Agent Notice before showing property.
    d. may not be a single agent.

11. In which status does a licensee NOT need to provide a written brokerage relationship disclosure notice?
    a. Single agent broker
    b. Transaction broker
    c. Designated sales associate
    d. When acting with no brokerage relationship

12. A broker must disclose known facts that materially affect the value of residential property when that broker is
    a. a licensee with no official brokerage relationship.
    b. a single agent.
    c. the transaction broker.
    d. all of the above.

13. A single agent for the seller has no brokerage relationship with a buyer. The buyer agrees to pay up to the listed price, if necessary, but first wants to submit an offer 10 percent below that price. The broker should
    a. tell the seller, "The buyer said he will pay up to the listed price."
    b. refuse to disclose the statement because of the broker's duty of limited confidentiality.
    c. suggest that the seller counteroffer, if desired.
    d. tell the seller, "The buyer is qualified."

14. For how many years must a broker retain required brokerage relationship disclosures?
    a. One
    b. Three
    c. Four
    d. Five

15. John and Bill are sales associates working for a commercial broker. The broker allows sales associate John to act as a single agent for the buyer and sales associate Bill to act as a single agent for the seller. Both the buyer and the seller have assets of more than $1 million and each agrees to this form of representation. The situation describes a
    a. transaction broker relationship.
    b. designated sales associate.
    c. single agency.
    d. dual agency.

16. A broker is showing a buyer a vacant site in Orange Park and tells the buyer that concurrency requirements may delay her building plans. When she asks her broker about the meaning of the word, the broker should respond,
    a. "It is a requirement that you get a building permit and an environmental audit at the same time."
    b. "You must provide a development of regional impact statement before building."
    c. "You must disclose whether the building plans cover any recreational leases."
    d. "There could be a lack of infrastructure in place that would put a moratorium on construction until the situation is remedied."

17. Henry has a capital gain of $197,000 on the sale of his home, which he owned for three years. The sales price was $425,000. Sales costs were $7,000, qualified fix-up costs were $1,000, and moving costs were $2,000. How much must Henry pay in capital gains taxes on this sale if his normal tax rate is 25 percent?
    a. $197,000
    b. $98,500
    c. $39,400
    d. $0

18. New concern about the presence of radon gas is the result of the increase in
    a. radon levels at large factories.
    b. the number of energy-efficient buildings.
    c. the depletion of the ozone layer.
    d. Freon® in air-conditioning systems.

19. There is special significance for licensees who sell homes built before 1978. That has to do with
    a. coastal management zones.
    b. lead-based paint disclosures.
    c. Americans with Disabilities Act properties.
    d. the end of freely assumable FHA loans.

20. To claim innocent purchaser status under the hazardous substance statutes, a purchaser should
    a. refuse to purchase former gas stations.
    b. pay for and obtain an extensive environmental audit.
    c. show that the seller did not reveal any problems.
    d. ask the real estate agent for a property warranty.

2 FAIR HOUSING AND THE AMERICANS WITH DISABILITIES ACT

LEARNING OBJECTIVES

Upon completion of this chapter, you should be able to:

1. list the categories of persons protected under the Fair Housing Act;

2. list at least five discriminatory practices prohibited by the Fair Housing Act;

3. describe the exception to "adult only" designations;

4. state which HUD form must be posted in all real estate offices;

5. describe at least four requirements of the Florida Americans with Disabilities Act; and

6. answer correctly each question on the short quiz on fair housing.

OVERVIEW

Title VIII of the Civil Rights Act of 1968, commonly known as the Fair Housing Act, prohibits discrimination in the sale, rental, and financing of dwellings based on race, color, religion, sex, and national origin. In 1988, Congress passed the Fair Housing Amendments Act (FHAA). The Amendments expand coverage of Title VIII to prohibit discriminatory housing practices based on disability and familial status. The Florida Fair Housing Act is modeled after the federal act, and affords victims of discrimination another, perhaps easier remedy than suing in federal court.

Another law directly affecting real estate practitioners is the Americans with Disabilities Act. This act sets the standards for building accessibility, goods, services, and employment. Florida has a law that mirrors this act.

Florida statutes prohibit housing discrimination against persons with human immunodeficiency virus (HIV) or acquired immune deficiency syndrome (AIDS).

PUBLIC PERCEPTIONS ABOUT FAIR HOUSING LAWS

Before going further, it may be interesting to take the short quiz in Figure 2.1 that the Department of Housing and Urban Development (HUD) has used to evaluate the general public's familiarity with the fair housing laws. When you have completed the quiz, you can check your answers and compare your scores.

Only 63 percent of those surveyed answered more than seven questions correctly. This survey demonstrates that many buyers and sellers of real estate don't understand fair housing laws. Customers sometimes make requests for licensees to act illegally on their behalf. It is the licensee's duty to describe the law and to scrupulously follow its requirements.

CIVIL RIGHTS ACT OF 1866

The **Civil Rights Act of 1866** was passed just after the Civil War to prohibit discrimination based on race. For many years, the law was not widely enforced, but in 1968 the U.S. Supreme Court upheld the law in the case of ***Jones v. Mayer***. Subsequent court actions requiring compliance with the law have been numerous and successful.

FIGURE 2.1 ■ A Short Quiz on Fair Housing

True or False?

1. Under federal law, it is legal for an apartment building owner to assign families with younger children to one particular building. ○ True ○ False

2. An apartment building owner has the right to reject an applicant because of poor housekeeping habits. ○ True ○ False

3. Not allowing the construction of a wheelchair ramp on the apartment building owner's property is permissible, even if the tenant agrees to remove it at his/her own expense upon leaving. ○ True ○ False

4. Under federal law, indicating a preference based on religion in advertising an available apartment is perfectly legal. ○ True ○ False

5. An apartment building owner may legally reject an applicant with a history of mental illness, though he/she is not a danger to others. ○ True ○ False

6. A rental application may be rejected by the landlord because of the applicant's religion. ○ True ○ False

7. When using a real estate agent, a family may sell their house only to a white buyer. ○ True ○ False

8. A real estate agent is allowed to limit a home search to certain neighborhoods based on the client's race/ethnicity. ○ True ○ False

9. A loan officer may turn down a black applicant because of the applicant's lack of steady job and income. ○ True ○ False

10. It is legal for a loan officer to require higher down payments from Hispanic families in order to get a mortgage. ○ True ○ False

Answer Key: 1. False 2. True 3. False 4. False 5. False 6. False 7. False 8. False 9. True 10. False

Source: Department of Housing and Urban Development

CIVIL RIGHTS ACT OF 1968

The **Civil Rights Act of 1968** included Title VIII, the **Fair Housing Act.** The act originally protected against discrimination in housing based on race, color, religion, sex, and national origin. In 1988 the **Fair Housing Amendments Act of 1988** (FHAA) added two new classes of protection: handicap and familial status. A discussion of each protected class follows.

Race and Color

Real estate advertisements should not indicate the racial makeup of a neighborhood. An ad that says, "Excellent area with many Asian families" would be a clear violation. Sales associates may never steer buying prospects into a neighborhood based on the buyer's description of racial or ethnic characteristics.

> **E X A M P L E :** An owner agrees to sell a house, but, after discovering that the buyers are black, pulls the house off the market, then promptly lists it for sale again. If the buyers file a discrimination complaint, HUD may authorize the U.S. Department of Justice to seek an injunction in Federal District Court to prevent the owner from selling the house to anyone else until HUD investigates the complaint.

In Practice

Don't advertise the words *Negro, Black, Caucasian, Oriental, American Indian, White, Black, Colored,* etc.

Religion

Licensees should not advertise that a home is "near St. Thomas Catholic Church," or that the neighborhood is "within walking distance to Temple Israel Day School."

> **E X A M P L E :** A Jewish person responds to a landlord's advertisement to rent an apartment. The owner says: "As a matter of principle, we rent to Christians only, and do not rent to Jewish, Muslims, or Hindus. There's a nice apartment down the street who will rent to you, and they have several vacancies."

In Practice

Don't advertise the words *Protestant, Christian, Catholic, Jew, Muslim,* etc.

Sex

Advertisements for single-family dwellings or apartments may not describe a preference or limitation based on sex. "Single female roommate wanted" is allowed as an exception for shared living advertising.

National Origin

Steering a Cuban family into an area because they want to live in a Spanish-speaking area is a violation. Advertising for "English-speaking tenant only" is a limitation and is illegal.

In Practice

Don't advertise the words *Mexican-American, Puerto Rican, Philippine, Polish, Hungarian, Irish, Italian, Chicano, African, Hispanic, Chinese, Indian, Latino,* etc.

Handicap

A **handicap** is defined in the act as:

1. a physical or mental impairment that substantially limits one or more of a person's major life activities;
2. a record of having such an impairment; or
3. being regarded as having such an impairment.

Not only can housing providers not discriminate against a person with a disability, but they must make reasonable accommodations to rules, policies, and practices to provide that person with the same enjoyment of a dwelling; to allow the person to make reasonable physical modifications of premises; and to require multifamily housing built since March 1991 to have basic wheelchair accessibility.

An **accommodation** is a change that the housing provider must provide. An example would be a tenant's request for a handicapped-accessible parking space close to the tenant's unit. A **modification** is a change that the housing provider must allow the tenant to provide at the tenant's expense. An example would be lowering cabinets and countertops for accessibility.

The Fair Housing Act's protection covers not only home seekers with disabilities but also buyers and renters without disabilities who live or are associated with individuals with disabilities

A number of cases have involved housing providers' responsibility to allow service or companion animals for people with disabilities even when they have a "no pets" rule in place. Licensees who advertise "not wheelchair accessible" violate the law. However, it is acceptable to advertise that a residence is "handicapped accessible," or "wheelchair ramp for accessibility."

In Practice

Don't advertise the words *crippled, blind, deaf, mentally ill, retarded, impaired, handicapped, physically fit,* etc.

Familial Status

Familial status is the presence or anticipated presence of children under age 18 in a household. Before the 1988 amendments were passed, a HUD study showed that 25 percent of apartment complexes had a "no children" policy. The policy decreased housing options for families with children.

The act defines *familial status* as:

1. a parent or another person having legal custody of such individual or individuals; or

2. the designee of such parent or other person having such custody, with the written permission of such parent or other person. The protections afforded against discrimination on the basis of familial status shall apply to any person who is pregnant or is in the process of securing legal custody of any individual who is not at least 18 years old.

Housing providers may not refuse to deal with families with children, segregate children into certain housing units, restrict children's activities with special rules, charge higher security deposits, restrict families with children only to some areas or floors of a property, restrict the number of children in a unit, or refuse to rent to children of a certain age. Owners may set reasonable rules for maximum occupancy in an apartment building, but owners should obtain legal advice before establishing such rules.

Under the **Housing for Older Persons Act**, a 1995 amendment to the Fair Housing Act, certain 55-and-older communities are exempt if at least 80 percent of the units have at least one occupant who is at least 55 years of age. While such communities can legally ban children they still may not discriminate on the basis of race, color, national origin, religion, sex, or disability.

In Practice

Don't advertise the words *children, adults, singles, mature persons,* etc.

Persons Covered by the Fair Housing Act

The law applies to persons who own four or more homes, multifamily properties (except properties with fewer than four units, one of which is occupied by the owner), brokers and sales associates who sell two or more homes in a year, and transactions in which a broker is involved. While it appears that a private owner may be able to discriminate under the 1968 Act, the 1866 Act clearly prohibits racial discrimination.

Who Is Not Covered by the Act?

The Fair Housing Act does not apply to all persons or organizations, as seen in the following three categories:

1. Religious organizations may limit the sale, rental, or occupancy of dwellings that it owns or operates for other than a commercial purpose to persons of the same

religion, and they may give preference to such persons, unless membership in such religion is restricted because of race, color, or national origin.

2. Private clubs that provide lodgings that it owns or operates for other than a commercial purpose may limit the rental of such lodgings to its members.

3. Owners of any single-family house may restrict the sale or rental of the house provided the following conditions are met:

   a. The owner does not own or have any interest in more than three single family houses at any one time.

   b. The house is sold or rented without the use of a real estate broker, agent, or salesperson. If the owner selling the house does not reside in it at the time of the sale or was not the most recent resident of the house prior to such sale, the exemption applies to only one such sale in any 24-month period;

   c. The rooms or units in dwellings contain living quarters occupied or intended to be occupied by no more than four families living independently of each other, if the owner actually maintains and occupies one of such living quarters as his or her residence.

Students and smokers are not protected. Income status, sexual orientation, marital status, and age are also not protected groups. These classes may, however, be protected under a local ordinance. Therefore before drafting a fair housing policy a housing provider should determine if local ordinances protect certain classes that are not protected by the state or federal law.

Violations

The following ten paragraphs describe behaviors that violate the fair housing laws:

1. Refuse to sell or rent a dwelling after a bona fide offer has been made, or to refuse to negotiate for the sale or rental of a dwelling because of race, color, religion, sex, familial status, or national origin, or to discriminate in the sale or rental of a dwelling because of handicap.

2. Discriminate in the terms, conditions, or privileges of the sale or rental of a dwelling, or in the provision of services or facilities in connection with sales or rentals, because of race, color, religion, sex, handicap, familial status, or national origin.

3. Engage in any conduct relating to housing that denies dwellings to persons because of race, color, religion, sex, handicap, familial status, or national origin.

4. Make, print, or publish any notice, statement, or advertisement with respect to the sale or rental of a dwelling that indicates any preference, limitation, or discrimination because of race, color, religion, sex, handicap, familial status, or national origin.

5. Represent to any person because of race, color, religion, sex, handicap, familial status, or national origin that a dwelling is not available for sale or rental when such dwelling is in fact available.

6. Induce for profit or attempt to induce a person to sell or rent a dwelling by representations regarding the entry into the neighborhood of persons of a particular race, color, religion, sex, familial status, or national origin or with a handicap. In establishing a discriminatory housing practice under this section

it is not necessary that there was in fact profit as long as profit was a factor for engaging in the **blockbusting** activity.

7. Deny access to or membership in any multiple-listing service, real estate brokers' association, or other service organization or facility relating to the business of selling or renting a dwelling because of race, color, religion, sex, handicap, familial status, or national origin.

8. Engage in **steering**, an illegal practice against a person or persons in a protected class, by:

   - discouraging that person from inspecting, purchasing, or renting a dwelling;
   - discouraging the purchase or rental of a dwelling by exaggerating drawbacks or failing to inform the person of desirable features of a dwelling or of a community, neighborhood, or development;
   - communicating to any prospective purchaser that he or she would not be comfortable or compatible with existing residents of a community, neighborhood, or development;
   - assigning any person to a particular section of a community, neighborhood, or development, or to a particular floor of a building.

9. Engage in prohibited activities relating to dwellings, including but not limited to:

   - discharging or taking other adverse action against an employee, broker, or agent because he or she refused to participate in a discriminatory housing practice;
   - employing **codes** or other devices to segregate or reject applicants, purchasers, or renters;
   - refusing to take or to show listings of dwellings in certain areas because of race, color, religion, sex, handicap, familial status, or national origin;
   - refusing to deal with certain brokers or agents because they or one or more of their clients are of a particular race, color, religion, sex, handicap, familial status, or national origin;
   - denying or delaying the processing of an application made by a purchaser or renter or refusing to approve such a person for occupancy in a cooperative or condominium dwelling because of race, color, religion, sex, handicap, familial status, or national origin.

10. Discriminate against any person in making loans for a dwelling, or which is or is to be secured by a dwelling, because of race, color, religion, sex, handicap, familial status, or national origin. Prohibited practices include, but are not limited to, failing or refusing to provide to any person the availability of loans, application requirements, procedures, or standards for the review and approval of loans or financial assistance, or providing information that is inaccurate or different from that provided others, because of race, color, religion, sex, handicap, familial status, or national origin. This violation is called **redlining.**

In Practice

Refuse to engage in discriminatory behavior with a buyer.

If a buyer asks you about the ethnic characteristics of a neighborhood, don't get involved in the conversation. This response may keep you out of trouble:

"I appreciate having the opportunity to work with you in finding a home. The law and our company's policy do not allow me to show you homes based on the racial, religious, or ethnic characteristics of a neighborhood. So I won't be able to place any such restrictions on showings or information about the availability of homes for sale or for rent."

ADVERTISING

Selective Use of Advertising Media or Content

The selective use of advertising content can violate the Fair Housing Act. For example, the use of the English language alone or the exclusive use of advertising catering to the majority population in an area, when there are also non-English speaking persons or other minority persons, may be discriminatory. The following are examples of the selective use of advertisements that may be discriminatory:

- **Selective geographic advertisements.** Such selective use may involve the strategic placement of billboards; brochure advertisements distributed within a limited geographic area by hand or in the mail; advertising in particular geographic coverage editions of major metropolitan newspapers.
- **Selective use of equal opportunity slogan or logo.** When placing advertisements, such selective use may involve placing the equal housing opportunity slogan or logo in advertising reaching some geographic areas but not others.
- **Selective use of human models when conducting an advertising campaign.** Selective advertising may involve an advertising campaign using human models primarily in media that cater to one racial or national origin segment of the population without a similar advertising campaign directed at other groups.

Evidence of Compliance with Fair Housing Laws

In the investigation of complaints, HUD will consider, as evidence of compliance, among other things:

- the use of the **Equal Housing Opportunity Logo**, statement, or slogan stating that the property is available to all persons regardless of race, color, religion, sex, handicap, familial status, or national origin; and
- that when photographic ads are used, human models should be representative of the majority and minority populations in the area, including both sexes and children, where appropriate.

F I G U R E 2.2 ■ Advertising Guide for Fair Housing Logos

As a guide to advertising the Equal Housing Opportunity logo, licensees can use this simple formula:

Size of advertisement	Size of logo in inches
1/2 page or larger	2 × 2
1/8 page up to 1/2 page	1 × 1
4 column inches to 1/8 page	½ × ½
Less than 4 column inches	Do not use

1   The choice of logo, statement, or slogan will depend on the type of media used
2   (visual or auditory) and, in space advertising, on the size of the advertisement. (See
3   Figure 2.2.)

4   In any other advertisements, if other logotypes are used in the advertisement, then
5   the Equal Housing Opportunity logo should be of a size at least equal to the largest of the
6   other logotypes.

7   In space advertising that is less than 4 column inches (one column 4 inches long
8   or two columns 2 inches long) of a page in size, the Equal Housing Opportunity slogan
9   should not be used.

10 Such advertisements may be grouped with other advertisements under a caption stat-
11 ing that the housing is available to all without regard to race, color, religion, sex, handi-
12 cap, familial status, or national origin.

**Forms
To Go**

13 Brokers should post the **Fair Housing Poster** in all offices. Failure to do so shifts the
14 burden of proof in discrimination actions to the broker. It is the broker's responsibility to
15 provide training and supervision to ensure compliance with the law. A poster is included
16 in Forms To Go, Appendix B.

In Practice

HUD says it's okay to use these words in your advertising: *master bedroom, desirable neighborhood, Santa Claus, Easter Bunny or St. Valentine's Day, Merry Christmas, Happy Easter, mother-in-law suite, bachelor apartment, great view, fourth-floor walk-up, walk-in closets, jogging trails, walk to bus stop, nonsmoking, sober, wheelchair ramp, two bedroom, cozy, family room, no bicycles allowed, quiet streets.*

DISCUSSION EXERCISE 2.1

EXAMPLES OF FAIR HOUSING VIOLATIONS
Match the letter of the prohibited action to the appropriate example.

Prohibited Action

A. Advertising any discriminatory preference or limitation in housing or making any inquiry or reference that is discriminatory in nature.

B. Denying membership or participation in a multiple-listing service, a real estate organization, or another facility related to the sale or rental of housing as a means of discrimination.

C. Falsely representing that a property is not for sale.

D. Altering the terms or conditions of a home loan, or denying a loan, as a means of discrimination.

E. Profiting by inducing property owners to sell or rent based on the prospective entry into the neighborhood of persons of a protected class.

F. Refusing to sell, rent, or negotiate the sale or rental of housing.

G. Changing the terms or conditions or services for different individuals as a method of screening.

Letter   Example of Violation

_____ William owns an apartment building with 160 residential units. When a Hispanic family asks to look at some of the apartments, he tells them to go away.

_____ Carolyn is quite religious, and when a Muslim family asks to look at a $900 apartment, she tells them that the $900 price is a discount for Christians. Their rent would be $1,000.

_____ A real estate developer runs a full-page ad in the Tampa Tribune that says: "Be a happy homeowner in Bellair Gardens." The only photo shows several African American families.

_____ Mildred is a person with disabilities. When she looks at a single-family home for rent, the owner says the home is not available. The next day, the house is advertised and a For Rent sign is posted.

_____ Sales Associate Sara sends a newsletter to homeowners in a predominantly white neighborhood. The cover of the newsletter has a photo showing several black persons. The title of the newsletter is "The Changing Face of Sunland Station."

_____ A lender requires that Jose, a Hispanic person, pay a higher rate of interest on a loan than is charged to other applicants who have similar jobs and credit scores.

_____ The Indian River Realty Council meets weekly to market available properties. The council has restricted membership to Caucasian males, rejecting applications from women and African Americans.

FAIR HOUSING ENFORCEMENT

HUD's Fair Housing Complaint Process

To report violations, contact:

> Office of Fair Housing and Equal Opportunity
> U.S. Department of Housing and Urban Development (HUD), Room 5204
> Washington, DC 20410-2000
> Toll-free hotline: 1-800-669-9777
> TDD: 1-800-927-9275
> Internet: *www.hud.gov/complaints/housediscrim.cfm*

Persons have one year to file a complaint with HUD. The complaint should include:

- the complainant's name and address,
- the name and address of the person or company who is the subject of the complaint,
- the address or other identification of the housing involved,
- a short description of the facts that caused the complainant to believe his or her rights were violated, and
- the dates of the alleged violation

A more detailed discussion of the complaint process is described below.

Intake. After HUD has received the initial information, an intake specialist will contact the complainant by phone to collect facts about the alleged discrimination. The specialist will then review the allegations to determine whether the matter is within HUD's jurisdiction. If the allegations do not fall within HUD's jurisdiction, for example if the complaint does not allege housing discrimination, HUD cannot accept the complaint and must close the case. If HUD has jurisdiction to investigate, HUD will file the complaint.

If the alleged discrimination occurred within a state or locality in HUD's Fair Housing Assistance Program, HUD will refer the complaint to that agency. That agency must begin to work with the complainant within 30 days, or HUD can take the complaint back.

Filing. If HUD accepts the complaint for investigation, the investigator will draft a formal complaint on HUD's standard form and mail it to the complainant. The complainant must sign the form and return it to HUD.

Within ten days after receiving the signed complaint, HUD will send the respondent notice that a fair housing complaint has been filed against him or her along with a copy of the complaint. Within ten days of receiving the notice, the respondent must submit to HUD an answer to the complaint.

Investigation. As part of the investigation, HUD will interview the complainant, the respondent, and pertinent witnesses. The investigator will collect relevant documents or conduct onsite visits, as appropriate. HUD has the authority to take depositions, issue subpoenas and interrogatories, and compel testimony or documents.

Conciliation. The Fair Housing Act requires HUD to bring the parties together to attempt to resolve every fair housing complaint. The choice to conciliate the complaint is completely voluntary on the part of both parties. If the parties sign a conciliation agreement,

HUD will end its investigation and close the case, but any conciliation agreement must protect the public's interests.

No cause determination. If, after a thorough investigation, HUD finds no reasonable cause to believe that housing discrimination has occurred or is about to occur, HUD will issue a determination of "no reasonable cause" and close the case. A complainant who disagrees can request reconsideration of the case. At that time, HUD will notify all of the parties that the request has been received and invite them to submit any additional evidence pertinent to the investigation.

HUD reviews all of the materials from the investigation and any additional evidence that the parties provide. HUD will then inform the parties if the Department has affirmed its finding of no reasonable cause or instead has decided to re-open the complaint. If HUD decides to re-open the complaint, it will resume investigation and conciliation. If HUD affirms its finding of no reasonable cause, HUD can take no further action on the complaint, but the complainant can appeal by filing a civil court action in the appropriate U.S. district court.

Cause determination and charge. If the investigation produces reasonable cause to believe that discrimination has occurred or is about to occur, HUD will issue a determination of reasonable cause and charge the respondent with violating the law. HUD will send a copy of the charge to the parties in the case.

After HUD issues a charge, a HUD Administrative Law Judge (ALJ) will hear the case unless either party elects to have the case heard in federal civil court. Parties must elect within 20 days of receipt of the charge.

Hearing in a U.S. district court. Within 30 days after either party elects to go to federal court, the Department of Justice (DOJ) will commence a civil action on behalf of the aggrieved person in U.S. district court. If the court finds that a discriminatory housing practice has occurred or is about to occur, the court can award actual and punitive damages as well as attorneys fees.

Hearing before a HUD ALJ. If neither party elects, a HUD ALJ will hear the case. An attorney from HUD will represent the aggrieved party before the ALJ. When the ALJ decides the case, the ALJ will issue an initial decision.

If the ALJ finds that housing discrimination has occurred or is about to occur, the ALJ can award a maximum civil penalty of $11,000, per violation, for a first offense, in addition to actual damages for the complainant, injunctive or other equitable relief, and attorneys' fees.

Within 15 days of the issuance of the ALJ's initial decision, any party adversely affected by the ALJ's initial decision can petition the Secretary of HUD for review.

The Secretary of HUD has 30 days after the initial decision to affirm, modify, or set aside the ALJ's initial decision, or remand the initial decision for further proceedings. If the Secretary does not take any action within 30 days, the decision will be considered the Department's final decision.

After the Department has issued a final decision, any party aggrieved by the Department's final decision can appeal to the appropriate court of appeals.

Testing

As part of its investigative process, HUD, as well as other organizations, visit rental and sales offices to monitor compliance with the law. The **testers** are usually organized in teams that have different ethnic, religious, or disability characteristics. Sometimes a black couple visits a real estate office in response to an ad for a specific house. They would be followed sometime later by a white couple wanting to see the same house. Of course, the test is to see whether the sales associate asks the same questions, establishes different financing requirements, shows the same houses, and offers equal service to both couples.

The Fair Housing Test forms ask the following questions:

- What was the date and time of visit?
- What is the name of the sales associate, as well as the associate's ethnicity, gender, and age?
- How long did you wait to meet with the person?
- What were you told about the availability of the home in the ad?
- Were there any other homes recommended to you? (Can you provide a list of those homes?)
- Did the agent talk about Fair Housing Laws?
- Were you referred to another associate?
- Did the agent tell you that you must go to a lender to be prequalified for financing?
- Can you list the qualifying questions you were asked, such as family size, income, savings, debts, reason for moving, etc.?
- Can you list comments made by the agent about neighborhoods and areas, such as noise, safety, schools, rising or declining values, racial characteristics, etc.?
- Did the agent make any remarks about race, religion, persons with disabilities, or families with children?
- What arrangements were made regarding future contact?

Of course, HUD is expecting that both couples would enjoy the same considerations.

Testing for violations against disabled persons. HUD also tests for violations of fair housing laws against persons who are disabled or handicapped as seen in the following examples.

EXAMPLE 1: A deaf tester who also had difficulty speaking understandably would visit a rental office in person to inquire about available housing. He used notes to communicate with the landlord or rental agent. Following the standard rental housing inquiries, the deaf tester asked whether the landlord would install flashing lights for the doorbell and alarm bells. If the landlord indicated that this accommodation would not be provided, the tester asked if he or she could pay for the installation of the flashing lights. The nondisabled tester also visited in person, simply making the standard rental housing inquiries.

EXAMPLE 2: A tester who was blind and accompanied by a guide dog visited a rental office in person to inquire about available housing. If a unit was available, the tester requested an accommodation—waiver of the "no pets" policy or of any special fees or restrictions on the presence of the dog. When rental agents were unsure or ambiguous about policies regarding service animals, testers made repeated call-backs until they received a definitive answer regarding this accommodation. If a unit was not available, the nondisabled tester also visited in person, making the standard rental housing inquiries, without any mention of a pet. In some cases, a unit is not available for the blind person that was available for the nondisabled person.

WEB LINK

National Fair Housing Advocate Online: *www.fairhousing.com*

Fair Housing Bookshelf: *www.hud.gov/library/bookshelf08/*

U.S. Department of Housing and Urban Development: *www.hud.gov/offices/fheo/index.cfm*

FLORIDA FAIR HOUSING ACT (CHAPTER 760, F.S.)

The **Florida Fair Housing Act** is modeled after the federal Fair Housing Act and prohibits discrimination based on race, color, religion, sex, national origin, familial status, or handicap. The principal reason that Florida has its own fair housing law is that suing in a state court gives victims of discrimination another, perhaps easier, remedy than trying to bring a federal case.

AMERICANS WITH DISABILITIES ACT

The **Americans with Disabilities Act** (ADA) prohibits discrimination based on **disability** in employment, programs, and services provided by state and local governments, goods and services provided by private companies, and commercial facilities. A *disability* is defined by the ADA as a physical or mental impairment that substantially limits a **major life activity**, such as walking, seeing, hearing, learning, breathing, caring for oneself, or working. The Department of Justice administers the law.

The ADA does not cover **temporary impairments** such as broken bones, nor sexual or behavioral disorders. Homosexuality, which is not a disability, is not covered under the law. The act does protect persons who are recovering from substance abuse, but it does not protect persons who are currently engaging in the current illegal use of controlled substances. Juvenile offenders and sex offenders, by virtue of that status, are not persons with disabilities protected by the act. Additionally, the act does not protect an individual with a disability whose tenancy would constitute a "direct threat" to the health or safety of other individuals or result in substantial physical damage to the property of others unless the threat can be eliminated or significantly reduced by reasonable accommodation.

Full compliance with ADA is required for new construction and alteration. Existing structures must be made **accessible** when that goal is **readily achievable**, meaning that the goal can be carried out without much difficulty or expense. The factors for determining whether changes are readily achievable are described in more detail in the ADA regulations issued by the Department of Justice, and the ADA regulations should be consulted for more detail. A tax deduction of up to $15,000 is available for removing barriers at existing places of business. Some of the ADA compliance requirements for various building areas are described on the following page.

Parking Areas

Parking areas should have one accessible space for every 25 total spaces. The accessible parking space should be eight feet wide for a car, with a five-foot access aisle. At least one space must be van accessible (eight feet wide with an eight-foot access aisle, and at least 98 inches of vertical clearance). The accessible spaces should be the closest available to the accessible entrance.

Access to Buildings

People with disabilities should be able to approach a building and enter as freely as everyone else. Curbs at the entrance should have curb cuts. The route of travel should be at least 36 inches wide, stable, and slip-resistant. An object must be within 27 inches of the ground in order to be detected by a person using a cane. Overhead objects must be higher than 80 inches for head room.

Ramps

For every inch of height, ramps should have at least one foot of length (1:12) and have a railing at least 34 inches high. There must be a 5-foot-long level landing at every 30-foot horizontal length of ramp, and at the top and bottom of the ramp and at switchbacks.

Entrances

Inaccessible entrances should have signs showing the closest accessible entrance. A service entrance should not be used as the accessible entrance unless there are no other options. Entrance doors should have at least 32 inches of clear opening, with at least 18 inches of clear wall space on the pull side of the door. Door handles should be no higher than 48 inches and operable with a closed fist. Doors in public areas should have at least a 32-inch opening.

Aisles and Pathways

Aisles and pathways to services should be at least 36 inches wide. Spaces in auditoriums should be distributed throughout the hall. Tops of tables or counters should be between 28 and 34 inches high.

Restrooms

Restrooms should be accessible to people with disabilities. If a restroom is inaccessible, there should be a sign giving directions to an accessible restroom. A wheelchair-accessible stall that is at least five feet square is necessary to make turns. Grab bars should be behind and on the side wall nearest the toilet. At least one lavatory should have a 30-inch-wide by 48-inch-deep clear space in front. The bottom of the lavatory should be no lower than 29 inches; the rim should be no higher than 34 inches. The faucets should be operable with one closed fist.

The ADA also requires that state and local governments provide access to programs offered to the public. The ADA also covers effective communication with people with disabilities and eligibility criteria that may restrict or prevent access, and the ADA requires reasonable modifications of policies and practices that may be discriminatory.

WEB LINK

U.S. Department of Justice: *www.usdoj.gov*

ADA Home Page: *www.usdoj.gov/crt/ada*

FLORIDA AMERICANS WITH DISABILITIES ACT (CHAPTER 760, F.S.)

The **Florida Americans with Disabilities Act** implements and mirrors portions of the Americans with Disabilities Act and includes other important provisions. Florida has its own act because suing in a state court gives victims of discrimination another remedy for violations.

AIDS VICTIMS AND HOUSING (CHAPTERS 689.25 AND 760.50, F.S.)

The fact that an occupant of real property is infected with HIV or diagnosed with AIDS is not a material fact that must be revealed in a real estate transaction. An owner of real property or his agent may not be sued for the failure to disclose to the buyer or tenant that an occupant of the property was infected with HIV or AIDS. [689.25, F.S.]

Such disclosure also would violate the law that prohibits discrimination against persons who have acquired immune deficiency syndrome (AIDS) and a human immunodeficiency virus (HIV). Any person with or perceived as having AIDS or HIV is entitled to every protection available to handicapped persons, including fair housing protections. [760.50, F.S.]

S U M M A R Y

The Civil Right Act of 1866 prohibits discrimination based on race. Title VIII of the Civil Rights Act of 1968 (the Fair Housing Act) prohibits discrimination based on race, color, religion, sex, and national origin. In 1988, Congress passed the Fair Housing Amendments Act (FHAA). The amendments expand coverage of Title VIII to prohibit discriminatory housing practices based on disability and familial status. The Florida Fair Housing Act is modeled after the federal act and affords victims of discrimination another, perhaps easier remedy than suing in federal court.

The Fair Housing Law applies to persons who own four or more houses, any multifamily property, except properties with four or fewer units when one is occupied by the owner. Brokers and sales associates who sell more than two homes a year are also required to abide by the law.

Religious organizations may restrict sales or rentals of their property to members of the organization. Private clubs that offer lodgings may restrict the use of the property to only their members. Other characteristics that are not covered by the law include smokers, students, low income persons, sexual orientation, marital status, and age.

Steering, blockbusting, and redlining are discriminatory practices that violate the laws.

When advertising, it is best to describe the attributes of the property. Avoid advertising the characteristics of the likely buyer or tenant. Selective advertisements, such as to certain geographic areas, or photos with models showing only one racial, sex, or ethnic characteristic are violations.

The Americans with Disabilities Act prohibits discrimination based on disability in employment, programs, and services provided by the government, goods and services provided by private companies, and commercial facilities. New construction must fully comply with ADA guidelines. Existing structures must be made accessible when that goal is readily achievable. Owners may be required to make accommodations to existing structures, policies, and practices to provide equal accessibility, and to allow tenants to make reasonable modifications to the premises.

KEY TERMS

accessible
accommodation
Americans with Disabilities
    Act
blockbusting
Civil Rights Act of 1866
Civil Rights Act of 1968
codes
conciliation agreement
disability

Equal Housing Opportunity
    Logo
Fair Housing Act
Fair Housing Amendments
    Act of 1988
Fair Housing Poster
familial status
Florida Americans with
    Disabilities Act
Florida Fair Housing Act
handicap

Housing for Older Persons
    Act
Jones v. Mayer
major life activity
modification
readily achievable
reasonable cause
redlining
steering
temporary impairments
testers

P R A C T I C E   E X A M

1. Which two classes were added to Title VIII of the Civil Rights Act of 1968 by the Fair Housing Amendments Act of 1988?
   a. Religion and sex
   b. Familial status and sex
   c. Familial status and age
   d. Handicap and familial status

2. Which is NOT a Fair Housing advertising violation?
   a. Home is close to the First Baptist Church and downtown.
   b. No university students!
   c. House is not modified for handicap access.
   d. Hispanic buyers welcome.

3. Due to the recent subprime loan problems, a lender has stopped making loans in a minority area. This is an illegal practice called
   a. redlining.
   b. blockbusting.
   c. steering.
   d. hammering.

4. It is NOT a potential violation of Fair Housing laws to advertise using
   a. the equal opportunity logo in some areas, but not in others.
   b. all black photographic models advertising for a housing development in a predominantly black area.
   c. human models that are representative of majority and minority populations in the area.
   d. a message such as "We specialize in sales to Asians."

5. A licensee is the single agent for a minority couple. He says, "Are you more comfortable buying a home in a neighborhood with people of your race?" Does this question violate any laws?
   a. Yes. This is an illegal act called "blockbusting."
   b. Yes. This is an illegal question that is considered "steering."
   c. No. If he is a single agent, he needs to know their housing needs.
   d. No. It is legal as long as the agent does not decide which neighborhoods to show.

6. A broker manages a single-family home. Harry, a disabled person, wants to rent the property and wants to make alterations, including installing a ramp at the entrance, lowering the kitchen counters, and widening some of the doorways. He agrees to pay for the remodeling and for restoring the premises at the end of the lease term. Which is correct?
   a. Owners of single-family homes are not required to comply with the Americans with Disabilities Act.
   b. The broker should suggest that Harry find another home that has already been renovated for the disabled.
   c. The owners could refuse to allow the alterations, but they must do so by stating that the renovations are "not readily achievable."
   d. If the broker explains that the owners will not allow the alterations, the law would be violated.

7. The vertical height for a wheelchair-accessible ramp is 30 inches. How many feet must the ramp be to meet the ADA guidelines?
   a. 18
   b. 24
   c. 30
   d. 36

8. If a broker complies with an owner's instructions to restrict prospective tenants to Christians, will the broker violate the Fair Housing Act?
   a. Yes, because it shows a preference or limitation based on religion.
   b. No, because single homeowners are not exempt from the act.
   c. No, because single homeowners are exempt from the act when using a broker.
   d. No, because religious preference is not a legal violation.

9. Which advertising term would be a violation of fair housing laws?
   a. Cool bachelor apartment
   b. Third-floor walkup
   c. Apartment for sober person
   d. English-speaking tenant wanted

10. A prospective tenant asks a landlord to provide a reserved handicapped-accessible parking space at the entrance to the apartment building. This is a request for a(n)
    a. accommodation.
    b. modification.
    c. waiver.
    d. conditional permit.

11. Which is NOT discrimination based on familial status?
    a. Requiring a couple to be married before occupancy
    b. Refusing to rent to a pregnant woman
    c. Refusing to show an apartment to a grandmother who has custody of two children
    d. Setting aside a section in the apartment complex near the playground for families with children

12. Which person or entity is covered by the Fair Housing Act?
    a. A religious organization renting its own property
    b. An owner of five single-family houses
    c. A private club providing lodging at its own property for a noncommercial purpose
    d. A duplex when the owner occupies one of the units

13. An example of steering is
    a. persuading a person to sell a dwelling by saying that persons of a particular race, color, religion, sex, familial status, or national origin, or with a handicap are moving into the area.
    b. discouraging the purchase or rental of a dwelling by exaggerating drawbacks or failing to inform the person of desirable features of a dwelling.
    c. representing to any person because of race, color, religion, sex, handicap, familial status, or national origin that a dwelling is not available for sale or rental when such dwelling is in fact available.
    d. refusing to sell or rent a dwelling after a bona fide offer has been made.

14. When the parties involved in a HUD complaint are brought together to attempt to resolve the issues, it is called
    a. mediation.
    b. arbitration.
    c. adjudication
    d. conciliation.

15. Unless either party elects to have a discrimination case heard in court the case will be heard by
    a. a HUD attorney.
    b. an assistant attorney general.
    c. an administrative law judge.
    d. civil court judge.

16. Which is NOT correct about accessible parking requirements of the Americans with Disabilities Act?
    a. Parking areas should have one accessible space for every 40 total spaces.
    b. The accessible parking space should be eight feet wide for a car, with a five-foot access aisle.
    c. The accessible spaces should be the closest available to the accessible entrance.
    d. At least one space must be van accessible (eight feet wide with an eight-foot access aisle, and at least 98 inches of vertical clearance).

17. Which is NOT correct about access to buildings under the Americans with Disabilities Act?
    a. Curbs at the entrance should have curb cuts.
    b. The route of travel should be at least 24 inches wide.
    c. Overhead objects must be higher than 80 inches for head room.
    d. An object must be within 27 inches of the ground in order to be detected by a person using a cane.

18. Accessibility standards for restrooms do NOT require that
    a. the bottom of the lavatory should be no lower than 21 inches, and the rim should be no higher than 42 inches.
    b. a wheelchair-accessible stall that is at least five feet square is necessary to make turns.
    c. grab bars should be behind and on the side wall nearest the toilet.
    d. at least one lavatory should have a 30-inch-wide by 48-inch-deep clear space in front.

19. Which parties are protected under the Americans with Disabilities Act?
    a. Homosexuals
    b. Persons who are abusing alcohol
    c. Persons with broken legs
    d. Persons recovering from drug abuse

20. Mary is showing her listing to William. John, the owner of the property, has been diagnosed with AIDS. What should Mary do with respect to disclosure?
    a. Mary should not volunteer the information, but if asked, is permitted to disclose the information.
    b. Mary has the duty to make disclosure because the information may materially affect the value of the property.
    c. Disclosure of the fact would be a violation of the law.
    d. Mary must ask John when taking the listing if it is all right to disclose the information to prospective buyers.

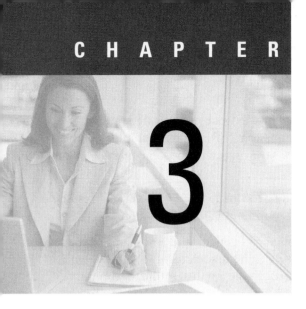

CHAPTER 3

BUSINESS PLANNING AND TIME MANAGEMENT

LEARNING OBJECTIVES

Upon completion of this chapter, you should be able to:

1. explain why a real estate sales associate needs additional knowledge and experience to become more professional;

2. describe three types of communication skills that the professional real estate sales associate must master;

3. list the three types of knowledge a real estate sales associate needs and distinguish the differences between each type;

4. describe the five requirements for effective goal setting; and

5. list at least ten services that an unlicensed personal assistant can perform.

OVERVIEW

Probably the most important characteristics of a successful real estate professional are professionalism and the ability to plan and manage time. The level of professionalism comes from following strong ethical guidelines and enhancing communication skills.

Because professionals are normally paid for their time and expertise, it is important to understand the benefits of goal-setting, business planning, and time management. A business plan sets goals and tells how those goals are to be achieved. Goals should be written, measurable, and attainable, and should contain deadlines.

Once the business plan has been completed, it's up to the licensee to make the most efficient use of time to maximize results and achieve all the goals. ■

ACHIEVING PROFESSIONALISM

Customers of real estate licensees expect them to be knowledgeable, organized, and effective in their duties. The Florida Real Estate Commission (FREC) has established the requirement for post-licensing education to help new sales associates become proficient in the day-to-day practice of real estate.

Professionalism is not easily achieved. Professional knowledge and behavior result from additional study and hard work and go beyond minimum legal requirements.

The sales associate who provides honesty, service, diligence, and knowledge tends to be more successful than the stereotypical "hard sell" sales associate who "closes" with manipulative techniques. This chapter deals with the basic qualities that better serve clients and customers:

- Professional ethics
- Communication skills
- Professional education
- Goal setting
- Time management

PROFESSIONAL ETHICS

A distinct difference exists between what is *ethical* and what is *legal*. License laws set a minimum standard of professional behavior, while codes of ethics set the higher standard of what is honest and fair to all parties involved in a real estate transaction.

Even the appearance of impropriety may cause customers to avoid doing business with a sales associate and his or her brokerage firm. The expression "perception is reality" is true; such shortcomings are very damaging to a real estate career.

The National Association of REALTORS® (NAR) has standardized a code of **professional ethics,** so that all members are aware of and follow their professional responsibilities. NAR's Code of Ethics is extremely influential, not only for REALTORS® but for other licensees, because ethical codes often later become license laws. The code may be the best available guideline for ethical behavior, whether or not a licensee is a member of NAR.

COMMUNICATION SKILLS

Communication is the core of the real estate brokerage business. A licensee may be knowledgeable, competent, and ethical, yet because of a lack of communication skills, be unable to help customers successfully. The four types of communication skills necessary are:

1. Listening skills
2. Oral communication skills
3. Written communication skills
4. Nonverbal communication skills

Listening Skills

One of the most important communication skills is listening. Good listening takes practice and has three basic steps:

1. **You must hear.** For example, if your customers say, "The price of the house is too high," you would be able to repeat the thought.

2. **You must understand.** Think about what the customers are saying. What do they mean when they say that? Should you ask some questions? Do they believe it's overpriced or that it's more than they can afford?

3. **You must evaluate.** Do the customers' comments make sense? Based on the information, should you change the type houses you show?

In Practice

Focus. Don't let your mind wander. Give your full attention. If you feel your mind wandering, lean forward into the conversation. Don't think about what you're going to say while the customers are still speaking.

Hear them out. Don't talk until they have finished. Let them say everything they want to say without being interrupted.

Listen for the main points. This is what they really want to say. The main points may be repeated. Pay special attention when they say, "The point of this is…"

Ask questions to be certain you've got it right. For example, you could say, "When you said that it's too high, did you mean that it's overpriced, or that it's more than you'd be comfortable buying?"

Oral Communication Skills

Talking to buyers, sellers, appraisers, surveyors, and other licensees enables the professional to share information, ask questions, and better understand the needs of others. The professional must be able to express information completely, honestly, and clearly. The individual who fails to master **oral communication skills** may be misunderstood, appearing incompetent or even dishonest.

Community colleges and universities offer communication and public speaking classes to the public. One inexpensive way to learn to speak effectively is by joining a Toastmasters Club, a nonprofit service organization devoted to enhancing oral communication skills. Many real estate licensees point to their years in Toastmasters as a key factor in their success.

WEB LINK

Toastmasters International: *www.toastmasters.com*

When licensees prepare for oral presentations, they should know exactly what they are going to say and organize the presentations logically.

Word choice is important. For instance, the statement "We can finish the deal by the end of the month" would sound better as "We should be able to close the transaction by the end of the month."

Jargon is a word or an expression related to a specialized vocation that a layperson might not understand. Licensees should avoid using jargon. For example, the term *floor duty* describes the period during which a sales associate is entitled to take all customer calls. While it's a well-known expression in real estate circles, it is not as familiar to consumers. A customer who calls the office for information on a listed property and is told "Just a minute, I'll let you talk to the associate on the floor" may wonder whether there has been an accident or just a lack of chairs. By avoiding jargon, real estate professionals help clients and customers better understand the information they are trying to relate.

Written Communication Skills

Letters, e-mail, flyers, and other forms of written communication are often the first impression licensees make on members of the public. Bad grammar and misspellings may reflect poorly on the licensee and the brokerage firm. Written communications skills are even more important for writing a contract provision. An ambiguous clause may result in a lost sale, a lawsuit, and disciplinary action by the FREC.

DISCUSSION EXERCISE 3.1

Les shows a townhome to a married couple who are interested in purchasing it despite the fact that the property has been poorly maintained. The seller has told Les that he would be willing to make reasonable repairs if the buyers include them in the sales contract. So Les writes the following special clause in the contract:

"Seller agrees to remodel the townhome and put everything into first-class condition."

Based on this clause, what will the buyer expect?

What will the seller want to do?

Is there a possibility for miscommunication here?

How should this clause have been written?

Written communication skills may be enhanced by taking courses at community colleges, by reading books to improve writing skills, or by purchasing a book of ready-made real estate letters, such as *Power Real Estate Letters*, by William H. Pivar (Dearborn Real Estate Education). A dictionary, a spell-checker, and a grammar checker on a software program are minimum requirements for achieving better written communication.

Nonverbal Communication Skills

Nonverbal communication, often called **body language,** can be very important in sales. The real estate sales associate who understands body language will be better able to read the attitudes of customers and develop body language that can make a customer comfortable and establish rapport. Often, nonverbal communication can be far more revealing than what a person says. Some obvious body language styles include those described in Figure 3.1.

F I G U R E 3.1 ■ Body Language Indicators

Body Language	Probably Means...	Comments
Pyramiding fingertips—the classic "banker" look	I'm superior to you, and I'm making some judgments about you	Don't do this when talking to a customer
Pyramiding, leaning back in the chair with hands joined behind the head—the "boss"	I'm superior to you; you have less status here	Don't do this when talking to a customer
Arms folded across the chest	Closed, defensive	Bad sign; you'll get nowhere in this presentation until you get the listener loosened up
Legs crossed at the knee away from the listener with body facing to the side	Closed, defensive	Bad sign; you'll get nowhere in this presentation until you get the listener loosened up
Customer looking away (no eye contact) during a sales presentation	Closed, often unfriendly	Bad sign; unlikely to buy until you can establish rapport
Palms toward the person just before speaking	Stop talking; I have more important things to say	Don't do this when talking to a customer
Stroking the chin (mostly males); fingertips to the neck (mostly females)	Sign of seriously considering the proposal	Get ready to write the offer
Scratching the head	Thinking; may be about to make a decision	Ask to help with any questions the customer may have
Staring at the ceiling	Thinking; trying to remember a fact	Ask to help with any questions the customer may have
Leaning forward into sales presentation	Interested, attentive	Good sign; you're doing something right

1 **Reflecting.** When **reflecting** what the other person has said, you show not only that you
2 have understood, you indicate interest in the other person and help establish rapport.

3 ***Testing understanding.*** The best way to use reflection is to test your understanding of
4 what the customer has said. This could also help to build rapport. If you repeat the words
5 exactly, it's called *parroting*. Rephrasing in your own words is called *paraphrasing*.

6 ***Creating rapport.*** Reflecting what a person says can create a bond of agreement. You can
7 reflect their *words* by echoing what they say. You can reflect their *style* by using their modes
8 of speech. However, poor use of this technique can have the opposite effect.

9 ***Nonverbal reflecting.*** You can also reflect nonverbal body language by repeating what
10 they do, rather than what they say.

11   *Mirroring* is displaying the same body language as the other person. If they lean for-
12 ward, you lean forward. However, it's easy to recognize and may backfire. A better way to
13 relate is by matching. *Matching* reflects nonverbal signals, but it is less obvious and not
14 copying. If they cross their arms, you can cross your legs. If they nod in agreement, you
15 can smile and occasionally nod.

1   Matching will build rapport only when the customer registers it intuitively not con-
2   sciously. There is a limit to how much matching will help in the sales presentation.

In Practice

To be more effective with your customers:

- Your handshake should be firm, but not too hard.
- Usually, direct eye contact when you are talking or listening is good. Staring without blinking or looking away occasionally may be disconcerting to the listener. Persons from certain cultures may perceive constant direct eye contact as disrespectful.
- Don't cross anything. Arms and legs should be open and relaxed.
- Lean forward into the conversation to display your interest. If you lean backward, especially if hands are joined behind the head, it may be perceived as a sign of superiority or aloofness.

WEB LINK

Center for Nonverbal Studies—a site rich in observations of nonverbal communication:
http://center-for-nonverbal-studies.org/

DISCUSSION EXERCISE 3.2

In this exercise, fill in the circle denoting the message you are receiving from a customer, then discuss your answers.

Customer Action	Aggressive	Bored	Closed	Ready to Buy	Deceptive
Arm around your shoulders	○	○	○	○	○
Leaning forward	○	○	○	○	○
Ignores distractions	○	○	○	○	○
Doodling as you talk	○	○	○	○	○
Sweating	○	○	○	○	○
Stifled yawn	○	○	○	○	○
Hands on hips	○	○	○	○	○
Biting inside of mouth	○	○	○	○	○
Looking down	○	○	○	○	○
Drumming fingers	○	○	○	○	○

PROFESSIONAL EDUCATION

Licensees enhance their professionalism through continuing education. The law requires continuing education before renewal of a license, but many professionals take more courses than are required by the law. National organizations award professional designations to graduates of their educational programs. The designations make consumers aware of those persons who have exceeded the legally required continuing education.

Other types of education, when combined with formal instruction, also enhance a licensee's competence. In *Real Estate Brokerage: A Success Guide,* by Cyr, Sobeck, and McAdams (Dearborn Real Estate Education), the authors describe three types of knowledge sales associates need:

1. Technical knowledge
2. Marketing knowledge
3. Product knowledge

Technical Knowledge

Technical knowledge provides the tools of the business, such as completing contracts properly, knowing sellers' and buyers' costs, and understanding the comparative market analysis process.

This course includes technical knowledge in the following areas:

- State and federal laws
- Preparing a comparative market analysis (CMA)
- Preparing a listing contract
- Qualifying a buyer
- Understanding financing plans
- Preparing a sales contract
- Reviewing closing statements
- Analyzing real estate investments

Sales associates should not work in the field without the appropriate technical knowledge. For example, sales associates will feel quite incompetent if they cannot fill out the cost disclosure statement or contract form. One of the purposes of this course is to provide the new licensee with the technical knowledge to become competent and confident with consumers. Technical knowledge also includes knowledge about state and federal laws, such as fair-housing and antitrust laws.

DISCUSSION EXERCISE 3.3

Traci has been in the real estate business for about a month and is working with her first buyer customers, referred to her by a close friend. She shows them a home listed by another sales associate in her office. The buyers immediately start to talk about where to place their furniture. "We think this is the one," they tell Traci.

It is Saturday afternoon, and Traci is unable to contact the broker to answer some questions about how to complete the required forms. Nervously, she tells the buyers, "You know, I hate to see you rush into anything. There are some other houses out there you might like better. I can show them to you tomorrow, if you like. That'll give you time to think about it all, too!"

What is Traci's main objective at this moment?

How could Traci have been better prepared for this situation?

Marketing Knowledge

Learning how to sell real estate comes from **marketing knowledge.** It encompasses the knowledge of psychology and the ability to assess a consumer's specific housing needs. This course includes marketing knowledge in some of the following areas:

- Business planning (section on self-marketing)
- Prospecting for listings
- Making an effective listing presentation
- Prospecting for buyers
- Showing and selling the property

Many sales training books and tapes are available commercially. Institutes and societies of the National Association of REALTORS® as well as local Boards of REALTORS® offer sales training classes. Many brokerage firms and franchise companies hold regular sales training courses for sales personnel. Marketing knowledge is an important tool and a major part of the service consumers expect when buying and selling real estate.

Product Knowledge

Customers expect their real estate sales associates to know the market. They want the benefits of that product knowledge in marketing a property or finding the right property for purchase. A new practitioner should work hard to get that knowledge as quickly as possible to best serve the consumer. This course cannot help you acquire **product knowledge.**

In Practice

If you really want to know the market, see lots of property.

If you don't know the inventory, take as much time as you can to see as many listings as possible, then schedule at least a half-day each week to update your knowledge with new listings. Make a list of the best properties in each price range.

SETTING GOALS, BUSINESS PLANNING, AND TIME MANAGEMENT

Setting realistic goals is extremely important in real estate sales. Because real estate sales associates are usually independent contractors, they receive little supervision. Without a clear set of goals and a strong plan, the licensee may lose focus and direction. Goals should be written, measurable, attainable, and flexible, and they should contain deadlines. Once goals have been set, a business plan should show how to achieve the goals. Time management is an important part of that plan.

A distinction can be made between goals, plans, and time management. For example, an automobile trip from Orlando to St. Louis requires all three:

1. The goal is St. Louis.
2. The plan is the road map on which is drawn the route and mileage.
3. **Time management** consists of the daily objectives: When do we leave, when do we stop for food, and how far should we go today?

Goal setting should begin with a long-term view: What accomplishments does a person want to achieve in his lifetime? Once this long-term view is established, the next step is to work back to the present, using smaller increments of time. By working from the long term to the short term, it becomes clear what a licensee must do this year, this week, and today to achieve the long-term goal.

When setting these goals, the professional should always include personal and family objectives. An example of professional goal setting follows. (See Figure 3.2.)

A licensee's five-year goals are:

■ earning the following professional education designations: CRS and CRB;

■ obtaining a broker's license;

■ owning a brokerage firm with 15 associates; and

■ acquiring $150,000 in additional net worth.

Once the licensee establishes her one-year goal, she converts it into monthly and weekly goals—short-term tasks.

In Practice

Remember, because you're not salaried, you'll have to pay your own taxes, health insurance, advertising expenses, Board of REALTORS® dues, and license fees. Estimate those costs at about 35 percent of gross income. So if you need to net $50,000 annually, you'll have to set your goal at about $77,000! To calculate: 100% − 35% = 65%. $50,000 ÷ .65 = $76,923.

F I G U R E 3.2 ■ Sample Long-Range Plan

Year 5	CRS designation	Own brokerage firm	$150,000 net worth
Year 3	Finished 2 courses	Open office	$90,000 net worth
Year 1	Finished first course	Pass course and state exam	Must save at least $30,000 this year
Month 1	Check class schedule	Check class schedule	Must save at least $2,500 this month

F I G U R E 3.3 ■ Goals Worksheet

1. During the next 12 months, I want to earn	$48,000
2. That works out to be monthly earnings of (Line 1 ÷ 12)	$4,000
3. Probably 60% of my earnings should come from listings sold (Line 2 × .60)	$2,400
4. Probably 40% of my earnings should come from sales made (Line 2 × .40)	$1,600

Achieving my listing income:

5. In my market area, the average listing commission amount is (Figure used here should be changed to fit your market.)	$1,800
6. So I must have the following number of listings sold (Line 3 ÷ Line 5)	1.5
7. If only 75% of my listings sell, I have to get this many listings (Line 6 ÷ .75)	2
8. It may take this many listing appointments to get a listing (Get this number from your broker.)	5
9. So I need to go on this many listing appointments (Line 7 × Line 8)	10
10. It may take this many calls to get an appointment (Get this number from your broker.)	15
11. So I have to make this many calls per month (Line 9 × Line 10)	150
12. Which means I must make this many calls per week (Line 11 ÷ 4.3 weeks per month)	35

Achieving my sales income:

13. In my market area, the average sales commission is (Figure used here should be changed to fit your market.)	$1,800
14. So I've got to make this many sales per month (Line 4 ÷ Line 13)	0.9
15. It takes about this many showings to make a sale (Get this number from your broker.)	20
16. So I must show this many properties per month (Line 14 × Line 15)	18

Source: *30-Day Track to Success* by Edward J. O'Donnell, O'Donnell Publishing, Tallahassee, 2003

**Forms
To Go**

Use the worksheet shown in Figure 3.3 to see what you must do today to achieve a $48,000 income. If the assumptions shown are appropriate for your market area, it is simple to project how you can accomplish the goal. This example focuses on income goals, but the same exercise could be completed for other goals.

A blank worksheet for *your* personal goals is included in Forms To Go, Appendix B.

When the licensee is aware of what she must do today to achieve her long-term goals, she writes out the goals in contract form. It can be a private contract or a public document, with copies delivered to the broker and a mentor. Giving a copy to another person usually strengthens a commitment to succeed in the goals. A sample goals contract might look like the one in Figure 3.4.

The licensee then posts the goals where they are visible. "Out of sight, out of mind" is true where goals are concerned.

F I G U R E 3.4 ■ **Goals Contract**

I, _____, have determined my career and financial goals voluntarily, independently, and without coercion. I now formally commit to the following:

During the next 12 months, I will earn (from Line 1)	$48,000
I will obtain at least this number of listings per month (from Line 7)	2
I will go on this number of listing appointments weekly (Line 9 ÷ 4.3)	2.3
I will make this many listing calls weekly (from Line 12)	35
I will make this many sales each month (from Line 14)	0.9
I will show this many properties each week (Line 16 ÷ 4.3)	4

If I begin to fall behind, I request that my broker remind me of this commitment and prod me to stay on schedule so that I can achieve my goals.

Date _____   My signature _____

Date _____   My broker's signature _____

Date _____   My mentor's signature _____

Source: *30-Day Track to Success* by Edward J. O'Donnell, O'Donnell Publishing, Tallahassee, 2003.

Daily Goals and Time Management

Time management goes hand in hand with goal setting. Goals don't work without a schedule. Besides being measurable and attainable, a deadline must be set for achieving the goals. For example, the goal of "making as many calls as possible to prospective sellers" is attainable, but it is also immeasurable because no time deadline has been established. The statement "I will make five calls to prospective sellers by 6 PM today" is clear, measurable, and more likely to accomplish the goal.

The licensee should make a **to-do list** before each workday starts. The licensee should keep the list nearby and check off each item as it is completed. This provides a sense of accomplishment and motivation to continue. Some helpful points to remember about the list:

- Transfer unfinished tasks from the previous day.
- Include those daily tasks from the goals worksheet that are necessary to achieve long-term goals.
- **Prioritize** items on the list.
- Put the least pleasant items at the beginning of the list. ("Eat the frog first.") Completing the tough tasks results in the ability to get on with achieving important goals.
- Establish times for completing each task. Even if they need to be adjusted later, you have established a basic guideline to follow.
- Make notes for items to include on tomorrow's list.

FIGURE 3.5 ■ Sample Daily Activity Log

A Direct $	Hours [Goal]	Hours [Actual]	Comments
Prospecting for sellers	1	1	Pretty good. Got a lead for a listing.
Prospecting for buyers	1	0	Just couldn't get to this.
Make appointments with buyers or sellers			
Showing homes			
Presenting offers			
Making listing presentation			
Other activities that will directly produce $:			
Calling friends for referrals	1	1	Jane said she has a good friend who needs to sell a house. Maybe I'll call her tomorrow.
TOTAL	3	2	I need to do better at this.
B Office and Administrative			
Prepare CMAs			
Write ads	.5		
Attend office meetings	1	0	
Look at properties	2	1	Just didn't have time to see more.
Attend education meeting		1	
Other administrative activities:			
Prepare announcement and mail out	1	0	I'll try to do this tomorrow.
TOTAL	4.5	2	
C Wasted Time			
Stopped to shop at Dillard's	0	1	Had a sale; shouldn't have, but…
Friend stopped by office	0	1	She had a day off and wanted to talk. Should have arranged to see her at lunch.
TOTAL		2	Makes me mad at myself.
? Personal			
Scheduled time off			
Other (Describe):			
Renew driver's license	.5	1.5	Went to tax collector's office, traffic snarled. Should have just mailed it.
TOTAL	.5	1.5	
GRAND TOTAL HOURS	8.5	7.5	

Time Management Hints

A licensee can do many things to help manage his or her time more effectively:

■ Schedule time off for family, recreation, exercise, and relaxation. Failing to plan for these items can result in guilt feelings, discontent, poor health, or burnout.

■ Make a time log of all activities in 15-minute segments for about two weeks. This will show where time is wasted and may give clues for being a more effective time

**Forms
To Go**

manager. Your time can be rated as *A*, *B*, or *C* with respect to productivity. *A* time is most productive because it represents time actually spent with customers. *B* time is necessary work that can sometimes be handled by a personal assistant. *C* time is wasted time. Doubling your income may require only moving more of your workday to A time, not working twice as many total hours. See Figure 3.5 for a sample daily activity log. And find a blank worksheet in Forms To Go, Appendix B.

- Qualify sellers and buyers based on their financial ability to complete a transaction, as well as on their motivation. Working with unqualified buyers and sellers is both a disservice to the consumers and a nonproductive use of time.

- Be on time for appointments. Being late is a quick way to lose the confidence of customers. Plan for contingencies such as rush-hour traffic, last-minute phone calls, and weather-related inconveniences.

- Understand how much each hour of your day is worth. For example, if you earn $48,000 per year and work 290 days per year, nine hours per day, you work 2,610 hours, and the hourly rate is approximately $18.39.

- Make cost-effective decisions. If you make $18.39 per hour, hiring a personal assistant for $10 per hour is more cost-effective than doing your own mail-outs and clerical work. Going home to wash the car Monday afternoon may cost you $18.39 versus $9.95 at a car wash.

- Utilize technology to increase productivity.

Time Management and the Use of a Personal Assistant

Personal assistants are becoming more and more valuable and popular in the real estate business, and they assist real estate salespeople by doing two different types of work, as seen in the descriptions below of licensed personal assistants and unlicensed personal assistants.

Licensed personal assistants. Licensed personal assistants are very valuable and can provide all real estate services for the customers of the employing licensee, including showing and listing properties, calling prospects, and providing access to a listed property. A licensed personal assistant must be registered under the employing broker and may be paid for brokerage activities only by the broker. A sales associate may pay the licensed personal assistant for nonselling activities but may not compensate a personal assistant for performance of brokerage activities that require a license.

Unlicensed personal assistants. Many licensees now employ unlicensed assistants to help complete routine office activities, such as mass mailings, writing ads, and preparing comparative market analyses. Sales associates who employ such assistants and their brokers must ensure that the assistant does not perform any activities that violate the law. A list of activities that may be performed by unlicensed personal assistants is shown in Figure 3.6.

An unlicensed individual may *not* negotiate or agree to any commission split or referral fee on behalf of a licensee.

Unlicensed personal assistants, because they are paid by salary and may not be paid commissions, are under the control of their licensee employers. They may not be classified as independent contractors. The employers must withhold and pay FICA and income taxes and file withholding tax reports on a timely basis. Penalties for noncompliance can

FIGURE 3.6 ■ **Unlicensed Personal Assistant Activities**

1. Answer the phone and make telephone calls.
2. Fill out and submit listings and changes to any multiple-listing service.
3. Follow up on loan commitments after a contract has been negotiated and generally secure the status reports on the loan progress.
4. Assemble documents for closing.
5. Secure documents (public information) from courthouse, utility district, etc.
6. Have keys made for company listings and order surveys, termite inspections, home inspections, and home warranties with the licensed employer's approval.
7. Write ads for approval of licensee and supervising broker (newspaper ads, Web site updates, etc.), and prepare flyers and promotional information for approval by licensee and supervising broker.
8. Receive, record, and deposit earnest money, security deposits, and advance rents.
9. Only type the contract forms for approval by licensee and supervising broker.
10. Monitor licenses and personnel files.
11. Compute commission checks.
12. Place signs on property.
13. Order items of repair as directed by the licensee.
14. Prepare flyers and promotional information for approval by licensee and supervising broker.
15. Act as a courier service to deliver documents, pick up keys.
16. Place routine telephone calls on late rent payments.
17. Schedule appointments for licensees to show listed property.
18. Be at an open house
    a. for security purposes, and
    b. to hand out materials (brochures).
19. Answer questions concerning a listing for which the answer must be obtained from the licensed employer–approved printed information and is objective in nature (not subjective comments).
20. Gather information for a comparative market analysis (CMA).
21. Gather information for an appraisal.
22. Hand out objective, written information on a listing or rental.

be substantial. Licensed personal assistants may be paid by commission, but commissions may be paid only by the broker. If the licensed assistant is paid a salary or assigned specific working hours or told how to do the work, she would be an employee rather than an independent contractor.

A licensee also should be aware of the liability of having employees. An accident on the job could make the licensee's employer liable, as could an employee who injures another person while running errands for the licensee.

DISCUSSION EXERCISE 3.4

Do a role-playing session, assigning parts to Sharon, John, and the broker.

Sharon:

(*Excited*) I did it! I got that FSBO over on Killearney Way! Now I have another showing appointment. I *love* this business.

 Gotta go! See you later!

John:

(*Dejected, shaking head*) How does she keep doing it? She seems to get one appointment after another. I'm still slogging along trying to finish up my daily plan. I've got eight more things to do!

Broker:

(*Sympathetically*) Tell me what you have done today, John.

John:

Well, I had to make copies of the plat book pages for my farm area, make up a list of all the people on Scenic Drive, take my clothes to the cleaners, shop for a financial calculator, go to the title insurance company to get a rate card, and get my car washed. I did all that.

Broker:

What is still on the to-do list?

John:

I still need to find some listings for the guy who called on my floor duty yesterday and tell him about some property. I've got to get back in touch with the buyer I showed property to last week to set up another appointment.

 Oh! And I need to get a market report back to my wife's friends who said they're interested in selling their house. I also got a response to the notice of sale cards I mailed last week. I need to call those people back. They said they might consider selling. And the tenants on Jackson Bluff Road think they may be ready to buy. I need to call them and set up a time.

 There's just not enough time in the day!

 Can you help John evaluate his time management skills so he can be as productive as Sharon?

SUMMARY

Licensees who meet only the minimum education requirements of the license law cannot be called professionals in the true sense of the word. To be perceived as a professional, a real estate sales associate will:

- acquire oral, written, and nonverbal communication skills to share information clearly in order to reduce the chance of misunderstandings and misrepresentation;

- acquire technical knowledge, marketing knowledge, and product knowledge;

- practice effective time management; and

- set goals that are written, measurable, attainable, flexible, and that establish deadlines.

Setting goals allows new licensees to achieve those business and personal objectives that provide the ability to grow professionally and provide better customer service. Time management allows sales associates to meet commitments and maximize their efforts to provide good service.

KEY TERMS

body language	prioritize	time management
jargon	product knowledge	to-do list
marketing knowledge	professional ethics	written communication
nonverbal communication	reflecting	skills
oral communication skills	technical knowledge	

PRACTICE EXAM

1. A new agent at a realty hires an unlicensed personal assistant for $7 per hour. The unlicensed assistant may NOT
   a. write ads for approval by the licensee and her supervising broker and place classified advertising.
   b. place signs on properties.
   c. show a buyer several listed properties (inside and out), provide complete information, and help the buyer write the offer.
   d. gather information for a CMA.

2. When a sales associate pyramids his fingers during a discussion, a customer is likely to perceive that the sales associate is
   a. listening carefully.
   b. closed and defensive.
   c. not speaking honestly.
   d. acting in a superior way.

3. Within five years, Cindy wants to have $50,000 in cash in the bank. She is just starting out in real estate and has just enough cash available for her living expenses. Without considering interest on the funds, how much cash should Cindy have by the end of year three to be on target to reach her goal?
   a. $35,000
   b. $32,000
   c. $30,000
   d. $24,000

4. Sales associates, to make the best impression, would NOT
   a. keep their arms open and relaxed.
   b. cross their arms across the chest.
   c. have a firm handshake.
   d. lean forward into the conversation.

5. You can improve your written communication skills by
   a. attending a community college course on writing.
   b. joining Toastmasters.
   c. reading books on the subject.
   d. doing both a and c.

6. Jonathon calls a realty to speak with Arthur about a property he wants to see. Arthur's secretary tells him, "Arthur is on the caravan." Puzzled, Jonathon hangs up with thoughts of the desert. This expression is an example of
   a. Jonathon's lack of communication skills.
   b. jargon.
   c. nonverbal communication.
   d. a common expression that buyers and sellers of real estate should understand.

7. Jan is in the office when she gets a call from a property owner who wants to list her home. Jan is uncertain about how to do a CMA and how to complete the necessary forms. Based on this information, Jan lacks
   a. technical knowledge.
   b. product knowledge.
   c. marketing knowledge.
   d. communication skills.

8. What is NOT true about an unlicensed personal assistant?
   a. The employing licensee may be financially liable for accidents involving the personal assistant.
   b. The employing licensee may be responsible for violations of the license law or FREC rules.
   c. The licensee's employing broker may be financially responsible for acts of the personal assistant, as well as for violations of the license law or FREC rules.
   d. Assistants rarely help increase the income of the sales associate enough to cover the assistant's compensation.

9. Setting and meeting goals does NOT involve
   a. starting with short-range increments.
   b. starting with long-term goals, then breaking them down into short-term objectives.
   c. writing the goals down.
   d. giving a copy of the goals to a mentor to help strengthen commitment.

10. Tim's goal is to make $58,000 in gross collected commissions next year. He feels that his listings should contribute about 50 percent of the required income. The average commission per transaction in his office is $1,200, and about two-thirds of his listings are expected to sell. He gets about three listings in five listing presentations. Approximately how many presentations must he make monthly to stay on target?
    a. Two
    b. Three
    c. Five
    d. Ten

11. Larry's goal is "to make as much money as I can next year." What is TRUE about his goal?
    a. As long as he works toward the goal, it is effective.
    b. It is not measurable.
    c. It is not attainable.
    d. It should be combined with a time management plan that says "I'll work until I get tired most days."

12. An effective method of finding out where time is wasted in a daily schedule is to
    a. keep good goal sheets.
    b. make a time log of activities.
    c. ask your spouse.
    d. measure the distance from appointment to appointment.

13. According to the text, sales associates should make a log of daily activities and
    a. try to move most activities into Section B (Office and Administrative).
    b. attempt to move hours spent on Section A (Direct $) to Personal Time.
    c. spend more time on Section A (Direct $).
    d. reduce personal time to 0 hours.

14. A new sales associate needs to earn $40,000 the first year. If expenses such as Social Security, Medicare, and operating expenses average 35 percent of gross income, what should the sales associate's goal be for gross income received from real estate commissions?
    a. $14,000
    b. $29,630
    c. $56,615
    d. $61,538

15. Guilt feelings, discontent, and burnout are likely to result from
    a. wasting time in the office.
    b. working too hard.
    c. failing to schedule time off for family, recreation, and exercise.
    d. not staying focused on business.

16. Which is LEAST likely to be one of a sales associate's five year goals?
    a. Obtaining names of customers who are likely to list their homes
    b. Earning a GRI designation
    c. Increasing net worth by $100,000
    d. Opening a brokerage firm

17. John works nine hours every day but Sunday. Last year he made $68,000. What is his gross hourly rate, assuming he worked 50 weeks?
    a. $34.00
    b. $25.19
    c. $22.35
    d. $17.92

18. When making a to-do list for the day, a sales associate should NOT
    a. establish times for completing each task.
    b. save the least pleasant tasks for after lunch.
    c. transfer unfinished tasks from the previous day.
    d. make notes to include on tomorrow's list.

19. A customer who observes a sales associate covering his mouth while giving a listing presentation most likely would perceive that the sales associate
    a. has chapped lips.
    b. feels superior.
    c. is closed and defensive.
    d. may not be speaking honestly.

20. A productive sales associate should NOT
    a. stay out of the office as much as possible.
    b. employ a personal assistant.
    c. work with unqualified buyers.
    d. prioritize his or her time.

APPLY WHAT YOU'VE LEARNED!

The author suggests the following actions to reinforce the material in *Section I—Laying the Foundation for a Successful Career:*

- ❏ List the customer contacts you have had in the previous two weeks. If you acted as a transaction broker, did you tend to favor one party over another?

- ❏ Write a script that you could use with a seller for introducing and explaining the property condition disclosure statement.

- ❏ Select a federal law in this section. Go to the Internet and find a site that includes the statutes. Print the statutes and then read the law, highlighting the important parts.

- ❏ List your personal characteristics that you believe will be of most value to you in your real estate career, then refine the list by showing which activities will best use those strengths.

- ❏ List your personal characteristics that you believe need improvement to enhance your career. Make one action plan focusing on ways to achieve those improvements and another focusing on ways to reduce the impact of those personal characteristics that are hard to change.

- ❏ At the next meeting of your Board of REALTORS®, don't hesitate to give an opinion on the subject under discussion or to market your listing during the marketing time.

- ❏ Prepare a to-do list for tomorrow, arranged by priority.

- ❏ Set a goal of getting one new listing within the next seven days, and write out an action plan to achieve the goal.

- ❏ Prepare a short-term goal that includes the number of customer contacts you intend to make each day for the next ten days.

OBTAINING LISTINGS THAT SELL

This section of the text leads the new associate through the activities with the most important goal in real estate—obtaining salable listings. Listings generate sales leads. Those persons with a large inventory of salable listings will make the highest income because listers are the only sales associates who can get paid on both sides of the transaction.

Chapter 4 shows how to build a strong prospecting program to generate a substantial listing inventory. Power prospecting is hard work that separates the highly successful professional from the making-a-living licensees.

Chapter 5 shows how to make that listing salable by pricing it to sell.

Chapter 6 shows how to turn the hard work of prospecting into signed listing agreements through effective listing presentations.

Chapter 7 describes the listing contract, showing licensees how to explain the agreement to the sellers.

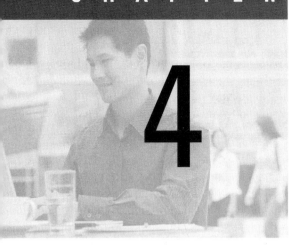

CHAPTER 4

PROSPECTING FOR LISTINGS

LEARNING OBJECTIVES

Upon completion of this chapter, you should be able to:

1. list the five principal sources of listings;

2. describe at least three types of properties a licensee should not attempt to list;

3. explain why a listing commission seems much higher than the stated percentage to the seller;

4. list at least three circumstances under which a FSBO might be ready to list right away;

5. describe the three transactions that can be generated from a call to a for-rent-by-owner;

6. state the principal reason that listings expire; and

7. list the five categories in a leads database.

OVERVIEW

Listings are the lifeblood of the real estate industry. Without listings to advertise, a brokerage firm gets few prospective buyers and makes few sales. This chapter describes some very effective methods for prospecting for listings, including how to work with FSBOs and FRBOs, how to communicate effectively with an owner whose listing has expired, how to organize a listing farm, and how to canvass for leads.

An important part of working with prospective sellers is the need to understand the situation and to tailor your presentation and problem-solving techniques to their particular needs.

At the end of the chapter is a section on how to use advanced prospecting techniques to become a listing superstar. It will take a lot of work and money, but the results can be truly amazing.

PROSPECTING OBJECTIVES

The main objective when prospecting for listings is to get an appointment to make a listing presentation. Because listings are the lifeblood of the real estate business, sales associates must know how to find sellers who need their professional services. In Chapter 4, the new sales associate will learn the most productive sources of listings and how to effectively approach the sellers and obtain an appointment to make a listing presentation.

The most important sources of listings for a *new* sales associate are:

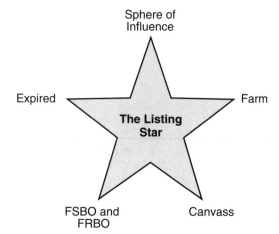

1. Sphere of influence
2. Expired listing
3. Farm
4. For sale by owners (FSBOs) and for rent by owners (FRBOs)
5. Canvass

Notice that the discussion began with sources of listings for *new* sales associates. In two, three, or four years, the new sales associate who uses these sources will have the most powerful listing source of all: previous customers.

No matter which method a sales associate uses to locate prospective listings, he must prepare for listing appointments carefully. The comparative market analysis (CMA) is necessary to help price the listing. The sales associate also must understand what costs the seller can be expected to pay, how to complete and explain the listing agreement, and how to market and service the listing.

YOU DON'T WANT THEM ALL

When prospecting for listings, qualify the properties and prioritize your efforts. Be picky. Your time is limited, and there are only so many listings you can work to get. The amount of effort required for prospecting and making a listing presentation is the same for a good listing as for a poor one. Don't spend time working to get a listing if:

- the seller is not motivated;
- the seller suggests you break the law by nondisclosure or discriminatory practices;
- the listing is outside your target market, such as in an adjoining community or is a warehouse opportunity if you're a residential sales associate;
- the listing is outside of your preferred price ranges;
- the property condition is so bad you would be embarrassed to show it; or
- the owners are so rude or demanding you don't want to work with them.

The secret is to prioritize your efforts and focus only on those listings that will sell within a reasonable time with reasonable effort on your part. For those you don't want, send a referral.

F I G U R E   4.1 ■ **List of Friends and Acquaintances**

Name	Address	Phone	Date Mailed	Date Called

SPHERE OF INFLUENCE

For a new sales associate, this source is the best source of new listings and sales. Your sphere of influence will include family, friends, and past customers.

Close Friends and Family

This category will be very small, probably having no more than 30–50 names, but it can be a powerful listing generator. Your close friends and members of your family will do business with you and send you referrals, but you may need to ask. The term "close friend" suggests a very strong, usually long-term relationship with mutual trust, care, and respect. Sometimes even close friends are reluctant to do business with friends for fear that the relationship could be affected. Your friends must be convinced of your professionalism and dedication. You must let them know when you do business that you will wear your "professional hat." The contacts within this group are natural and frequent, and all requests for business will be low key.

Friends and Past Customers

These are people we know reasonably well, but who are not close friends. Perhaps we have had lunch together or worked on a committee together. The size of this category will grow with the number of years you are in real estate (past customers). This group is a significant source of new business and referrals. Work it diligently! Each person on the list should hear from you by mail or phone at least twice monthly.

You should start by making a contact list of your friends and acquaintances. (See Figure 4.1.) The number will vary depending on your social activities, but try to list at least 50 people. You should call your family members to ask for business. Because of the do-not-call registry rules, depending on your relationship, you should contact most of them with a handwritten note. Handwritten notes are much more personal than a typed letter. A sample note is included in Figure 4.2.

If your friend is not on the do-not-call registry, follow up in about a week with a phone call.

FIGURE 4.2 ■ Sample Note to Your Friends

Hi Sheryl,

Just a note to tell you hello, and to let you know I'm working full-time in real estate with Crystal Springs Realty.

If you should hear of anyone getting ready to buy or sell, I'd really appreciate your calling to let me know.

I hope Randy and the boys are all well. Let's have lunch soon!

(signed)

EXPIRED LISTINGS

Expired listings can be a profitable source of business for licensees if they understand why listings expire, how to locate them, and when and how to approach the owners of expired listings.

Why Listings Expire

Some listings don't sell during the listing period for a variety of reasons, including:

- market conditions (oversupply of homes available for sale);
- property condition;
- listing period too short;
- uncooperative owner or tenant;
- overpriced; or
- poor marketing effort.

Except for the uncooperative owner or tenant, the major reason listings expire *is almost always price*. If there is an oversupply of homes on the market, the price should have been reduced. If the property condition is poor, it was probably overpriced. A short listing period calls for a low price.

Finding Expired Listings

Listings expire from the multiple-listing service (MLS) every day. They are shown in the change-of-status section where you can also find sales and price changes. Without the MLS, it is more difficult to work this market. An excellent way to find expired listings is to get a recommendation from sales associates who have a listing about to expire when the owner won't relist. You can either pay a referral fee or have a cooperative arrangement to send your sellers to them at the end of a listing period.

How to Approach Owners of Expired Listings

The owner whose property did not sell may be disillusioned with brokers and nonreceptive to your approach. To effectively work expired listings, you must have empathy. The seller whose home was on the market for six months and didn't sell might:

- wonder why he or she bought a home that no one else likes;

■ feel the broker did little or nothing to market the property; or

■ believe the home was overpriced during the listing period.

Once you understand how the owner might feel, you will be better able to tailor your approach to the situation.

Using the same methods used with FSBOs or FRBOs, licensees can prospect for expired listings by:

■ direct mail,

■ telephone, or

■ visit.

Direct mail may be too late because owners who want to sell often list with another broker immediately after the listing expires. A visit may not be as time-effective as first telephoning, but visiting the owner is more likely to result in getting the listing. When the owner answers the door, you might ask the questions in the telephone calling guide in Figure 4.3. Your objective is to be invited inside to view the home, getting an opportunity for a listing presentation.

FARMING

Think of farming as the cultivation of listings, much like establishing an orange grove. You can't get rich planting one tree. The more trees you plant, the greater the harvest. The grove takes a lot of work for some time without any apparent return. But when the grove begins to produce, it can shower you with fruit for years to come. And as the trees grow larger, the size of the harvest increases and can make you rich.

The listing **farm** requires lots of hard work to get established and for a time may have no apparent return. Many listing farmers abandon the grove just before it produces. If you decide to farm an area, you must make a commitment to continue for at least three years.

What's the Payoff?

Farming is a disciplined approach to prospecting. It is intended to expand a sales associate's sphere of influence, thus increasing listings and sales. Joyce Caughman's book, *Real Estate Prospecting*, 2nd ed. (Dearborn Real Estate Education, 1994), describes how farming should produce 20 percent of the listings in the farm area in the second year, 50 percent in the third year, and up to 75 percent of the listings after that.

F I G U R E 4.3 ■ **Expired Listing Telephone Calling Guide**

1. Check the do-not-call registry before calling.
2. Introduce yourself, your company, and say why you're calling.
3. Tell the seller the listing has expired and ask if he or she still wants to sell.
   ■ If the answer is yes, get an appointment.
   ■ If the answer is no, ask if the seller would like to know why the house didn't sell. Get an appointment, and make a CMA study.
   ■ If the answer is no, say thanks and place another call.

Assume that owners in your farm area move once every six years and your farm has 800 houses. That means 133 homes will be listed this year (800 ÷ 6). If you're in the third year of your farm and get 50 percent of those listings, you'll get 67 listings, or 5½ each month. Assuming further that the average sales price is $200,000, ⅔ of your listings sell, and your share is 1.5 percent, your listing commissions alone would be over $134,000 ($200,000 × 67 × ⅔ × .015).

How Many Homes Should Be in a Farm?

Because the farm may take six months before generating listings, a sales associate must also prospect using other methods. A new licensee should start a farm with no more than 200 homes but should select an area that allows for expansion of the farm. Many successful sales associates ultimately develop farms with a total of 800 to 1,000 homes located in several neighborhoods.

How to Choose the Farm Area

You must carefully select your listing farm. It should have the following characteristics:

- Middle to upper price range
- High turnover
- Increasing property values
- Not currently being farmed by any other sales associate

The five steps to take are as follows:

1. Select at least six potential farm neighborhoods. Check the MLS or the tax appraiser's office for all sales during the previous year.
2. Of those sales, review the listing office and sales associate so you can see if one person is getting a large market share. This would indicate that person is farming the area.
3. Get the total number of homes in the area by looking at the subdivision plat map.
4. Divide the number of sales by the number of homes in the neighborhood to get the turnover index.
5. Select the neighborhood that is not currently being farmed that has the highest turnover index.

Figure 4.4 is an example of the evaluation process. Blackwater Farms and Green Valley are currently being farmed, so it's not worthwhile to try to compete if other good areas are available. Orangewood has a 25 percent turnover ratio, and the home prices are in the $200,000 range. Orangewood is our choice.

Make Farm Contacts Now, Organize Over Time

Some sales associates spend too much time preparing to farm and too little time making contacts. While it's nice to have a wall map, a database of information about each homeowner, or prepared mailings for the next six months, that can be done later. It's tempting to "play office" rather than risk rejection by talking with prospective sellers.

FIGURE 4.4 ■ Farm Area Evaluation

Neighborhood	Currently Farmed?	Home Prices	Sales Last Year	Homes in Neighborhood	Turnover Index
Rustling Woods	No	$175,000	88	521	17%
Blackwater Farms	Yes	$200,000	86	416	21%
Dolphin Downs	No	$150,000	145	740	20%
Glass Springs	No	$250,000	52	345	15%
Orangewood	No	$200,000	172	685	25%
Green Valley	Yes	$250,000	68	534	13%

One task that you should do up front, however, is to prepare a CMA for the neighborhood, showing listings and sales for at least three years. This will help you discuss prices and also to know what prospective sellers paid when they purchased. Preparation of a CMA is discussed in Chapter 5.

How to Make Contacts in Your Farm Area

Contacts in your farm area should be a combination of direct mail, telephone, and a visit. Remember, direct mail is passive prospecting that works well as long as personal contact is part of the farming program. A multi-colored newsletter with your name and company logo is inexpensive and can result in more business. You can also send a letter of introduction, a postcard, or any other mailing piece that keeps your name in front of the owners. Notice of listings and sales in the farm area can be one of the most effective and cost-efficient mailings but should be followed up with a phone call or a visit. (See Figure 4.5.)

Calling persons in a farm area can be effective, but there should be a good reason for the call. Some of those reasons include telling about a new listing, a sale, or that you will be holding an open house. Remember to check the do-not-call registry.

The best way to cultivate your farm is by visiting owners in the neighborhood. Saturdays are wonderful visit days. A drive through the neighborhood will allow you to stop and meet people out walking or doing yard work. A cold canned drink is a good "ice-breaker."

Of course, just knocking on doors is one of the best activities. Give the homeowner a gift such as a calendar or yardstick with your name (and company name) imprinted on it. The owners may remember you when it's time to sell their homes.

You should make at least one contact each month with everyone in your farm area. If you work 25 days each month and farm 500 homes, you must make at least 20 contacts each day. Rotating between mailings, phone calls, and visits may reduce your workload. After you become fairly well known, you can increase the mail contacts and reduce the personal contacts.

FIGURE 4.5 ■ **Notice of Sale Card**

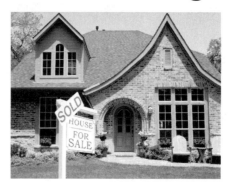

We've done it again!

We have just participated in the sale of your neighbor's home located at

724 Oak Street.

Your neighborhood is very attractive and much in demand by buyers. You might be pleasantly surprised when you learn the market value of your home. I'd be glad to furnish information to you about prices and marketability.

Please call me right away if you might be considering selling your home.

Hilda Cummings, Sales Associate
(312) 555-4300 • Floyd Realty, Inc.

FOR-SALE-BY-OWNER

The only potential prospect we know *for sure* who wants to sell his house is the **for sale by owner (FSBO).** It is surprising that so few new sales associates use this outstanding source of listings in their daily plan. The myths many sales associates quote to avoid prospecting the FSBO market include the following:

■ It takes more organizational skills to make the prospecting pay off.

■ Sometimes FSBOs are not courteous to licensees who phone or visit (but remember, you can phone only if the owner is not on the National Do Not Call Registry).

■ They won't agree to add the commission to their price.

■ It takes significant selling skills to get a listing from a FSBO.

■ FSBO houses are overpriced already.

Sales associates who master the FSBO market by adapting to its unique characteristics are able to significantly increase their listing inventories.

WHY FSBOs ARE FSBOs

If you were an owner of a property, try to think why you might consider selling it yourself rather than listing it. Assume your home is worth $200,000. A broker's commission of 6 percent would result in your paying $12,000, a pretty substantial amount. But if you further assume you bought the home two years ago for $185,000, with a 10 percent down payment, your equity is now approximately $35,000.

Calculation: $200,000 minus the original mortgage of $166,500 (.90 × $185,000) less some principal paid back.

Now, you see, the $12,000 is much greater than 6 percent. It's actually closer to 34 percent of the equity, perhaps explaining why a seller might want to try it alone. It also explains why you will need a good presentation to show them why they need you.

FSBO Characteristics

First, anyone in sales can be much more effective with a healthy supply of empathy. *Empathy* is the sensitivity to the thoughts and feelings of others. To be able to persuade an owner to list, the licensee must first understand the mindset of that owner.

Those of us who have sold a car directly, rather than trading it in, usually did it to make more money from the sale. Whether that savings occurs is not the point; the fact is we did it for that purpose.

It's fair to assume that of all the FSBOs out there, at least 90 percent are trying to sell without a broker in order to save the commission. It's also likely that only a certain set of circumstances will change that mindset. The FSBO may be ready to list if he or she is:

- moving out of town right away;
- concerned about personal security;
- baffled by the home-selling process;
- not available during normal hours to show the home;
- uncomfortable negotiating with people; or
- convinced that a buyer will reduce the price offered by *at least* the amount of the commission.

The sales associate who has made a positive contact with the sellers when those circumstances exist is most likely to get the listing. While "moving out of town right away" on the list above is based on external conditions, the licensee may be able to change the sellers' minds on the others during the listing presentation (covered in Chapter 6).

Finding and Tracking the FSBOs

An important part of the FSBO prospecting process is finding and tracking FSBOs. Most sellers use a yard sign, classified ad, or a note on a community bulletin board.

F I G U R E 4.6 ■ For-Sale-by-Owner E-Mail Service

From: Landvoice.com
Sent: Thursday, May 13, 2007 3:29 AM
To: AliceNewby@Hendricksrealty.com
Subject: May 13 2007 - FSBO Information

(1 of 2)
FL: Tallahassee (All) Source: TAL Newspapers A
First Advertised: 05/13/2007
850-555-0001   Do Not Call Registry

Sam Seller

5555 Main Rd., Tallahassee, FL 32310-4635
HOME in TALLAHASSEE $525,000
Bd: 3 Ba: 4 Style: Ga:
Sq Ft: 3645   Year Built: Lot Size:

1   Most sales associates locate FSBOs in the classified ads. The licensee may assume that
2   all ads that don't have the name of a brokerage firm are FSBOs. A broker's ad without the
3   firm name is a *blind ad*, a violation of Chapter 475.

4   *LandVoice.com* provides a daily e-mail service to subscribers in most cities for about $40
5   monthly, showing all new FSBOs advertised in the local newspapers that day. It includes the
6   owner's name, phone number (with do-not-call registry status), address, and other advertised
7   information. See Figure 4.6 for a sample of e-mail data. Subscribers can also view complete
8   data on the LandVoice Web site and search FSBOs by city area or price range.

WEB LINK

http://landvoice.com

9   A list of all FSBOs coming on the market for the previous week or month is also avail-
10   able with *LandVoice.com*, so it becomes easier to track time on the market.

11   Because not all FSBOs advertise in the newspaper, the licensee can find those proper-
12   ties by driving through neighborhoods and asking friends and family to call when they see
13   a sign or notice on a bulletin board.

14   If you don't use an FSBO service such as the one shown, you should organize the
15   FSBOs by phone number. Even though this is the age of technology, many sales associates
16   keep index cards with the phone numbers prominently placed in the upper right corner
17   of the card. If you use this system, you then sort the cards by the number. When going
18   through the paper, look for the number, then compare it with the cards. If it's not there,
19   this is a new property. See Figure 4.7 for an example of the file card system. To find the
20   owners' information, use a cross-reference directory as described later in this chapter.

21   It's easier to sort the ads if the records are on your computer. A spreadsheet or a data-
22   base program such as Access makes it easier. Even your word processor makes it simple to
23   sort using the "table" function. (See the sample of table function in Figure 4.8.) Contact
24   programs such as *Top Producer* or *Act!* are specifically designed for this purpose, have many
25   more functions, and are more user-friendly.

F I G U R E 4.7 ■   **FSBO Index Card**

W. H. Lister (305) 555-4369
0123 Street Way
Miami, 33165

Contacts:
4/15   Phoned, said he did not want to list now.
4/20   Stopped by and gave him sample contracts. "Thanks!"
4/25   He got my "thanks" card. Called to ask me if I could give him an opinion of value.
4/26   Went over my CMA with him at the house.
4/27   He called me to come over and list his house at $220,000.

FSBO Prospecting Techniques

Licensees who work the FSBO market must be persistent, organized, and disciplined (POD). The first approach to an FSBO can be done by:

- direct mail,
- telephone call, or
- visit.

**Forms
To Go**

Direct mail is a low-risk exercise that is likely to have a fairly low reward ratio. Direct mail is **passive prospecting,** which should always be followed by a phone call or a visit. When used in conjunction with one of the other methods, it can be an effective way to prospect. The objective of sending direct mail is to introduce yourself to the seller. See Forms To Go, Appendix B, for a sample FSBO letter.

Before telephoning a FSBO, be certain to reread the section covering the National Do Not Call Registry in Chapter 1. The liability for a violation of the law is quite substantial. If an FSBO's phone number is on the list, make a note such as <DO NOT CALL LIST> in all data. (See Figure 4.8.)

F I G U R E 4.8 ■   **Sample Table for FSBO Information Sorted by Phone Number**

Phone	Name / Address	Price	Contacts
(305) 555-2527	J. B. House 1111 Another St. Miami, 33185	$175,000	4/12 Phoned. Made listing appointment 4/13 Got listing at $175,000.
(305) 555-2421 <DO NOT CALL LIST!>	Mary Mover 2222 Avenue Miami, 33134	$215,000	4/16 Stopped by. Told me she wasn't interested, but took sample contract.
(305) 555-4369	W. H. Lister 0123 Street Way Miami, 33165	$220,000	4/15 Phoned, said he did not want to list now. 4/20 Stopped by and gave him sample contracts. "Thanks!" 4/25 He got my "thanks" card. Called to ask me if I could give him an opinion of value. 4/26 Went over my CMA with him at the house. 4/27 He called me to come over and list his house at $220,000.

F I G U R E 4.9 ■ FSBO Telephone Calling Guide

1. Check the do-not-call registry before calling.
2. Introduce yourself, your company, and say why you're calling.
3. Ask to visit the home at a specific time.
4. If the seller declines, you could ask if the seller would agree to pay a commission if you bring a buyer.
5. If the seller agrees to pay a commission, get an appointment to see the home.
6. If the seller doesn't agree, ask if he'd sell if the buyer agreed to pay the commission.
7. If the seller says no, ask if you can call again in the future.

The objective for the call is to get an appointment to give a listing presentation. (See Figure 4.9.)

The most effective way to get a listing is by visiting the house. Many licensees don't like to do this because of the risk of rejection. When you see a FSBO sign, just stop the car and walk to the door. You can also set up the visits by geographic area, using your FSBO data cards. Asking questions is the best approach. The objective for the visit is to get an appointment to give the sellers a listing presentation. (See Figure 4.10.)

At the FSBO's Front Door

The following seven questions may help you build rapport with the sellers:

1. How much are you asking for the home?
2. How long has it been for sale?
3. Are you moving out of town?
4. Have you had any offers?
5. If I brought a buyer to you, would you pay commission?
6. Do you have a sales contract?
7. Would you like to see a market report on your neighborhood?

F I G U R E 4.10 ■ So, You've Got an FSBO Appointment?

If an owner accepts your request to visit, set the appointment for a time when both parties will be home and available to talk. Ask that the sellers have several items ready for you, if possible:

■ a copy of the paperwork when they purchased, especially the deed and title insurance documents;
■ their homeowners' insurance policy;
■ a copy of the property survey, if available; and
■ an extra set of front door keys.

Why do you need these items now?

1. Because they will be helpful when you list the home
2. Because when you get there and find all these items neatly stacked on the table, it's your signal that they are ready to list their home

In Practice

Don't forget, sellers are also buyers. You have to find out what they intend to buy, and where, when this house is sold. If the seller tells you they are moving to another city, you have an opportunity to send a referral to a broker in that area. Referral commissions can be a significant part of your annual income if you always get the information about where people are moving.

FOR-RENT-BY-OWNER

The most common way to find many **for rent by owners** (FRBOs) is by reading the classified ads in the newspaper or other classified-ad publication. Owners trying to rent a house are good prospects for either a listing, a sale, or property management.

FRBO Characteristics

The following analysis demonstrates that while they are similar to FSBOs in some ways, FRBOs struggle with entirely different problems, requiring a more appropriate problem-solving approach by licensees who want to list their properties.

FRBO as listing prospect. Those who own rental homes experience difficulties such as vacancies, uncollectible rent, evictions, and damage to the property. When the home is currently for rent, the sales associate must understand that some or all of those problems may have occurred very recently.

FRBO as buying prospect. Sometimes investors have factored such problems into their business plan, understanding the characteristics of rental property. Those investors frequently plan to continue investing in rental property.

FRBO as property management prospect. Persons who have their property for rent may be weary of the time and effort involved in managing their own property. They may have had difficulty showing the property because of other commitments, and sometimes rental prospects are "no-shows." Your call may come at the right moment and may turn into an opportunity for management. If your company does not have a property management department, ask your broker to send a referral to a local company that will pay a referral fee for the business.

FRBO Prospecting Techniques

The first approach to an FRBO can be made by:

- direct mail,
- telephone, or
- visit

Because the phone number in the ad is that of the owner's home, not the rental, it's difficult to learn where the rental property is located. The first contact can be direct mail followed by a phone call. Before telephoning a FRBO, be certain to check the National Do Not Call Registry. (See Figure 4.11.)

F I G U R E 4.11 ▨ FRBO Telephone Calling Guide

1. Check the do-not-call registry before calling.
2. Introduce yourself, your company, and say why you're calling.
3. Ask if the owner has considered selling rather than renting.
    - ■ If the answer is yes, suggest you do a market report, and get an appointment.
    - ■ If the answer is no, go to the next step.
4. Ask if the owner might consider buying other income property.
    - ■ If the answer is yes, get an appointment to discuss other properties.
    - ■ If the answer is no, go to the next step.
5. Ask if the owner has considered hiring a professional property manager.
    - ■ If the answer is yes, get an appointment for your company's property manager.
    - ■ If the answer is no, thank the owner for his or her time and say goodbye.

The objective for this call is to get an appointment to give a listing presentation. Remember, the advertised phone number matches the owner's address, not the rental property.

Another mailing, a phone call, or a visit should always follow direct mail. When used in connection with one of the other methods, it can be an effective way to prospect. The objective of sending direct mail is to get a call from the seller.

Because the owner does not live at the rental property, visiting is probably the least effective method.

CANVASSING

Every sales associate who aspires to attaining top producer status understands the power of canvassing. While this is the last prospecting tool mentioned as a listing source, it is likely the most important.

Canvassing is prospecting by mail, telephone, and in person, not necessarily in your farm. All **power prospecting** programs include canvassing.

Power Prospecting

Setting high income goals requires a commitment to prospect. The three keys to prospecting success are as follows:

1. Numbers

2. Consistency

3. Organization

Numbers. The difference between making a living and becoming a real estate sales superstar is numbers. Following these tips will help you become a successful prospector:

- ■ Follow all laws when prospecting, paying particular attention to the federal Do Not Call Registry.

- ■ A cross-reference directory can give you information on area residents and businesses. Cross-reference directories are arranged by street addresses and numerically by phone number. Listings arranged by street addresses allow you to find all the residents and businesses on a particular street in sequence. Listings arranged by phone number allow you to find all the numbers and names for a particular area code and exchange. The product is available in print, online, or on CD. An annual subscription (costing from $150 to $400, depending on the location) will give current information, and can filter out phone numbers that appear on the National Do Not Call Registry.

WEB LINK

Hill-Donnelly Corp. sells cross-reference directories for many market areas: *www.hill-donnelly.com*

- Use a prospecting tool like The Daily 100 Power Prospecting Points Chart. (See Figure 4.12.) Note that this chart awards more weight to activities that are more likely to result in a listing or a sale. For example, sending a mailing to for-sale-by-owners is worth one point, but visiting in person gives five points because it is a more productive activity.

- Work out of the office as much as possible. The only people you'll see there are other sales associates.

- Avoid time-wasting activities such as idle conversation, poor organization and planning, and uncontrolled interruptions. If you're worth $18.40 per hour, four hours per week of idle conversation with associates in the office costs you nearly $75!

It's all about prospecting. If a sales associate can just reduce wasted hours and hours spent on administrative "support" functions and shift them to A-level activities, talked about in Chapter 3, income should show a dramatic rise.

For example, if a sales associate decides to make a commitment to do power prospecting, and is able to increase contacts, the income should show a dramatic increase. Figure 4.13 and Figure 4.14 show what can happen to the income stream in seven months if a person goes from little or no prospecting to power prospecting. The amounts shown won't magically work for every sales associate, but depend on the following two assumptions:

1. The sales associate is articulate, likes people, and is disciplined.

2. The sales associate has finished training and knows how to:

   a. prepare a CMA,
   b. make an effective listing presentation,
   c. show properties,
   d. ask closing questions, and
   e. ask for the order.

For example, John is a sales associate who has been "drifting" through his startup-training program. After he completes the program, he decides to work smarter and increase his prospecting time. The first month he works 20 days and gets 700 points (35 per day). He continues to work the program, becomes more focused, and is finally able to achieve a 2,500-point month. His business increases dramatically. He finally understands that "prospecting is the name of the game." While some licensees may be skeptical of the income levels shown, power prospectors know the numbers *work*.

Figure 4.14 is a graphic illustration of the results of the power prospecting program.

F I G U R E 4.12 ■   The Daily 100 Power Prospecting Points Chart—How to Survive and Make Money Selling Real Estate

Directions: Complete any combination of the activities listed below. If you consistently "earn" at least 100 Daily Power Prospecting points, your personal income will increase dramatically!

Name:_____ Week Beginning:_____ Goal for Wk:$_____

Suggested Activity	Points	Mon.	Tue.	Wed.	Thu.	Fri.	Sat.	Sun.	Total
Listings:									
FSBO (For Sale by Owner)—Mail	1								
FSBO—Phone	2								
FSBO—Visit	5								
Expired Listing—Mail	1								
Expired Listing—Phone	2								
Expired Listing—Visit	5								
Notice of Listing—Mail	1								
Notice of Listing—Phone	2								
Notice of Sale—Mail	1								
Notice of Sale—Phone	2								
FRBO (For Rent by Owner)—Mail	1								
FRBO—Phone	2								
Cold Call Completed	2								
Follow up on Listing Prospect	2								
Listing Presentation Made	10								
Listing Taken	20								
Servicing Listing by Mail	2								
Servicing Listing by Phone	3								
Servicing Listing by Visit	5								
Listing Price Change	5								
Listing Term Extended	5								
Contract on Listing Presented	10								
Listing Sold	20								
Sales:									
Office Caravan (per home seen)	3								
Previewing Listings	3								
Prospecting Calls to Renters	2								
Open House	10								
Name and Phone from Ad Call	5								
Follow up on Buying Prospect	2								
Property Shown to Buyer	5								
Contract Written	10								
Contract Accepted	20								
Sales Servicing Call	3								
Referral Requested from Buyer	2								
Referral Sent to Another City	5								
Closing Attended	10								
Other:									
Attend Office Meeting	10								
Attend MLS Marketing Session	10								
Attend Education Meeting (hr)	10								
Past Customer Contacted	3								
Phone Friend about Real Estate	3								
Lunch with a Prospect	5								
Attend Civic Club Meeting	5								
Thank-You Card Mailed	3								
Personal Referral Received	5								
Newsletter Mailed	2								
Other Productive Activities	?								
Total Points									

Source: *30-Day Track to Success* by Edward J. O'Donnell, O'Donnell Publishing, Tallahassee, 2003.

F I G U R E 4.13   ■   John's Power Prospecting Program

	Month 1	Month 2	Month 3	Month 4	Month 5	Month 6	Month 7
Points on Daily 100	**700**	**1,000**	**1,200**	**1,400**	**2,000**	**2,200**	**2,500**
Following month business results							
Listings taken	1	1	1	2	2	2	3
Sales made	0	0	1	1	2	2	3
Listings sold	0	1	1	2	2	3	4
Total transactions	1	2	3	5	6	7	10
Commissions: ($150,000 price with a 1.5% commission to sales assoc.)	$0	$2,250	$4,500	$6,750	$9,000	$11,250	$15,750

F I G U R E 4.14   ■   Income-to-Effort Ratios Using the Daily 100

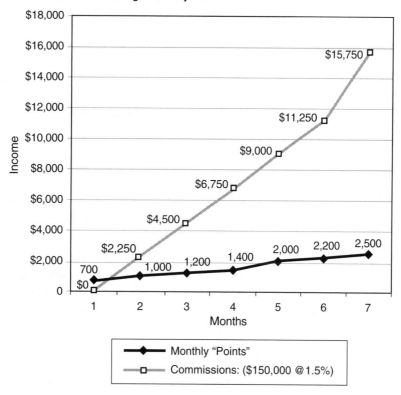

BECOMING A LISTING SUPERSTAR

This section is designed for sales associates who are not satisfied with the median net income but who want to be in the 90th percentile and above. The average licensee does some prospecting in small numbers and the results are modest. The superstar prospects to a huge base of leads and harvests huge rewards. You should go back to your goals worksheet and "kick it up a notch!" Make the worksheet show you want gross income of $200,000.

Your Leads Database

First, set up a software database. There are many databases available, including MS Outlook, Palm Pilot software, and Top Producer. One of the first steps is to organize your potential leads into the following five database categories:

1. Close friends and family
2. Friends
3. Customers
4. Acquaintances
5. Targeted strangers

You need the different categories because your prospecting methods depend on your relationship. Your close friends and family relationships were discussed as your sphere of influence earlier in this chapter, and the next sections concern acquaintances and targeted strangers. Customers are an obvious self-explanatory category.

There is another category of persons called "others" who won't be put in our database. They make up the general population, strangers whom we don't consider prospects.

Acquaintances

These are people we've met or spoken to by phone but don't yet know well. We will develop this group into a powerhouse of direct and referral business. One of the major objectives of our prospecting efforts is to move as many targeted strangers to this category as possible. We should have a combination of contacts with this group using mail and telephone at least twice monthly.

Targeted Strangers

Your **targeted strangers** list contains persons we don't know who are qualified by income, occupation, or residence address. This is by far the largest group in your database. The names might come from mailing list companies based on income levels, or from cross-reference directories, or from lists of doctors, attorneys, accountants, and business owners. This list should be very large, starting with at least 5,000 names and addresses. In the beginning you should send this list as a direct mail piece (it could be a postcard or newsletter) at least six times annually. Leads that are generated must be followed up immediately. If you generate one transaction for every 100 names (a modest goal), you will have an additional 50 transactions this year. If your average commission is $2,000 per sale, your income has increased by $100,000.

What will it cost? Postcards can be designed online through companies like *VistaPrint* *.com* using one of hundreds of templates. Five thousand glossy finish postcards, printed front and back, cost about $400 plus shipping. You can upload your photo and company logo. Send a different postcard each month. Your software will make label printing easy. Let's check the numbers:

Estimated gross income:		$100,000
Less prospecting costs:		
Postcards – $399 (for 5,000) for 12 months (12 × $399)	$4,788	
Estimated mailing costs	$ 612	
Postage (60,000 cards × .28)	$16,800	
Labor 6 hours × $8/hour × 12 months	$ 576	
Total Costs		$22,776
Net income generated		**$77,224**

Making Contacts

Following are the six important points to remember when you are prospecting:

1. **Success is in the numbers**. Be confident that this process will result in much higher income levels. You will discover that there is a strong correlation between your prospecting and the number of transactions you make. When you discover what your personal ratios are, it's easy to better control your income levels by your daily prospecting. If you get $3,000 extra income, on average, from every 100 contacts you make, you should assume that by making 1,000 additional contacts (20 per week) you can increase your income by $30,000.

2. **Be consistent.** Set the same time every day to make your contacts. Stick to the schedule, but if a closing or appointment is unavoidably scheduled, make sure the prospecting time is rescheduled for later in the day. It's like a diet; you might get off track, but success will come only if you get back to the plan.

3. **Call at your best time of day.** Some of us are great in the morning. Others are a little grumpy and should set their prospecting time later. Just be sure you have a high energy level. Because showing and listing appointments are usually set for afternoons or evenings, morning may be the best time for a prospecting routine.

4. **Make the first call!** The following calls will be easier. Think of the athletic slogan "Just do it!" The hardest call is the first call. Just think one call at a time.

5. **You'll get better.** As you make your daily calls, your contact skills will get better and your enthusiasm levels will increase.

6. **Remember the goal.** Before you make your calls, visualize what you want to happen as a result of the call. Put a sign above the phone that says "Get an appointment!" Another sign might read "Get a referral!"

Saturate and Remind

When you put a new entry into your "acquaintances" category, your strategy should be to "saturate and remind."

If you watch television, you have undoubtedly seen one or more companies start a major media campaign with saturation broadcasting. A three-hour sports program, for example, might have as many as ten 30-second commercials in the first two hours. For the next hour, the commercial is often abbreviated to 15 seconds, but because we know it well enough by then the short ad is as effective as the longer one. This is saturate and remind.

When you meet a new qualified prospect by phone or in person, that person is now put in the saturate mode, with at least a weekly contact for six weeks. Now they know who you are and what you do. If your contacts have been skillful, they also like you, will do business with you, and will send you referrals.

After the saturation period, you can reduce the number of contacts to twice monthly, and you'll have a steady source of business.

S U M M A R Y

The main objective of a licensee when prospecting is to get an appointment. The most important source of listings for new sales associates are spheres of influence, expired listings, farms, for sale by owners (FSBOs) and for rent by owners (FRBOs), and canvassing.

Licensees should be selective about which listings to try to obtain and avoid listing property if the seller is not motivated or wants you to break the law. Also avoid listings out of your market area or in poor condition.

Most FSBOs try to sell direct in order to save the commission. Licensees who work the FSBO market must be persistent, organized, and disciplined (POD). Most FSBOs advertise in the classifieds. Organize the FSBOs by telephone number. The most effective way to get a listing from an FSBO is to pay a visit.

A sales associate who prospects FRBOs has a chance of three types of transactions: the FRBO might 1) list the house, 2) buy another house, or 3) ask the licensee to manage the property.

Farming is a prospecting activity with long-term results. Persons who farm an area for several years may get up to 75 percent of the listings in a given neighborhood. The farm should be in a large area, but the associate should start with no more than 200 houses. The farm should be in a high-turnover neighborhood that is not currently being farmed.

Canvassing is the process of contacting prospective customers by mail, telephone, or in person. Licensees who want to engage in power prospecting must establish a leads database containing close friends and family, friends and past customers, acquaintances, and targeted strangers. Friends, past customers, and acquaintances should be contacted in some way at least twice monthly. New persons in the acquaintances category should have a contact program of saturate and remind, meaning weekly contacts for at least six weeks, then twice monthly.

K E Y   T E R M S

| farm | for sale by owners | power prospecting |
| for rent by owners | passive prospecting | targeted strangers |

P R A C T I C E   E X A M

1. Which is NOT a prospecting source to find listings?
   a. For-sale-by-owners
   b. Expired listings
   c. Buyer seminars
   d. Farming

2. The BEST listing source for new associates is
   a. referrals from previous customers.
   b. sphere of influence.
   c. farming.
   d. expired listings.

3. A sales associate who has limited time should NOT try to get a listing where the
   a. seller is motivated.
   b. property is in good condition.
   c. sellers don't need to sell.
   d. property is in the licensee's market area.

4. A sales associate is trying to list an FSBO house valued at $250,000 with a $220,000 mortgage. The seller says, "Your commission is too high!" The sales associate says, "But our listing commission is only 6 percent!" What is the commission as a percent of the seller's equity?
   a. 6
   b. 10
   c. 25
   d. 50

5. It is more likely that a seller will list if he or she
   a. does not need to move right away.
   b. is available during normal hours to show the home.
   c. does not like meeting and negotiating with people.
   d. understands the home-selling process.

6. The three keys to prospecting success are
   a. numbers, consistency, and organization.
   b. FSBOs, FRBOs, and expired listings.
   c. technical, marketing, and product.
   d. oral skills, written skills, and listening skills.

7. Finding new FSBOs in the classifieds is easier if the information is sorted by
   a. addresses.
   b. sellers' names.
   c. telephone numbers.
   d. city area.

8. What type of prospecting is direct mail?
   a. High risk
   b. Passive
   c. Stand-alone
   d. Wasted

9. What must be consulted before making telephone canvassing calls?
   a. The broker
   b. The National Do Not Call Registry
   c. The national No-Spam Directory
   d. Local ordinances

10. What is the most effective way to get an FSBO listing?
    a. Visit
    b. Telephone
    c. Direct mail
    d. Canvass

11. What is NOT a type of income transaction that can reasonably result from contacting a for rent by owner (FRBO)?
    a. Sale
    b. Listing
    c. Management contract
    d. Appraisal

12. When using direct mail as a prospecting tool for FSBOs, the mailing
    a. should stand alone as the principal activity.
    b. should be followed with a phone call or a visit.
    c. may be wasted time and effort.
    d. will generate many calls in response.

13. When prospecting for FRBOs, probably the LEAST effective contact method is
    a. direct mail.
    b. telephoning.
    c. visiting.
    d. direct mail with a follow-up call.

14. The principal reason a listing expires is
    a. market conditions.
    b. uncooperative owner.
    c. property condition.
    d. unrealistic price.

15. The best source for finding expired listings is through
    a. classified ads.
    b. multiple-listing service.
    c. a sign on the property.
    d. friends and family.

16. Direct mail is NOT usually a good idea for prospecting expired listings because
    a. by the time it gets there, a motivated seller has already listed.
    b. no one reads mail.
    c. it's too expensive.
    d. it violates Federal Trade Commission rules.

17. The principal drawback of a farm is
    a. farms have proven to be time-wasters.
    b. you may have to work for a long period before any returns are realized.
    c. ordinances that prevent such activities.
    d. too many sales associates are competing with you.

18. A listing farm should NOT have the following characteristic
    a. highly desirable area with low turnover.
    b. middle to upper price range.
    c. increasing property values.
    d. not currently being farmed.

19. A neighborhood has 480 homes. Last year, 69 homes were listed and 60 were sold. What is the turnover rate?
    a. 14%
    b. 12.5%
    c. 8.3%
    d. 7.2%

20. The largest number of names in your database will be in what category?
    a. Friends
    b. Acquaintances
    c. Targeted strangers
    d. Close friends and family

5

PRICING THE PROPERTY TO SELL

L E A R N I N G   O B J E C T I V E S

Upon completion of this chapter, you should be able to:

1. explain the types of appraisals a real estate licensee may provide for a fee;

2. differentiate between an appraisal and an opinion of value;

3. list four conditions that must be met in order to fairly use a comparable sale;

4. describe the three categories of properties shown in a comparative market analysis;

5. list at least three sources of information used in compiling a comparative market analysis; and

6. explain the adjustment process and direction of the adjustment.

O V E R V I E W

Single agents and transaction brokers have the duties of skill, care, and diligence. Assisting a seller in setting a realistic listing price or helping a buyer understand the market and assisting in setting a realistic offering price are two of the most important services a sales associate can offer.

Because all real estate activity is related to value, a valid estimate of property value has a significant effect on marketing a listing.

Market value is the most important value in a real estate transaction. The *market value* of real estate is the most probable price a property should bring in an arm's-length transaction occurring in a competitive and open market.

Real estate licensees use the **appraisal** process to produce opinions of value, comparative market analyses (CMAs), and nonfederally related appraisals.

Licensees must be familiar with the valuation of real property. While most licensees do not prepare formal real estate appraisals, they will go through the appraisal process to some degree when listing properties. Licensees must have a good working knowledge of the market in which they operate to be able to use evaluation methods competently. ▪

OPINION OF VALUE VERSUS CERTIFIED APPRAISAL

Real estate licensees may not refer to themselves as appraisers unless they are licensed appraisers or are certified appraisers. All active licensees may be paid for providing appraisals or appraisal services as long as they do not represent themselves or their reports as being certified. The appraisal may not be used in a **federally related transaction.** However, the lack of state certification as an appraiser does not prevent a real estate licensee from appraising a property for compensation in a nonfederally related transaction. An appraisal must be professionally, competently completed, and comply with the **Uniform Standards of Professional Appraisal Practice (USPAP).** Failure to do so leaves the licensee open to civil liability and disciplinary action. A licensee involved in the listing or sale of a property should not prepare an appraisal for that property.

A licensee may give an **opinion of value** when making a prospective sale or taking a listing. This opinion of value may not be referred to as an *appraisal* or a *certified appraisal* because the licensee has a personal interest in the transaction. Chapter 5 focuses primarily on preparing opinions of value.

Basic Principles of Value

Many economic principles influence the value of real property. They are interrelated, and their relative importance varies, depending on local conditions. The following principles are important to licensees attempting to estimate market value:

- Substitution
- Highest and best use
- Law of supply and demand
- Conformity
- Contribution
- Law of increasing and diminishing returns
- Competition
- Change
- Anticipation

Substitution. This is probably the most important factor in pricing residential property in a neighborhood with an active market. The value of a given parcel of real property is determined by using the principle of substitution. The maximum worth of the real estate is influenced by the cost of acquiring a substitute or comparable property.

DISCUSSION EXERCISE 5.1

You have prepared a CMA for Savannah Cooley. Your opinion of value, based on sales of comparable homes, falls in a range between $192,000 and $203,000. Cooley needs $215,000 from the sale of her home to pay a number of obligations and requests that you list it at that price. Give four persuasive arguments for listing her property at market value.

Highest and best use. Of all the factors that influence market value, the primary consideration is the highest and best use of the real estate. A property's highest and best use is its most profitable legally and physically permitted use, that is, the use that provides the highest present value.

Law of supply and demand. As it does with any marketable commodity, the law of supply and demand affects real estate. Property values rise as demand increases or supply decreases. For example, when demand declined recently, the result was declines in property values throughout most of Florida.

Conformity. In neighborhoods of single-family houses, buildings normally should follow the principle of conformity; that is, they should be similar in design, construction, and age to other buildings in the neighborhood to realize their maximum value. An elaborate mansion on a large lot with a spacious lawn is worth more in a neighborhood of similar homes than it would be in a neighborhood of more modest homes on smaller lots. Subdivision restrictive covenants are designed to promote the principle of conformity to maintain and enhance values.

Contribution. Any improvement to a property, whether to vacant land or a building, is worth only what it adds to the property's market value. An improvement's contribution to the value of the entire property may be greater or smaller than its cost. A licensee's opinion should be governed by a feature's contribution to value, not its actual cost.

DISCUSSION EXERCISE 5.2

You have prepared a CMA for Phyllis, who lives in Scenic Heights, an area of $100,000 homes. Phyllis reviews the recent sales and sees that her house has a large swimming pool, a feature that is not present in the homes in the report. She produces the invoices for the cost of her pool, which total $25,000, and suggests a $125,000 list price. Sales data show that pools in the neighborhood add about $6,000 to the properties' list prices.

Do a role-playing exercise, with another person taking Phyllis' part, and discuss the pricing principles involved.

Law of increasing and diminishing returns. Improvements to land and structures can reach a point at which they have no positive effect on property values. As long as money spent on such improvements produces a proportionate increase in income or value, the law of increasing returns is in effect. When additional improvements bring no corresponding increase in income or value, one can observe the law of diminishing returns.

Smaller homes in a neighborhood of larger homes may experience increasing returns when improved. Homes that are the same size or larger than surrounding homes should not be improved significantly until the owners have considered the economics of their decisions.

DISCUSSION EXERCISE 5.3

Sandy purchased a two-bedroom home in Betton Hills for $200,000. She builds an extra bedroom and bath and finds that the value has increased by much more than the cost of the improvements. She continues improving the property by adding two more bedrooms and a large family room with a fireplace. Sandy decides to sell, and she calls you to list the property. Your CMA shows that the value increase was much less than the construction cost. Sandy disagrees with your findings.

Do a role-playing exercise, with another person playing the part of Sandy, while you explain to her why the value may not have increased as much as the cost of improvements.

---

1 **Competition.** All residential properties are susceptible to competition. The only house
2 for sale in a nice, well-maintained neighborhood has a better chance of selling at or near
3 market value than if several houses on the same street were for sale.

4 **Change.** All property is influenced by the principle of change. Because no physical or
5 economic condition remains constant, licensees must be aware of market forces when
6 preparing opinions of value.

7 **Anticipation.** Most buyers purchase real estate with the expectation that its value will
8 increase, and they have been rewarded when the anticipation proves to be correct. In
9 inflationary times, the anticipation of higher prices creates a multitude of buyers, driving
10 prices higher than can be supported for long periods. In Florida, the prices for oceanfront
11 properties have increased dramatically.

12 But when the market begins to top out, the anticipation of a price recession can
13 cause investors to dump property on the market, forcing prices lower. Anticipation also is
14 important to prices of property in times of decreasing interest rates, when builders rush to
15 fill the expected demand. Licensees must be aware of the importance of anticipation when
16 valuing property for sale.

17 # COMPARATIVE MARKET ANALYSIS

18 Most licensees use a **comparative market analysis (CMA)** for arriving at an opinion of
19 value. A CMA is a process of gathering and analyzing the **property characteristics** of
20 homes currently for sale, homes recently sold, and homes listed that did not sell. It may
21 range in form from a simple list of recent sales with no adjustments to a detailed adjust-
22 ment grid. Whether taking a simple or a complex approach, a licensee needs to ensure that
23 she has met all of the conditions for selecting comparables.

24 ## Gathering CMA Data

25 First, the sales associate must have knowledge of the **subject property.** If it is a standard
26 floor plan subdivision home, it may be possible to complete a market analysis without a
27 property inspection. However, if the seller has made many improvements or if the home
28 has other amenities not typical of the market, it may be difficult to make adjustments

during the CMA's presentation phase. The truly professional approach is to inspect the property before completing the CMA.

Once the property inspection has been completed, the licensee should select the best properties for comparison. The following three categories of comparison help sellers and buyers better understand the market:

1. Properties that have sold

2. Properties that are now on the market

3. Property listings that have expired

The CMA will be a good indication of value only when comparables exist in a reasonably active market and where sufficient, reliable market sales information is available.

A **comparable property** should meet the following four conditions before it is used in a CMA:

1. It should be similar to the subject property.

2. If this is a sale, it should have sold recently—within the past year.

3. It should be located in the same market area as the subject property.

4. It should have changed owners as a result of an arm's-length transaction.

Reviewing actual sales prices of comparable properties helps buyers and sellers see what buyers actually pay in the marketplace. Comparable sales data are important when new financing is necessary because an appraiser relies on these data to estimate market value. Many sales are contingent on financing the purchase price, so it is of no value to overprice a property only to lose the sale when the lender and buyer receive the appraisal report.

Reviewing the prices of comparable properties now on the market shows the seller what owners of properties with similar characteristics are asking. These are the properties that will compete with the seller's. The principle of substitution means that a buyer will select the property with the best price, all other things being equal. A seller who wishes to position the property in the most effective price window values it just above recent sales and just below competing properties. A properly priced listing should result in a reasonably quick sale at the optimum price.

The listing prices of properties that do not sell demonstrate the resistance level of buyers to overpriced listings. In almost every case, the expired listing has been priced too high for the amenities offered.

The best sources for gathering CMA information include:

■ multiple-listing service (MLS) records,

■ company files,

■ public records,

■ other licensees, and

■ data service companies.

MLS records are the most convenient and comprehensive method of getting listings and sales information. MLS computer records can be searched by address and subdivision for ease in finding comparable sales. The information can be retrieved for sold, current, or expired property listings.

Company files are limited in scope but may be more complete as to property descriptions and financing used in purchases.

The public records include information recorded in the clerk's office and information on file with the tax appraiser. Except for verification of sales data and identities of the parties, the information from the clerk's office is not as important as the information available at the tax appraiser's office. While the information from the property appraiser's records is sometimes outdated, the records are still a useful source of data. Because the "sold" section of the CMA should include for-sale-by-owner properties, the appraiser's office is often the best information source for such sales.

Licensees often know of properties that have just closed. The information given should be verified and added to the report to include current sales.

Data service companies compile property sales data and sell the information to interested parties. Because this information does not give complete property descriptions, it is best used as a checklist to ensure that all sales have been considered.

Selecting Comparable Properties

A licensee preparing a CMA has two choices when selecting properties to compare. The first choice is to report every sale and every listing in the neighborhood, together with features and prices. The other choice is to analyze only the properties that are comparable.

Reporting all properties gives the seller an overview of the entire neighborhood market. Some sellers believe a list is incomplete if they know of a neighbor's home that sold recently that is not on the list; therefore, a complete list may make sellers more comfortable. However, problems sometimes arise with this all-inclusive list. Properties that are not comparable may mislead a seller concerning values. Properties that should not be used as comparables when making CMA adjustments include those that have significant differences in construction quality or size. Properties sold to relatives may be suspect as to fair value of the price and should be excluded from consideration.

Listing only three or four comparable properties makes a clearer presentation for a seller and reduces the chance for confusion about values. This is the approach that appraisers use.

Perhaps the best approach for the licensee is to prepare a comprehensive list of all properties that have sold, are listed currently, or have expired and then select the most comparable properties from that list for analysis. This method satisfies the needs of completeness and clarity. The characteristics for comparison are described below.

Common Elements of Comparison

Clearly, the accuracy of the comparable sales approach relies on the elements of comparison selected for adjustment. The elements listed on the CMA chart in Figure 5.1 are some of the most common and significant factors that affect value in standard residential appraisals. In any given analysis, it may be necessary to include other adjustments. The easiest way to fill out the CMA is to list all of the details of the subject property, then evaluate each comparable with the data that have been gathered.

F I G U R E 5.1 ▓ Sample Property Characteristics*

Location	Number of bedrooms
Size and shape of lot	Number of bathrooms
Landscaping	Kitchen characteristics
Style	Condition of exterior
Construction quality	Condition of interior
Design	Garage
Age	Other improvements
Square feet of gross living area	General condition
Number of rooms	

*These are selected examples only; more or fewer characteristics may be applicable.

Location. What are the three most important determinants of property value? The old expression "location, location, location" is the best answer. Location is so important that only in very unusual circumstances would a licensee use a property outside the subject's neighborhood as a comparable sale. In such a case, the comparable should come from a similar neighborhood. Even within the same neighborhood, locations can result in significant variances. A property across the street from a park is more valuable than one across the street from a commercial area.

DISCUSSION EXERCISE 5.4

Sara wants a for sale by owner to list with her, but the FSBO says that the commission added to his price would make the property overpriced. Sara really wants the listing, so she finds several homes the same size as the FSBO's property and prepares a CMA. However, the comparables she uses are located in another, more upscale neighborhood. The owner looks at the CMA and lists with Sara.

   Has Sara prepared an acceptable CMA? Why or why not?
   Has Sara violated any ethical or legal code? Why or why not?

Size and shape of lot. Irregularities can make portions of a site unusable for building, impair privacy, or restrict on-site parking, which could require major adjustments. Street frontage and total square footage of the lot are other important considerations.

Landscaping. Trees, plantings, and other types of landscaping should be evaluated as to maturity, quantity, and quality.

Construction quality. If construction quality of a comparable is not equivalent to that of the subject property, a major adjustment must be made. It is possible that the difference in quality might disqualify the property as a comparable.

Style. Generally, the style of a house follows the rule of conformity (a house should not be the only one of its type in the neighborhood). An important aspect of style is the number of floors of the residence. A one-story ranch house probably could be compared to a split-level, with some adjustment made. A three-story house is not comparable to a one-story ranch house, however.

1   **Design.** Design must be viewed from both functional and aesthetic standpoints. Func-
2   tional aspects include the existing traffic patterns in a house, placement of doors and win-
3   dows, room-to-room relationships, and the usefulness of rooms. Aesthetic aspects focus on
4   how pleasant and attractive an interior appears to an observer.

5   **Age.** Because most subdivisions are built within a relatively short period of time, there
6   may not be significant age differences among comparables. A brand-new home is likely
7   valued by the builder according to actual costs, overhead, and profit. While overall upkeep
8   is important, the home's age may alert the licensee to outmoded design and fixtures or to
9   needed repairs.

10   **Square feet of gross living area.** This is one of the most common areas for making adjust-
11   ments because size differences among homes can be calculated easily. If licensees make
12   adjustments for square footage, they also must be careful when adjusting for number of
13   rooms or bedrooms because this could lead to double counting. Adjustments for gross liv-
14   ing area can be misleading if all properties are not comparable. For instance, a small house
15   normally sells for more per square foot than a large house in the same area. A one-story
16   house has a higher cost per square foot than a two-story house. Be sure that all properties
17   used are comparable to the subject property. Appraisers normally do not count any floor
18   area that is below grade as gross living area, so do not use such properties unless the subject
19   also has below-grade area.

DISCUSSION EXERCISE 5.5

Silas Dean is trying to set a price for a 1,500-square-foot home in Green Hills.
He finds the following comparable sales:

Price	Square Feet	Price per Square Foot
$49,500	980	$50.51
51,000	1,025	49.76
50,000	1,000	50.00
61,500	1,500	41.00

The average price per square foot for these properties is $47.82. Sam Wil-
liamson, who owns the home, asks, "What is it worth?" Dean replies, "Houses
sell for $47.82 per square foot in this neighborhood. Based on that, your property
should sell for about $71,700." Williamson agrees and lists at $71,500.

Do you agree with Dean's analysis? If not, why not?

---

20   **Measuring practice.** Measurement of a house is extremely important. An error could
21   cause problems in pricing the property if the home's square footage is given to buyers. Cal-
22   culate the square footage of gross living area of the house shown on the following page.

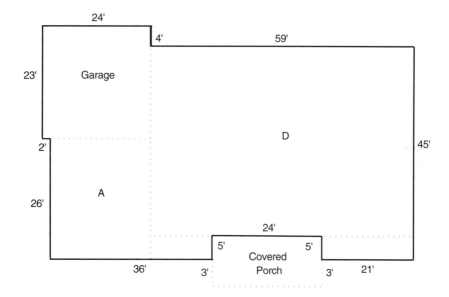

DISCUSSION EXERCISE 5.6

You have done a market report for the Meadows at Woodrun subdivision. Your analysis of property value, based on several 1,200-square-foot homes, indicates that homes sell at prices averaging $50 per square foot. When talking by phone with a prospective seller, you quote that figure after setting the listing appointment. When you arrive at the property with your listing information in hand, the seller proudly shows you the 500-square-foot two-car garage that has been converted into a heated and cooled family room. He indicates that the price at which you should list the home is $85,000, based on 1,700 square feet times your $50-per-square-foot figure. Role-play this situation, and explain why it may be difficult to market this home at $85,000. Also discuss some methods of arriving at a more realistic price.

Number of rooms. The total number of rooms in a house does not include the foyer or bathrooms and generally does not include basement rooms. Don't double count when adjusting for square feet and number of bedrooms.

Number of bedrooms. A major adjustment is needed if the subject property has two bedrooms and the comparables have at least three, or vice versa. Don't double count when adjusting for square feet.

Number of baths. Full baths (lavatory, toilet, and tub, with or without shower), three-quarter baths (lavatory, toilet, and shower), and half baths (lavatory and toilet) comprise this category. Modern plumbing is assumed, so an adjustment must be made for out-of-date fixtures if different from the subject property.

Kitchen. Licensees should focus on certain key factors, as follows:

■ Location

■ Counter space and storage

■ Service triangle

■ Appliances

The location of the kitchen is an important factor, based on its convenience to dining areas and accessibility for unloading groceries. Usually the market will not accept a kitchen with inadequate counter and storage space. The food service triangle is calculated by drawing straight lines connecting refrigerator, range, and sink. Most consumer polls show that the total length of the three lines combined should be greater than 12 feet but should not exceed 22 feet. Appliances represent a sizable portion of the home's cost, and their age and condition are important.

Other space. Unfinished attic, porch, utility room, Florida room, or any other room not part of the primary house area is included in this category.

Condition of exterior. An adjustment should be made for any needed repair work.

Condition of interior. An adjustment should be made for needed repairs. Luxurious finishing such as real wood paneling, adds to a home's value.

Garage. If the subject does not have one, any garage on a comparable property requires an adjustment. Garages on the subject and comparable properties must be compared for type of construction and size.

Other improvements. An adjustment should be made for differences between the subject property and the comparable. Landscaping, driveways, trees, and pools should be adjusted based on their contribution to value.

Adjusting for Differences

Ideally, the licensee wants to find comparable sales that are identical in characteristics to the subject property. In the real world, this doesn't always happen. While the CMA is not meant to be an appraisal, it is necessary to make **adjustments** for some of the differences discussed above. A major difference between the subject property and comparable property, such as a pool, could make an opinion of value very misleading if no adjustment is made for the pool. Many licensees recognize the difficulty in doing a CMA because when they look at a sold property, they see it as it is *today*, not how it looked when it went under contract. The important consideration in adjusting the comparable sale is how it looked at the time of sale.

> **EXAMPLE:** Whitney Cooley, a licensed sales associate, is preparing a CMA for Brian Edwards' three-bedroom, two-bath home in Eastgate. One of the comparable properties with the same floor plan sold recently for $73,000. The only difference between the properties is that the comparable property has a swimming pool. Whitney has done CMAs in Eastgate before and estimates that a pool contributes about $4,000 to value. The subject property doesn't have a pool, so Whitney makes a minus adjustment of $4,000 to the comparable's sales price. This indicates a value of $69,000 for the subject.
>
> How did Whitney determine that a pool contributes $4,000 to value in that neighborhood? The matched pair technique helped her make the estimate. She examined two recent sales in which the only difference was the fact that one property had a pool. The property with the pool sold for $4,000 more than the home without the pool. Because the pool was the only difference, the $4,000 must be attributable to that amenity. It would be better to make the comparison with several matched pairs to support the conclusion, but the technique is valid. The cost to build the pool is not added, just the value buyers and sellers place on the pool.

Adjustments are always made to the comparable property, never to the subject. Adjustments are subtracted from the comparable property if the comparable is bigger or better. Adjustments are added if the comparable is smaller or less desirable. An easy way to remember is "CIA, CBS":

- If the Comparable is Inferior, Add
- If the Comparable is Better, Subtract

Adjustments should be made for sold properties, listed properties, and expired properties; then each category should be reconciled.

Reconciliation

Reconciliation is the resolution of several adjusted values on CMAs into a single estimate of value. While an appraiser is expected to report a single-market value amount, a licensee making an opinion of value may prefer to report a range of values, from lowest to highest adjusted value of the comparables. Presenting a range rather than a single estimate of value allows a seller to price the property somewhat higher than the sold properties would indicate. The seller should understand that the home will likely sell at some price other than the list price and should consider all offers within the range of values.

Reconciliation enables the licensee to set the range differently. The first step is to estimate the value for each section of the report (sold properties, listed properties, and expired listings). Reconciliation is not simply the averaging of these values. The process requires the licensee to examine carefully the similarity of each comparable property to the subject property. If one comparable is nearly identical to the subject, including all relevant **transactional characteristics,** the sales price of that comparable might be the subject's estimated market value. When the comparables vary in their degree of similarity to the subject, the comparable property judged most similar is assigned the greatest weight in the reconciliation process.

The estimates for each section should be rounded. The range would then be calculated from the reconciled value of sold properties and the reconciled value of properties listed currently.

Another method for setting a range of values is to reconcile the sold properties to a value estimate, then check to see what properties sell for as a percentage of list price, then divide the value estimate by that amount. The two values comprise the range high and low.

DISCUSSION EXERCISE 5.7

You have just completed a CMA for Tim Palmer's home at 1112 Bristol Court. The reconciled market value of his home is $127,500. MLS statistics indicate that homes sell at approximately 95 percent of list price.

What is the range of value you quote to Tim?

F I G U R E 5.2 ■ **Plat Map of Neighborhood**

Prepared especially for
Ellen Johnson
3417 Jeannie Court
Tallahassee, FL 32301

A Visual Aid to the CMA

"A picture is worth a thousand words" is a timeworn expression because it is true. Sellers who review CMAs with licensees often have difficulty visualizing the comparable properties. The licensee who provides visual data can make a clearer presentation, and that may result in more realistic pricing. Owners who are motivated to sell do not set out to overprice their properties. Overpricing is usually the result of an inadequate understanding of the market, and that responsibility belongs to the listing sales associate.

Valuable visual aids include plat maps of the subdivision and pictures of the comparable properties. The plat map should be color-coded to show which properties were sold, which properties are now for sale, and which listings have expired. (See Figure 5.2.) Photographs can be printed from the MLS computer system or taken with a digital camera. The licensee should also include a photo of the seller's home. The seller will appreciate your personal touch and the extra photo for her scrapbook. Leaving a family home of some years can be a sentimental experience, and the seller will remember a licensee who is sensitive to those feelings.

C A S E   S T U D Y

COMPARATIVE MARKET ANALYSIS

Your CMA will require getting information from the owner, gathering information from the tax rolls through the MLS system, and analyzing the value contributed to the property by amenities.

Getting Information from the Owner

You have just received a request from John Halliburton to discuss listing his family's home. Mr. Halliburton gives you some basic information:

- The full name of all persons on the deed: *John Halliburton and Susan C. Halliburton, HW*
- The property address: *4316 Landtowne Drive, Orlando*
- The owner's home and office phone number: *407-555-3557; 407-555-3917*
- The number of bedrooms and baths in the home: *Four bedrooms, two baths*
- A description of extras in the home: *1,920 square feet of gross living area, two-car garage*
- A convenient time for an appointment: *This is the time to decide whether to do a pre-presentation inspection of the property (two appointments required: one to inspect the property, one to present the CMA). You decide to have one appointment at 6:20 this evening and will inspect the property at that time.*

Gathering Information from the Online Tax Rolls

The tax rolls for Orange County show the following information for the property:

- Legal description: *Lot 14, Block H, Landover Hills, Unit 2 - Orange County*
- Property tax appraisal: *$149,300*
- Annual taxes: *$2,986.45*
- Year built: *1989*
- Base area: *1,920 square feet (later verified by physical measurement)*
- Total area: *2,420 square feet (includes attached 2-car garage)*
- Last sale: *1996*
- Last sale price: *$128,000*
- Mortgage: *Sun Title Bank*

A search of the tax records shows seven sales in the subdivision within the previous year, ranging from $168,000 to $174,800. Six of the seven sales were reported in the MLS. The sales are shown in the first section of the CMA in Figure 5.3.

There are four properties currently for sale in the MLS, shown in the second section of the CMA, and three listings have expired within the last 12 months, shown in the third section.

F I G U R E 5.3 ■ **Comparative Market Analysis**

Comparative Market Analysis

Prepared for: _____

Property Address: _____

Date: June 8, 201____

Description: _____

Properties sold within the previous 12 months

Property Address	Sales Price	List Price	Days on mkt	Living Area	Features	Estimated Adjustment	Adjusted Sales Price	Comments
1816 Hibiscus	172,800	180,000	120	1820	Pool, FP, Screen Porch			
2412 Nasturtium	169,900	177,900	71	1920	FP			
1763 Camellia	173,500	182,000	45	1900	Pool			
1421 Azalea	168,900	175,000	52	2000	Screen Porch			
1640 Clover	171,200	179,500	61	2000	1 Car Garage			
2210 Hibiscus	168,000	175,900	32	1900				
1240 Camellia	174,800	182,500	70	1920	Screen Porch, FP			

Median $ _____

Percent sales price/list price _____

Properties currently on the market

Property Address	List Price	Days on Mkt.	Living Area	Features	Estimated Adjustment	As Adjusted	Comments
1818 Azalea	191,000	75	2100	Pool			
1740 Hibiscus	178,800	120	1900	FP			
2210 Clover	185,000	38	1820	Screen Porch, Pool			
1604 Magnolia	177,000	45	1920	Screen Porch			

Median $ _____

Properties which were listed but failed to sell during the previous 12 months

Property Address	List Price	Days on Mkt.	Living Area	Features	Estimated Adjustment	As Adjusted
2212 Camellia	192,800	180	1900	Pool, FP, Screen Porch		
1812 Hibiscus	185,500	240	2000	Screen Porch		
2211 Azalea	186,600	140	1800	FP		

Median $ _____

The suggested marketing range is $ _____ to $ _____

This information is believed to be accurate, but is not warranted.

Analysis of Value Contributed to the Property by Amenities

Over a period of time, in reviewing data on sold properties, we can estimate what a pool, a garage, an extra bedroom, or a fireplace contributes to value. The matched pair technique would compare similar houses with and without a particular feature. The difference in price would tend to show what the feature contributes in value.

For purposes of this CMA, we shall assume that sold properties in the neighborhood have shown the following value contributions over time:

- The contribution of a pool is $7,000.
- The contribution of a fireplace is $1,800.
- The contribution of an extra garage stall (2 cars, rather than 1) is $2,800.
- The contribution of extra square footage differences is $50 per square foot.
- The contribution of a screened porch is $2,000.

The CMA has been filled in with the exception of the adjustments shown above. Please compare the subject property with the comparable properties and make adjustments to the comparable properties. Then complete the analysis and estimate the marketing range for the property. Presenting this CMA to the sellers will be discussed in Chapter 6.

CMAs Using Comparable Sales and Listings (No Adjustments)

Licensees commonly use a "no-adjustments" CMA method in pricing property. It involves listing properties for sale now, properties sold in the previous year, and expired listings, without making adjustments. Its simplicity is appealing to licensees and sellers alike because it provides an overview of the market. However, if properties on the chart are not comparable and the subject property is priced from an average of sales prices or square-foot calculations, the pricing method can be misleading.

DISCUSSION EXERCISE 5.8

In this role-playing session, assume the CMA has been explained, but the seller is attempting to set an unreasonably high listing price. Discuss as many persuasive points as possible to encourage the seller to price the property in the range suggested.

Computer-Generated CMAs

As computers have become more important in every phase of the real estate business, software programs help make impressive presentations to buyers and sellers. Many of these programs are formatted to print out an entire listing presentation to the sellers, tailored to their specific needs. In many cases, the time required is less than that of handwriting the old CMA grids. Most of the computer programs are designed to interface directly with the MLS system program and download the necessary data. This saves time because the licensee does not have to type the information. Most programs provide raw sales data without adjustment, although the sales associate, by selecting only comparable properties, can come quite close to market value.

SUMMARY

A real estate licensee may prepare an appraisal in a transaction that is not federally related. F.S. 475 requires that the appraisal be done in conformity with the Uniform Standards of Professional Appraisal Practice. Normally, when listing or selling property, licensees prepare a comparative market analysis (CMA) and give their opinion of value. Many important principles of value exist, including highest and best use, substitution, supply and demand, contribution, and conformity.

The comparable sales approach to estimating value is the most appropriate method appraisers use to value homes and vacant sites. The comparative market analysis is the method most licensees use to prepare an opinion of value. The three sections of a CMA are properties that have sold recently, properties for sale now, and properties that did not sell during the listing periods. Data for the CMA are gathered primarily from the MLS and county property appraiser's records. Only comparable properties should be used in the analysis. A range of values is provided to the seller because it is more meaningful than a single value.

KEY TERMS

adjustments	federally related transaction	transactional characteristic
appraisal	opinion of value	Uniform Standards of
comparable property	property characteristic	Professional Appraisal
comparative market	reconciliation	Practice (USPAP)
analysis (CMA)	subject property	

P R A C T I C E   E X A M

1. An appraisal of real property is a(n)
   a. accurate determination of its value.
   b. process of arriving at its value.
   c. estimate of its value.
   d. reconciled statement of just value.

2. Of all the factors that influence market value, the most important is the
   a. principle of substitution.
   b. highest and best use.
   c. law of increasing and diminishing returns.
   d. principle of conformity.

3. The Joneses live in a 2,100-square-foot home. Home sizes in the area range from 1,200 square feet to 2,100 square feet. Sales Associate Sam found seven comparable sales from different sized homes. He calculated the sales price per square foot for each home, averaged all the prices, and applied it to the square feet in the subject home. In preparing the CMA, Sam
   a. has prepared the CMA properly.
   b. should have asked the Joneses how they wanted him to do it so they could get the best price for their home.
   c. has violated Chapter 475 because he did not follow the USPAP.
   d. should have used only the sales prices of similar size homes.

4. The most profitable legally and physically permitted use of real property is called its
   a. market value.
   b. appraised value.
   c. location.
   d. highest and best use.

5. A comparative market analysis would be LEAST effective when trying to establish value for a
   a. residential property.
   b. duplex.
   c. public school property.
   d. vacant property.

6. Which is designed to promote the principle of conformity to maintain and enhance value in a subdivision?
   a. Restrictive covenants
   b. Zoning codes
   c. Comprehensive plans
   d. Land use codes

7. When Mr. Wilson added a family room to his house, which was already too large for the area, he did not see the value increase as much as the cost of the addition. What principle was demonstrated?
   a. Highest and best use of the land
   b. Increase in value at least equal to the cost of construction
   c. Law of increasing returns
   d. Law of diminishing returns

8. When listing a property in the ordinary course of business, any active real estate licensee in Florida is authorized to prepare an
   a. opinion of value.
   b. appraisal report.
   c. appraisal assignment report.
   d. analysis assignment report.

9. A mansion in a neighborhood of smaller, more average homes would violate the principle of
   a. change.
   b. conformity.
   c. competition.
   d. contribution.

10. In a neighborhood of three-bedroom, two-bath homes, an owner added a second bathroom at a cost of $1,600. An appraiser adjusted the value of the home upward by $2,000 due to the improvement. This is an example of the principle of
    a. change.
    b. conformity.
    c. competition.
    d. contribution.

11. Traci is preparing a CMA for property located in Arbor Hills. She finds three homes that sold recently: a four-bedroom home with a pool that sold for $90,000; a three-bedroom home with no pool that sold for $81,000; and a three-bedroom home with a pool that sold for $85,000. Based solely on the above information, what does a swimming pool contribute to value in Arbor Hills?
    a. $9,000
    b. $5,000
    c. $4,000
    d. $0

12. The ideal kitchen service triangle should be from
    a. 9 to 25 feet.
    b. 12 to 22 feet.
    c. 120 square feet.
    d. 12 by 24 feet.

13. The comparable sales approach to value is based primarily on what principle of valuation?
    a. Conformity
    b. Substitution
    c. Supply and demand
    d. Highest and best use

14. Which is NOT important in comparing properties using the comparable sales approach?
    a. Date of sale
    b. Size of house
    c. Original cost of improvements
    d. General condition and appearance

15. You are preparing a CMA and want to be certain that it reflects comparable sales of properties sold directly by owners. The best place to find the information is in
    a. either the clerk's office or the tax appraiser's office.
    b. city hall.
    c. the MLS records.
    d. the tax collector's office.

16. When the term *recently* is used to describe a comparable sale, it is generally understood to mean that the property sold within the past how many months?
    a. 12
    b. 8–15
    c. 12–18
    d. 18

17. Which is NOT a condition that a licensee must meet when selecting comparable properties using the comparable sales approach to value?
    a. Similar
    b. Sold recently
    c. Same market area
    d. Same floor plan

18. Which is correct if a broker charges a $400 fee for preparing an appraisal that will not be used in a federally related transaction?
    a. The broker may prepare an appraisal but may not charge a fee.
    b. The broker must follow the Uniform Standards of Professional Appraisal Practice.
    c. The broker has violated Chapter 475, F.S.
    d. The broker must call the appraisal an opinion of value.

19. You are estimating the value of a vacant lot zoned for single-family residence use. One year ago, a comparable lot sold for $25,000. Your analysis of market conditions and property characteristics produced the following needed adjustments: subject lot, $2,000 inferior; subject site location, $3,000 superior. These adjustments result in an estimated market value for the subject lot of
    a. $26,000.
    b. $23,000.
    c. $24,000.
    d. $27,000.

20. A home has dimensions of 35 feet by 57 feet that include an attached 24-foot by 22-foot garage and a 200-square-foot screen porch. How many square feet of gross living area does the home have?
    a. 1,267
    b. 1,467
    c. 1,995
    d. 2,354

6

MAKING THE LISTING PRESENTATION

LEARNING OBJECTIVES

Upon completion of this chapter, you should be able to:

1. enumerate at least four requirements for a proper listing presentation;

2. list the five major steps in a listing presentation;

3. describe the steps in explaining a CMA;

4. list two visual aids for a CMA presentation;

5. list the three major sections in a Sellers' Net Proceeds Form;

6. list at least eight costs that a seller may be expected to pay at closing;

7. explain why insurance and escrow amounts usually are not included in the Seller's Net Proceeds Form;

8. explain the reasons for rounding all figures used in the Seller's Net Proceeds Form;

9. prepare a Seller's Net Proceeds Form; and

10. describe the problems a FSBO may face when selling his or her house.

OVERVIEW

As a licensee's ability to deliver an effective listing presentation increases, the "close" rate for listing appointments will be higher. Prospecting is a numbers game. It may take up to 50 calls to get one listing appointment. What a shame it would be to have all that effort rendered worthless by failing to prepare carefully before sitting down with the sellers. ■

REQUIREMENTS FOR THE LISTING PRESENTATION

This presentation is a "sit down at the dining room table" discussion when both husband and wife are present. It will be successful *only* if you:

- know all the parties who need to sign your listing are available;

- are fully prepared to list the property, meaning you must have all the forms ready for signature when the parties agree to list;

- know this presentation thoroughly;

- know about the house you are trying to list by using the information you gathered from the tax appraiser's office, the plat books, or from your own personal inspection;

- have prepared a comparative market analysis (CMA) to help you show the sellers a fair value for their house and to protect you from the overpriced listing, a nemesis that will cost you time and aggravation, and make for unhappy customers;

- have your information organized in a businesslike fashion and your mind organized as well;

- are properly dressed and professional in appearance and manner; and

- are on time for the appointment.

THE FIVE MAJOR SEGMENTS OF THE PRESENTATION

A **listing presentation** consists of the following five major segments:

1. Building rapport with the sellers
2. Explaining the pricing process (going over the CMA)
3. Estimating the seller's proceeds (the Seller's Net Proceeds Form)
4. Discussing the reason most FSBOs don't sell their homes
5. Asking for the listing

Building Rapport with the Sellers

The following five strategies, if followed conscientiously at a listing presentation, will help almost any real estate salesperson build rapport with sellers:

1. Greet the sellers at the door with a smile, and be yourself. Thank them for the opportunity to visit their home and, after some initial small talk, begin taking control of the interview.
2. If you haven't already made a preliminary visit to the property, ask the sellers to give you a tour. Have a note pad to record your observations for each room. Ask questions about the house while on the tour. If you see any features that indicate the sellers' hobbies, awards, or family photos, try to acknowledge them. Show the owners that you've done your homework by confirming some of the information you've gotten from the tax appraiser.
3. Inspect the property boundaries; make notes of exterior features, then ask the sellers to help you measure the exterior of the house. Confirm that total with the information you have from the tax appraiser.

4. After returning indoors, arrange to have all parties sit at a dining or kitchen table. Suggest that the TV be turned down (or off) so that you can hear them well.

5. Find out why they are selling. If they are moving to a new town, find out how they feel (not think) about the move. Is it scary? Has he or she met the new boss? How do they feel about the new job? Let them know you care about them as individuals.

Explaining the Pricing Process

The presentation should provide information the sellers need to fully understand the listing process. Agents who give a value without first going over the CMA may lose the opportunity for realistic pricing if the sellers are surprised and offended at the value. A proper presentation should proceed in the following 11-step sequence:

1. Help the sellers understand the current market conditions. You can get this information from MLS statistics or from your broker. Give statistics for the overall market. The CMA will help show the neighborhood statistics. For example, tell the sellers the:

   a. number of houses currently listed,
   b. number of homes sold last month, and
   c. month's supply of homes on the market (divide listed homes by sales).

2. Give the sellers your analysis of the market:

   a. Is it a buyers' or a sellers' market?
   b. Are prices rising or falling?
   c. What is likely to happen if interest rates rise (or fall)?

3. Explain the importance of pricing the property within the selling range. Use the pricing pyramid in Figure 6.1.

4. Inform the sellers that the purpose of the CMA is to determine the best list price for the property.

5. Explain the report and how you researched the material in it. If your conclusions of market value are less than the sellers' desired price, you may have a problem. Do not state your conclusions at this time. Wait to see what the sellers conclude from the comparable sales. (Often sellers will quickly realize that their price is too high and, if motivated to sell, will agree to reduce the price.)

6. Explain how each section of the CMA is important in the decision-making process by giving the sellers an overview of the following:

   a. Sold listings prove what selling prices have been and what bank appraisals might show.
   b. Homes now for sale illustrate the importance of competitive pricing.
   c. Expired listings demonstrate the futility of pricing property at an unrealistically high price.

7. Review individual properties on the report while referring to visual aids such as a subdivision map and photos.

8. Ask the sellers for questions or comments.

9. Give the sellers time to arrive at a range of values independently.

10. If the sellers want to price the property too high, discuss the reasons why that approach is unproductive.

11. When a realistic listing price has been agreed upon, complete the Seller's Net Proceeds Form.

FIGURE 6.1 ■ **The Pricing Pyramid**

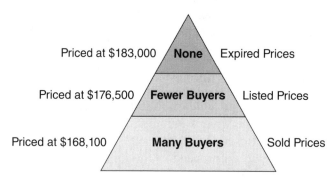

The Number of Potential Buyers Is
Related to Your Home's Price

Priced at $183,000 — **None** — Expired Prices

Priced at $176,500 — **Fewer Buyers** — Listed Prices

Priced at $168,100 — **Many Buyers** — Sold Prices

This chart helps sellers to visualize the effect pricing
may have on the activity level the house will experience.
The lower the price, the more buyers will be attracted.

CASE STUDY

PRESENTATION OF A CMA

Assumptions

Use the CMA from Chapter 5.

You visited the house yesterday when Mrs. Halliburton was home to measure it, evaluate its features, and take some digital photos for the presentation this evening. This allowed you to prepare a CMA with confidence that there would be no surprises.

Cast: **Sales Associate:** Alice Newby
    Sellers: John Halliburton, Susan Halliburton

Alice: Mr. and Mrs. Halliburton, thanks for inviting me into your home. Helping you get the most dollars for your home in a reasonable time is one of my most important responsibilities in my real estate practice. One of the ways I can really be helpful is by carefully preparing a market report. It's called a *comparative market analysis*. Have you seen one of these before? [Hand them a copy of the CMA.]

John: No, we haven't. But this is our first home.

Alice: OK, it will take us a few minutes to go over it, but it's well worth the time. The decisions we make based on this analysis are going to be very important to you as we go forward.

You can see I've put your names and addresses here at the top.

You can see that the report is broken into three main sections [pointing]: Here are the sales in your neighborhood for the last 12 months. The sold properties section will tell us what homes appraisers can use and will give us an idea of the value for a homebuyer's bank appraisal. The section on properties that are now listed shows your competitors.

And here are the properties that failed to sell, usually because they were overpriced. All of these properties are going to help us to decide at what price we should offer your home. Here's a map of the neighborhood so you can see where each of these homes is located. Do you have any questions so far?

Susan: Well, I don't see one of our neighbor's homes on your list, and I know he sold his house last May. The address is 4425 Landtowne Drive.

Alice: Right. Let me see [looks at another list of every sale in the area]. Yes, you're right. Here it is on this list [shows list]. As you can see, his house had only 1,500 square feet, while yours has more than 1,900. I didn't use it in our pricing guide because it's just not comparable, don't you agree?

Susan: Yes, I see.

Alice: On each of the homes included on our list, I've made some adjustments based on major differences from your house. For example, the house at 1640 Clover has only a one-car garage, and yours has a two-car garage. The price difference for that feature is about $2,800, so your house should sell for about $2,800 more.

John: OK, that makes sense.

Alice: You can see that in the first section, sold properties, the median sales price of properties—and what yours will probably appraise for—is about $168,100. In the second section, your competition has a median listed price of $176,500. Now our best chance at a sale within reasonable time frames is to price your home somewhere above the sold properties and below the competing properties. Does that make sense?

John: Sure does.

Alice: Here are the properties that were overpriced and stayed on the market a long time. They didn't sell. You can see they had a median price of $183,000. We want to avoid being in this group, don't you agree? [Shows them the pyramid (such as the one found in Figure 6.1).] Let me show you the Pricing Pyramid. As you can see, if you price the home at the median of the sold homes in your area, you'll attract the most buyers. If you price at what the other homes are listed for, you'll get some activity, but not as much. And if you price it too high, you won't see many buyers at all. The more buyers we can get to look, the better the chance of a sale.

John: Yes, we'd like to get it sold within the next few months.

Alice: Great. Based on what you've seen here, what do you think would be the best listing price for us to put it on the market?

Susan: Well, I think we've got to be somewhere in between the sold ones and the listed ones. Do you think we could list it at the higher end, like $176,500?

Alice: What do you think, John?

John: I'd like to get as much as possible, Susan, but two of the homes for sale now are at $175,000. I think maybe $174,500 might get it sold faster.

Susan: Yes, that's true. I'm cool with $174,500.

Alice: I wholeheartedly agree. Could we schedule your home for our office inspection next Monday, or will the following week give you more time to get it ready? (This is the first time you ask for the order.)

Susan: Well, we may not be quite ready to do anything yet. Can we think about it and let you know?

Alice: Absolutely. Maybe it would be helpful if I showed you what you are likely to clear from the sale after paying off the mortgage and all your expenses. Would that be helpful?

John: Sure would.

DISCUSSION EXERCISE 6.1

Using the CMA report in Figure 5.3 role-play the complete presentation of a CMA without referring to the script above. The instructor might assign several persons to present the different sections of the material. Assign a classmate to represent a "reasonably motivated" seller who is kind to the agent.

ESTIMATING THE SELLER'S PROCEEDS

A seller generally is reluctant to enter into a listing agreement until she understands what expenses she must pay at closing. The **net proceeds** after paying off the mortgage and expenses of a sale are of primary interest to the seller and are often a factor in setting a list price. It is extremely important that a licensee use skill, care, and diligence in estimating the seller's proceeds from the sale. The following is a discussion of the **Seller's Net Proceeds Form.** (See Figure 6.2.)

Seller's Net Proceeds Form

A section for the seller's name and the property address should be completed. The left side of the form itemizes income and expenses related to the sale. Two columns are provided for calculations:

- *When listing the property.* The licensee might use column 1 when calculating an estimate based on a recommended price; the licensee would use column 2 if the seller wanted to know how much a different list price would net.
- *When giving the seller a range of values.* The sales associate could provide for the seller a high-end list price and a low-end list price.
- *At the time of listing.* Column 1 could be used for showing the net proceeds if customary seller's expenses were paid; column 2 could be used if the seller were asked to pay the buyer's loan closing costs. This is much like a best-case, worst-case scenario.
- *For estimates given at the time of listing.* Column 1 is for listing proceeds; column 2 could be used when an offer is submitted.
- *At the time an offer is submitted.* Column 1 shows the seller's net if the offer was accepted; column 2 shows the seller's net if a counteroffer was accepted.

Seller's equity section. The seller's **equity** section consists of the sales price, less mortgage balances and other encumbrances. Special assessment liens and construction liens would be shown in the space provided for other encumbrances. All items should be rounded because this is an estimate. An exact mortgage balance is unnecessary because of the closing date's

F I G U R E 6.2 ■ Seller's Net Proceeds Form

Seller's Name: _____

Property Address: _____

Selling Price	$	$
Less: 1st Mortgage 　　　2nd Mortgage 　　　Other		
Seller's Equity	$	$
Less: Expenses		
Doc Stamps on Deed		
Termite Inspection and Treatment		
Title Insurance		
Homeowner's Warranty		
Buyer's Closing Costs 　Buyer's Origination Fee 　Buyer's Discount Points		
Repairs and Replacements		
Seller's Attorney Fee		
Brokerage Fee		
Other Miscellaneous Costs		
Other		
Total Expenses	$	$
Less: Prorations		
Property Taxes		
Interest		
Homeowner's Dues		
Rents and Deposits		
Total Prorations	$	$
Net Proceeds to Seller	$	$

These figures are estimates and intended only as a guide. They will vary at closing because of prorations, the mortgage balance, and unforeseen costs. An exact itemization will be provided to you at closing. Please read this and all other documents relating to this sale carefully. If you require further explanation, please consult an attorney.

Date: _____   Prepared by:_____

Seller: _____   Seller: _____

uncertainty. Uneven dollars and cents amounts should not be included. Exact amounts imply an accuracy that does not exist in the estimate.

Expenses section. Any expenses that the seller might be required to pay should be listed. It is better to overestimate than to underestimate the expenses. Sellers will not be unhappy if they receive more at the time of closing than they had expected, but they likely will be upset if expenses have been underestimated. Even though the bottom of the form provides a disclaimer, the licensee must be careful to avoid errors. Some expenses that should be discussed follow:

- Documentary stamps on deed are $.70 per $100 or fraction thereof of the sales price. The seller normally pays the cost of these stamps.

- Termite inspection (treatment and repairs) could be a substantial expense to the seller but is not known at the time of listing or contract. A conservative approach would be to show the cost of both in this section. A licensee should stay current on the costs of inspection and treatment in the property's market area. In many areas, the inspection is the buyer's expense.

- When making the seller's statement, the licensee would include the typical charge a seller might be expected to pay for title insurance and related costs based on local practice.

- Homeowner's warranty costs often are associated with the seller's need to assure the buyer that the home is in good condition and will be warranted against many defects by an independent home warranty company. Depending on the company, these costs may range from $300 to $500.

- Buyer's closing costs, the origination fee, and discount points can be very substantial expenses to the seller if the seller agrees to pay them. When taking a listing, a sales associate should include these items if the custom in the market area dictates. When preparing this estimate at the time of contract, the sales associate should take extra care if the seller will pay the buyer's costs. The licensee should use the lender's good-faith estimate, with a maximum amount agreed to in the contract. Leaving this open-ended in a contract can be problem if the discount points or other costs increase between the time of acceptance and the time of closing.

- Repairs and replacements usually are those that a lender might require. They also could be the result of wood-destroying organisms or nonfunctioning appliances. The licensee should overestimate somewhat as a cushion for such contingencies.

- The seller's attorney fee is an expense left to the seller to decide. The licensee should list the normal closing review fee for the seller in his market area.

- The brokerage fee is the commission the brokerage firm charges.

- Other miscellaneous costs include items like express mail fees for mortgage payoffs and recording mortgage satisfactions. The licensee should overestimate somewhat as a cushion here to allow for contingencies. A seller on a tight budget cannot afford unpleasant surprises. This line also could be used to round uneven expense amounts into even amounts. For example, if the expenses were $8,945.60, the miscellaneous costs could be estimated at $54.40, resulting in total estimated expenses of $9,000.

Prorations section. This section, if not carefully estimated, could result in an unpleasant surprise for the seller because most prorations are debits (charges) to the seller. Because the closing date is not certain, it is not necessary to do exact prorations; approximations are satisfactory if amounts are rounded higher. The statement offers no provision for insurance prorations or proceeds from a lender's escrow account. Insurance should *not* be prorated;

the buyer should purchase her own policy, and the seller should get a cancellation refund. Because the insurance refund and escrow refund from loans paid off are not received at closing, the net proceeds statement does not include these items. (If the mortgage is to be assumed, the prorations could be offset by the amounts held in escrow, as the buyer will be expected to reimburse the seller for those amounts.)

- Property taxes should be estimated for the year if tax information is not available. An assumed closing date is used to estimate prorations. If the closing were anticipated for June 28, for example, the licensee would show a charge to the seller for half the year's taxes.

- Interest prorations can be difficult to calculate. The amount depends on the time of month for the closing. Most interest is paid in arrears, but not all loans have that feature. The safest policy, if the loan is current, is to show a charge for a full month's interest.

- Homeowners' association dues can be substantial in some areas, particularly with condominiums and other properties having substantial common maintenance areas. The dues may be paid in advance but often are paid in arrears. The homeowner should be questioned about the status of the dues.

- Rents and deposits can be major charges to the seller of an income property. If the seller has collected rent in advance, the buyer is entitled to the rent for the part of the month after the closing. The buyer also should be paid the security deposits.

Net proceeds to seller. The net proceeds equal the seller's equity less expenses and prorations. The amount of the seller's proceeds should be rounded to the next lowest $100.

Exercise: Estimating Net Proceeds to Seller

Estimating the seller's net proceeds properly is extremely important. This exercise should be completed carefully using the Seller's Net Proceeds Form found in Figure 6.2. Round up on expenses, prorations, and mortgages, and do not use cents. The final estimate should be rounded to the lowest hundred, using the following information:

Seller's name	Cindy Lewis
Property address	1947 Oldfield Circle
Prepared by	Janice Brown
Estimated closing date	August 26
Sales price	$93,800.00
Existing first mortgage (8.5%)	47,425.67
Home equity loan (11%)	14,659.42
Brokerage fee	7%
Termite inspection and treatment	400.00
Buyer's title insurance	650.00
Repairs and replacements	450.00
Seller's attorney fee	350.00
Homeowner's warranty	375.00
Discount points	2,100.00
Annual taxes	1,325.00
Interest	?
Annual homeowner's dues	150.00

> **DISCUSSION EXERCISE 6.2**
>
> Using the Seller's Net Proceeds Form prepared in the above exercise, role-play the presentation of the form to the seller. The instructor might assign several persons to present the different sections of the material. Assign a reasonably motivated seller who is kind to the agent. The licensee should ask a closing question when showing the net proceeds from the sale.

Ask for the Order

Show the sellers the net amount to be received and ask, "Can you live with this figure?" If the answer is yes, follow up with, "Do you have any objections to my making the property available to all the REALTORS® in the city through the multiple-listing service?" If the answer is OK, ask for the current mortgage information, and proceed to fill out the listing forms. You have obtained the listing!

If the answer is "We are not ready to list at this time," say, "I understand," then go to the next step.

DISCUSS THE REASONS MOST FSBOS DON'T SELL THEIR HOMES

During any listing presentation, be prepared if necessary to carefully explain to your potential clients that FSBOs usually don't sell their homes for a variety of reasons, the most serious of which are discussed below.

The Problem of Showing the Property

FSBOs must be made aware of the following three reasons why showing their home themselves is extremely difficult, annoying, and exasperating:

1. Explain that the sign in front of the home invites any passersby to come to the front door and ask to be let inside. Normally, a resident of a home would never allow the person access, but it's now more difficult to say no. Talk for a moment about the family's security and that trained real estate professionals will escort all buyers after they are qualified.

2. Remind the owners that a buyer cannot know everything about their property by simply looking at the front of the house. This is a very important point, especially if the home has only average curb appeal but the inside is far nicer than average. Without knowing about the good features, a buyer might drive right by. You should explain that when their home is shown, trained real estate professionals will escort qualified buyers inside, the only place they can truly evaluate this home.

3. You can remind the sellers that if they are not home all day and on the evenings and weekends to show the home, the buyer may not call back. Every time they go shopping or to work, their property is "off the market." Explain that when they list with you, the property will be on the market 24 hours a day, because they can reach a licensee who will have the information the buyer wants.

The Problem of Financing

Because the buyers will likely need new financing on the property, you could explain that they may want assistance in deciding where to go for a home mortgage and may not understand the process. Because of that reason, many buyers ask for the help of a real estate professional.

The Problem of Oral Negotiations

Discuss with the sellers the disadvantage of direct negotiations with a buyer. Many buyers buy direct because their negotiation skills give them an advantage. Buyers will ask questions about the reason for selling and about how much lower the sellers might go. If the sellers remain firm, explain that the buyers may leave. But the sellers should also know that if they give a buyer a lower figure, that buyer may later try to negotiate even lower.

The sellers should be told that when a buyer wants to make an offer, the licensee will put it in writing and ask for a good-faith deposit so that if the price offered by the buyer is acceptable, all the sellers need to do is sign it.

The Problem of Writing a Purchase Contract

You can ask sellers whether they have a contract form and whether they feel comfortable filling it in for the buyers to sign. If the sellers have a contract form and think they can fill it in, let them know about the education process most licensees undergo so they can write one that will not end up in court.

If the sellers say they have an attorney to write the contract, suggest that it's important for the attorney to be qualified in real estate practice. You might also raise the question of how quickly a good, but busy, attorney could get a contract written when a buyer is ready to buy.

The Major Problem: FSBOs Want to Save the Commission

In this last part of your discussion, you want to get the sellers' agreement that they are willing to try to overcome these obstacles in order to save the commission. When they agree, you must answer their objection to listing with you by letting them see their efforts won't save a commission. Ask the sellers why they believe a buyer would be willing to take the time and make the effort to buy a house directly from a seller when the buyer could get much more help from a licensee. Then explain to them that the reason is that the buyer is also buying direct solely to save the commission and that it won't be possible for both parties to save the full commission. In the unlikely event that both seller and buyer complete the transaction without help from a licensee, why couldn't both parties save the full commission?

ASKING FOR THE LISTING

A closing question such as "Can you see how most persons who try to sell their homes turn to a real estate professional?" might generate a positive answer. You can then ask if they'd like you to try to get the home into the MLS as soon as possible, or bring your office staff over on Monday morning to see it, or whether they would like you to hold an open house next Sunday. If their response is positive, you can begin filling out listing paperwork.

In many cases, the sellers won't be ready to list with your company. You should ask for the reason, and if they want to think about it, you should tell them why, when they decide to list the property, the listing person should be you.

Show the seller why the REALTOR® should be you. Tell the sellers about you and your brokerage firm. For example, explain that you

- have an office in a high traffic location;
- went through a rigorous training program that makes all your associates more professional and successful;
- generate more sales through your office listing caravans;
- will put their home into the MLS immediately;
- will be advertising the home;
- pride yourself on holding successful open houses;
- are a member of an out-of-town referral agency,
- offer a warranty program, explaining how that will help to sell the property;
- will call them each week to tell them of your progress;
- will give them your special "Seven-Step Service" program.

SEVEN-STEP SERVICE

A seller wants to know what the brokerage firm will do to earn the commission, and a chart similar to the one shown in Figure 6.3 may be helpful. While the chart itself is rather sparse, for easy understanding, the sales associate might tell the seller about each step in more detail. After you have finished your presentation, you should clearly and directly ask for the order. "Mr. and Mrs. Halliburton, may I help you sell your property?"

If the answer is no, you should review every point of the presentation point-by-point, then ask for the order again. In many cases, the presentation will result in a listing. If for any reason you do not get a listing, arrange to visit again in three days. You may never get the listing, but it won't be because you gave up too soon.

S U M M A R Y

Making an effective listing presentation will result in a much higher close rate for listing appointments. Several conditions must be met in order to succeed:

- All parties on the deed must be present.
- All forms must be ready for the sellers' signature.
- The licensee must know each step of the presentation.
- The licensee must have complete information about the property to be listed.
- A comparative market analysis must be prepared.
- The licensee must be organized, have a professional appearance, and be on time.

[The material in the listing presentation section is from *30-Day Track to Success,* ©1984, 1996, and 2007 by Edward J. O'Donnell.]

F I G U R E 6.3 ■ **Seven-Step Service Chart**

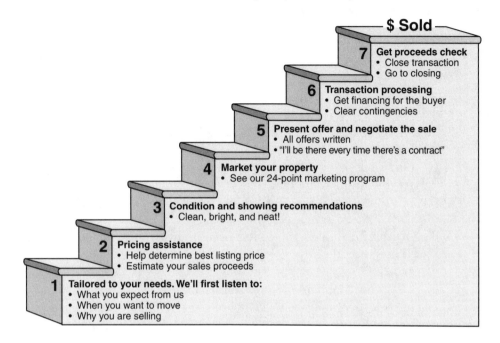

Seven-Step Service
We're with You Every Step of the Way!

$ Sold

7 **Get proceeds check**
• Close transaction
• Go to closing

6 **Transaction processing**
• Get financing for the buyer
• Clear contingencies

5 **Present offer and negotiate the sale**
• All offers written
• "I'll be there every time there's a contract"

4 **Market your property**
• See our 24-point marketing program

3 **Condition and showing recommendations**
• Clean, bright, and neat!

2 **Pricing assistance**
• Help determine best listing price
• Estimate your sales proceeds

1 **Tailored to your needs. We'll first listen to:**
• What you expect from us
• When you want to move
• Why you are selling

The five major parts of a listing presentation are as follows:

1. Building rapport with the sellers

2. Explaining the pricing process

3. Explaining the Seller's Net Proceeds Form

4. Discussing the importance of listing with your brokerage firm

5. Asking for the listing

A seller usually is more interested in the net proceeds from the sale of his property than the home's actual sales price. The Seller's Net Proceeds Form—the financial disclosure to the seller—consists of three major sections. The seller's equity section provides the sales price less mortgage balances, with the difference being the seller's equity. The expenses section shows expenses the seller must pay at closing. The prorations section includes taxes, interest, rents, and homeowner's dues.

K E Y   T E R M S

equity   net proceeds   Seller's Net Proceeds Form
listing presentation

PRACTICE EXAM

1. When presenting a CMA, a licensee should NOT
   a. discuss current market conditions for the overall market, only for the sellers' neighborhood.
   b. recommend a price for the property before going over the data in the CMA.
   c. give the seller a range of values rather than a single value.
   d. ask for the order after the explanation.

2. Where is the best place in the house to make the listing presentation?
   a. Living room sofa
   b. On the deck outside
   c. At the dining room table
   d. In front of the TV

3. The reason for eliminating cents and rounding to the nearest $100 on the Seller's Net Proceeds Form is to
   a. avoid giving the impression that the figures will be exactly as shown at closing.
   b. make the statement easier to understand.
   c. provide a cushion in the estimate.
   d. accomplish all of the above.

4. The components of the seller's equity section of the Seller's Net Proceeds Form include
   a. seller's equity, expenses, and seller's net proceeds.
   b. sales price, prorations, and expenses.
   c. seller's equity, prorations, and seller's net proceeds.
   d. sales price, mortgages, and seller's equity.

5. What is the proper order for a complete listing presentation?
   a. CMA, sellers' net, building rapport with the sellers, reasons for listing with your brokerage firm, ask for the order
   b. Ask for the order, CMA, sellers' net, building rapport with the sellers, reasons for listing with your brokerage firm
   c. Building rapport with the sellers, ask for the order, CMA, sellers' net, reasons for listing with your brokerage firm
   d. Building rapport with the sellers, CMA, sellers' net, reasons for listing with your brokerage firm, ask for the order

6. When explaining the current market conditions to the seller, one piece of information that would NOT normally be included is the
   a. aggregate square footage of all listed homes.
   b. number of houses currently listed.
   c. month's supply of homes on the market.
   d. number of homes sold last month.

7. Which part of the CMA would indicate overpriced listings?
   a. Sold houses
   b. Houses currently for sale
   c. Expired listings
   d. Withdrawn listings

8. The preferable approach to setting the listing price is to:
   a. list at the price the seller wants.
   b. go over the CMA carefully and to help the seller to arrive at an appropriate range of values.
   c. tell the seller the maximum price at which you will list the house at the beginning of the meeting.
   d. find out what the seller needs from the sale and add your commission.

Use the following information to answer questions 9 through 12.

Broker Sharon is compiling a Seller's Net Proceeds Form for Ellen Johnson. The figures she gathers are as follows:

Brokerage fee	7%
Title insurance	$ 780.00
Termite inspection and treatment	300.00
Sales price	127,500.00
Existing first mortgage @ 10%	98,601.60
Documentary stamps on deed	?
Property taxes for the year	1,745.60
Interest proration (paid in arrears)	?
Closing date	June 30

9. What is the seller's equity, rounded to the nearest $100?
   a. $29,000
   b. $28,900
   c. $20,000
   d. $16,300

10. What are the total expenses, rounded to the next highest $100?
    a. $10,100
    b. $10,800
    c. $10,900
    d. $11,800

11. What are the total prorations, rounded to the nearest $100? Will the prorations be added or subtracted from the equity?
    a. $2,600 added
    b. $900 subtracted
    c. $1,300 subtracted
    d. $1,700 subtracted

12. What are the seller's net proceeds, rounded to the nearest $100?
    a. $14,500
    b. $15,400
    c. $16,300
    d. $17,100

13. Patti is making a listing presentation to a FSBO. She completes the CMA and gets the sellers to accept the net amount on the Seller's Net Proceeds Form. She should be able to take the listing now primarily because
    a. she has completed all steps of the listing presentation.
    b. the commission is included on the Seller's Net Proceeds Form, and the sellers have agreed to the amounts shown.
    c. the FSBOs should know they would not be able to sell the property themselves.
    d. she has not gone over the reasons the sellers should list with her firm.

14. The reason it is NOT practical for a licensee to determine the exact prorations on the Seller's Net Proceeds Form when taking a listing is that
    a. it takes too long.
    b. a mistake will likely lose the listing.
    c. most sellers refuse to list when they see the prorations.
    d. the exact closing date is unknown.

15. When preparing the interest proration on a Seller's Net Proceeds Form, the best policy is to enter
    a. zero on the line, with a note that it can't be determined at this time.
    b. a full month of interest.
    c. one-half month of interest.
    d. two months of interest.

16. Which is NOT one of the three major problems in showing the property a FSBO should be told to expect?
    a. The risk to personal safety exists because of letting all prospective buyers into the house.
    b. The fact is that most new buyers will need financing.
    c. It is hard to get prospective buyers inside if the exterior of the house is not particularly attractive
    d. The house is off the market when the seller is away from home.

17. The reason most FSBOs won't be able to save the commission is that
    a. they may not understand how to help the buyer get financing.
    b. they may show the house to an unqualified buyer.
    c. the prospective buyer is buying direct to save the same commission.
    d. the seller may not know how to write a binding contract.

18. The final step in the listing presentation is
    a. explaining to the sellers why they should list with your brokerage firm.
    b. asking for the order.
    c. delivering the CMA.
    d. putting the listing into the MLS.

19. If the sellers want to list the property before you have completed the listing presentation, you should
    a. politely request a little more time to cover the presentation.
    b. suggest they may wish to think about it overnight, and leave the paperwork for them to sign later.
    c. ignore the interruption and continue with your presentation.
    d. take the listing.

20. On the Seller's Net Proceeds Form, which proration should NOT be included?
    a. Property taxes
    b. Insurance
    c. Interest
    d. Rents, if this is a rental property

7

LISTING CONTRACTS

LEARNING OBJECTIVES

Upon completion of this chapter, you should be able to:

1. explain the wording that could be used to protect both seller and broker from commission disputes caused by a buyer who improperly tries to leave the broker out of the transaction in an open listing;

2. state the legally required elements in a listing contract;

3. explain the distinguishing characteristics of each of the following types of listings: open, exclusive agency, and exclusive-right-of-sale;

4. discuss the purpose of an owner's warranty in a listing contract;

5. discuss the purpose of the latent defects disclosure in the process of listing real property for sale;

6. explain the steps required to complete a residential profile sheet;

7. complete the residential profile sheet;

8. complete a listing contract;

9. explain each paragraph of the listing agreement that applies to your market area; and

10. design a listing servicing program for your personal listings.

OVERVIEW

A listing contract is an agreement between a real estate broker and a property owner. The listing contract specifies the duties of both the broker and the owner in the sale of the owner's real property. Without listing contracts, there would be little or no inventory to sell, exchange, lease, rent, or auction. It is important to understand that a listing agreement is a personal services (employment) contract that requires that the broker perform one or more professional services to fulfill the agreement. The broker may seek assistance from other licensees, but the primary responsibility remains with the listing broker. The listing contract is a broker's employment contract, and all listings should be in writing. If litigation should result from some misunderstanding, default, or breach, it is much easier to resolve by showing the terms of a written contract than by obtaining testimony to prove the terms or conditions of an oral listing. Because the statute of frauds does not cover listing contracts, oral listing contracts are enforceable with the proper amount of evidence and testimony. ◼

TYPES OF LISTING CONTRACTS

In this chapter, three types of listing contracts are identified. The exclusive-right-of-sale listing contract is emphasized because of its predominance in residential property transactions.

Open Listing

An **open listing** is a contract in which an owner reserves the right to employ any number of brokers. Brokers may work simultaneously, but the first broker who produces a ready, willing, and able buyer at the terms accepted by the seller is the only one who earns a commission. If the owner himself sells the property without the aid of any of the brokers, he is not obligated to pay any commission; but if a broker can prove she was the procuring cause of the transaction, she may be entitled to a commission. While most residential brokers will not accept open listings, commercial and agricultural property brokers sometimes work with sellers with this type of listing.

Any listing contract normally creates an open listing unless the contract is worded in a manner that specifically provides for a different type of listing. While open listings may be either oral or implied, a contract does not exist until terms are negotiated. For example, a for-sale-by-owner sign that indicates "brokers protected" or in some other way invites offers from brokers does not create a listing contract.

Either or all parties may terminate an open listing at will, and in the absence of formal notification, an open listing may terminate after a reasonable time. The owner principal is not obligated to notify any of the brokers that the property has been sold.

Exclusive-Agency Listing (Exclusive Listing)

The **exclusive-agency listing** is the preferred listing agreement of an owner who has selected one particular broker as his or her exclusive agent, for a specified period of time, to sell real property according to the owner's stated terms. In an exclusive-agency listing, the owner appoints the broker but reserves the right to sell the property without paying a commission to the broker if the broker has not introduced or identified the buyer. If the broker performs by selling the property before the owner can do so, the broker is entitled to a commission. Exclusive-agency residential listings are less common than exclusive-right-of-sale listings.

A common problem with exclusive-agency and open listings is the exposure to lawsuits for procuring cause between the broker and the seller.

DISCUSSION EXERCISE 7.1

Arthur Cody lists Donald Wilson's home under an exclusive-agency listing agreement. Arthur shows the property to William Farkas. William notices that the seller has a sign on the property saying For Sale by Owner—555-1145. Arthur drops William off and writes a letter to Donald, registering William as a prospect. Immediately after Arthur drops him off, William calls Donald directly. Donald does not know that Arthur has shown the property and agrees to a reduced price because no commission is involved. Donald and William enter into a contract for sale. It is only after the contract is signed that Donald gets Arthur's prospect registration letter. When the sale closes, Arthur brings suit for commission as the procuring cause of the sale.

Role-play the court argument: Arthur, arguing for a commission on the sale, and Donald, explaining why no commission is due.

---

1 In the discussion exercise above, Donald, whom we assume to be an honest person,
2 was sued because of the buyer's actions, not his own. How can a broker prevent this type
3 of misunderstanding? Registration is not enough, because the notification may come after
4 the parties have entered into a contract.

In Practice

Protect your seller by suggesting that when he or she sells directly to put these words in the contract:

This property is listed with a broker under an agreement that the broker will be paid a commission for procuring a buyer for the property. Buyer warrants to seller that he or she was not shown or made aware of this property by any real estate broker or sales associate. Buyer agrees that if a broker claiming a commission provides information to the contrary, buyer will reimburse seller for commissions due to said real estate broker as well as legal fees.

5 A buyer who has seen the property with a broker will refuse to sign such a statement,
6 putting the seller on notice that the buyer is trying to save the commission by excluding
7 the broker.

8 Two other problems can arise from an exclusive-agency agreement. First, a broker
9 is reluctant to show property to a buyer if the owner's phone number is displayed promi-
10 nently on a sign in front of the property. The sign invites the buyer to exclude the broker
11 to get a better price. If the broker takes the listing under an exclusive agency, the broker
12 should get the owner's agreement to remove the sign.

13 Another problem the broker faces is the possibility of the owner's advertising a lower
14 price (broker's price less commission). The broker likely will lose the buyer if the buyer
15 sees the owner's ad. The broker and the owner should quote the same price.

Exclusive-Right-of-Sale Listing

The **exclusive-right-of-sale listing** is the most advantageous listing from the broker's viewpoint and the most common type of listing. The listing is given to a selected broker, who then becomes the exclusive broker for the sale of the property. The broker is due a commission regardless of who sells the property. That is, if the owner sells the property during the contract period, the broker still earns a commission. Also, if the owner sells the property within a designated time period after the listing contract has expired to a buyer originally introduced to the property by the broker, the owner usually is liable for a sales commission to the broker.

To be enforceable, this type of listing contract should be in writing and include valuable consideration. Only exclusive-right-of-sale and exclusive-agency listings may be entered into the MLS by the listing brokers.

Florida Laws Regulating Listing Agreements

Florida law recognizes written, oral, or implied listings assuming evidence is available to support a claim for compensation. If a listing is written, it must include a definite expiration date, a description of the property, the price and terms acceptable to the sellers, the amount of commission due upon the broker's performance, and the signature of the parties. A written listing agreement may not have wording that makes it self-renewing, or the listing will be rendered void. The broker, or the broker's authorized representative, must deliver to the sellers a copy of the listing agreement within 24 hours of signature.

Warranties by the Owner

If the listing broker is a single agent for the seller, both the broker and the seller have obligations under the listing agreement. The principal has legal obligations to the broker, including performance of all promises made in the contract, as well as the obligation to engage in honest, straightforward dealing. The actions and misrepresentations of a seller can become a liability to the agent. For example, if a seller tells a sales associate that the plumbing pipes are copper and the sales associate passes along that information to a buyer without qualification, both the seller and the brokerage firm may be liable for damages if the buyer later discovers the plumbing pipes are polybutylene. Litigation may result in damages assessed against both the seller and the broker.

THE EXCLUSIVE-RIGHT-OF-SALE AGREEMENT

The sales associate should complete as much of the paperwork as possible before the listing appointment. Because the task can be done in a controlled environment without distractions, it is more likely to be correct. The advance preparation also results in a more efficient process once the sales associate is with the seller.

Understanding the Exclusive-Right-of-Sale Listing Agreement

The real estate licensee is expected to be knowledgeable about the listing contract and able to explain the provisions clearly and completely. Sellers lose confidence in a sales associate who stumbles through an explanation of the agreement or who doesn't know the meaning of a clause.

F I G U R E 7.1 ■ Exclusive-Right-of-Sale Listing Agreement

Exclusive Right of Sale Listing Agreement
FLORIDA ASSOCIATION OF REALTORS®

1   This Exclusive Right of Sale Listing Agreement ("Agreement") is between

2* _____ ("**Seller**") and

3* _____ ("**Broker**").

4   **1. AUTHORITY TO SELL PROPERTY: Seller** gives **Broker** the EXCLUSIVE RIGHT TO SELL the real and personal property
5   (collectively "Property") described below, at the price and terms described below, beginning the _____ day of
6   _____, _____, and terminating at 11:59 p.m. the _____ day of _____, _____
7   ("Termination Date"). Upon full execution of a contract for sale and purchase of the Property, all rights and obligations of this
8   Agreement will automatically extend through the date of the actual closing of the sales contract. **Seller** and **Broker**
9   acknowledge that this Agreement does not guarantee a sale. This Property will be offered to any person without regard to race,
10 color, religion, sex, handicap, familial status, national origin or any other factor protected by federal, state or local law. **Seller**
11 certifies and represents that he/she/it is legally entitled to convey the Property and all improvements.

12 **2. DESCRIPTION OF PROPERTY:**
13*   **(a)** Real Property Street Address: _____
14*   _____
15*   Legal Description:_____
16*   _____ ❏ See Attachment _____
17*   **(b)** Personal Property, including appliances:_____
18*   _____
19*   _____ ❏ See Attachment _____
20*   **(c)** Occupancy: Property ❏ is ❏ is not currently occupied by a tenant. If occupied, the lease term expires _____.

21 **3. PRICE AND TERMS:** The property is offered for sale on the following terms, or on other terms acceptable to **Seller:**
22*   **(a) Price:** _____
23*   **(b) Financing Terms:** ❏ Cash ❏ Conventional ❏ VA ❏ FHA ❏ Other _____
24*   ❏ **Seller** Financing: **Seller** will hold a purchase money mortgage in the amount of $_____ with the
25*   following terms: _____
26*   ❏ Assumption of Existing Mortgage: Buyer may assume existing mortgage for $_____ plus
27*   an assumption fee of $_____. The mortgage is for a term of _____ years beginning in _____, at
28*   an interest rate of _____% ❏ fixed ❏ variable (describe) _____
29*   Lender approval of assumption ❏ is required ❏ is not required ❏ unknown. Notice to **Seller**: You may remain liable for an
30   assumed mortgage for a number of years after the Property is sold. Check with your lender to determine the extent of your
31   liability. **Seller** will ensure that all mortgage payments and required escrow deposits are current at the time of closing and will
32   convey the escrow deposit to the buyer at closing.
33*   **(c) Seller Expenses: Seller** will pay mortgage discount or other closing costs not to exceed _____% of the purchase
34   price; and any other expenses **Seller** agrees to pay in connection with a transaction.

35 **4. BROKER OBLIGATIONS AND AUTHORITY: Broker** agrees to make diligent and continued efforts to sell the Property until
36 a sales contract is pending on the Property. **Seller** authorizes **Broker** to:
37   **(a)** Advertise the Property as **Broker** deems advisable including advertising the Property on the Internet unless limited in
38   (4)(a)(i) or (4)(a)(ii) below.
39   **(Seller opt-out)(Check one if applicable)**
40*   ❏ (i) Display the Property on the Internet except the street address of the Property shall not be displayed on the Internet.
41*   ❏ (ii) **Seller** does not authorize **Broker** to display the Property on the Internet.
42   **Seller** understands and acknowledges that if **Seller** selects option (ii), consumers who conduct searches for listings on
43   the Internet will not see information about the listed property in response to their search.
44*   _____/_____ **Initials of Seller.**
45   **(b)** Place appropriate transaction signs on the Property, including "For Sale" signs and "Sold" signs (once **Seller** signs a sales
46   contract) and use **Seller's** name in connection with marketing or advertising the Property.
47   **(c)** Obtain information relating to the present mortgage(s) on the Property.
48   **(d)** Place the Property in a multiple listing service ("MLS"). **Seller** authorizes **Broker** to report to the MLS this listing
49   information and price, terms and financing information on any resulting sale for use by authorized Board / Association
50   members, MLS participants and subscribers; and

51* **Seller** (____) (____) and **Broker/Sales Associate** (____) (____) acknowledge receipt of a copy of this page, which is Page 1 of 4 Pages.

ERS-14tb   Rev. 11/09   © 2009   Florida Association of REALTORS®   All Rights Reserved

F I G U R E 7.1 ■ **Exclusive-Right-of-Sale Listing Agreement (continued)**

52 (e) Provide objective comparative market analysis information to potential buyers; and
53* (f) (Check if applicable) ❏ Use a lock box system to show and access the Property. A lock box does not ensure the
54 Property's security; **Seller** is advised to secure or remove valuables. **Seller** agrees that the lock box is for **Seller's** benefit and
55 releases **Broker**, persons working through **Broker** and **Broker's** local Realtor Board / Association from all liability and
56* responsibility in connection with any loss that occurs. ❏ Withhold verbal offers. ❏ Withhold all offers once **Seller** accepts a
57 sales contract for the Property.
58 (g) Act as a transaction broker of Seller.
59 (h) **Virtual Office Websites:** Some real estate brokerages offer real estate brokerage services online. These websites are
60 referred to as Virtual Office Websites ("VOW"). An automated estimate of market value or reviews and comments about a
61 property may be displayed in conjunction with a property on some VOWs. Anyone who registers on a Virtual Office Website
62 may gain access to such automated valuations or comments and reviews about any property displayed on a VOW. Unless
63 limited below, a VOW may display automated valuations or comments/reviews (blogs) about this Property.
64* ❏ **Seller** does not authorize an automated estimate of the market value of the listing (or hyperlink to such estimate) to be
65 displayed in immediate conjunction with the listing of this Property.
66* ❏ **Seller** does not authorize third parties to write comments or reviews about the listing of the Property (or display a hyperlink
67 to such comments or reviews) in immediate conjunction with the listing of this Property.

68 **5. SELLER OBLIGATIONS:** In consideration of **Broker's** obligations, **Seller** agrees to:
69 (a) Cooperate with **Broker** in carrying out the purpose of this Agreement, including referring immediately to **Broker** all
70 inquiries regarding the Property's transfer, whether by purchase or any other means of transfer.
71 (b) Provide **Broker** with keys to the Property and make the Property available for **Broker** to show during reasonable times.
72 (c) Inform **Broker** prior to leasing, mortgaging or otherwise encumbering the Property.
73 (d) Indemnify **Broker** and hold **Broker** harmless from losses, damages, costs and expenses of any nature, including
74 attorney's fees, and from liability to any person, that **Broker** incurs because of (1) **Seller's** negligence, representations,
75 misrepresentations, actions or inactions, (2) the use of a lock box, (3) the existence of undisclosed material facts about the
76 Property, or (4) a court or arbitration decision that a broker who was not compensated in connection with a transaction is
77 entitled to compensation from **Broker**. This clause will survive **Broker's** performance and the transfer of title.
78 (e) To perform any act reasonably necessary to comply with FIRPTA (Internal Revenue Code Section 1445).
79 (f) Make all legally required disclosures, including all facts that materially affect the Property's value and are not readily
80 observable or known by the buyer. **Seller** certifies and represents that **Seller** knows of no such material facts (local
81* government building code violations, unobservable defects, etc.) other than the following: _____
82* _____
83 **Seller** will immediately inform **Broker** of any material facts that arise after signing this Agreement.
84 (g) Consult appropriate professionals for related legal, tax, property condition, environmental, foreign reporting requirements
85 and other specialized advice.

86 **6. COMPENSATION: Seller** will compensate **Broker** as specified below for procuring a buyer who is ready, willing and able to
87 purchase the Property or any interest in the Property on the terms of this Agreement or on any other terms acceptable to
88 **Seller. Seller** will pay **Broker** as follows (plus applicable sales tax):
89* (a) _____ % of the total purchase price plus $_____ OR $_____, no later than
90 the date of closing specified in the sales contract. However, closing is not a prerequisite for **Broker's** fee being earned.
91* (b) _____ ($ or %) of the consideration paid for an option, at the time an option is created. If the option is exercised,
92 **Seller** will pay **Broker** the paragraph 6(a) fee, less the amount **Broker** received under this subparagraph.
93* (c) _____ ($ or %) of gross lease value as a leasing fee, on the date **Seller** enters into a lease or agreement to
94 lease, whichever is soonest. This fee is not due if the Property is or becomes the subject of a contract granting an exclusive
95 right to lease the Property.
96 (d) **Broker's** fee is due in the following circumstances: (1) If any interest in the Property is transferred, whether by sale, lease,
97 exchange, governmental action, bankruptcy or any other means of transfer, regardless of whether the buyer is secured by
98 **Broker, Seller** or any other person. (2) If **Seller** refuses or fails to sign an offer at the price and terms stated in this Agreement,
99* defaults on an executed sales contract or agrees with a buyer to cancel an executed sales contract. (3) If, within _____ days after
100 Termination Date ("Protection Period"), **Seller** transfers or contracts to transfer the Property or any interest in the Property to any
101 prospects with whom **Seller, Broker** or any real estate licensee communicated regarding the Property prior to Termination Date.
102 However, no fee will be due **Broker** if the Property is relisted after Termination Date and sold through another broker.
103* (e) Retained Deposits: As consideration for **Broker's** services, **Broker** is entitled to receive _____% of all deposits that
104 **Seller** retains as liquidated damages for a buyer's default in a transaction, not to exceed the paragraph 6(a) fee.

105 **7. COOPERATION AND COMPENSATION WITH OTHER BROKERS: Broker's** office policy is to cooperate with all other
106* brokers except when not in **Seller's** best interest: ❏ and to offer compensation in the amount of _____% of the
107* purchase price or $_____ to **Buyer's** agents, who represent the interest of the buyers, and not the interest of **Seller** in

108* **Seller** (____) (____) and **Broker/Sales Associate** (____) (____) acknowledge receipt of a copy of this page, which is Page 2 of 4 Pages.

ERS-14tb   Rev. 11/09   © 2009   Florida Association of REALTORS®   All Rights Reserved

F I G U R E 7.1 ■ Exclusive-Right-of-Sale Listing Agreement (continued)

109* a transaction; ❏ and to offer compensation in the amount of _____% of the purchase price or $_____ to a
110* broker who has no brokerage relationship with the **Buyer** or **Seller**; ❏ and to offer compensation in the amount of
111* _____% of the purchase price or $_____ to Transaction brokers for the **Buyer**; ❏ None of the above (if this is
112 checked, the Property cannot be placed in the MLS.)

113 **8. BROKERAGE RELATIONSHIP:** Under this Agreement, **Broker** will be acting as a transaction broker. **Broker** will deal
114 honestly and fairly with **Seller**, will account for all funds, will use skill, care, and diligence in the transaction, will disclose all
115 known facts that materially affect the value of the residential property which are not readily observable to the buyer, will present
116 all offers and counteroffers in a timely manner unless directed otherwise in writing and will have limited confidentiality with **Seller**
117 unless waived in writing.

118 **9. CONDITIONAL TERMINATION:** At **Seller's** request, **Broker** may agree to conditionally terminate this Agreement. If **Broker**
119 agrees to conditional termination, **Seller** must sign a withdrawal agreement, reimburse **Broker** for all direct expenses incurred
120* in marketing the Property and pay a cancellation fee of $_____ plus applicable sales tax. **Broker** may void the
121 conditional termination and **Seller** will pay the fee stated in paragraph 6(a) less the cancellation fee if **Seller** transfers or
122 contracts to transfer the Property or any interest in the Property during the time period from the date of conditional termination
123 to Termination Date and Protection Period, if applicable.

124 **10. DISPUTE RESOLUTION:** This Agreement will be construed under Florida law. All controversies, claims and other matters
125 in question between the parties arising out of or relating to this Agreement or the breach thereof will be settled by first
126 attempting mediation under the rules of the American Mediation Association or other mediator agreed upon by the parties. If
127 litigation arises out of this Agreement, the prevailing party will be entitled to recover reasonable attorney's fees and costs, unless
128 the parties agree that disputes will be settled by arbitration as follows: **Arbitration:** By initialing in the space provided, **Seller**
129* (_____) (_____), Listing Associate (_____) and Listing Broker (_____) agree that disputes not resolved by mediation will be settled
130 by neutral binding arbitration in the county in which the Property is located in accordance with the rules of the American
131 Arbitration Association or other arbitrator agreed upon by the parties. Each party to any arbitration (or litigation to enforce the
132 arbitration provision of this Agreement or an arbitration award) will pay its own fees, costs and expenses, including attorney's
133 fees, and will equally split the arbitrators' fees and administrative fees of arbitration.

134 **11. MISCELLANEOUS:** This Agreement is binding on **Broker's** and **Seller's** heirs, personal representatives, administrators,
135 successors and assigns. **Broker** may assign this Agreement to another listing office. This Agreement is the entire agreement
136 between **Broker** and **Seller**. No prior or present agreements or representations shall be binding on **Broker** or **Seller** unless
137 included in this Agreement. Signatures, initials and modifications communicated by facsimile will be considered as originals.
138 The term "buyer" as used in this Agreement includes buyers, tenants, exchangors, optionees and other categories of potential
139 or actual transferees.

140* **12. ADDITIONAL TERMS:** _____
141* _____
142* _____
143* _____
144* _____
145* _____
146* _____
147* _____
148* _____
149* _____
150* _____
151* _____
152* _____
153* _____
154* _____
155* _____
156* _____

157* **Seller** (_____) (_____) and **Broker/Sales Associate** (_____) (_____) acknowledge receipt of a copy of this page, which is Page 3 of 4 Pages.

ERS-14tb   Rev. 11/09   © 2009   Florida Association of REALTORS®   All Rights Reserved

F I G U R E 7.1 ■ Exclusive-Right-of-Sale Listing Agreement (continued)

158* Date: _____ **Seller's Signature:** _____ Tax ID No: _ _ _ - _ _ - _ _ _ _

159* Home Telephone: _____ Work Telephone: _____ Facsimile: _____

160* Address: _____

161* Date: _____ **Seller's Signature:** _____ Tax ID No: _ _ _ - _ _ - _ _ _ _

162* Home Telephone: _____ Work Telephone: _____ Facsimile: _____

163* Address: _____

164* Date: _____ **Authorized Listing Associate or Broker:** _____

165* Brokerage Firm Name: _____ Telephone: _____

166* Address: _____

167* | Copy returned to **Customer** on the _____ day of _____, _____ by: ❏ personal delivery ❏ mail ❏ E-mail ❏ facsimile. |

The Florida Association of REALTORS® makes no representation as to the legal validity or adequacy of any provision of this form in any specific transaction. This standardized form should not be used in complex transactions or with extensive riders or additions. This form is available for use by the entire real estate industry and is not intended to identify the user as a REALTOR®. REALTOR® is a registered collective membership mark which may be used only by real estate licensees who are members of the NATIONAL ASSOCIATION OF REALTORS® and who subscribe to its Code of Ethics.
The copyright laws of the United States (17 U.S. Code) forbid the unauthorized reproduction of this form by any means including facsimile or computerized forms.

168* **Seller** (_____) (_____) and **Broker/Sales Associate** (_____) (_____) acknowledge receipt of a copy of this page, which is Page 4 of 4 Pages.

ERS-14tb   Rev. 11/09   © 2009   Florida Association of REALTORS®   All Rights Reserved

The Florida Association of REALTORS® distributes the listing agreement shown in Figure 7.1. If you use a different form, the clauses in your listing agreement probably are very similar. The numbered paragraphs below correspond to the 13 paragraphs in the agreement.

Parties. The parties are the owner(s) of the property and the brokerage firm, not the sales associate. All persons owning an interest in the property should be included here. The licensee should check the seller's deed to ensure that all persons on the deed sign the listing. Corporations, partnerships, trusts, and estates require special treatment. See the broker or an attorney for advice.

1. *Authority to sell property.* This paragraph gives the broker an exclusive right to sell the property. The listing term also is shown here. Many brokerage firms have policies for the listing term, depending on the type of property. A typical residential period is six months. The licensee should examine that policy carefully, however, in light of the best marketing period. For instance, in many areas of Florida, the best sales period is from May through August. If that is the case, a six-month listing taken on January 2 expires July 2, with two months remaining in the best selling period. A far better approach is a minimum of six months, provided all listings remain active at least through August 31. A contract written during the listing period extends the listing until the closing. The seller agrees to offer the property without unlawful discrimination. The seller warrants that he can convey the property legally.

2. *Description of property.*

   a. *Real property street address.* The property address is entered here. The legal description should be taken from the public records or from the owner's deed, if available. If it is a metes-and-bounds description, it should be attached. A description taken from the tax records or from former listing information is not satisfactory, as these sources are not always reliable.

   b. *Personal property.* Fixtures as well as other personal property must be listed here. Often a seller agrees to leave a refrigerator, drapes, or a washer/dryer; however, the licensee should discuss with the seller the possibility of holding back the offer of these items, using them as negotiating tools when an offer is made. (For example, "The seller says that if you can increase your offer by $1,000, she will give you her washer-dryer.")

   Some items are not included as part of the agreement. The licensee should ask the seller an important question: "Is any item attached to the property that you *do not want to be included with the sale?*" The agreement does not provide a section for this exclusion, but the licensee should be certain to include any such items on an addendum. If possible, the fixture should be removed before the home is shown.

   c. *Occupancy.* This section covers the seller's representation about occupancy rights by another party. If a third party is in possession of the property, the buyer's rights are subject to those of the tenant.

3. *Price and terms.*

   a. *Price.* Here the licensee records the price at which the property will be offered.

   b. *Financing terms.* The terms are important to the seller and the listing broker, particularly in the way the property is marketed. If the seller agrees to seller financing, the terms of such financing are stated here. If there is an existing mortgage on the property, the seller is asked whether it can be assumed with or without lender approval. The seller is warned about liability in case of an assumption. The seller also agrees that the loan is current in case of assumption.

   c. *Seller expenses.* This section limits the amount the seller agrees to pay for discount points and other closing costs as a percentage of the sales price. The licensee should take care to ensure that the amount shown here is enough to pay typical costs of sale, including a commission. Of course, the seller could agree to pay more when signing a contract for sale. The licensee should disclose anticipated seller's costs on the Seller's Net Proceeds Form before presenting the listing agreement and each time an offer is presented to the seller.

4. ***Broker obligations and authority.*** The broker makes promises in this section (the consideration is what makes this a bilateral contract) that include working diligently to sell the property. The seller authorizes the broker to take the following steps:

   a. Advertise the property as the broker deems advisable, place an appropriate sign on the property, and use the seller's name in marketing the property. This section also allows the seller to opt out of displaying the property on the Internet.

   b. Place appropriate signs on the property, including "For Sale" and "Sold" signs.

   c. Obtain information about the mortgage (usually a signed request from the seller for a status letter).

   d. Place the property in the MLS. Some brokers hold a listing out for an extended period of time, during which the broker attempts to sell the property himself. If the licensee is a single agent, this could be considered as subordinating the principal's interests to the broker's personal interests, a clear violation of fiduciary duties.

   e. Provide a CMA to potential buyers.

   f. Place a lockbox on the property if the seller specifically authorizes it. The seller is asked to relieve the broker, staff, and Board of REALTORS® from liability due to loss. The seller may request that the broker withhold oral offers and *all* offers once the seller accepts a contract.

   g. Act as a transaction broker.

   h. Virtual office Web sites that allow automated estimates of value or comments or reviews about the property. This section allows the seller to opt out of the value estimates or comments.

5. ***Seller obligations.*** The seller agrees to:

   a. cooperate with the broker to obtain a sale and refer all inquiries to the broker;

   b. give keys to the broker and make property available for showing during reasonable times;

   c. inform the broker before leasing or mortgaging the property;

   d. hold the broker harmless because of (1) the seller's negligence or misrepresentations, (2) losses from the use of a lockbox, (3) the existence of undisclosed facts about the property, or (4) arbitration or lawsuits against the broker by another broker (This serves as a warranty that the seller's statements to the broker are true and that indemnifies the broker against representations made by the seller that the broker passes on to a buyer. The warranty against seller misrepresentations is commonly called the *warranty of owner clause*.);

    e. comply with the Foreign Investment in Real Property Tax Act (FIRPTA) requirements in case the seller is a foreign national (This could require that the buyer withhold 10 percent of the sales proceeds and forward the funds to the IRS.);

    f. make legally required disclosures affecting the property's value. This usually involves the seller completing the "Sellers' Real Property Disclosure Statement" (See Forms-To-Go Section). The sales associate should not complete this form for the seller. This is often referred to as a *latent defects addendum*; and

    g. consult with qualified professionals for legal, tax, and other matters, the intent of which is to reduce the licensee's liability.

6. *Compensation.* This is an agreement to find a purchaser who is ready, willing, and able to buy, either at the list price or any other price agreeable to the seller. It is not dependent on a closing (as in a listing "to effect a sale").

    a. This paragraph sets the commission as a percentage of the price or as a dollar amount. The commission is due no later than closing but may be due whether or not a closing occurs.

    b. In case the seller and a buyer agree to an option contract, this paragraph sets the commission as a percentage of the option amount or as a dollar amount. The commission is due at the time the option is created. The total commission, less the commission received from the option, is due when the option is exercised.

    c. In case a lease agreement is created, this paragraph sets the commission as a percentage of the price or as a dollar amount. The commission is due when the seller enters into an agreement to lease. An exception occurs if the seller employs another broker under an exclusive-right-to-lease agreement.

    d. Broker's Fee. This paragraph describes when the broker's fee is due:

        (1) if any interest in the property is transferred, whether by sale, lease, exchange, government action (e.g., eminent domain), or bankruptcy, no matter who finds the buyer;

        (2) if the seller refuses to sign an offer at full price and terms, defaults on a contract, or agrees with a buyer to cancel an executed sales contract; or

        (3) if, after the listing's expiration, a prospect who learned about the property through a broker buys the property within the protection period. An exception occurs if another broker has subsequently listed the property.

    e. Retained Deposits. This paragraph entitles the broker to a specified percentage of all deposits that the seller retains as liquidated damages for a buyer's default. The amount cannot exceed the total commission as shown in paragraph 6(a).

7. *Cooperation and compensation with other brokers.* This section states that the broker's policy is to cooperate with all other brokers except when it would not be in the seller's best interests. It authorizes the listing broker to offer commission splits with other brokers. The seller checks her approval for splits with (1) buyers' agents, (2) nonrepresentatives, (3) transaction brokers, or (4) none of the above. If the seller checks "none of the above," the listing broker may not put

the listing into the MLS, because the MLS requires an offer of compensation to a cooperating broker.

8. ***Brokerage relationship.*** As described in Chapter 1, brokers may work with buyers or sellers as nonrepresentatives, single agents, or transaction brokers. The listing contract includes the disclosure forms for single agent or transaction broker. The seller should sign the forms, or, if the seller declines to do so, the licensee should so indicate on the listing contract form. If the broker is starting as a single agent and may become a transaction broker, the transition notice *must* be signed.

9. ***Conditional termination.*** If the seller decides not to sell the property, the broker may agree to terminate the contract. The seller must sign a withdrawal agreement, then pay the broker's direct expenses and a specified cancellation fee. If the seller contracts to transfer the property during the protection period, the broker may cancel the termination and collect the balance of the commission due.

10. ***Dispute Resolution.*** This paragraph requires that conflicts be submitted to a mediator agreed to by the parties. If the mediation is not successful, and unless the parties agree in advance to arbitration, either party may sue. The prevailing party is entitled to recover attorney's fees and costs.

11. ***Arbitration.*** This section allows the parties (seller, listing associate, and listing broker) to agree to settle disputes by binding arbitration in the county where the property is located. The parties agree to split the costs equally. The inclusion of the listing associate in the contract is curious because the listing agreement is between the seller and the broker, and only the broker is authorized to take action for a commission. If the intent was to protect the broker from the sales associate's later claims for a commission if arbitration was unsuccessful, that might be better handled in the employment agreement. The agreement suggests that the costs will be split among the three parties.

12. ***Miscellaneous.*** The agreement may be assigned to another listing office, which is a departure from the former practice. Fax communications are enforceable.

13. ***Information and signature section.*** This section provides space for additional terms and personal information, including tax ID numbers as well as signature lines. Note that the listing sales associate may be authorized to sign the listing for the broker. This facilitates giving the seller a copy of the agreement immediately, satisfying the 24-hour requirement. The box at the bottom of the contract indicates when the seller's copy was legally delivered.

Explaining the Agreement to the Seller

The presentation of the listing agreement to the seller needs to be thorough to ensure that the seller fully understands. Sales associates sometimes take a casual approach to explaining the listing agreement or offer no explanation at all to the seller. A sales associate may say, "Don't worry, it's the standard agreement. Sign here." Or the sales associates might try an explanation even though they don't understand the agreement themselves. This misleads the seller and is not acceptable. The licensee's job is to give the seller an understanding of the important provisions the agreement contains.

New sales associates should understand the agreement totally and explain each paragraph clearly. If a seller asks, "What happens during the listing period if I decide I want to lease the property to a tenant?" the sales associate should answer, "If you'll look at paragraph 6(c), you'll see that the property can be leased. You agree to pay my company a fee of _____ percent, but the fee does not include management."

The professional sales associate explains the listing agreement in language that the seller understands easily. Role-playing is an excellent method of learning this skill. When the role-playing results in wording that sounds appropriate, the sales associate should write it down so she can then refer to the written explanation during the listing appointment.

The following scenario might result from a licensee's role-playing exercise:

"Mr. Jones, this is the standard agreement all brokers use for homes listed in the MLS system. Let's go over it together, paragraph by paragraph.

"This top section shows your name as the seller and _____ Realty as the broker. Do I have your names spelled correctly?

"Section 1 shows that you give my company the authority to sell your property starting today and ending on _____. You understand that I can't *guarantee* a sale of the property. I must offer property without violating any fair housing laws. And you agree that you can legally sell the property.

"Section 2 shows that the address of the property is _____. And the legal description of the property taken from your deed is shown here."

The sales associate continues to explain sections 3 through 11 of the listing contract in a similar manner. She refers to the checklist in Figure 7.2 to be certain she has completed all the necessary documents and taken all the necessary actions in regard to the listing.

DISCUSSION EXERCISE 7.2

Using the listing agreement for your market area, paraphrase the legal words in everyday language that will help a seller understand the agreement better. In a group situation, each person should be assigned a paragraph. The person then explains the paragraph to the group in lay language, and the group provides constructive criticism. Because each person would explain each paragraph differently, every sales associate should prepare his own written text for use in presentations.

Closing for the Listing

All necessary forms should be completed by this time. The best approach would be to have the seller sign all forms at the same time rather than sign each as they are presented. A sample discussion of the conversation is shown in Figure 7.3.

Marketing the Listing

The seller employs the listing broker to market the property. Many sellers believe that the licensee has not done her job unless the listing broker actually sells the listing. The licensee should discuss this misconception with the seller during the listing presentation.

F I G U R E 7.2 ■ Listing Procedure Checklist

You must complete Brokerage Relationship Disclosures in accordance with Chapter 475, F.S.
This form should accompany all listings.

Property Address: _____

Listing Associate: _____

Listing Packet Contents (bold print indicates seller's signature is required):

- ❏ Comparative Market Analysis
- ❏ Brokerage Relationship Disclosures
- ❏ **EXCLUSIVE-RIGHT-OF-SALE AGREEMENT**
- ❏ MLS Profile Sheet
- ❏ **MORTGAGE STATUS REQUEST**
- ❏ **PROPERTY CONDITION DISCLOSURE STATEMENT**
- ❏ **HOME WARRANTY AGREEMENT**
- ❏ **SELLER'S NET PROCEEDS FORM**
- ❏ Survey, if available
- ❏ Copy of mortgage and note
- ❏ Copy of deed restrictions
- ❏ Title Insurance Policy
- ❏ Key to property
- ❏ Floor plan, if available
- ❏ Copy of seller or buyer referral sent out
- ❏ Three ads
- ❏ Sign installation form
- ❏ Lockbox installation form
- ❏ Client contact sheet
- ❏ Copy of computer printout

Office Action:

- ❏ Get office manager's approval on listing forms.
- ❏ Enter listing data into computer.
- ❏ Put copy of printout into Floor Duty Book.
- ❏ Distribute copies of printout to all sales associates.
- ❏ Turn in listing packet to secretary.

Follow-up Action:

- ❏ Return all original documents to seller.
- ❏ Send seller copy of the MLS listing book photo and information.
- ❏ Contact seller weekly.
- ❏ Send seller copy of mortgage status letter when received.
- ❏ Send copies of all ads to seller

The seller should understand that if the licensee does her job properly, the house will sell through the licensee's marketing efforts—both to potential buyers and to other licensees, who will show the property to their buyers.

The broker has been hired to get the best price in the shortest time and with the least inconvenience to the seller. This requires the licensee to market the property in ways other than just showing it herself. Some of these activities include

■ disseminating the property information to all agents in the company;

■ putting the sign on the property;

F I G U R E 7.3 ■ **Getting Signatures on Listing Documents**

Mr. and Mrs. Jackson, I've prepared this letter to your mortgage company to send us the current balance and payoff amount. We'll use this when we have your house sold. They'll send it to me, and I'll give a copy to you for your records. They require your approval, so I'll need your signatures right here, please. [When they sign the form, put it back in your stack.]

Now, we agreed to market the property at $_____. Based on that, you remember we went over the statement showing your expenses of the sale and what you would receive as proceeds. Here's a copy for your records, and I need you to OK this form for our records. [After they sign the form, put it back in your stack.]

OK, you completed the disclosure statement that we'll give to buyers when they are interested in the home. This will protect you from later claims that you held back important information. I need your signatures here please. [After they sign the form, put it back in your stack.]

Great. We've gone over the agreement for us to market your home. I need your OK right here. [After they sign the form, put it back in your stack.]

I appreciate your confidence, and I'll start the marketing of your home right away. I'm going to try to get back to the office and prepare information to put the property into MLS. Before I leave, do you have any questions?

1 ■ putting an MLS lockbox on the property (if approved by the seller and available
2 in the market area);

3 ■ arranging for all company sales associates to inspect the listing on caravan day;

4 ■ getting the information into the MLS as soon as possible (it is unethical and self-
5 serving to withhold the information from other brokers and sales associates while
6 the agent attempts to sell the property herself);

7 ■ announcing the listing at company sales meetings and at Board of Realtors®
8 marketing meetings;

9 ■ preparing a brochure to place in the home for prospective buyers and cooperat-
10 ing licensees;

11 ■ scheduling an open house if appropriate for the listing;

12 ■ writing at least three good ads to generate potential buyers;

13 ■ putting listing on Web sites (personal page, company page, and other advertiser's
14 pages);

15 ■ using e-mail auto responders to get immediate feedback for customers who ask
16 for information from a Web site;

17 ■ preparing Web advertising and virtual tour;

18 ■ preparing mail-outs to send to potential buyers;

19 ■ preparing a property brochure for potential buyers and other sales associates;

20 ■ telling 20 neighbors about the listing by mail;

21 ■ calling the neighbors to ask for help in finding buyers;

22 ■ holding a Realtors® luncheon at the property to increase activity; and

23 ■ reviewing sales and listing activity in the neighborhood. Update the CMA at
24 least once a month.

25 A detailed marketing program such as this could be the basis for a "Satisfaction
26 Guarantee" or "Steps to a Successful Sale" listing presentation.

> ## DISCUSSION EXERCISE 7.3
>
> In small groups, prepare a 30-point marketing plan for a brochure you use in your listing presentation. Brainstorm to come up with different marketing ideas.

Staging the Home

Chefs say the first taste of a meal is with our eyes. Presentation is extremely important! That wisdom is true also when we market a home. Home presentation, or *staging*, can make your listing stand out from comparable homes, and is especially effective in a buyer's market. Many of the cable channels have very popular programs showing house makeovers, and many of the ideas presented will be helpful in marketing your listing.

Sometimes when buyers are shown a property, the sales associate will have to say "Try to look past the clutter and you'll see how much potential there is here." When there are many homes for sale in the area, it's unlikely that the potential buyer will *want* to look past the clutter.

Steps to get the house ready to sell include:

- **Get it clean.** After living in the home for years, owners tend to overlook some of the surface buildup and strange odors. One way to help them be more objective about the condition of the house is to suggest you take them to see other houses on the market in their price range. When they see how spotless many of the homes are, it may convince them to put some elbow grease on those frayed areas.

- **Get it light.** When you get it clean, light it up! When the home is shown every light in the house should be on and drapes open. Cut back bushes around windows. Kitchens and baths should be bright. It's fine to use candles, but fire safety is an important concern.

- **Decorating is not staging.** Many homeowners have pretty homes, and they have decorated them to match their personalities. Red flocked wallpaper may be nice for some, but anathema for others. Take "personality" out of the house and stage it so that it will appeal to the largest number of people.

- **Staging is cosmetic.** When you look at an appraisal report, there are two categories of depreciation: curable and incurable. Curable depreciation, when the problem is fixed, adds more to the property value than the cost to fix it. That's the object of staging: to make only those cash outlays that are returned in the sale price. That can include painting, wallpapering, decluttering, and focusing on dramatic, cosmetic transformations.

- **Go for the model home look.** Warm and cozy without your "personality." Get the kids toys packed up after they use them; remove the family pictures that cover the wall in the hallway; take down Dad's electric train layout in the family room.

- **Remove excess furniture and accessories.** Make the space seem larger by having less clutter. In some model homes smaller than normal beds are used. While you don't want to do that, you can probably get rid of 50 percent of the contents of a room. Take the excess furniture to mini-storage.

- **Get rid of the old stuff.** Remove furniture and paintings over ten years old unless they are true antiques. Accessories should be used to give the house an updated look.

- **Have appropriate furniture in rooms.** A computer station in the dining room simply may not feel right to a buyer, so relocate it.

- **Highlight with color.** For years, real estate professionals suggested to paint it all beige. A great home stager can work wonders with dramatic accent walls. Owners should be careful if not trained in staging skills, as bad choices can ruin the effect.

- **It should smell and sound luscious.** We all know the trick of freshly baked cookies in the home (you can buy a spray product that saves the trouble of baking). But don't forget that when a buyer will be escorted through the home, soft music often sets the stage.

- **Healthy houseplants and throws on the sofa.** Make the house very livable so your buyers can picture themselves enjoying the home. Set the dining table as if for company and put a book next to the easy chair.

- **The best stage is empty.** When the house is being shown by an agent, the owners should leave (and take the dogs). Let the buyers have emotional possession, ask questions, sit on the sofa, and make themselves *at home!*

Servicing the Listing

Servicing the listing often is more important than acquiring it. "I never hear from him!" is probably the complaint sellers make most often about their sales associates. If a seller does not hear from his listing sales associate, the seller perceives that she is not doing her job.

DISCUSSION EXERCISE 7.4

You are a real estate sales associate who is quite busy and disorganized. You have had a listing for six months that is about to expire, and you wish to renew it. Despite your best intentions, you have failed to contact your clients, Harold and Deidra, for more than two months. As the time progressed, it became even harder for you to make the call. You set an appointment to visit the home at 7:30 PM. Because you are caught in traffic, you are 20 minutes late when you walk up to the house. You are surprised to see that a competitor has listed the property next door. Even worse, it has a "contract pending" sign attached. Harold answers the door, nods his head seriously, and says, "Well, stranger. Long time no see!"

Role-play this situation. Try your best to reestablish the trust and rapport you had at the beginning of the listing period. It may be instructive enough that you will never allow this situation to happen in your career.

Those professional licensees who are successful consistently do not accomplish this on the strength of salesmanship alone. The licensees are successful because they provide service to their clients and customers. Often, a family's home is the largest asset it will ever have, so a sales associate never must take the marketing of the home lightly.

1 Failure to maintain regular contact with a seller is a detriment to a sales associate's
2 future success.

In Practice

Select one evening each week, such as Thursday night, to service your listings.

Contact every seller in person, by phone, or if personal contact is not successful, by mail or e-mail. If you call and the seller does not answer, write a card
immediately to let them know you called.

Clip every ad from every paper and homes magazine, then paste it on a note
card and mail it with a note that says, "Thought you'd like to see a recent ad on
your home. Regards."

Ask every seller to call immediately if another licensee shows the property.
Then follow up to help make the sale.

Call the seller after talking to a cooperating broker and give feedback about
the showing.

---

3 Often sales associates lose touch with sellers because they don't know what to talk
4 about and feel that they sound like broken records because they say the same things over
5 and over.

6 Each sales associate should prepare a Listing Servicing Schedule, which provides a
7 basic format for the servicing of every listing. A sample form is shown in Figure 7.4.

WHEN LISTINGS DON'T SELL

9 Occasionally, sales associates feel that they are wasting their time listing property. "I make
10 more money working with buyers. I have ten listings and haven't earned a dime!"

11 Sales associates who feel that way may need to evaluate their listing inventory using
12 the Listing Quality Report in Figure 7.5.

13 Notice that the bottom part of the listing evaluation indicates that the sales associate
14 who thinks he or she has five listings has the equivalent of only 1.65 listings (adding the
15 percentages of chance of sale). The associate may boast of a listing volume of $1,160,700
16 (average of $232,140) but really has the equivalent of only $419,070 (average of $83,814)
17 when considering the chance of sale.

18 Overpriced listings result in frustration for the sales associate and resentment by the
19 owner, who may become more demanding and tell friends of the lack of effort on the part
20 of the sales associate. Sometimes, if the seller will not price the property appropriately, it
21 may be best for the sales associate to give the listing back to the seller. A comment such as
22 "We value our relationship with you and don't want you to feel we are not being produc-
23 tive. I feel you may be mad at us later on if we didn't give you the opportunity to talk with
24 other agencies."

25 If the sales associate internalizes this evaluation and mentally reviews it when taking
26 a listing, it is more likely that only salable listings would be taken thereafter.

F I G U R E 7.4 ■ Listing Servicing Schedule

Property Address_____ H Phone: _____ W Phone: _____

Sellers' Names _____ Children: _____

First Day:
- ❏ Verify tax information and legal description.
- ❏ Send out mortgage status request.
- ❏ Write three ads.
- ❏ Place listing on Web page.
- ❏ Send thank-you card to seller.
- ❏ Enter listing information in computer.
- ❏ Put copies of listing information in floor book.
- ❏ Distribute copies of listing information to all sales associates.
- ❏ Put sign and lockbox on property.

Second Day:
- ❏ Mail out notice of listing cards to at least 20 neighbors.
- ❏ Call or e-mail seller to tell of above steps.

End of First Week:
- ❏ Send letter to seller signed by broker.

Day after Caravan:
- ❏ Collect caravan comment sheets.
- ❏ Visit with seller to evaluate results of caravan and comments.

Second Week:
- ❏ Clip ads of property. Send to seller in postcard format.
- ❏ Check MLS information on computer, verify information, then e-mail to seller.
- ❏ Call seller to tell of progress. Ask seller to call when house is shown.

Third Week:
- ❏ Clip ads of property. Send to seller in postcard format.
- ❏ Run MLS computer check for new listings and listings under contract, then e-mail information to seller.
- ❏ Call or e-mail seller to find out who has seen home.
- ❏ Check with sales associates who have shown home; give feedback to seller.

Fourth Week:
- ❏ Clip ads of property. Send to seller in postcard format.
- ❏ Run MLS computer check for new listings and listings under contract, then e-mail information to seller.
- ❏ Call or e-mail seller to find out about who has seen home.
- ❏ Check with sales associates who have shown home; give feedback to seller.

Fifth Week:
- ❏ Clip ads of property. Send to seller in postcard format.
- ❏ Run MLS computer check for new listings and listings under contract, then e-mail information to seller.
- ❏ Visit seller in the home, and go over CMA. Get price reduction if appropriate.
- ❏ Walk through property again. Point out areas needing attention.

F I G U R E 7.4 ■   **Listing Servicing Schedule (continued)**
Sixth Week:

- ❏ Clip ads of property. Send to seller in postcard format.
- ❏ Run MLS computer check for new listings and listings under contract, then e-mail information to seller.
- ❏ Call or e-mail seller to find out who has seen home.
- ❏ Check with sales associates who have shown home; give feedback to seller.
- ❏ Schedule open house for the property, if appropriate.
- ❏ Send notice of open house to at least 20 neighbors.

Seventh Week:

- ❏ Run open house, and leave a note for seller on results. Call later.
- ❏ Clip ads of property. Send to seller in postcard format.
- ❏ Run MLS computer check for new listings and listings under contract, then e-mail information to seller.
- ❏ Call or e-mail seller to find out who has seen home.
- ❏ Check with sales associates who have shown home; give feedback to seller.
- ❏ Send out notice of listing to additional 20 homes in neighborhood.

Eighth Week:

- ❏ Clip ads of property. Send to seller in postcard format.
- ❏ Run MLS computer check for new listings and listings under contract, then e-mail information to seller.
- ❏ Call or e-mail seller to find out who has seen home.
- ❏ Check with sales associates who have shown home; give feedback to seller.

Ninth Week:

- ❏ Clip ads of property. Send to seller in postcard format.
- ❏ Run MLS computer check for new listings and listings under contract; then e-mail information to seller.
- ❏ Call or e-mail seller to find out who has seen home.
- ❏ Check with sales associates who have shown home; give feedback to seller.
- ❏ Do another CMA. Visit with seller, and get price reduction and extension.
- ❏ Schedule luncheon for sales agents.

Tenth Week:

- ❏ Clip ads of property. Send to seller in postcard format.
- ❏ Run MLS computer check for new listings and listings under contract, then e-mail information to seller.
- ❏ Call or e-mail seller to find out who has seen home.
- ❏ Check with sales associates who have shown home; give feedback to seller.

Continue this pattern until listing has been sold.

FIGURE 7.5 ■ **Listing Quality Report**

	123 Main St.		412 First St.		821 Jones St.	
	Yes	No	Yes	No	Yes	No
Listed at recommended CMA price?		✓		✓		✓
House in good condition?	✓			✓		✓
Seller motivated?	✓		✓			✓
Yard sign?	✓		✓		✓	
Easy showing access? (Lockbox, etc.)	✓		✓		✓	
Good curb appeal?		✓	✓			✓
Recommend price reduction	$10,000		$15,000		$17,500	

A. Address	B. Time Left	C. List Price	D. Chance of Sale During Term	E. Quality Volume [CxD]	F. Recommended Price Change
123 Main St.	3 months	$205,000	25%	$51,250	$10,000
412 Monroe St.	1 month	$178,200	10%	$17,820	$15,000
821 Jones St.	2 months	$312,500	40%	$125,000	$17,500
1250 Sipa Rd.	4 months	$285,000	60%	$171,000	$10,000
116 Third St.	5 months	$180,000	30%	$54,000	$10,000
TOTAL	**Avg 3 mo.**	**$1,160,700**	**1.65 listings**	**$419,070**	**$62,500**

KEY TERMS

exclusive-agency listing	latent defects addenda	servicing the listing
exclusive-right-of-sale listing	open listing	warranty of owner
	profile sheet	

SUMMARY

Three major types of listing agreements are open listings, exclusive-agency listings, and exclusive-right-of-sale listings. An owner's warranty in a listing indemnifies the broker from false statements the owner makes to the broker. A latent defects addendum to a contract holds the owner accountable for failing to disclose existing defects to the property that are known or should have been known.

Licensees should review carefully and understand thoroughly the listing contracts they use. A licensee should be able to explain clearly to a seller the important provisions of a listing agreement.

A licensee must market property with skill, care, and diligence. A major part of the licensee's professional duties, in addition to listing and selling, is servicing listings and keeping in touch with sellers on a regular basis.

P R A C T I C E   E X A M

1. If an owner reserves the right to sell the property himself, but allows many brokers to work simultaneously, he has given the brokers
   a. exclusive agency listings.
   b. no listings.
   c. exclusive-right-to-sell listings.
   d. open listings.

2. An open listing is created by
   a. written document only.
   b. a sign that says "brokers protected."
   c. negotiation.
   d. a broker putting a sign on property.

3. A broker just listed a house for six months. The listing will automatically renew for an additional three months unless canceled in writing by either party. This type of agreement
   a. is advantageous to the seller and is endorsed by the National Association of REALTORS®.
   b. is a violation of the license law.
   c. is permissible provided full disclosure is made to the seller of its self-renewing provision.
   d. may be used only by single agents and is not available to transaction brokers.

4. What clause in a listing contract contains a promise by the owner certifying that all of the information related to the property is true and accurate?
   a. Property owner's
   b. Property condition
   c. Warranty of owner
   d. Owner's certification

5. What addendum to a listing contract states that the owner has a duty to disclose any facts materially affecting the property's value?
   a. Caveat emptor
   b. Latent defects
   c. Special clauses
   d. Hold harmless

6. What type of listing is used when an owner selects one brokerage firm to sell his property but reserves the right to sell the property personally and not pay a commission?
   a. Exclusive-right-of-sale
   b. Exclusive-agency
   c. Open
   d. Option contract

7. A seller refuses to allow the listing broker to split commissions with buyers' brokers, transaction brokers, or nonrepresentation brokers. Based on this information, which of the following statements is correct?
   a. The seller's viewpoints are perfectly acceptable and understandable; the broker may take the listing and enter it in the MLS.
   b. The broker may not take the listing under these circumstances.
   c. The broker may take the listing but may not enter it in the MLS.
   d. The listing may be placed into MLS only if it is an exclusive-right-of-sale listing.

8. Seller Diane tells Sales Associate Todd that she intends to take the ceiling fan when she moves, so he should be sure the listing information shows that it is not part of the sale. In this case, what should Todd do?
   a. Tell Diane that the ceiling fan is a fixture and must stay with the property.
   b. Tell Diane, "Let's wait and see if it's mentioned in the purchase contract; if it is not specifically itemized, you can take it."
   c. Strongly urge Diane to leave the fan.
   d. Tell Diane to remove the fan before the property is shown.

9. The legal description entered into the listing agreement and into MLS
   a. should be taken from the owners' deed or the public records.
   b. is usually omitted in listing and sales contracts.
   c. should be either the lot and block number or the seller's mailing address.
   d. is not a significant piece of information for listing or sales contracts.

10. If sellers, when listing the property, offer to leave a washer/dryer combination, the sales associate should
    a. warn them of the sales tax liability.
    b. tell them not to leave it.
    c. suggest it not be included until an offer is received.
    d. disregard the offer without discussing it with the sellers.

11. The section of the FAR listing agreement titled "Cooperation and Compensation with Other Brokers" indicates that the
    a. broker need not cooperate with other brokers.
    b. broker's policy is to cooperate with other brokers except when it would not be in the seller's best interests.
    c. broker pays the cooperating broker at least 50 percent of the total listing commission.
    d. broker may not cooperate with any other broker without prior written approval.

12. The FAR listing agreement has a dispute resolution clause that
    a. requires the parties to seek redress in a court of law.
    b. allows only the broker and the seller to settle disputes by binding arbitration.
    c. allows the broker, the sales associate, and the seller to settle disputes by binding arbitration.
    d. requires the parties to seek resolution at a hearing before the Florida Real Estate Commission.

13. A broker lists a large townhome in Pebble Creek. The broker has to give the seller a signed copy of the agreement
    a. before leaving the seller's presence.
    b. within 48 hours.
    c. in 7 days.
    d. within 24 hours.

14. Broker Sandy is talking with Robert about listing his home. If Robert says that he is ready to list but has two people he wants to exclude from the listing for three weeks, Sandy should
    a. wait three weeks, then come and get the listing.
    b. have Robert sign an open listing.
    c. have Robert sign an exclusive-right-of-sale listing.
    d. have Robert sign an exclusive-right-of-sale listing with an addendum that excludes the two prospective buyers.

15. Two problems faced by a licensee who has taken an exclusive-agency listing result from
    a. a dishonest seller and a dishonest broker.
    b. other brokers and other sales associates.
    c. an owner's sign on the property and the owner advertising a different price.
    d. a buyer going to another broker and the other broker failing to disclose his bro-kerage relationship.

16. The maximum period between a listing sales associate's calls to the seller should be how many days?
    a. 1
    b. 7
    c. 10
    d. 14

17. An open listing
    a. may be terminated at will.
    b. must be written to be enforceable.
    c. may be given to only one broker at a time.
    d. requires the owner to notify the broker if the property is sold.

18. On June 18, Broker Susan listed the Smiths' house for six months. On August 16, the Smiths terminated the listing, paying Susan a cancellation fee of $250. In Sep-tember, the Smiths listed their house with Cobble Realty. They accepted a contract in October, which closed on November 28. Based on the conditional termination clause of the FAR listing agreement, the Smiths
    a. are liable to Broker Susan for the full commission.
    b. have acted in violation of state law.
    c. have terminated the original listing and need pay only Cobble Realty.
    d. may owe Broker Susan up to 1 percent of the sales price of the home.

19. The parties to a listing agreement are the
    a. seller and buyer.
    b. seller and sales associate.
    c. sales associate and broker.
    d. seller and broker.

20. Susan lists property with Jack Smith, a multimillion-dollar producer. Jack's agreement calls for him to enter the listing into the MLS within three working days. On the second day, Jack shows the property to Sally Shuler, who loves it. She is leaving town the next day, she tells him, but will be back in one week to purchase it if it is still on the market. Jack wants to double his commission by selling his own listing, so he withholds the information from the MLS for ten days. Based on this information, Jack
    a. is following a legal, time-honored tradition in real estate by working to sell his own listing.
    b. may be liable to the seller for violating duties required by the listing agreement.
    c. will not be disciplined by FREC if he does in fact sell the property.
    d. is likely to be more successful in real estate.

APPLY WHAT YOU'VE LEARNED

The author suggests the following actions to reinforce the material in *Section II—Obtaining Listings That Sell:*

❏ Set up your Power Prospecting database. Start with your close friends and family, then list all the friends and past customers you can think of. After that, try to think of anyone, even vaguely familiar, that you have met and get the names down. You can get the addresses and contact information later.

❏ If you own a home, estimate its current value, then prepare a CMA. If you do not own your home, do this exercise for a friend. Does the CMA support the value you guessed?

❏ Based on the CMA you did on your own house, or your friend's house, prepare a Seller's Net Proceeds Statement.

❏ Complete a listing agreement for your home, along with other forms required by your broker. Ask your broker to review them.

❏ Write three practice ads to market your home.

❏ Pick a large neighborhood in your city with lots of sales activity. Find as many sales as possible for the previous 12 months. Using the matched pair technique, identify the dollar contribution from

  ❏ a swimming pool,

  ❏ an extra bedroom,

  ❏ an enclosed garage, and

  ❏ a corner lot.

❏ Using the same analysis, calculate the percentage difference between listing price and selling price.

❏ Using MLS data, divide the number of houses on the market by the number of house sales last week to find how many weeks' supply of homes are on the market. Do this at least once a month. It's an excellent indicator of market activity.

❏ Write a script for the explanation of a CMA to a prospective seller. Record your presentation on audiotape to hear how it sounds. Edit as necessary until it sounds just right.

❏ Record your explanation of the listing agreement used in your office. Edit your remarks until you are satisfied.

SELLING REAL PROPERTY

A sales associate must understand the buyer's needs and financial abilities. Licensees should understand how to find buyers and live up to the buyers' expectations. Buyers expect licensees to have broad knowledge about properties on the market and market values. They also want to know how much they can afford to pay for a house, based on their income.

The sales associate must be able to estimate the buyer's costs so that the buyer who contracts for a property is aware of the cash requirements expected at closing.

Knowledge of contracts is extremely important to sales associates. Not only do licensees need to know how to prepare purchase agreements, they must be able to explain the basic terms of the agreements so that buyers and sellers are aware of their rights and responsibilities.

Once a licensee shows the right property, the licensee must be ready to write the offer. Chapter 8 has a case study on writing and presenting the offer that will help the new licensee understand the process of presenting offers and negotiating counteroffers.

WORKING WITH BUYERS

LEARNING OBJECTIVES

Upon completion of this chapter, you should be able to:

1. list four methods that will enhance your product knowledge;

2. list at least five sources of buyers;

3. give at least three methods to show a buyer why an appointment with you will benefit him or her;

4. list two important reasons for qualifying a buyer;

5. explain how prioritizing buyers benefits both the buyers and the sales associate;

6. qualify a buyer using the Fannie Mae/Freddie Mac housing expense ratio and the total obligations ratio;

7. calculate the total monthly payment (PITI) on a mortgage loan;

8. qualify a buyer using the do-it-yourself prequalification form;

9. list two benefits in having a buyer prequalify at a mortgage lender's office;

10. list the steps between setting up an initial appointment with a buyer and writing a contract for purchase; and

11. explain why you would show a limited number of homes to a potential buyer in one day.

OVERVIEW

Working with buyers is an important function of the professional real estate sales associate. Buyers are interested in working with knowledgeable, caring sales associates, and they generally are reluctant to make appointments without evaluating the sales associate's skills. A sales associate must be adept at handling telephone inquiries, must know the inventory, and must stay current with available financing plans. Above all, the sales associate must understand and observe the laws with respect to required disclosures and fair housing. ▧

PRODUCT KNOWLEDGE

A buyer usually benefits from working with a licensee, regardless of the brokerage relationship, because of the licensee's product knowledge. It is hard work to acquire the extensive product knowledge that buyers expect. To become proficient, sales associates should accomplish the following goals:

- Spend a majority of the first few weeks in real estate looking at property.

- See at least 30 new properties each week.

- Keep a record of listings they have viewed by using a contact program like Top Producer or Act! or even by using index cards grouped by price range and outstanding features. Sales associates may use the cards like flash cards to remember five good listings in each price range or five with pools or five fixer-uppers. With practice, sales associates can remember more listings than five.

- Constantly practice matching neighborhoods with price ranges or house sizes.

- Prepare a "Five-Star Home List" showing the best-buys-on-the-market sheet for each price range (for instance, $175,000 to $200,000). See a sample "Five-Star Homes" listing in Figure 8.1.

If a buyer calls to ask for an address of one of the sales associate's listings, the sales associate should provide the information to the caller and, if needed, use "my five favorite homes on the market in your price range" to get an appointment with the buyer.

DISCUSSION EXERCISE 8.1

If you actively sell residential properties, try to name from memory the location of at least three single-story, four-bedroom listings. Try to name the location for four listed homes with swimming pools.

FIGURE 8.1 ■ Five-Star Homes

★ ★ ★ ★ ★
FIVE-STAR Homes
(BEST BUYS ON THE MARKET)
Price Range: $175,000–$200,000

Price	Address	MLS #	Comments
$176,900	116 Belmont Rd.	15432	Great deck, vaulted ceiling
$179,500	1272 Scenic Rd.	16523	Brick, large oak in front
$185,000	784 Wilson Ave.	16132	Wood frame colonial
$185,000	1216 Kara Dr.	15478	Huge back yard with hot tub
$188,500	8754 Skate Dr.	15843	Heavily wooded, secluded
$199,900	124 E. Call St.	16021	Downtown, arched doorways

FINDING BUYERS

Some good sources of buyers include:

- calls resulting from advertising,
- calls resulting from signs,
- past customers and clients,
- friends and family,
- open house visitors,
- canvassing prospects,
- buyer seminar attendees, and
- buyer farm.

DISCUSSION EXERCISE 8.2

Carol is on floor duty when she receives a call from a buyer who says, "I'm looking for a four-bedroom home with a pool, northeast, but it's got to have a large workshop. Do you have anything like that listed in the $150,000 range?"

"No, I don't have any listings like that," she says, "but I can show you another company's listing that may be just right for you. I saw it last week. It's very spacious, in an elegant setting with a great view. I believe it's priced at $148,500. I'm available to show it to you this afternoon at 4:30, or I have another time available at 6:15. Which is better for you?"

Is Carol likely to get an appointment to show the property? Why or why not? Is there something she said that you would say differently?

Calls Resulting from Advertising

If a licensee wants his or her personal name to appear in a brokerage firm's ad, the licensee's last name must be included at least once in the ad. The brokerage firm's name must be included to avoid charges of "blind" advertising. For example, Joseph J. Perkins, a sales associate, could place an advertisement with "call Joe for more information," provided the ad includes the brokerage firm's name and Joe's last name somewhere in the ad. [61J2-10.025(2)]

Advertisement calls are an extremely important source of buyers. A buyer calls for more information to determine whether a house is right for him. A buyer seldom calls to make an appointment with a sales associate, but the sales associate's objective is *always to get the appointment with the buyer.* The sales associate must remember two important points when answering buyer advertisement calls:

1. It is difficult for the sales associate to talk intelligently about properties that she has not seen. For this reason, the sales associate *should see every company listing before answering calls on ads or signs.*

2. The sales associate should review all company advertising in newspapers and homes magazines. The licensee should clip each ad and paste it on a separate piece of notebook paper or index card. A **fallback list,** sometimes called a *switch*

F I G U R E 8.2 ■ **Fallback List**

"FALLBACK LIST" FOR 3415 MONITOR LANE

Address	MLS #	Price	Comments
1546 Merrimac Dr.	16546	$189,500	Large workshop, lots of trees, 2 streets over
1247 Thresher Ln.	16478	$194,500	20' × 30' deck, screened pool area, spotless
1687 Woodgate Way	16521	$195,000	2 stories, 4 bedrooms, close to town
1856 Hoffman Dr.	16493	$185,000	Huge oak in front, lots of azaleas, big kitchen
1260 Dunston Ct.	16470	$192,500	Quiet street off Meridian, very clean, bright

list or *pivot list*, should be prepared for each ad. A fallback list comprises three to five properties that are similar to the property being advertised. The list can consist of the sales associate's personal listings, the brokerage firm's listings, or other brokers' listings. If a caller isn't satisfied after learning more about the property in question, the sales associate can refer to the fallback list of other properties that might be suitable. The fallback list becomes invaluable in getting the appointment and helping the buyer find the right property. A sample fallback list is shown in Figure 8.2.

> ### DISCUSSION EXERCISE 8.3
>
> Do a role-playing exercise, with a class member calling on an ad for 3415 Monitor Lane. Try to get an appointment using one of the methods discussed.

Often, a caller wants a property's address but is unwilling to give her name or phone number. "I just want to ride by to see whether I like it," the caller says. The sales associate will not get the appointment unless the caller feels she will benefit by meeting with the sales associate. The best-buys sheet and the fallback list may come in handy to get the appointment. Most buyers would feel that the sales associate had market information that would make it worthwhile to make an appointment.

In Practice

If a buyer resists giving a name and phone number, try this approach:

"I understand your feelings. You know, many properties that come on the market are sold before they are even advertised because they have a sales associate who watches the market and calls immediately. Would you like to have the first opportunity to see these prime properties right away?" This question will often get their contact information.

When a caller is adamant about wanting an address but will not make an appointment, some sales associates do not give the address because they will lose the call. It is not worthwhile, however, to generate ill will with the consumer. Perhaps a better approach is to be helpful in every way. Ask how many property ads the caller has circled in the newspaper or homes magazine. Tell the caller you will give him an address and information on each listing advertisement, even though other real estate companies hold the listings. You should have a copy of the classified ad section and a homes magazine handy. Follow along with the caller, mark each ad, and set a time that you can get together. Prepare a list with addresses, prices, square footage, and other property features. What is the attraction to the buyer? One call gets it all because the consumer sees a benefit to meeting with the licensee. The attraction to the sales associate? The buyer places no calls to the competition, and an appointment has been set.

Once an appointment is made, it is time to evaluate the buyer's needs and financial capabilities. This is called **qualifying** the buyer.

Often the first visit with the buyer is simply a get-acquainted visit, meant for making required disclosures and for qualifying. After this is completed, a second appointment is set to show properties.

Calls Resulting from Signs

Another source of buyers is calls on property signs. Callers on real estate ads generally want the properties' addresses. Callers on signs generally want the prices because they already know the locations. A sales associate should handle a sign call like an ad call, with the exception of the information provided.

Past Customers and Clients

One of the best sources of buyers is past customers and clients because they already have enjoyed the benefits of the sales associate's services. Agency representation may be a problem, however. If the sales associate listed a client's property in a prior relationship, the person may feel that the same agency relationship exists in the purchase of a new home. The sales associate must give the buyer the appropriate brokerage relationship disclosures.

Friends and Family

Among the sales associate's first sources of buyers when he starts in real estate are friends and family. The agent should write to everyone he knows and stay in contact for news of potential customers. When working with a friend or family member, the sales associate must evaluate the loyalty issue to decide whether being a single agent for the buyer is more appropriate than being a transaction broker.

Open House Visitors

Holding open houses is a good way to find prospective buyers. The primary objective of an open house is *not* to make the seller happy (a sale makes the seller happy) but to get buyer prospects. If the buyer purchases the home on display, so much the better. The sales associate should prepare a brochure for the home with the sales associate's name and picture prominently placed.

Usually, open house visitors are just looking. The sales associate should tell them that they are welcome to walk through the home but that she wants to point out a few features that are not readily apparent. If this home is not right for the visitors, the licensee should have ready her list of the five best homes in the price range as well as a fallback list, then set an appointment to talk.

Canvassing Prospects

Canvassing is an excellent method of finding buyers and is discussed in detail in Chapter 4. The same canvassing call can be a source of either buyers or sellers. The sales associate might ask, "Do you know someone who may be getting ready to buy or sell real estate?" Often the answer is yes, and the sales associate can set an appointment. Remember, you may not call anyone on the national or state Do Not Call Registry.

Buyer Seminar Attendees

Many sales associates and brokers consider buyer seminars to be outstanding prospecting tools and offer them to the public to attract large numbers of buyers at one time. Some real estate companies have impressive materials and workbooks for attendees of the classes, which run over two or three evenings. Often attendees pay a nominal fee to cover the cost of books. Most seminars entitle an attendee to schedule a one-hour consultation with the seminar leader about a specific real estate problem or need. This can benefit both the consumer and the licensee if a business relationship results. Remember that the appropriate brokerage relationship disclosures must be made.

Buyer Farm

Buyer farms are organized in much the same way as listing farms, requiring good selection techniques, strong organizational skills, and periodic, effective communications. The farmer could contact renters or buyers who might want to trade up.

Renters. One source of buyers is contacting occupants in rental properties, but the success of farming tenants will depend on local market conditions. In the late 1990s, when interest rates were low, it was easy to show renters how they could buy a home and actually have lower payments. The recent increases in home prices, higher insurance costs, and high property tax rates have reduced housing affordability to levels not seen since the early 1980s. In some areas of the state rent prices are now substantially below the monthly mortgage payments of similar properties, so convincing tenants to become owners is more difficult. Additionally, the subprime loan fallout has greatly reduced the chances for marginal buyers to get loans. That said, many tenants continue to buy homes, and a consistent approach to contacting tenants may result in many sales.

Because most apartment properties will not allow door-to-door solicitation, a licensee can phone renters who are not on the do-not-call registry or send direct mail. The materials mailed to the tenants could be as simple as a postcard showing listings available in an appropriate price range or as robust as a company folder with brochures, information about financing available, and photos of current listings.

Buyers who might want to trade up. Perhaps a better source is an owner of a house who wants to trade up to a larger home. This buyer will likely have enough equity in the current home to make a down payment on a new home, and, because his or her home has appreciated recently, won't feel the price "sticker shock" as keenly. This person can be found in "first-time buyer" neighborhoods that have a large turnover of homes. Farming an area like this can result in many listings as well as buyers.

QUALIFYING THE BUYER

It is a waste of time to show properties the buyer does not like or cannot afford. So, before showing properties, the sales associate must get the answers to two important questions: (1) What are the buyers' housing objectives? (2) What can the buyer afford to pay?

What Are the Buyers' Housing Objectives?

Some of the information the sales associate should get from the buyers includes the following:

- What features do they want in the home?
- How quickly do they need to move?
- Must the buyers sell their current home?
- If they're leasing now, when does the lease expire?
- Have the buyers already spoken to a lender and been preapproved?
- Is there a specific area they want?

Desired features. The sales associate should ask the buyers what features the home *must have* and what features would be *nice to have*. The *must have* could be features like a particular area of town, four bedrooms, and a two-car garage. The *nice to have* might be features like high ceilings, heat pump, or a wood deck. See 20 Questions for Prospective Buyers in Figure 8.3

Urgency level. The sales associate also needs to know the buyer's urgency level. Each buyer should be classified based on urgency and motivation to purchase. (See Figure 8.4.) A person needing to move within the next 30 days, for example, is a Priority 1 buyer, needing immediate attention. A person who doesn't have an immediate need, but who should not be ignored, is classified as Priority 2. A buyer who either will not or cannot purchase immediately is Priority 3 and should be contacted regularly for showings. If a buyer relocating to the city is in town just for the weekend to purchase a home, the sales associate knows this is a Priority 1 buyer. After financial qualifying shows the buyer to be capable of making a purchase, the sales associate might say, "It sounds like your situation needs my full attention. If you approve, I'll clear my calendar so we can find the right home for you." A buyer whose present lease expires in six months has less urgency to purchase now and is classified as Priority 3.

Current housing situation. If the buyers currently own a home that must be sold, one of the first actions should be to look at their home and make a listing presentation. After their home is listed, the best way to motivate the buyers-sellers to price their present home competitively is to show homes they might want to purchase during that listing period. When they see the right home, they will be prepared to sell their own quickly.

If the buyers are currently leasing, the licensee must determine when the lease expires. That will help in prioritizing the buyer.

F I G U R E 8.3 ■   20 Questions for Prospective Buyers

1. What part of town do you want to live in? _____
2. What price range would you consider? $_____ to $_____
3. How soon do you need to move? _____ Months
4. Have you been preapproved for a mortgage loan?   ❑ yes   ❑ no
5. Do you have a home you need to sell first?   ❑ yes   ❑ no
6. Are you leasing?   ❑ yes   ❑ no   If yes, when is your lease up? _____
7. Do you want a specific school? _____
8. Do you want ❑ an older home or ❑ a newer home (less than 3 years old)?
9. What kind of houses would you be willing to look at?
   ❑ 1 story   ❑ 2 story   ❑ townhouse or condo   ❑ mobile home
10. What style house appeals to you most?
    ❑ contemporary   ❑ traditional   ❑ Spanish   ❑ no preference
11. How much fixing up would you be willing to do?   ❑ A lot   ❑ A little   ❑ None
12. Do you have to be close to public transportation?   ❑ yes   ❑ no
13. Do you have any physical needs, such as wheelchair access?   ❑ yes   ❑ no

14. The site:	Must have	Would like to have
Large yard (¼ acre or more)	❑	❑
Small yard (less than ¼ acre)	❑	❑
Fenced yard	❑	❑
Garage	❑	❑
Carport	❑	❑
Patio/deck	❑	❑
Pool	❑	❑
Extra parking	❑	❑
Other buildings (barn, shed, etc.)	❑	❑

The Interior:

15. How many bedrooms must you have? _____ would you like to have? _____
16. How many bathrooms do you want? _____
17. How big would you like your house to be (square feet)? From _____ to _____ Sq Ft.

18. Features	Must have	Would like to have
Air conditioning	❑	❑
Wall-to-wall carpet	❑	❑
Ceramic tile	❑	❑
Hardwood floors	❑	❑
Eat-in kitchen	❑	❑
Separate dining room	❑	❑
Formal living room	❑	❑
Family room	❑	❑
Separate den or library	❑	❑
Separate laundry room	❑	❑
Fireplace	❑	❑
Workshop	❑	❑
No interior steps	❑	❑
"In-law" apartment	❑	❑

Community features

19. Neighborhood Amenities	Must have	Would like to have
Community pool	❑	❑
Golf course	❑	❑
Basketball court	❑	❑
Tennis courts	❑	❑
Gated community or doorman	❑	❑
Clubhouse/activities	❑	❑

20. Other special features _____

F I G U R E 8.4 ■ **Prioritizing Your Buyers**

Buyer's Situation	Priority Level
Needs to move within 30 days or in town for the weekend to find a house	1
Wants to buy a house within the next three to six months	2
Can't buy right now but is just starting to look; perhaps on a lease expiring next year	3

Buyer's family helping in the decision. The sales associate must also find out whether someone other than the buyers will be involved in making the final purchasing decision. If the buyers' uncle will evaluate the final choice, the sales associate should try to get the uncle to see each property along with the buyers. Why? The uncle may have a better grasp of the market and of property values and may help the buyers reach a decision sooner.

Best times to see property. The licensee must find out what times are most convenient for the buyers to look at properties. Are they available during the day? Can they come immediately to see a property if the right one comes on the market? Or does their job situation require that they see property only in the evenings after work or on weekends?

Describing the Buying Process to the Buyer

At the first meeting with the buyer, the sales associate should provide, in addition to the agency disclosure form, a clear picture of the entire process, from the time of this first meeting right up until the day the buyer moves into his new home. The buyer who understands the process is less likely to become uneasy or reluctant to purchase when he finds the right property. The buyer should be given a copy of the purchase agreement, and the sales associate should explain important provisions in the agreement. A buyer's cost disclosure should be prepared for the home the buyer desires. This also helps in the financial qualifying process.

Financial Qualification

Financial qualification is crucial to a successful sale. If the buyer contracts for a home and applies for a loan that is later denied, the seller, buyer, and sales associate have wasted time and effort. In addition, loan application fees ranging from $250 to $500, depending on the lender, could be lost. Licensees should explain both issues to their customers to help them understand the importance of financial qualifying.

Financial qualification is designed to determine how much money the buyer can borrow for the purchase of property.

Lender prequalifying versus preapproval. Having a lender preapprove the buyer is the best approach and should be used whenever possible, but certainly before the buyer actually contracts for property. Preapproval is given only after the buyer has been interviewed and the buyer's credit report has been reviewed and the income verified.

A lender's preapproval letter makes the buyer's offer much stronger in the eyes of a seller and will result in more contracts.

Most lenders adhere to the Fannie Mae/Freddie Mac standards in reviewing loan applicants. Those agencies recommend the maximum housing expense ratio (front) of 28 percent and the maximum total obligations ratio (back) of 36 percent for qualifying potential buyers for first mortgage (conforming) loans. The Federal Housing Administration's (FHA's) maximum housing expense ratio is 31 percent, and the maximum total obligations ratio is 43 percent. These figures are guidelines only. Some lenders will vary from these guidelines, so a prospective buyer who does not meet the guidelines may still be able to talk with a lender that will make the loan.

The common reason buyers don't qualify under the Fannie Mae/Freddie Mac standards is usually the back ratio: total obligations. If that's too high, perhaps a creative lender can still help by increasing the qualifying income or suggesting prepaying some installment debt to less than 10 months so that it's no longer counted. A very high credit score could also help get the loan. Other compensating factors include:

- having a good record of promotions and raises;
- having little or no installment debt if housing expense ratio is too high;
- making a down payment greater than 20 percent;
- having saved money while making rent payments higher than the mortgage payments of the new mortgage; and
- having a job with great benefits, such as a company car, free health plan, and high company contributions to a 401(k) plan.

DISCUSSION EXERCISE 8.4

The following role-playing skit, designed to highlight mistakes some sales associates make in their first meetings with prospective buyers, allows both spectators and participants to learn from the process. Three actors are needed—a sales associate and two buyers. The persons in the skit should be enthusiastic and as realistic as possible. During the presentation, if the sales associate says something that may violate the law or ethics, group members should shout "Zap!" to signify their disapproval. At the end of the skit, group members should be able to itemize the sales associate's errors and recommend responses to the buyers' questions.

SKIT

Buyers' First Meeting with a Licensee

Buyers walk in, are greeted by sales associate.

Licensee: Hello, may I help you?
Husband: Yes, we are here to see Lee Wilson.
Licensee: I'm Lee. You must be Mr. and Mrs. Camp?
Wife: Yes, we are. Very nice to meet you.
Licensee: Great. Please sit down. (*Pause while they sit.*)
Husband: Our mutual friends, the Joneses, recommended we get in touch with you.
Licensee: Yeah, the Joneses send me lots of people. By the way, if you send me anyone who buys a house, I'll give you $50.

Wife: That's what they told us. I hope you can find us a good deal, too.

Licensee: I love working with buyers, Mrs. Camp, and because I'm a transaction broker, I can work harder on your behalf.

Wife: Well, do you have any distress sales of houses in the $200,000 range that we could take advantage of?

Licensee: As a matter of fact, my company just listed one. The listing sales associate suggested that I look at it. Confidentially, the owners' business is in trouble, and they need to sell quickly. The listing sales associate says they are desperate and probably would come off the price as much as $20,000, but we should start even lower to get the best counteroffer.

Husband: Tell us about it.

Licensee: Well, it's in Bent Tree Estates, close to Lake Jackson. It's got three bedrooms, two baths, a large lot, and a two-car garage. It's in absolutely perfect condition.

Wife: The newspaper ran an article last week suggesting that buyers get a home inspection. Is that a good idea?

Licensee: It is if you want to spend $300 for nothing. I've looked over the house, and it's just perfect. No problems whatsoever.

Husband: I need to tell you that we may have a problem qualifying for a new loan. I had some credit problems last year, and we got turned down on another house we tried to buy. We really need to get an assumable loan with no qualifying.

Licensee: If you like this house, maybe we can structure a wraparound loan to beat the due-on-sale clause with the seller carrying some of the financing. Can you work with $20,000 down?

Husband: I think we can come up with that much, if we can get the price right. Can we put some kind of contingency in the contract in case I can't get the money?

Licensee: Hey! I can write up a contract with contingencies that will let you out at any time with no risk. Don't worry about that. But let's go see it.

Husband: Should we have an attorney?

Licensee: You know what's wrong with five attorneys up to their necks in sand?

Husband: (*Smiles*) No, what?

Licensee: Not enough sand. (*He laughs.*) Seriously, folks, you don't need an attorney. I can help you with anything an attorney can.

Wife: Can we ask you some more questions first?

Licensee: Sure. Go ahead.

Wife: Is it a good neighborhood?

Licensee: Oh, yeah, there are hardly any minorities living there!

Wife: Well, I didn't mean that. I meant is it pleasant and well maintained?

Licensee: Uh-oh, sorry. Yes, it's really nice.

Husband: Well, let's go looking. I hope it works out.

Licensee: I'll do everything I can for you. (*The Camps leave; to an associate in the office*) Hey, Jim! I'll be back in a while. I've got some flakes with no money again, but I'm going to show a house!

Is it possible to learn from mistakes? The mistakes made in this skit may seem ridiculous, but these statements are actually made—although probably not all in a single transaction. Sales associates must be alert in their presentations and when answering questions to avoid these mistakes.

After qualifying the buyer, the sales associate should prepare the customer to buy.

PREPARING THE CUSTOMER TO BUY

The successful sales associate will prepare the customer for signing the contract long before the right property is found. After qualifying the buyer's needs, the sales associate should give the buyer a copy of the contract for purchase and sale and explain the more important paragraphs to the buyer.

This explanation of the contract serves two important functions:

1. If the buyer receives important information from the sales associate at their first meeting, this works to cement the buyer's loyalty to the associate.
2. Because the buyer is given a copy of the contract along with an explanation, the contract becomes the buyer's property. When the buyer becomes interested in a particular property, he or she is not startled when the sales associate pulls out a contract form.

> **In Practice**
>
> Keep a contract on a clipboard along with the MLS information on the property. It's always in sight so the buyer can see it. If the buyer asks questions like, "Can the seller leave the draperies?" you would ask, "Shall I put that in the agreement?" while writing on the contract.

BUYER BROKERAGE AGREEMENT

While licensees nearly always require a written agreement from sellers, they often work with buyers on an open-listing basis. A licensee may give the customer valuable information on the market and other ideas on purchasing a home but may end up working for nothing. Many successful licensees are requesting that buyers also enter into a written **buyer brokerage agreement** for representation by the licensee, either as a single agent or as a transaction broker.

Some prospective buyers will be reluctant to sign such an agreement because they may be required to pay a commission. They may not be aware that the agreement calls for the broker to offset the commission from monies received from a seller if the property is listed with a cooperating broker. A buyer who understands the benefits will be more likely to sign the agreement. When the buyer agrees to pay a commission, the broker can show the buyer unlisted property (FSBOs, properties being foreclosed, real estate owned by banks, etc.). Buyers would not see such properties without a commission agreement.

The real estate licensee should understand the Exclusive Buyer Brokerage Agreement (Figure 8.5) and be able to explain its provisions clearly and concisely. The numbered paragraphs following the form correspond with the 14 sections of the agreement.

F I G U R E 8.5 ■ Exclusive Buyer Brokerage Agreement

Exclusive Buyer Brokerage Agreement
FLORIDA ASSOCIATION OF REALTORS®

1. PARTIES: _____ ("**Buyer**") grants

    _____ ("**Broker**")

    Real Estate Broker   /   Office

    the exclusive right to work with and assist **Buyer** in locating and negotiating the acquisition of suitable real property as described below. The term "acquire" or "acquisition" includes any purchase, option, exchange, lease or other acquisition of an ownership or equity interest in real property.

2. **TERM:** This Agreement will begin on the _____ day of _____, _____ and will terminate at 11:59 p.m. on the _____ day of _____, _____ ("Termination Date"). However, if **Buyer** enters into an agreement to acquire property that is pending on the Termination Date, this Agreement will continue in effect until that transaction has closed or otherwise terminated.

3. **PROPERTY: Buyer** is interested in acquiring real property as follows or as otherwise acceptable to **Buyer** ("Property"):

    (a) Type of property: _____

    (b) Location: _____

    (c) Price range: $_____ to $_____.

    ❏ **Buyer** has been ❏ pre-qualified ❏ pre-approved by _____

    for (amount and terms, if any) _____

    (d) Preferred terms and conditions: _____

    _____

    _____

    _____

4. BROKER'S OBLIGATIONS:
    (a) **Broker Assistance. Broker** will
       * use **Broker's** professional knowledge and skills;
       * assist **Buyer** in determining **Buyer's** financial capability and financing options;
       * discuss property requirements and assist **Buyer** in locating and viewing suitable properties;
       * assist **Buyer** to contract for property, monitor deadlines and close any resulting transaction;
       * cooperate with real estate licensees working with the seller, if any, to effect a transaction. **Buyer** understands that even if **Broker** is compensated by a seller or a real estate licensee who is working with a seller, such compensation does not compromise **Broker's** duties to **Buyer**.
    (b) **Other Buyers. Buyer** understands that **Broker** may work with other prospective buyers who want to acquire the same property as **Buyer**. If **Broker** submits offers by competing buyers, **Broker** will notify **Buyer** that a competing offer has been made, but will not disclose any of the offer's material terms or conditions. **Buyer** agrees that **Broker** may make competing buyers aware of the existence of any offer **Buyer** makes, so long as **Broker** does not reveal any material terms or conditions of the offer without **Buyer's** prior written consent.
    (c) **Fair Housing. Broker** adheres to the principles expressed in the Fair Housing Act and will not participate in any act that unlawfully discriminates on the basis of race, color, religion, sex, handicap, familial status, country of national origin or any other category protected under federal, state or local law.
    (d) **Service Providers. Broker** does not warrant or guarantee products or services provided by any third party whom **Broker**, at **Buyer's** request, refers or recommends to **Buyer** in connection with property acquisition.

Buyer (____) (____) and **Broker/Sales Associate** (____) (____) acknowledge receipt of a copy of this page, which is Page 1 of 3 Pages.

F I G U R E 8.5 ■ Exclusive Buyer Brokerage Agreement (continued)

5. **BUYER'S OBLIGATIONS: Buyer** agrees to cooperate with **Broker** in accomplishing the objectives of this Agreement, including:
    (a) Conducting all negotiations and efforts to locate suitable property only through **Broker** and referring to **Broker** all inquiries of any kind from real estate licensees, property owners or any other source. If **Buyer** contacts or is contacted by a seller or a real estate licensee who is working with a seller or views a property unaccompanied by **Broker**, **Buyer** will, at first opportunity, advise the seller or real estate licensee that **Buyer** is working with and represented exclusively by **Broker**.
    (b) Providing **Broker** with accurate personal and financial information requested by **Broker** in connection with ensuring **Buyer's** ability to acquire property. **Buyer** authorizes **Broker** to run a credit check to verify **Buyer's** credit information.
    (c) Being available to meet with **Broker** at reasonable times for consultations and to view properties.
    (d) Indemnifying and holding **Broker** harmless from and against all losses, damages, costs and expenses of any kind, including attorney's fees, and from liability to any person, that **Broker** incurs because of acting on **Buyer's** behalf.
    (e) Not asking or expecting to restrict the acquisition of a property according to race, color, religion, sex, handicap, familial status, country of national origin or any other category protected under federal, state or local law.
    (f) Consulting an appropriate professional for legal, tax, environmental, engineering, foreign reporting requirements and other specialized advice.

6. **RETAINER:** Upon final execution of this Agreement, **Buyer** will pay to **Broker** a non-refundable retainer fee of $_____ for **Broker's** services ("Retainer"). This fee is not refundable and ❏ will ❏ will not be credited to **Buyer** if compensation is earned by **Broker** as specified in this Agreement.

7. **COMPENSATION: Broker's** compensation is earned when, during the term of this Agreement or any renewal or extension, **Buyer** or any person acting for or on behalf of **Buyer** contracts to acquire real property as specified in this Agreement. **Buyer** will be responsible for paying **Broker** the amount specified below plus any applicable taxes but will be credited with any amount which **Broker** receives from a seller or a real estate licensee who is working with a seller.
    (a) Purchase or exchange: $_____ or _____% (select only one) of the total purchase price or other consideration for the acquired property, to be paid at closing.
    (b) Lease: $_____ or _____% (select only one) of the gross lease value, to be paid when **Buyer** enters into the lease. If **Buyer** enters into a lease-purchase agreement, the amount of the leasing fee which **Broker** receives will be credited toward the amount due **Broker** for the purchase.
    (c) Option: Broker will be paid $_____ or _____% of the option amount (select only one), to be paid when **Buyer** enters into the option agreement. If **Buyer** enters into a lease with option to purchase, **Broker** will be compensated for both the lease and the option. If **Buyer** subsequently exercises the option, the amounts received by **Broker** for the lease and option will be credited toward the amount due **Broker** for the purchase.
    (d) Other: Broker will be compensated for all other types of acquisitions as if such acquisition were a purchase or exchange.
    (e) Buyer Default: Buyer will pay **Broker's** compensation immediately upon **Buyer's** default on any contract to acquire property.

8. **PROTECTION PERIOD: Buyer** will pay **Broker's** compensation if, within _____ days after Termination Date, **Buyer** contracts to acquire any property which was called to **Buyer's** attention by **Broker** or any other person or found by **Buyer** during the term of this Agreement. **Buyer's** obligation to pay **Broker's** fee ceases upon **Buyer** entering into a good faith exclusive buyer brokerage agreement with another broker after Termination Date.

9. **EARLY TERMINATION: Buyer** may terminate this Agreement at any time by written notice to **Broker** but will remain responsible for paying **Broker's** compensation if, from the early termination date to Termination Date plus Protection Period, if applicable, **Buyer** contracts to acquire any property which, prior to the early termination date, was found by **Buyer** or called to **Buyer's** attention by **Broker** or any other person. **Broker** may terminate this Agreement at any time by written notice to **Buyer**, in which event **Buyer** will be released from all further obligations under this Agreement.

10. **DISPUTE RESOLUTION:** Any unresolveable dispute between **Buyer** and **Broker** will be mediated. If a settlement is not reached in mediation, the matter will be submitted to binding arbitration in accordance with the rules of the American Arbitration Association or other mutually agreeable arbitrator.

11. **ASSIGNMENT; PERSONS BOUND: Broker** may assign this Agreement to another broker. This Agreement will bind and inure to **Broker's** and **Buyer's** heirs, personal representatives, successors and assigns.

12. **BROKERAGE RELATIONSHIP: Buyer** authorizes **Broker** to operate as (check which is applicable):
    ❏ single agent of **Buyer.**
    ❏ transaction broker.
    ❏ single agent of **Buyer** with consent to transition into a transaction broker.
    ❏ nonrepresentative of **Buyer.**

Buyer (_____) (_____) and **Broker/Sales Associate** (_____) (_____) acknowledge receipt of a copy of this page, which is Page 2 of 3 Pages.

F I G U R E 8.5 ■ **Exclusive Buyer Brokerage Agreement (continued)**

13. SPECIAL CLAUSES: _____

_____

_____

_____

_____

_____

14. ACKNOWLEDGMENT; MODIFICATIONS: **Buyer** has read this Agreement and understands its contents. This Agreement cannot be changed except by written agreement signed by both parties.

Date: _____   **Buyer:** _____   Tax ID No: __ __ __ - __ __ - __ __ __ __

Address: _____

Zip: _____   Telephone: _____   Facsimile: _____

Date: _____   **Buyer:** _____   Tax ID No: __ __ __ - __ __ - __ __ __ __

Address: _____

Zip: _____   Telephone: _____   Facsimile: _____

Date: _____   **Real Estate Associate:** _____

Date: _____   **Real Estate Broker:** _____

Buyer (_____) (_____) and **Broker/Sales Associate** (_____) (_____) acknowledge receipt of a copy of this page, which is Page 3 of 3 Pages.

EBBA-4x   Rev. 10/06   © 2006   Florida Association of REALTORS®   All Rights Reserved

1. **Parties:** The parties are the buyer and the broker. This paragraph also defines the terms of "acquisition" to be purchase, option, exchange, lease, or other acquisition or ownership or equity interest in real property.

2. **Term:** This paragraph sets forth the dates the agreement will be effective. Notice that if there is a contract pending on the expiration date of the agreement, the agreement is extended until the contract is closed or terminated.

3. **Property:** This section shows the

   a. *Type of property:* for example, residential, agricultural, office, etc.
   b. *Location* would normally be used to describe a city or county, or another geographic area.
   c. *Price range* would set the minimum and maximum limits the broker should use in selecting properties to show. This section also discloses that the buyer may have already been preapproved for a mortgage.
   d. *Preferred terms and conditions* sets out the buyers' preferences, such as owner financing, small down payment, lease-purchase, and so forth.

4. **Broker's Obligations:**

   a. *Broker assistance:* The broker agrees to cooperate with seller's brokers to complete a transaction. It also states that even if the broker is paid a commission split from the seller's broker, the broker's duties to the buyer are not reduced.
   b. *Other buyers:* This section discloses to the buyer that the broker may work with another buyer interested in the same property but must maintain confidentiality as to the terms of any offers.
   c. *Fair housing:* Broker states he or she will not participate in unlawful discrimination.
   d. *Service providers:* Broker shall not be responsible for acts of a third party recommended by the broker, such as a home inspector or title insurance company.

5. **Buyer's Obligations:** In this section, the buyer agrees to tell sellers or other brokers he is working under contract with a broker, to conduct all negotiations through the broker, to give the broker personal financial information and allow the broker to run a credit check, to hold the broker harmless for any damages, and to consult an appropriate professional for tax, legal, and other services.

6. **Retainer:** Many licensees ask prospective buyers for a nonrefundable retainer at the time this contract is signed. It has an option for the retainer to be credited to the total compensation.

7. **Compensation:** This obligates the buyer to pay a commission to the broker, offset by any commissions the broker may receive from a seller or a broker working with the seller. The broker is entitled to his or her commission if the customer purchases, leases, or options the property. The commission may be stated as a percentage of the sale, lease, or option, or it can be a fixed fee. The broker is also entitled to a commission if the buyer defaults on any contract.

8. **Protection Period:** If the broker has shown property to the buyer and the buyer purchases the property within the agreement period, the buyer will owe the commission unless the buyer has entered into a buyer brokerage agreement with another broker after the termination date.

9. **Early Termination:** The buyer may terminate the agreement, but if the buyer buys property the buyer learned about during the contract term, the buyer owes the commission. The broker may terminate the agreement at any time by giving written notice.

10. **Dispute Resolution:** Disputes must be mediated first. If mediation is not successful, the parties must agree to submit the dispute to binding arbitration.

11. **Assignment; Persons Bound:** The broker is allowed to assign the agreement to another broker.

12. **Brokerage Relationship:** This section has several checkboxes for the parties to indicate what type of broker relationship they will have. *Note:* The fact that a box is checked does not discharge the broker from giving the buyer the prescribed brokerage relationship notice before showing a property or entering into this agreement.

13. **Special Clauses:** This gives the parties additional space to add other provisions to the agreement.

14. **Acknowledgment; Modifications:** Indicates the buyer has read and understands the agreement. There are spaces for signatures of the buyer(s), sales associate, and broker.

SHOWING THE PROPERTY

Once the buyer has been qualified, it is time to show properties that meet the buyer's needs. The sales associate should use the following sequence in the showing and contracting process:

1. Setting the appointment
2. Previewing the properties
3. Planning the route
4. Entering and showing the properties
5. Evaluating the buyer's level of interest
6. Estimating the buyer's costs and making required disclosures
7. Writing the contract

Steps 1 through 5 are discussed in the following sections. Step 7, writing the contract, is the subject of Chapter 9. Step 6, estimating the buyer's costs and making required disclosures, is covered in Chapter 10.

Setting the Appointment

This step is important not only for the obvious reason (nothing can happen until a meeting occurs) but also from a timing standpoint. Many times a sales associate will not set an appointment until he has previewed homes and is confident that good choices are available to show. The advantage of this method is that the sales associate can describe properties that meet the buyer's needs. Two disadvantages in this approach follow:

1. The sales associate might spend a lot of time looking at properties, only to find that the buyer is working with another licensee.
2. If the sales associate can't find anything just right and puts the buyer off, the buyer might decide to work with another licensee.

> **In Practice**
>
> Set the appointment—you'll find the properties. Showing homes helps the buyer focus on likes and dislikes and showing homes that are not quite right is better than not showing homes at all.

It is important to keep in contact with the buyer regularly, based on priority status. At least weekly, the sales associate should match the buyer's profile with new listings, then call the buyer for an appointment. If the sales associate wants a Saturday showing appointment, the appointment must be made far enough in advance that the buyer can make the necessary arrangements. Saturday morning is too late to make the call. Early in the week is the best time to call for weekend showing appointments.

The best way to match a buyer with property is to use a contact program like Top Producer or Act! A separate card may be printed for each property. Match-ups between buyers and properties also are possible using some of the MLS system software. If the sales associate does not have access to a computer, it is simple to enter the buyer information on prospect cards. Spread out the cards on a tabletop and group them by price range when reviewing new listings. Listings should be matched to the buyer, and the sales associate should call the buyer about the properties. The more frequently the sales associate makes the buyer aware that the sales associate is continually searching for the right property for the buyer, the more likely it is that the buyer will call about properties he has seen.

Previewing the Properties

The sales associate should preview properties before actually showing them to the buyers. The sales associate would be surprised and embarrassed if, after telling the buyers, "I think you'll like this next one!" takes them to a property in terrible condition.

Each time the sales associate sees a new property, whether on a showing appointment, a preview day, or an office caravan of new listings, the sales associate should match that property with a buyer, taking careful notes before contacting the appropriate buyer.

> **In Practice**
>
> One of the most important factors in "closing the sale" is being prepared. That means having the objective firmly in mind that today you will write the contract. So before showing property, you should have a number of things in your file folder:
>
> 1. a copy of the lender's good-faith estimate for the top price the buyer can qualify for so you're ready to write the buyer's estimated cost disclosure, and
> 2. all the necessary forms, including the cost disclosure estimate sheet and the contract for sale and purchase.

Planning the Route

Normally, the sales associate should show no more than five properties in one tour. However, if a Priority 1 buyer is in town for the weekend for the purpose of buying a home, the sales associate must continue to show homes or risk losing the buyer.

When setting the appointment to show properties, the sales associate must consider in which order the homes will be shown. Buyers go through a continual evaluation process during the inspection tour, and the sales associate should help that process. Many sales associates like to schedule the home they consider just the right property as the last on the tour. While there are good arguments for this procedure, there are also disadvantages. The biggest problem is that if the houses get better between numbers one and five, and five is the best, the buyer wants to see house number six. Most brokers recommend showing the best house early in the tour. This sets a standard against which all other homes are measured. It usually makes the tour faster because the buyer can decide quickly that the home shown earlier was more to his or her liking.

Once the route has been decided, the sales associate should make appointments for the showings with the property owners. The time scheduled for each showing should not be fixed but should fall in a range, because it is often difficult for the sales associate to judge how long the buyer will stay in each home on the tour. The seller should be asked to prepare the home for showing by opening the drapes and turning on all the lights so that the house will be bright and pleasant. The sales associate should ask the seller to vacate the property during the showing so that the buyer can have emotional possession of the property. If the sales associate has a cell phone, she should call the seller when leaving the previous house on the tour. If the seller owns a dog, the sales associate should ask that the seller make arrangements to contain the pet. If the sales associate will be later than scheduled or must cancel, common courtesy as a professional dictates that the sales associate should call the seller to explain the circumstances. Nothing is more disappointing to a seller than to needlessly prepare the home for a showing.

The route taken on the way to each property also is important. A trip past a beautiful park nearby makes the home site more interesting to the buyer, as does a trip past the shopping areas and schools closest to the home. While the initial route might avoid unsightly areas, they should be shown on the way out. Failure to show such surroundings is misrepresentation.

In Practice

■ If the property has negative features, discuss those features on the way to the property—for example, "When I previewed the home yesterday, the housekeeping was not up to its usual standard because the kids are out of school this week. I hope that's OK." This reduces the shock the buyer might feel when entering. Often, the buyer defends the property: "Considering everything, the house is surprisingly clean!"

■ Avoid exaggerating a home's positive aspects to the buyer. This may create an expectation that the house will not meet. Let the buyer be pleasantly surprised when discovering the features.

Entering and Showing the Properties

This process depends on a property's general appearance. If the home's exterior is outstanding, the presentation should give the buyer time to appreciate this feature. Many sales associates park across the street so that a buyer's walk to a house is as pleasant as possible.

When highlighting a property's features, the sales associate must remember the most important words in any sales presentation:

- Fact
- Bridge
- Benefit
- Picture

The sales associate often points out facts that she believes to be important to the buyer and expects the buyer to be able to translate each fact into a benefit. "This house is on a cul-de-sac" might be a typical comment when driving up to the property. The sales associate believes this is important information to the buyer. The buyer might be thinking, "Yes, that's quite obvious. So what?" The full presentation should include fact, bridge, benefit, and picture.

The *fact* is that the property is on the cul-de-sac. The *bridge* might be "What that means to you, Mr. and Mrs. Jones, . . ." The *benefit* is the rest of the sentence: "is that because there is no through-traffic, automobiles travel very slowly, resulting in greater safety to your children." The *picture* is a word picture: "Imagine being out here on the street while your children roller-skate safely."

DISCUSSION EXERCISE 8.5

Picture a house that you have been in recently. Try to think of as many features of the house as you can, then express those features to represent fact, bridge, benefit, and picture statements.

Set up a group contest to see who can come up with the most fact-bridge-benefit-picture statements about a house that is familiar to all of you.

The sales associate should practice this technique whenever she can: when driving in the car alone, when **previewing properties,** or when on the office caravan of listings. Once this technique becomes a habit, buyers will find the sales associate's statements clearer and more interesting, and the sales associate will make more sales.

Many times, the listing office gives out the key to the back door, or the back door key may be the only key provided in the lockbox, or **keysafe,** at the house. Although the sales associate must go in through the door for which she has a key, the buyer always should enter through the front door.

In Practice

Don't overshow a property. Let the buyer discover some of the best features on his own. (Overshowing is walking through a property making statements such as "This is the dining room.")

Making the Buyers' Decision Easier

Normally, a sales associate will only show five to seven homes during a showing appointment. This is usually recommended so the buyer can have an opportunity to give feedback and not become confused by a huge number of homes. In some cases, however, many homes are shown to a buyer during one appointment. This might happen if the buyer is making a trip from out-of-town and needs to find the right house during this trip.

If a buyer sees 20 to 30 homes in a tour, the buyer will certainly be confused about which home had what feature. To make it easier, an experienced associate will have the buyer make a decision after seeing each home. You would say, "Which home do you like best—this house or the house on Hibiscus Lane?" If the answer were "Hibiscus Lane," you would say, "OK, forget all the other homes." At the last home on the tour, it is then easy to close with the question, "Well, which home do you want to buy, this one or the one on Hibiscus Lane?"

If you show more homes tomorrow, and the buyer liked Hibiscus Lane best, start the tour by taking the buyer back to Hibiscus Lane, with a comment like, "OK, so this is the house we're ready to buy if we don't find one better today, right?"

Evaluating the Buyer's Level of Interest

A buyer usually knows he or she is not interested shortly after entering the house. The sales associate should stop showing the property and proceed to the next. Because this is not the right house, it would be pointless to answer any of the buyer's objections. If the seller is at home, the sales associate should explain tactfully that the house does not satisfy the buyer's needs.

Handling Objections

Here are some important points to remember about buyers' objections:

- An objection can be an opportunity to make the sale. Many objections can be turned into immediate selling points. "The house needs paint" could provoke an argument from an unprofessional sales associate. The empathetic sales associate simply asks, "Would you paint it yourself, or would you hire someone to paint it for you?" With a positive response from the buyer, both parties are happy.

- Be certain you understand the objection; restate it. For example, a buyer may say, "This house costs too much money!" You may follow with a question like, "If I understand you, you feel that the house is overpriced?" The buyer may answer, "No, I'm just not certain I want to buy a house at this price level." By clarifying with a question, you avoid being argumentative.

Don't answer an objection until you have isolated it; if there are many more objections, this is not a suitable property. "If it were not for the problem about the house price, would you buy this house?" A yes answer tells you this: "Satisfy me regarding this problem, and I'll buy."

If you don't feel you can answer an objection to the buyer's satisfaction, especially if the objection is valid and you believe it is a "deal-breaker," you shouldn't. You should agree with the buyer and go to the next property.

Make a list of as many objections you can think of, then write out at least two plausible answers to the objection. Try them in your office sales meetings and practice them regularly.

Chapter 9 covers the legal document called a Contract for Sale and Purchase. It is very important for licensees to understand the wording of the agreement they will ask buyers and sellers to sign. Chapter 10 discusses writing and presenting an offer.

S U M M A R Y

When working with buyers, a sales associate must be certain to make required agency disclosures on a timely basis. A buyer benefits most when a licensee represents the buyer and no one else. Extensive product knowledge is necessary if a sales associate is to provide the best service to a consumer. The sales associate has many ways to acquire product knowledge, but all consist of looking at properties. Index cards or client contact software helps the licensee remember properties, and a best-buys-on-the-market list helps the sales associate better exhibit her product knowledge.

Sales associates draw buyers from a number of sources: calls on ads or signs, past customers or clients, friends and family, open house visitors, canvassing, and buyer seminars. When handling an ad or a sign call, a licensee's primary objective is to get an appointment. Sales associates should prepare carefully for ad calls, know the properties advertised, and have fallback lists.

A sales associate should qualify a buyer's housing objectives and have the buyers preapproved for a loan, as well as prioritize buyers based on the immediacy of their needs. When showing properties, the sales associate should describe benefits and be careful not to overshow the properties. The sales associate can help reduce buyer confusion by helping the buyer decide which house the buyer favors, or likes best, after each house is shown.

K E Y   T E R M S

buyer brokerage agreement	keysafe	previewing properties
canvassing	prequalification	qualifying
fallback list		

PRACTICE EXAM

1. Most brokers recommend showing the best house
   a. last.
   b. early in the tour.
   c. second to last.
   d. whenever—it doesn't matter.

2. Before showing properties to a buyer, a sales associate should NOT
   a. qualify the buyer's financial abilities and housing needs.
   b. preview the homes to be shown.
   c. make the required brokerage relationship disclosures.
   d. find out what church they would like to live near.

3. A Priority 1 buyer is one who
   a. has an immediate need to buy.
   b. is important but not as important as Priority 3.
   c. will not buy right away but should be contacted regularly.
   d. is not highly motivated.

4. Normally, the prospective buyer calling about a property with a For Sale sign wants information from the sales associate about the property's
   a. location.
   b. lot size.
   c. price.
   d. address.

5. According to the FAR Exclusive Buyer Brokerage Agreement, if there is a dispute between the buyer and the broker that they are unable to resolve, the parties
   a. must submit to a decision of the local Board of REALTORS® Professional Standards Committee.
   b. must submit first to binding arbitration.
   c. have the option of arbitration or litigation.
   d. must first submit to mediation, and if that is not successful, to arbitration.

6. Broker John entered into an agreement with prospective buyer Clifford, using the FAR Exclusive Buyer Brokerage Agreement. Broker John showed a property at 1816 Curtis Drive, but Clifford said he really didn't care for it. After their agreement expired, Clifford signed a similar agreement with Broker Maxwell. About one month later, Maxwell showed Clifford the house at 1816 Curtis Drive and Clifford bought it. Which is correct?
   a. Broker Maxwell committed a violation of Chapter 475 by interfering with a previous contract.
   b. According to the terms of the contract, Broker John is entitled to the commission as the procuring cause of the sale.
   c. According to the terms of the contract, Broker Maxwell is entitled to the commission as the procuring cause of the sale.
   d. Buyer Clifford is not liable to either party.

7. What is the best approach if a prospective buyer who has called on an ad says, "I'd just like to have the address of the property, and I'd rather not give you my name at this time."
   a. "If you don't give me your name, I can't give you the address."
   b. "Our company policy is to not give out addresses."
   c. "Some of the best listings are never even advertised. Would you like me to call you when a great listing comes on the market?"
   d. "I'm sorry, but the law doesn't permit me to give out that address."

8. Because of high prices, high property taxes, and high insurance rates, the best buyer farms are likely to be in areas
   a. of high-priced houses.
   b. where the occupants need subprime loans.
   c. of owner occupants who are ready to trade up to a larger house.
   d. owned by elderly people.

9. How does a buyer benefit by agreeing to pay a brokerage commission to her broker?
   a. The commission will be lower than if the seller has to pay a commission.
   b. The broker will automatically be the buyer's single agent.
   c. The broker will be able to work harder on the buyer's financing alternatives.
   d. The broker can show the buyer unlisted properties like FSBOs and foreclosures.

10. For a buyer to decide to work with a licensee, the most important factor probably is the licensee's
    a. low fee.
    b. product knowledge.
    c. dress code.
    d. automobile make and model.

11. When making an appointment with a seller to show her property, a sales associate should NOT
    a. set the time as a range rather than a specific time.
    b. tell the seller to turn on the lights.
    c. tell the seller to leave the home during the showing.
    d. fail to call if it looks like the visit will be much later than the time specified.

12. A sales associate's primary objective when answering a sign call or an ad call is to
    a. give out the information requested.
    b. make a friend.
    c. make an appointment.
    d. get a name.

13. A fallback list consists of
    a. past customers.
    b. answers to objections.
    c. places to find part-time employment.
    d. properties similar to those advertised.

14. If a property is particularly attractive from the front, the best way to show the property is by
    a. parking in the garage.
    b. parking at the street.
    c. sending a photo to the buyer.
    d. driving up and down the street first.

15. Before a buyer begins seeing properties, the sales associate should NOT
    a. give the buyer a brokerage relationship notice.
    b. qualify the buyer.
    c. ask the buyer about his feelings about having minorities living in the neighborhood.
    d. find out what area of town the buyer would prefer.

16. A sales associate asks a seller to vacate the property while it is being shown because the
    a. seller can't hear what the sales associate is saying about the property.
    b. buyer can take emotional possession of the property during the showing.
    c. children of the buyer can use the bathroom if necessary.
    d. buyer can inspect the structure for defects without interruption.

17. Generally, the only features a sales associate should discuss with a buyer on the way to viewing a property are the
    a. home's most outstanding attributes.
    b. negative features if any.
    c. beautiful Jacuzzi and huge master suite.
    d. features previously discussed.

18. One way to find lots of buyers at one time is
    a. calling friends.
    b. calling past customers.
    c. canvassing.
    d. conducting buyer seminars.

19. A sales associate's statement that "the house is built of brick" should be followed immediately by the
    a. fact.
    b. bridge.
    c. benefit.
    d. picture.

20. The safest way for a sales associate to determine whether a buyer is qualified is to use
    a. the services of a lender to do it.
    b. national mortgage market guidelines.
    c. Fannie Mae/Freddie Mac underwriting guidelines.
    d. any of the above methods.

9

SALES AND OPTION CONTRACTS

LEARNING OBJECTIVES

Upon completion of this section, you should be able to:

1. explain the exceptions to the statute of frauds that are recognized as valid real estate transactions;

2. list at least three transactions that are not suitable for using the Florida Association of REALTORS® Residential Sale and Purchase Contract;

3. describe the legal test for the sufficiency of a legal description;

4. complete a sales contract; and

5. list the requirements for completing an option contract.

OVERVIEW

Contracts are part of our everyday lives. When a person orders telephone service, buys a refrigerator, or pays for an airline ticket, a contract has been formed.

Licensees regularly work with many different kinds of contracts. The broker's employment agreement, listing contracts, buyer brokerage agreements, leases, options, and sales contracts are just a few. Understanding the information in a contract and being able to correctly explain it to sellers and buyers is an important function of a sales associate. Licensees may legally prepare listing contracts, sales contracts, and option contracts. Preparing notes, mortgages, or deeds is unauthorized practice of law.

ANALYSIS OF REAL ESTATE CONTRACTS

A **contract** is a promise or set of promises that must be performed. Once the promise is given, the law recognizes performance of that promise as a duty. If the promise is broken or breached, the law provides a legal remedy for the injured party. However, one promise, standing alone, does not constitute a contract. Some specific act by the party to whom the promise is made, or a mutual promise from that party, is required to conclude a contract. For example, if you promise to fix your neighbor's roof and the neighbor thanks you, no contract exists because you asked for nothing in return for your promise. If your neighbor promises to give you $1,000 to fix her roof and you promise to do it, mutual promises have been exchanged, and a contract has been made.

DISCUSSION EXERCISE 9.1

You are a sales associate who has listed John Wilson's home in Foxcroft. Mr. Wilson would rather not repair several property defects (such as a cracked foundation). He suggests the use of an "as is" clause in the contract so that a buyer can do any inspection desired. "Based on this clause," Wilson tells you, "we have no need to disclose."

Does the use of an "as is" clause in a sales contract excuse a broker from disclosing material facts regarding a property? Explain.

Statute of Frauds

Before the enactment of the **statute of frauds,** it was not uncommon for a person to pay "witnesses" to falsify testimony to support a nonexistent oral contract for the sale of real property. The law commonly called the *statute of frauds* requires that certain types of contracts, in order to be enforceable, be in writing and be signed by the party against whom enforcement is sought. Contracts that must be in writing and signed are of two general types: those that will not be performed fully within a short period of time and those that deal with specific subjects.

In Florida, an agreement or a promise that cannot be performed by both parties within one year after the contract date must be evidenced by a written document. Also, an agreement to sell or the actual sale of any interest in real property is subject to the statute of frauds and must be in writing and signed by all parties bound by the contract to be enforceable. Witnesses are not required.

Two common exceptions to the statute of frauds are recognized:

1. *Executed contracts.* Performance of the promise made proves the contract existed; therefore, the function of the statute of frauds has been accomplished, and a written form is not required.

2. *Partial performance.* Usually, the statute of frauds does not apply to partially performed contracts as long as two conditions have been met: (1) partial or full payment has been made and (2) the buyer has either taken physical possession of or made improvements to the subject property. For example, if a buyer has evidence of a $500 payment toward the purchase of a parcel of land, then moves onto the property and plants a crop of tomatoes, the statute's function has been accomplished. The payment and possession are regarded as evidence that a valid contract exists.

> **In Practice**
>
> When a buyer or seller wants to change anything in a contract, such as moving the closing date beyond that required in the contract, be sure to get a written addendum to the contract signed by both buyer and seller. An oral agreement isn't worth the paper it's not written on.

SALES CONTRACTS

A **sales contract,** also referred to as a *purchase and sale contract* or a *contract for sale and purchase,* is a written agreement setting forth the terms for the transfer of real property from seller to buyer, with both signing the document. The standard contract for sale and purchase developed by the Florida Association of REALTORS® (Residential Sale and Purchase Contract) is the most widely used preprinted sales contract form in the state. (See Forms To Go, Appendix B.) This section of the chapter presents specific instructions for the correct preparation of that contract, providing licensees with hands-on practice in preparing contracts to increase their professional skills. If licensees in your area use a different sales contract form, substitute that form for the FAR contract. The discussion that follows applies to your contract form as well.

**Forms
To Go**

Online Contracts for REALTORS®

Members of the Florida Association of REALTORS® have a very helpful tool called "Form Simplicity Library," containing a library of forms. Using this Web site, users can accomplish the following:

- Fill in forms such as listing and sales contracts
- Save forms as internal data or flat PDF files
- Print forms
- E-mail forms to customers
- Link common information between forms, providing the quick processing of contract-related forms
- Create a Form Transaction, managing forms as a group and for the auto-filling in of information common to the deal such as names and addresses
- Save their own special clauses to insert into contracts
- Use their contact list information on customers, cooperating licensees, title companies, and loan institutions to automatically populate their contracts
- Set up a brokerage office database account so the broker can review all contracts

Whether to Use a Printed Form

No two real estate transactions are exactly alike. Even two nearly identical houses located adjacent to one another may require different contractual handling. The earnest money deposits, mortgage sources, and prices, as well as many other items, must be considered. Even the tried-and-proven clauses in a standard form may need to be adapted to the requirements of a particular transaction. Therefore, licensees should use printed form contracts cautiously. Two contracts are widely used by licensees: the **FAR Residential Sale and Purchase Contract** and the FAR/BAR Contract for Sale and Purchase. This text will describe the features of the FAR contract. Both contracts are similar and are intended for use in routine transactions involving the sale of single-family dwellings or unimproved real property. If a licensee is involved in any one of the following types of transactions, the contracts are *not* suitable:

- Business purchase or sale
- Construction or improvements contract
- Contract for deed (installment contract, agreement for deed)
- Exchange agreement (contract for exchange of real property)
- Lease with option to buy
- Option contract (to be described later in this chapter)
- Unique or complex transactions

If vacant land, other than a single-family vacant lot, is involved in a transaction, special provisions should be included in the contract concerning the concurrency status of the property for development purposes, as well as suitability for its intended use relative to the area's comprehensive plan.

Responsibility for Preparation

The sales contract is the most important instrument for closing a real estate transaction. Because it is the final agreement after all the offers and negotiations that have taken place, a licensee must be very careful when preparing it. Any time a licensee is not certain whether an attorney is required in preparing any special clause or type of contract, the best course of action is to advise the buyer and seller to consult an experienced real estate attorney.

The sales associate and his or her employer may be held financially responsible for any mistakes in the agreement. If any errors, omissions, or ambiguities exist regarding material terms, the courts will not go outside the contents of the contract to determine intent. The licensee who prepared the contract will not be allowed to explain later intent not indicated in the contract contents. If the contract is vague and unenforceable, the result could be no transaction at all, loss of commission, and a possible civil lawsuit against the licensee.

"Time Is of the Essence" Provision

A single sentence in Paragraph 11, **"Time is of the essence** for all provisions of this Contract,"** has important legal effects. If a party fails to perform the duties or promises made within the exact time limits in the contract, it causes an automatic default. This default then creates a right of cancellation on the part of the other party (**voidable contract**).

F I G U R E 9.1 ■ Stated Performance Dates

Some important contract performance dates and deadlines are in Paragraph:

- •2(b)   Additional deposit;
- •3(b)   Financing period: time for buyer to qualify for and obtain financing;
- •3   Buyer to apply for financing;
- •4   Closing date;
- •6 and 8   Inspection period and wood-destroying organisms report;
- •7(c)   Buyer cancellation period for flood zone floor level problems;
- •10   Delivery of title evidence;
- •11   Effective date definitions;
- •16   Dispute resolution;
- •Signature   Offer, counteroffer, and effective date of contract.

In Practice

Because of the importance of meeting requirements with dates and times, licensees should:

- ■ use realistic time periods,

- ■ check that the time periods complement and are consistent with times in other blank spaces, and

- ■ set up calendar deadlines in the file to monitor performance by the parties to the sales contract once it has been signed. (See Figure 9.1.)

Gathering Contract Data

Collecting the information required to complete all of the entry blanks in the FAR contract is a sizable task. Information may become available or should be obtained as the real estate licensee helps negotiate the contract. Once the licensee gathers all of the information, she or he must verify it for accuracy and currency. Including obsolete information in a contract may be more harmful to a successful closing than having insufficient information to complete the contract. The licensee should pay particular attention to and be sure to verify the following two categories of data:

1. *The owner/seller's name and address and the property's legal description.* MLS data, property appraiser information, and even listing agreements have been in error on occasion. Place more reliance on an existing or a prior title insurance policy, a deed, or a survey for the information.

2. *Financial information.* Financial data tend to change frequently and require last minute updating. Check with local lenders to make certain that times allowed for obtaining financial commitments are realistic and that the rates and terms contemplated actually are available.

PREPARING SALES CONTRACTS

While the following guidelines are provided as an aid in understanding and preparing each element in the FAR Residential Sale and Purchase Contract, these instructions are generic in description and should apply to most other sales contracts. Each specific provision of the form is described separately to help licensees examine the contract thoroughly. Paragraph numbers in this section refer to contract paragraph numbers. The current FAR Residential Sale and Purchase Contract is reproduced in its entirety in Forms To Go, Appendix B.

**Forms
To Go**

Residential Sale and Purchase Contract

1. Sale and Purchase.

Seller: Seller's name(s) should be shown in the manner in which title is held, showing the marital status of each seller. You can get this information from the seller's title insurance policy or a copy of the recorded deed.

Residence: If a married person owns the property individually, you should obtain the signature of the spouse to avoid possible future litigation.

Joint Ownership: If the property is jointly owned, obtain the signatures of all joint owners. If a residence is located on the property, obtain the signatures of joint owners and their spouses.

Corporations, Partnerships, Estates, Trusts, and Use of Powers of Attorney: Each requires special attention and instructions. Seek broker or legal counsel, as appropriate.

Buyer: Buyer's name(s) should be shown in the same manner as the buyer wishes title to be taken at closing. Other points to consider include:

- Each buyer shown on the contract must execute the contract.
- If the buyer later desires to take title in some other manner and this is permitted by the contract, an appropriate assignment or amendment to the contract should be obtained at closing.
- Buyers often seek advice as to the manner in which they should take title to property—for example, tenancy by the entireties, tenants in common, and so on. If the buyer asks how title should be taken, advise him to see his attorney. Under no circumstances express an opinion.
- *Non–U.S. Corporations, U.S. Corporations, Partnerships, etc.:* Seek broker or legal counsel, as appropriate.
- *Addresses and Telephone Numbers:* Include complete information concerning these items to make handling the transaction easier for all involved.
- *Address:* If the street address, city, and ZIP code are available, insert them. This may render an otherwise insufficient legal description legally sufficient.

Legal Description: *Material Term:* The legal description of the property to be sold is an essential provision of the contract. A defective legal description can render the contract unenforceable.

Sufficiency Test: The classic test of the sufficiency of a legal description is whether a surveyor can locate the property by reference to the description used.

Reliable Information: Do not rely on tax roll descriptions. The tax rolls are filled with errors and abbreviated descriptions that could be regarded as legally insufficient. Also, do not rely on descriptions contained in MLS listing sheets because they may only repeat errors others have made. Instead, rely on copies of prior deeds, prior title insurance policies, or prior surveys.

Description Not Known at Time of Contract: If any question remains as to the property's exact location, size, or description, and if the question cannot be resolved before the execution of the contract, agreement must be reached as to the survey of the property and as to who will bear the expense of the survey. Furthermore, agreement must reflect that the contract will be amended to conform to the legal description. The buyer also should have the right to terminate the contract if the property location and size are not substantially as represented.

Easements, Other Interests: The legal description should include any interest in the property being conveyed—for example, private right-of-way or common elements. This information usually is found on the deed or title insurance policy.

Quantity: From the seller's point of view, references to exact acreage in the legal description should be avoided. This could give rise to a right on the part of the buyer either to cancel the contract or to reduce the purchase price should the actual acreage prove to be materially different.

Minimum Description Requirements—Platted Subdivision

- County in which property is located
- Lot and block numbers
- Name of subdivision (include phase or unit if applicable)
- Plat book and page number of recorded plat

Minimum Description Requirements—Condominium

- County in which property is located
- Condominium unit or parcel number
- Name of condominium complex
- Identification of common elements—for example, parking spaces and storage spaces if applicable
- Recording information (official record book and page number) of original declaration of condominium and any amendments
- Reference to ground lease or recreational lease and recording information if applicable

Minimum Description Requirements—Unplatted Property

- County in which property is located
- Legal description provided by survey or prior deed(s)
- Reference to section, township, and range

Improvements and Attachments: The contract includes all improvements and attached items, and further describes fixtures, built-in furnishings, built-in appliances, ceiling fans, light fixtures, attached wall-to-wall carpeting, rods, draperies, and other window coverings (unless any of these items are specifically excluded). It has a section to add other items of personal property. If personal property is to be included, you should prepare an accurate description. Because personal property may be regarded as a material term of the contract, inaccurate, incomplete, or insufficient descriptions can render the contract voidable or unenforceable. To reduce appraisal problems and potential sales tax liability, the contract has these words: "Personal property listed in this contract is included in the purchase price, has no contributory value, and is being left for Seller's convenience."

What to Include: In the normal residential transaction, a detailed inventory of all personal property (with defects disclosed if applicable) should be prepared and attached to the contract. The list should include all kitchen equipment and appliances, plus other equipment and appliances, such as outside television antennas and satellite dishes, pool equipment, lawn furniture, and other easily removable "fixtures." Quantify items where applicable. Failure to provide an accurate and complete inventory of all property included in the sale can lead to closing day problems, and the broker may have to make up any difference to close the transaction.

Florida Sales Tax on Personal Property: The Florida Department of Revenue has made several rulings on the tax liability of personal property included in the sale of real property. If itemized in the sales contract, with a separately stated value for each item, sales tax must be paid. No sales tax is due if the contract simply lists the property, such as a "refrigerator, range, microwave, and washer/dryer combination."

Price and Financing

2. Purchase Price.

Fixed Purchase Price: The format of the preprinted contract calls for a fixed purchase price to be expressed in monetary terms.

Variable Price: If the full purchase price cannot be expressed in monetary terms, the manner in which it might be determined accurately should be stated in the contract in an addendum. For example, if acreage is involved and the parties agree on a price per acre, that price per acre should be set forth in an addendum (under "Special Clauses," check "Addendum is attached") together with a provision for an accurate survey determination. Whenever an addendum is used, it should have the date of the original contract, the complete names of the parties, and a complete legal description. It also must be dated and signed by the parties.

Method of Payment: The subparagraphs set forth the manner in which the purchase price is to be paid. The sum total of the monetary amounts set forth in these subparagraphs should equal the purchase price.

DISCUSSION EXERCISE 9.2

You are writing a contract for the purchase of a tract of land that is to be subdivided. The parties mark on the actual property lines where the division is to be made but can only estimate the size of the property at about 24 acres. Both parties agree on a price of $12,500 per acre.

Write a special clause that will set forth the parties' agreement and be legally binding.

Deposit Received.

2(a): with the amount of the deposit, the date, and the escrow agent.

2(b): This line is used when the payment of the deposit is split between the initial deposit and an additional deposit. Typically, the second deposit is much larger than the initial deposit. The amount of the additional deposit and the date or the number of days within which it must be made should be inserted. The contract allows the seller to recover not only the initial deposit but also any unpaid deposit. If the buyer defaults by failing to make the additional deposit, the seller is faced with having to initiate litigation to recover the balance. While the seller has an alternate remedy of specific performance, the seller's best remedy in the event of buyer default is a forfeiture of the deposit.

2(c): Enter the amount of total financing in this line. It can be shown as a dollar amount or as a percent, but a dollar amount is usually better to determine whether the balance to close is correctly added.

2(d): This line can be used for items that are not cash or financing. For example, it could be a boat taken as part of the purchase price.

2(e): State the balance of the cash to be paid after deducting from the purchase price the cash deposit, financing, and other payments. Note that this figure does not include closing costs, prepaid items, or prorations. The contract requires either cash or a locally drawn certified or cashier's check, not a personal check, in order to speed up disbursement of funds at closing.

3. Financing.

There are two options that can be selected in this section:

    a. A cash transaction with no financing contingency
    b. A financing commitment no later than the date specified or the closing date, whichever is sooner, by

        1. a new loan (fill in the amount or percentage of value) or
        2. seller financing (use an addendum to describe).

Prompt Application. The number of days the buyer will have to make an application is inserted. Except under unusual circumstances, it should be possible for the buyer to make an application for the mortgage almost immediately. The broker or sales associate should ensure that the buyer proceeds diligently to make a loan application. Keep in mind that paragraph 11 of the contract makes time of the essence, and failure to make a timely application may be a default.

In Practice

Monitor the buyer.

You should make sure the buyer applies on time, or the seller may declare a default and require the buyer to forfeit the deposit. If additional time is needed to obtain a loan commitment and the parties agree, get a written amendment, signed by the parties, to extend the time.

New Mortgages

Financing Contingency: If the buyer cannot qualify for the loan in time after making all necessary good-faith efforts, if the buyer is turned down, or if the appraisal is too low to get the financing, the buyer may elect not to proceed, return all seller's documents, and, after all interested parties agree, get the deposit back.

Know the Mortgage Market: All active licensees should have current information on the local mortgage market, including data on available interest rates (fixed and adjustable), points, time for processing applications, and so on.

Contingency Should Be Broad: Whether the buyer or the seller is the principal, make certain that the financing contingency clause describes a mortgage that is obtainable by the buyer.

Time to Get Commitment: The number of days the buyer has to obtain a loan commitment is sometimes based on how much time the seller will give the buyer to find financing. In any event, the broker or sales associate should know approximately how long local institutions take to process loan applications. Then a reasonable period of time should be inserted.

Type of Mortgage: A mortgage loan can be obtained on the basis of either a fixed rate or an adjustable rate, and the appropriate box should be checked. If the buyer has not decided, the third block should be checked, indicating that the buyer will seek a commitment for either a fixed-rate or an adjustable-rate loan. If the buyer seeks a different type of mortgage, address this in an addendum.

Principal Amount: The principal amount of the third-party mortgage that the buyer seeks is inserted. Licensees should have a working knowledge of what is available in the local financial market.

Closing

4. Closing Date; Occupancy.

Time is of the essence: The failure of either party to close on the closing date, assuming the closing date is not extended, causes a default.

Conditions: The closing date should be set for a reasonable period of time after any conditions have been satisfied and the title evidence delivered.

DISCUSSION EXERCISE 9.3

You are writing a FAR/BAR contract for the sale of a 160-acre farm and home. All parties have agreed that the buyer should have 40 days from the contract date to produce a written commitment for financing the purchase.

What would be an optimum time for the contract closing date?

Extensions: Note the phrase "unless extended by other provisions of this Contract." As previously stated, the contract sets forth many deadlines for performance. Where any of these provisions would require or allow performance to take place after the closing date, the closing date will be deemed extended.

Swept Clean: Notice that the seller's personal items are to be removed by the closing date and the property swept clean. Junk items that are not included in the sale should be removed from the property.

Insurance suspension: When a hurricane is in a specific geographic area called the "box" (see Chapter 12), insurance underwriters no longer issue policies. This provision allows the date of closing to be extended for up to five days after the suspension is lifted. The buyers should be advised to get insurance coverage well before closing.

5. Closing Procedure; Costs.

This section allows an electronic closing. If there is gap title insurance during the period from closing to recording, the closing agent will disburse at closing to the seller and the broker.

a. **Seller Costs:** This section shows the expenses to be paid by the seller, including taxes on the deed; documentary stamps on the deed; and repairs up to 1.5 percent for repairs on warranted items, wood-destroying organism treatment, and costs associated with permits.

b. **Buyer Costs:** Buyer agrees to pay taxes on notes and mortgages and recording fees on deed and financing statements. Buyer also agrees to pay for lender's title insurance, inspections, survey, and flood insurance.

c. **Title Evidence and Insurance:** This section lets the parties determine what type of title evidence is appropriate and who will pay for title insurance.

d. **Prorations:** Expenses of the property will be prorated between the parties. The buyer agrees to be responsible for property tax increases due to a change in ownership. The intent of this is to protect the seller in case the property taxes have been capped under the "Save Our Homes" amendment.

e. **Tax Withholding:** Parties agree to abide by the Foreign Investment in Real Property Tax Act if the seller is a "foreign person," as described in the law.

f. **Home Warranty:** The parties may agree on a homeowners' warranty and who will pay for it.

Property Condition

6. Inspection Periods.

This paragraph sets the date by which all inspections must be completed.

7. Real Property Disclosure.

This paragraph requires that the seller disclose all known defects that materially affect the value of the property other than those that are readily observable.

Other disclosures are required, including energy efficiency, radon gas, flood zone, and the homeowners' association disclosure.

8. Maintenance, Inspections, and Repair.

a. **Warranty, Inspections, and Repair:** This section requires the seller to keep the property in the same condition until closing except required repairs. If seller can't complete the repairs by closing, the seller must pay for the repairs at closing.

1. *Warranty:* Seller warrants that appliances; heating, cooling, mechanical, electrical, security, sprinkler, septic, and plumbing systems; seawall; and dock and pool equipment are in working order at closing.

Seller need not repair any cosmetic conditions, as defined in the contract, nor bring any item into compliance with existing building code regulations.

2. *Professional Inspection:* Buyer may have an inspection made of warranted items and has five days after the inspection period to notify seller of items that are not in the condition warranted. After five days, the buyer must accept the items "as is."

3. *Repair:* This section describes remedies if the seller disagrees with the buyer's inspection results. It also describes the process if the repair costs exceed the amount the seller had agreed to pay.

b. **Wood-Destroying Organisms:** This section describes the wood-destroying organism (WDO) inspection and the steps a seller must take if damage or active infestation is discovered.

c. **Walk-Through Inspection:** The walk-through inspection is solely to determine that the seller has made the required repairs and has met the contractual obligations. If the buyer does not make the walk-through inspection, the seller's repair and maintenance obligations are deemed fulfilled.

9. Risk of loss.

This section describes the remedies available in case the improvements are destroyed before closing.

Title

10. Title.

Either the seller or the buyer may pay the cost of either a **title insurance** policy or an up-to-date **abstract of title.** The title insurance premium must be charged for the title insurance commitment or binder whether or not a policy is issued. There is no charge for a policy issued pursuant to an issued commitment.

a. **Title Evidence:** The time limit for delivery of title evidence may depend on several factors, such as the satisfaction of contingencies. Generally speaking, however, it is desirable to provide for delivery of title evidence as quickly as possible so that if any title problems are discovered, there will be as much time as possible to deal with them. Where the time period between the date of the contract and the closing date is prolonged, it is desirable to provide in the contract a provision that the title insurance binder will be updated by endorsement to reflect any intervening title matters that might have arisen.

b. **Title Examination:** This paragraph describes the steps available to the buyer in case title is found to be defective.

c. **Survey:** The contract provides that if the survey shows an encroachment or a violation, the fact of such encroachment or violation will be regarded as a title defect, and the curing provisions of Paragraph (b) will apply. If, for example, zoning setback violations are found, these curing provisions would give the seller an opportunity to seek an appropriate variance from zoning authorities. There is also a sentence requiring compliance with the coastal construction control line.

Miscellaneous

11. Effective Date; Time.

This paragraph makes the effective date the date that the last of the parties initialed or signed the latest offer. It also has the wording that "time is of the essence." Time periods do not include Saturdays, Sundays, or holidays, and the periods end at 5 PM.

12. Notices.

Notices may be made by mail, personal delivery, or electronic media. The paragraph emphasizes that if the buyer does not make the required notices about contingencies to the seller on time, the contingency will no longer exist.

13. Complete Agreement.

Except for brokerage agreements, this is the only agreement between the parties. Handwritten portions of the agreement supersede preprinted portions if the two conflict. This sentence is meant to protect the contract if a licensee fails to delete an inconsistent provision covered in handwritten clauses or to protect any riders or addenda that are designed to show the parties' true intent. To know whether it is necessary to revoke, amend, or replace a printed provision, a licensee must know the content of the printed provisions.

14. Assignability; Persons Bound.

The contract may not be assigned without the seller's consent.

Default and Dispute Resolution

15. Default.

   a. **Seller Default:** If the seller defaults, buyer can either get the binder back and cancel the contract or seek damages, or can sue for specific performance. Seller will also owe the broker a commission.
   b. **Buyer Default:** If the buyer defaults, the seller can collect the deposits as liquidated damages, agreeing to pay the broker 50 percent of the deposits up to the full brokerage fee.

16. Dispute Resolution.

   a. **Disputes Concerning Entitlement to Deposits:** In case of disputes over the escrow deposits, buyer and seller can go through mediation for up to 30 days. If that fails, the escrow agent will submit the dispute to arbitration, a Florida court, or the Florida Real Estate Commission for a resolution.
   b. **All Other Disputes:** In disputes other than over escrow deposits, the parties have 30 days to go through mediation, after which they must seek binding arbitration of the issues.
   c. **Mediation and Arbitration; Expenses:** The parties agree to equally split the fees paid to mediators or arbitrators.

Escrow Agent and Broker

17. Escrow Agent.

This paragraph authorizes the escrow agent to accept and disburse funds and releases the escrow agent from liability unless there has been willful breach of the contract or gross negligence. If the escrow agent has to interplead the subject matter with a court, the court costs and attorney's fees may be paid from the deposit.

18. Professional Advice; Broker Liability.

This section advises the buyer to get legal and other professional advice. The buyer agrees to look solely to the seller for property condition, square footage, and other facts that affect property value. If the buyer or seller makes misstatements, the broker is entitled to collect court costs and attorney's fees to defend against damage claims.

19. Brokers.

Parties agree in this paragraph that the broker is the procuring cause of the sale, and they direct the closing agent to disburse brokerage fees according to the brokerage agreements and the cooperating broker arrangements for commission splits. In the absence of such brokerage agreements, the paragraph is set up to fill in the brokers' names and the amount of their commissions.

Addenda and Additional Terms

20. Addenda.

Licensee should check the appropriate boxes for addenda that apply to this agreement. The Comprehensive Addendum to the Residential Sale and Purchase Contract has many of the most common clauses. Various laws and regulations require that some riders be attached to the contract and that other riders expand and clarify contract terms. All of the riders listed are available as preprinted forms.

21. Additional Terms.

This is the area for special clauses specific to the needs of this particular transaction.

Practicing with the Contract for Sale and Purchase

The discussion above was meant to familiarize the student with some of the contract language. In Chapter 10 the student will have an opportunity to complete another FAR Residential Sale and Purchase Contract along with a cost disclosure statement, and prepare a counteroffer.

OPTION CONTRACTS

An **option contract** is a contract between a property owner (optionor) and another (optionee) in which the optionee, for a consideration, has the right (not the obligation) to purchase or lease the property at a specified price during a designated period. To be enforceable in Florida, an option must contain all of the essential elements of a contract.

Strictly speaking, it is important to distinguish between an *option contract* and an *option* (in actual practice, the terms are often used interchangeably). If you offer to sell your house to a friend for $100,000 and your friend says she wants to think about the offer for a day or so, your friend might have an option, but she does not have an option contract. Therefore, you could revoke your offer to sell and no breach of contract would occur because no contract exists when there is a lack of consideration (exchange of promises). Had your friend paid you $1,000 in consideration of a 30-day or 60-day period to decide about your offer and you agreed to those terms, an option contract would have been concluded. The consideration given legally may be applied as part of the purchase price in the event the option is **exercised.**

An option creates a contractual right; it does not create an estate in the optioned property. When first written and executed, an option contract is unilateral. The owner/optionor is obligated to sell if given proper notice by the buyer/optionee, but the buyer/optionee is not obligated to purchase and may allow the option to expire. Options frequently are used to give a developer or buyer time to resolve problems related to financing, zoning, title, or feasibility before committing to purchase or lease. Options also are useful instruments in the land assemblage process.

In addition to the required information in an option contract, other provisions should or may be included. For example, a statement of the method of notice required to exercise the option normally is provided. Also, some provision should be included concerning the option money (the consideration) if the option is not exercised. Unless expressly prohibited by the wording of the terms, an option normally is assignable.

Option contracts often are written with less care and attention than they deserve. Keep in mind that an option contract is converted into a sales contract when the option is exercised. However, if the option fails to include all the terms material to the transaction and leaves some terms or decisions for future agreement, the option contract normally is not enforceable. For example, if the option calls for a purchase-money mortgage as part of the method of payment and does not include the mortgage interest rate or the duration, courts normally would refuse to enforce the contract. Generally, it pays to have a competent real estate attorney construct an option agreement.

DISCUSSION EXERCISE 9.4

Oscar paid Silvio $2,000 for a 30-day option to buy Silvio's house for $160,000. Two weeks later, Silvio sold his house to Benny for $175,000.

Can Oscar enforce his option and require the property to be sold to him? Why or why not?

The optionee may wish to record the option. This establishes the optionee's rights back to the option date and gives priority over subsequent rights of third parties. Good title practice requires that a release of option be recorded later in the event a recorded option is not exercised. Otherwise, the expired option may create a cloud on the title. Many times, an option is constructed to include a defeasance clause stating that the recorded option will automatically cease to be a lien on the property upon expiration of the exercise date.

SUMMARY

A contract is a legally enforceable agreement that can be classified in a number of ways, such as bilateral, unilateral, express, implied, executory, executed, quasi, voidable, and void. Each classification has specific legal effects in a court of law. The licensee is permitted to "prepare" three types of real estate contracts: listing, sales, and option contracts. A sales contract is an agreement for the sale and purchase of real property. The various provisions and standards contained in a sales contract include information on the parties to the agreement, a legal description of the property, the purchase price and method of payment, deadline times and dates, information about financing, and riders to the contract.

KEY TERMS

abstract

contract

exercised

FAR Residential Sale and
    Purchase Contact

option contract

statute of frauds

time is of the essence

title insurance

voidable contract

P R A C T I C E   E X A M

1. Your neighbor promises to paint your house while you are on vacation. You tell the neighbor you would like him to paint it white. At that point, your neighbor and you have
   a. an implied contract.
   b. no contractual agreement.
   c. an employment contract.
   d. an option contract.

2. A good practice when writing an offer to purchase a house owned separately by the wife is to
   a. have a title search performed before allowing the seller to accept the offer.
   b. require that the seller's signature be notarized.
   c. insist that two witnesses sign the contract.
   d. have both the wife and her spouse sign the contract.

3. The FAR Residential Sale and Purchase Contract is LEAST suitable for transactions involving the sale of a
   a. single-family home.
   b. condominium dwelling unit.
   c. vacant residential site.
   d. business.

4. Tim is trying to close on his new home. The required closing date was August 26. The previous day, a hurricane in the Caribbean caused insurance underwriters to suspend writing new policies. If Tim fails to close on the 26th, what effect will this have on Tim's FAR contract?
   a. His contract will be void.
   b. His contract will be voidable by the seller.
   c. He has three days to close after the suspension is lifted.
   d. He has five days to close after the suspension is lifted.

5. When "time is of the essence," failure of any party to perform within established time limits can result in automatic
   a. cancellation of the contract.
   b. liability for damages.
   c. default by the tardy party.
   d. forfeiture of all contractual rights and deposits.

6. When a licensee verifies contract information, one of the preferred sources regarding the owner/seller and the legal description is
   a. the MLS databank.
   b. a previous title insurance policy.
   c. the listing agreement.
   d. the latest appraisal report.

7. Which statement is NOT correct regarding a violation of the statute of frauds?
   a. It may not constitute an illegal act, but it invalidates a sales contract.
   b. It carries with it prescribed time frames for enforcement.
   c. It questions the contract's validity.
   d. It normally has to do with whether a contract is in writing.

8. What is FALSE about a valid real estate sales contract?
   a. It is legally enforceable in a court of law.
   b. It has five essential elements.
   c. It requires witnessing.
   d. It deals with the transfer of an interest in real property.

9. Sales tax liability is triggered on a real estate purchase contract when personal property is
   a. described in a contract.
   b. itemized and a separate value for each item is placed in the contract.
   c. said to add value.
   d. said to be left for the convenience of the parties.

10. Rob purchased a home using the FAR Residential Sale and Purchase Contract. Before closing, he was approached by an investor who offered him a substantial profit if he would sell him his contract. Which is correct about the contract's assignability?
    a. He can freely assign the contract.
    b. He cannot assign the contract without the seller's written consent.
    c. He cannot assign the contract because it would violate Florida law.
    d. He can assign the contract as long as the property is not the seller's homestead.

11. A prospective buyer signs a sale and purchase contract form offering to pay the seller $175,000. The seller counteroffers for the full list price of $190,000. The buyer refuses the counteroffer. Later, the seller signed the original $175,000 offer. Which is correct?
    a. No enforceable contract exists because the counteroffer terminated the original offer.
    b. The contract is enforceable.
    c. The seller owes the broker a commission.
    d. The buyer owes the broker a commission.

12. A sales associate wrote a special clause into paragraph 21 of the FAR Residential Sale and Purchase Contract that contradicted one of the preprinted clauses in Paragraph 4. The special clause as written
    a. has no effect.
    b. has no effect because she failed to cross out the preprinted clause.
    c. is valid and binding.
    d. was improper and is considered unauthorized practice of law.

13. What is the classic test of the sufficiency of a legal description?
    a. It is the one used on the property tax bill.
    b. It is the one recorded in the clerk's office.
    c. It includes the address as shown by the U.S. Postal Service.
    d. A surveyor can locate the property by reference to the description.

14. Under the Florida Association of REALTORS® Residential Sale and Purchase Contract, the party responsible for a property tax increase because of a change in ownership is the
    a. buyer.
    b. seller.
    c. both parties equally.
    d. broker, if the broker did not specifically write the provision into the contract.

15. The minimum description requirement in a contract for a platted subdivision does NOT include the
    a. lot and block number.
    b. number of acres in the parcel.
    c. plat book and page number of recorded plats.
    d. county in which the property is located.

16. The date of the FAR contract is the date the
    a. buyer signs the contract and gives the earnest money deposit.
    b. seller signs the contract.
    c. transaction will close.
    d. last one of the buyer or seller signs the contract and communicates it to the other.

17. If the buyer asks to have occupancy of a house before closing, the BEST suggestion from the sales associate to the seller would be
    a. "Let's put the early occupancy in the contract so that if the sale falls through, the buyer easily can be required to vacate."
    b. "We should require that the buyer give an additional deposit of up to $1,000."
    c. "Don't let them move in if you can avoid it."
    d. "Because I know the buyers, I'm sure it will be OK."

18. An option contract is
    a. bilateral and binds the optionor.
    b. bilateral and binds the optionee.
    c. unilateral and binds the optionor.
    d. unilateral and binds the optionee.

19. Calvin, a sales associate, writes up a six-month option agreement for Ricky Field on property located on Capital Circle. Ricky pays $2,000 option money. Calvin writes, "Terms of owner financing will be negotiated when this option is exercised." When Ricky later exercises the option, the seller wants a higher interest rate and a shorter loan term than Ricky will accept. In this case, which is correct?
   a.   Ricky can sue and the court will force the seller to a lower interest rate.
   b.   If Ricky sues, the court probably will decide that the option contract is not enforceable because it is too vague.
   c.   The seller can sue Ricky and force him to close at the higher interest rate.
   d.   The parties must go to binding arbitration.

20. A man purchases an option on property. He requires that the option contract be acknowledged and recorded. The seller asks his agent about the best way to proceed. How should the agent answer?
   a.   Option contracts cannot be recorded under Florida law.
   b.   Don't ever sell an option because they never close.
   c.   The option should include a defeasance clause stating that the recorded option will automatically cease to be a lien on the property upon expiration of the exercise date.
   d.   Option contracts are illegal in Florida.

CHAPTER

10

WRITING AND PRESENTING THE OFFER

LEARNING OBJECTIVES

Upon completion of this section, you should be able to:

1. prepare and explain a buyer's cost disclosure;

2. write a contract for sale and purchase and be able to explain it in easy-to-understand language;

3. list the steps involved in presenting an offer;

4. list the three possible seller responses to an offer;

5. prepare a counteroffer using information given in the problem; and

6. describe the process involved when a seller makes a counteroffer.

OVERVIEW

Licensees hope that at the end of the showing process, the buyers will have found the right house. Sometimes the buyers will tell the licensee, "This is the house; we'd like to make an offer." More often, a buyer will say, "This is our favorite so far, but we'd like to think it over." The professional licensee can help the buyer make the decision by ensuring that the buyer has been preapproved by a lender and by describing the process of making an offer. Chapter 10 will help sales associates become familiar with that decision-making process. ▪

HELPING THE BUYER TO DECIDE TO MAKE AN OFFER

A buyer who feels information is lacking may be reluctant to make an offer. What if I don't have enough cash? What if the lender turns me down? Could I lose my deposit?

A professional sales associate can ensure that the buyer will have this information before showing properties. The steps would be to:

1. get the buyer preapproved by a lender, and get a good faith estimate (GFE),
2. show the buyer the important financial aspects of the purchase, and
3. describe the sales process to the buyer

Good-Faith Estimate

One result of the 2008 financial crisis was the redesign of the Good Faith Estimate, which must be given to the borrower at the time of loan application or within three business days after the receipt of the loan application. Effective January 1, 2010, the form was changed from a one-page to a three-page document. Among other things, the GFE now has certain tolerances for accuracy. Some of the costs quoted may not increase at settlement, and other costs may increase no more than 10 percent. A sample Good Faith Estimate is shown in Figure 10.1.

There is concern among many lenders that the new GFE is inferior to the one it replaced. Two very important items are missing from the form:

■ Only the principal and interest portion of the mortgage payment is shown, not the total monthly mortgage payment (including taxes and insurance).
■ Total settlement costs are shown, but not the total cash needed to close.

Many lenders are filling in the gaps by giving borrowers a worksheet to provide the information. Interestingly, the worksheets are very similar to the old GFEs.

F I G U R E 10.1 ■ **Good Faith Estimate**

OMB Approval No. 2502-0265

Good Faith Estimate (GFE)

Name of Originator	Security Atlantic Mortgage Company
Originator Address	3500 NE Parkway Destin, FL 32541
Originator Phone Number	850-555-9087
Originator Email	Sally.Linder@xyzlender.com

Borrower	Robert Smith and Sandy Smith, a married couple
Property Address	1854 West Chancery Court Destin, FL 32541
Date of GFE	February 18, 201_

Purpose	This GFE gives you an estimate of your settlement charges and loan terms if you are approved for this loan. For more information, see HUD's *Special Information Booklet* on settlement charges, your *Truth-in-Lending Disclosures,* and other consumer information at www.hud.gov/respa. If you decide you would like to proceed with this loan, contact us.
Shopping for your loan	Only you can shop for the best loan for you. Compare this GFE with other loan offers, so you can find the best loan. Use the shopping chart on page 3 to compare all the offers you receive.
Important dates	1. The interest rate for this GFE is available through ⟦March 18, 201_ at 4:00 pm⟧ . After this time, the interest rate, some of your loan Origination Charges, and the monthly payment shown below can change until you lock your interest rate. 2. This estimate for all other settlement charges is available through ⟦March 18, 201_⟧ 3. After you lock your interest rate, you must go to settlement within ⟦30⟧ days (your rate lock period) to receive the locked interest rate. 4. You must lock the interest rate at least ⟦15⟧ days before settlement.

Summary of your loan		
Your initial loan amount is	$ 200,000.00	
Your loan term is	30	years
Your initial interest rate is	4.5	%
Your initial monthly amount owed for principal, interest, and any mortgage insurance is	$ 1,013.37	per month
Can your interest rate rise?	☒ No ☐ Yes, it can rise to a maximum of %. The first change will be in	
Even if you make payments on time, can your loan balance rise?	☒ No ☐ Yes, it can rise to a maximum of $	
Even if you make payments on time, can your monthly amount owed for principal, interest, and any mortgage insurance rise?	☒ No ☐ Yes, the first increase can be in and the monthly amount owed can rise to $. The maximum it can ever rise to is $	
Does your loan have a prepayment penalty?	☒ No ☐ Yes, your maximum prepayment penalty is $	
Does your loan have a balloon payment?	☒ No ☐ Yes, you have a balloon payment of $ due in years.	

Escrow account information	Some lenders require an escrow account to hold funds for paying property taxes or other property-related charges in addition to your monthly amount owed of $ ⟦1,013.37⟧ . Do we require you to have an escrow account for your loan? ☐ No, you do not have an escrow account. You must pay these charges directly when due. ☒ Yes, you have an escrow account. It may or may not cover all of these charges. Ask us.

Summary of your settlement charges		
A	Your Adjusted Origination Charges (See page 2.)	$2,160.00
B	Your Charges for All Other Settlement Services (See page 2.)	$4,722.86
A + B	Total Estimated Settlement Charges	$ 6,882.86

FIGURE 10.1 ■ **Good Faith Estimate (continued)**

Understanding your estimated settlement charges

Your Adjusted Origination Charges

1. **Our origination charge**
   This charge is for getting this loan for you. | $2,000.00

2. **Your credit or charge (points) for the specific interest rate chosen**
   ☐ The credit or charge for the interest rate of [   ] % is included in
     "Our origination charge." (See item 1 above.)
   ☐ You receive a credit of $ [   ] for this interest rate of [   ] %.
     This credit **reduces** your settlement charges.
   ☒ You pay a charge of $ [2,000.00   ] for this interest rate of [4.5   ] %.
     This charge (points) **increases** your total settlement charges.
     The tradeoff table on page 3 shows that you can change your total settlement charges by choosing a different interest rate for this loan. | $2,000.00

A | Your Adjusted Origination Charges | $ **4,000.00**

Your Charges for All Other Settlement Services

Some of these charges can change at settlement. See the top of page 3 for more information.

3. **Required services that we select**
   These charges are for services we require to complete your settlement. We will choose the providers of these services.

Service	Charge	
Appraisal/Credit Report	POC/$55.00	
Amortization Schedule	$25.00	
Courier Fee	$20.00	

   $100.00

4. **Title services and lender's title insurance**
   This charge includes the services of a title or settlement agent, for example, and title insurance to protect the lender, if required. | $700.00

5. **Owner's title insurance**
   You may purchase an owner's title insurance policy to protect your interest in the property. | $850.00

6. **Required services that you can shop for**
   These charges are for other services that are required to complete your settlement. We can identify providers of these services or you can shop for them yourself. Our estimates for providing these services are below.

Service	Charge	
Survey	350	

   $350.00

7. **Government recording charges**
   These charges are for state and local fees to record your loan and title documents. | $52.50

8. **Transfer taxes**
   These charges are for state and local fees on mortgages and home sales. | $1,100.00

9. **Initial deposit for your escrow account**
   This charge is held in an escrow account to pay future recurring charges on your property and includes ☒ all property taxes, ☒ all insurance, and ☐ other [Mortgage Insuranc■] . | $2,630.00

10. **Daily interest charges**
    This charge is for the daily interest on your loan from the day of your settlement until the first day of the next month or the first day of your normal mortgage payment cycle.
    This amount is $ [24.66   ] per day for [17   ] days (if your settlement is [5/15/201_   ]). | $419.18

11. **Homeowner's insurance**
    This charge is for the insurance you must buy for the property to protect from a loss, such as fire.

Policy	Charge	
Insurses-all, Inc.	$2,050.00	

    $2,050.00

B | Your Charges for All Other Settlement Services | $ 8,251.68

A + **B** | Total Estimated Settlement Charges | $ 12,251.68

Good Faith Estimate (HUD-GFE) 2

F I G U R E 10.1 ■ Good Faith Estimate (continued)

Instructions

Understanding which charges can change at settlement

This GFE estimates your settlement charges. At your settlement, you will receive a HUD-1, a form that lists your actual costs. Compare the charges on the HUD-1 with the charges on this GFE. Charges can change if you select your own provider and do not use the companies we identify. (See below for details.)

These charges **cannot increase** at settlement:	The total of these charges **can increase up to 10%** at settlement:	These charges **can change** at settlement:
■ Our origination charge ■ Your credit or charge (points) for the specific interest rate chosen *(after you lock in your interest rate)* ■ Your adjusted origination charges *(after you lock in your interest rate)* ■ Transfer taxes	■ Required services that we select ■ Title services and lender's title insurance *(if we select them or you use companies we identify)* ■ Owner's title insurance *(if you use companies we identify)* ■ Required services that you can shop for *(if you use companies we identify)* ■ Government recording charges	■ Required services that you can shop for (if you do not use companies we identify) ■ Title services and lender's title insurance (if you do not use companies we identify) ■ Owner's title insurance (if you do not use companies we identify) ■ Initial deposit for your escrow account ■ Daily interest charges ■ Homeowner's insurance

Using the tradeoff table

In this GFE, we offered you this loan with a particular interest rate and estimated settlement charges. However:

- If you want to choose this same loan with **lower settlement charges,** then you will have a **higher interest rate.**
- If you want to choose this same loan with a **lower interest rate,** then you will have **higher settlement charges.**

If you would like to choose an available option, you must ask us for a new GFE.

Loan originators have the option to complete this table. Please ask for additional information if the table is not completed.

	The loan in this GFE	The same loan with lower settlement charges	The same loan with a lower interest rate
Your initial loan amount	$ 200,000.00	$ 200,000.00	$ 200,000.00
Your initial interest rate [1]	4.5 %	5 %	5.5 %
Your initial monthly amount owed	$ 1,013.37	$ 1,073.64	$ 1,135.58
Change in the monthly amount owed from this GFE	No change	You will pay $ 60.27 **more** every month	You will pay $ 122.21 **less** every month
Change in the amount you will pay at settlement with this interest rate	No change	Your settlement charges will be **reduced** by $ 2,000.00	Your settlement charges will **increase** by $ 4,000.00
How much your total estimated settlement charges will be	$ 12,251.68	$ 10,251.68	$ 8,251.68

[1] *For an adjustable rate loan, the comparisons above are for the initial interest rate before adjustments are made.*

Using the shopping chart

Use this chart to compare GFEs from different loan originators. Fill in the information by using a different column for each GFE you receive. By comparing loan offers, you can shop for the best loan.

	This loan	Loan 2	Loan 3	Loan 4
Loan originator name	XYZ Mtg Lndrs			
Initial loan amount	$200,000.00			
Loan term	30 Years			
Initial interest rate	4.5%			
Initial monthly amount owed	$1,013.37			
Rate lock period	30 Days			
Can interest rate rise?	No			
Can loan balance rise?	No			
Can monthly amount owed rise?	No			
Prepayment penalty?	No			
Balloon payment?	No			
Total Estimated Settlement Charges	$12,251.68			

If your loan is sold in the future

Some lenders may sell your loan after settlement. Any fees lenders receive in the future cannot change the loan you receive or the charges you paid at settlement.

 Good Faith Estimate (HUD-GFE) 3

PRACTICE EXERCISE 10.1

Using the blank form in Figure 10.2, estimate the buyer's cash needed to close and monthly payments based on the following information:

Purchaser	Kyle and Kari Buyers
Property address	1460 Lime Drive
	Orlando, FL
Date of contract	March 20, 20__
Mortgage lender	Security First
Sales price	$200,000
First mortgage:	$160,000
Closing Costs:	Take from GFE
Escrow/ Prepaid Items:	
Taxes—3 months	$600
Hazard insurance (1 year)	$900
Hazard insurance (2 months)	$150
Prepaid interest (1 month)	$935

Mr. and Mrs. Buyers will provide a deposit of $4,000.

---

1 Let's do a little exercise to show what else would be needed to give the buyer a better pic-
2 ture of what it will take to close (use Figure 10.2). First, we'll use the lender's GFE showing
3 total settlement costs (less charges paid in advance) and then add the down payment and
4 prepaid items for the escrow reserves to show the cash necessary to close. Next, we'll use
5 the lender's figure for the principal and interest payment and add the monthly amounts for
6 taxes and insurance to estimate the total monthly payment for principal, interest, taxes,
7 and insurance (PITI).

WRITING THE REAL ESTATE CONTRACT

9   In the case study below, you will prepare the buyers' offer using the figures from the GFE
10 and Figure 10.2. You are a sales associate for Sunny Hills Realty, Inc. In March of this
11 year, a past customer referred Bob and Sandy Smith to you. At your request, they visited
12 Security Atlantic Mortgage Company, which preapproved them for a mortgage loan of up
13 to $200,000.

DISCUSSION EXERCISE 10.1

After the disclosure has been completed, do a role-playing session in class, with two students playing Mr. and Mrs. Smith and one student playing the sales associate. The sales associate should present the completed form to the Smiths, who should ask some simple questions in a positive way.

F I G U R E 10.2 ■ Buyer's Estimated Cash to Close

Purchasers:_____ Property address:_____

Date:_____ Mortgage lender: _____

Purchase price:	$ _____
Less new mortgage:	− _____
Equals down payment:	$ _____
Plus total settlement costs from GFE:	+ _____

Plus prepaid items for escrow reserve:

_____ mo. property taxes   @ ____ = $ _____

_____ mo. insurance   @ ____ = $ _____

_____ mo. mtg. insurance @ ____ = $ _____

_____ mo. ppd. interest   @ ____ = $ _____

Total prepaid items:	$ _____
Less earnest money deposit:	− _____
Equals cash needed to close:	$ _____

Estimated monthly payments

Principal and Interest (from GFE):	$ _____
Property taxes (annual taxes/12 months):	+ _____
Hazard insurance (annual insurance/12 months):	+ _____
Mortgage Insurance (from lender):	+ _____
Other:	+ _____
Total monthly payments:	$ _____

1 You learned that they wanted a three- or four-bedroom home with two baths and a
2 two-car garage. They wanted a home in the northeast less than five miles from the regional
3 hospital, where Bob is a pharmacist.

4 You described the entire process of buying a home, from showing homes through mov-
5 ing into their new home.

6 You went over the lender's good-faith estimate and worksheet with them and dis-
7 cussed the important clauses in the purchase agreement. You gave them copies of the
8 paperwork along with a transaction broker notice. Because they have enough cash for a
9 20 percent down payment (80 percent loan), you can show homes in the $250,000 range
10 ($200,000 ÷ .80).

11 ## Finding the Right Home

12 You set a showing appointment for Saturday and begin previewing homes that might sat-
13 isfy your customers' requirements. You find five houses that seem like real possibilities; one
14 of them is just about perfect. It is located at 816 Harrison Court, a quiet street in a well-
15 kept neighborhood, just two miles from the hospital. The owners have kept it in wonder-
16 ful condition. And it has great "curb appeal." It was listed by Blue Sky Realty, Inc., and is
17 priced at $270,000. Perfect! You make appointments with the sellers to show the homes.

18 On Saturday morning you show the Smiths your favorite home first. They love every-
19 thing about it. You give them a copy of the sellers' disclosure statement that was available

on the kitchen counter. It has no apparent problems. After entering each house after that, it doesn't take long to walk through, because they love the first home. You suggest a return visit and clear it with the sellers. The sellers tell you they are going out for several hours and the house will be available most of the day. After returning to the home, you stay unobtrusive and let the Smiths discover more features of the home. They want to think it over.

Writing the Offer

You suggest that, even if they end up "sleeping" on the decision, it might be helpful if they had the contract filled out. Bob says to make the paperwork out as if they were paying $245,000. Because Bob wants to see the backyard again, you suggest Bob and Sandy look around the property some more while you complete the paperwork.

You will ask the buyers to give you a good-faith deposit of $5,000. Based on previous conversations, the Smiths will want to be in the home in 20 days. Because the sellers are in town, and because the market is so active, you will give them until 10 PM tonight to accept or reject the offer.

In Practice

Make the acceptance time short. The seller is more likely to decide more quickly and not "shop" the offer.

You pull out the MLS data from the house that shows the following information:

Sellers' names: Larry and Wilma Palmer

Street address: 816 Harrison Court, Sunny Hills, FL

Legal description: Lot 18, Block C, Old Hills as recorded in book 126, page 368, Houser County.

Personal property included: range, draperies, rods, and window treatments (as shown by the MLS information). The Smiths also want to include the washer, dryer, and the riding lawn mower. You explain that these items are not included in the sale, but they want to try for them anyway.

PRACTICE EXERCISE 10.2

Preparing the FAR Residential Sale and Purchase Contract.   (Remove the Residential Sale and Purchase Contract from Forms To Go, Appendix B, and complete the form with the information you have been given so far.)

Just as you are finishing the contract, Sandy and Bob return to the kitchen. You tell them it's a great home, and well priced at $270,000. You ask if there is anything they want to do to the home after they buy it, and Bob says he wants to pour a concrete patio. At your request, they write a short note to the sellers about why they want to buy this house, then both sign it.

You go over the cost-disclosure statement, and attach it to the lender's good-faith estimate. Then you go over the contract form carefully. Sandy says it all looks good. You say, "You could go home and worry about this tonight, or I could take this to the seller and you might have great news to celebrate tonight. Wouldn't it be better if we went ahead?" Wait for the answer, because in many cases, the buyer will agree.

If the Smiths agree, ask them to:

1. approve the cost disclosure first;

2. sign a receipt for the sellers' property disclosure statement; and

3. approve the agreement with their signatures.

Ask for the good-faith deposit and clip all the paperwork together. To prepare them for a counteroffer, ask that they not be too disappointed if the seller does not accept the offer at $245,000. After dropping them off, you should immediately contact the listing agent, Hillary Jenkins.

Presenting the Offer

Hillary answers her mobile phone right away. After you tell her that you have an offer that expires at 10 PM, she asks if you'd like to fax it to her office. Because you want to present the offer with her, you arrange to meet at her office 45 minutes before her appointment with the Palmers. You ask if there are any other offers to be presented, and she says there are not. You request that you be called if that situation changes, and she agrees. In some cases, especially if you are a buyers' agent, the listing sales associate will be reluctant to let you present your offer. Explain that you will not stay during the discussions, but that it may be helpful if you tell them about the buyer, present the offer, and see if they have any questions about the flexibility of the buyers, for example, on the closing date.

Hillary calls back and says she has an appointment with the Palmers at 7 PM, and will see you at her office at 6:15 PM. Following are some suggestions that will prove helpful in presenting an offer to purchase:

■   Present it with the listing agent. You are the only one who can answer questions about the buyers, and give the buyers a "face" to the sellers. But this is top priority time and your buyer's dreams and lots of your money is riding on your performance.

- If you are the listing associate, have the selling associate help you present. It also stops second-guessing about the quality of your presentation if his or her offer is not accepted.
- If the other associate is a buyers' single agent, you should tell your sellers not to show reactions that may affect their negotiating position.

In Practice

Go with your offer. Teamwork will get it through.

If you are the listing sales associate, prepare your sellers for a low offer before the cooperating sales associate arrives to present the offer. If a seller has raised expectations, a low offer may insult the sellers and make it very difficult to put a transaction together.

If the parties are far apart on the offered price, try to keep the buyers and sellers from taking it personally. It is your job to be sure personalities are not a factor in the negotiations.

Going to the Sellers' House

You make extra copies of the offer, gather all the documents, and arrive at the Blue Sky Realty office at 6:15 PM. You show Hillary the bank's preapproval letter and give her a copy of the offer. If she has no questions about the offer, you ask if she'd like you to present it to the sellers and she agrees. She also suggests that after presenting the contract, if the sellers have no questions, that you might excuse yourself so they have time to discuss the offer. This is very gracious on her part as she will not ask to you leave; it will be your idea.

You go in separate cars to the house. Hillary waits outside so you can go in together.

In Practice

If it's a good offer, bring a "Sold" sign on top of your folder.

At the door Hillary introduces you to the seller and takes charge, asking if we can all sit at the kitchen table. The sellers agree.

In Practice

While you're presenting, be sure to do the following:

- Be courteous to the cooperating sales associate—always. Nothing can derail the presentation of an offer more than distrust and dissension between the licensees.

- Don't give the offer out to the sellers until you have summarized the important parts. It is hard to maintain control if the parties are looking at all different parts of the contract, interrupting by asking questions.

- Cover all points of the agreement, making price last. Have all the buyers' requirements depend on "getting the price right."

- Make enough copies for everyone so they don't have to read over your shoulder.

- Give copies, never the original offer, so it doesn't get marked.

1 Hillary starts the presentation by complimenting you. You look at her with gratitude
2 and admiration, understanding why she is successful.

3 She continues: "I'm going to let _____ tell you a little about the prospective buyers
4 and go over the offer with you, if that's OK." The sellers nod in agreement and look in
5 your direction.

In Practice

Following are tips in how to handle low offers carefully:

- If you are the listing associate and the selling associate brings in a very low offer, have the cooperating associate present the offer to your sellers.

- If the offer is low and the sellers are angry, let them vent their frustration before starting to work on a counteroffer.

6 "Hi, Mr. and Mrs. Palmer," you say. "I'd like to say how pleased I am to be working
7 with Hillary again. You made a great choice when you listed your home with her. Before I
8 go over the offer, I'd like to tell you a little about the buyers. Their names are Robert and
9 Sandy Smith. Robert is a pharmacist at Sunny Hills Regional Hospital. They have two
10 children, Mary, who's three, and Brett, who's one.

11 "They have owned a condominium since they've been married, so this is their first
12 home. They have been approved for financing by the bank to buy your home. And they
13 love it! They have written you a note about your house and why they want to buy it."
14 Hand them the note. (See Figure 10.2.)

15 Mr. Palmer says, "They sound like pretty nice people. But let's see what they're willing
16 to pay."

17 And you present the contract. Save the offered price until last. Ask if they will let
18 you cover the highlights before starting a discussion on any one item, and that you'll give

F I G U R E   10.3   ■   Handwritten Note

Dear Mr. and Mrs. Palmer,

We just want to tell you how much we love your home. We can tell that you love it too, by the way you keep it so beautiful.

We can't think of a home that would be better to raise our two young children in. Their names are Mary and Brett.

We hope you will let us have it.

And we hope you'll be happy in your new home, too.

Sandy Smith
Bob Smith

them copies of the agreement in a moment. Then cover the contingencies first before talking about price.

"The buyers need to close and move in 20 days. I've spoken with the lender who says they can close it on time.

"They're including your refrigerator, range, washer and dryer, riding mower, and the window treatments.

"They're getting new financing and have been preapproved for their loan."

Now tell them the offer is $245,000. Reassure the sellers that the buyers' offer is not meant to insult them, but they can qualify to buy a $250,000 home and are hoping to keep $5,000 to build a concrete patio. Give statistics about sales: "Listings sell at 94 percent of list price," etc., so this offer is right on target.

> **In Practice**
>
> If the parties are far apart on the offered price, try to keep the buyers and sellers from taking it personally. It is your job to be sure personalities are not a factor in the negotiations.

Tell the sellers that if they have no questions for you about the buyers or the offer, you'd like to excuse yourself to give them an opportunity to discuss the offer with Hillary. You can tell them you have some calls to make anyway, and will do it from your car, so you'll be close by if any other questions arise.

Sellers' Responses to an Offer

Sellers who receive an offer on their home have the following three possible responses:

- Acceptance
- Rejection
- Counteroffer

1 **Acceptance.** Obviously, the selling sales associate hopes the response will be an accep-
2 tance. The offer is signed and becomes a contract between the buyer and the seller.

3 **Rejection.** If the price offered is very low, and is obviously a "fishing expedition," the
4 seller may be advised to reject the offer outright. A better approach might be to reject the
5 offer with an invitation to come back with a more serious offer. The market is currently
6 a strong buyers' market in Florida, so sellers should be cautious in rejecting offers, and
7 even when making counteroffers. Many sellers have refused to accept low offers who later
8 regretted missing the opportunity to sell. As their counselor, be certain that the sellers are
9 aware of market conditions.

10 **Counteroffer.** If the offer is not acceptable but is close enough to be considered serious,
11 a **counteroffer** should be used. A counteroffer keeps the parties "at the table," making
12 continued negotiations easier.

13 Keep notes when the sellers are discussing the pros and cons of the offer. When the
14 sellers reach a decision on the terms of the counteroffer, a counteroffer form should be
15 used rather than marking on the contract. This is a good idea for legibility and enforce-
16 ability purposes.

17 In 15 minutes, Hillary comes to the door and motions you inside. Back at the table,
18 Hillary says, "Mr. and Mrs. Palmer want the Smiths to have this home, but want to make
19 several changes. First, they feel the house is worth the asking price of $270,000, but they
20 will split the difference with the buyers at a price of $257,000. They will include the
21 range and window treatments, but want to take the other items of personal property. Also,
22 because they cannot get into their new home, the closing date will have to be 30 days from
23 now. Do you think you can help me prepare several copies of the counteroffer? "

**Forms
To Go**

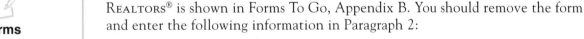

PRACTICE EXERCISE 10.3

Preparing the Counteroffer. A counteroffer form from the Florida Association of
REALTORS® is shown in Forms To Go, Appendix B. You should remove the form
and enter the following information in Paragraph 2:

Clause	Counteroffer Terms
1.	Washer, dryer, and riding lawn mower are not included in the sale.
2.	Price shall be $257,500
3.	Closing date shall be 30 days from the date of this contract

24 In paragraph 3 of the counteroffer, check that the counteroffer must be delivered to
25 Seller or Seller's licensee within 24 hours from 11 PM the 18th day of October.

26 After the counteroffer has been prepared and signed by the sellers, all it will take to
27 make the counteroffer into a contract will be the buyers' signatures on the counteroffer.

28 You say to the sellers: "Thank you all so much for your courtesy. I'll do everything I
29 can to sell your home. Hillary, I'll call you as soon as I've spoken with the buyers."

In Practice

Work the contract until it's either accepted or dead. Don't stop working it because it's nearly midnight. Sellers want to sell and buyers want to buy, and they respect professionals who work hard. Working late brings an urgency that gets lots of offers accepted.

When you arrive at the Smiths' house, tell them you have great news. "The sellers came off their price by $12,500! Let's go over their counteroffer."

They agree to all the terms of the counteroffer. You change the cost disclosure statement to reflect the new price, and have them sign the counteroffer. Call Hillary and tell her you'll take the counteroffer to her office or her house, and she should get it to the sellers. She agrees.

You have sold the house and made several people very happy.

In Practice

If you are the listing associate and there are multiple offers from both your company and other companies, get your broker involved. If your company has an offer to present, tell the other associates not to fax their offers. You don't want to know what they have so you won't be suspected of "shopping" the offer. The broker should meet with all the associates before the presentation to establish the ground rules. The broker should arrange for each selling associate to present his or her offer in the order received. Everything should be scrupulously fair and transparent.

SUMMARY

Because buyers are reluctant to commit to buy without understanding the financial commitment they must make, a sales associate should be sure the buyers have a GFE and a worksheet of total cash needed, which has been prepared by the lender.

A licensee should practice preparing offers on different types of properties with a variety of financing programs. Once the practice offer is written, you should role-play the explanation of the offer. Practice will give you the skills to help you get more transactions to the closing table.

A seller has three possible responses to a counteroffer: acceptance, rejection, or counteroffer. To counteroffer, the seller makes the appropriate changes, initials each change, and then signs the offer. To accept the counteroffer, a buyer need only initial the changes.

KEY TERMS

counteroffer   Good Faith Estimate (GFE)

P R A C T I C E   E X A M

1. John is preparing a buyer's cost disclosure statement. Because he wants to protect himself from later problems, he should
   a. use a disclosure form for a similar house from the office closed-sales files.
   b. talk to several licensees in the firm to get their ideas on current costs.
   c. ask his broker for the information on closing costs for a new loan.
   d. get the information from the lender's good-faith estimate.

2. A buyer has been prequalified for a $160,000 mortgage. If the buyer has enough cash for a 20 percent down payment, he or she can get a house priced at
   a. $320,000.
   b. $240,000.
   c. $220,000.
   d. $200,000.

3. According to the text, the sales associate who is presenting the offer should normally give copies of the offer
   a. before starting to present the information.
   b. only after summarizing the important parts of the offer.
   c. just before asking for a signature.
   d. to the listing sales associate by fax as soon as the associate is notified of the offer.

4. When presenting an offer, the sales associate should NOT
   a. give the seller the offer with the original signatures.
   b. make copies for all the parties who are present.
   c. work the offer until it's accepted or dead.
   d. present all terms of the offer before discussing the price.

5. When the seller wants to make a counteroffer
   a. it should be made orally.
   b. the seller should initial the changes but should not sign the offer.
   c. the seller should initial the changes and sign the offer.
   d. the sales associate should strongly object and try to get the original offer accepted.

6. If you are the listing sales associate and there are multiple offers to be presented, both from your company and other companies, you should
   a. present your company's offers first.
   b. tell the sales associates in your company the details of the other offers.
   c. get your broker involved.
   d. get the associates from the other companies to fax their offers.

7. When presenting an offer to the sellers, it is helpful to
   a. tell them first what price is being offered.
   b. make only one copy of the offer in order to keep better control of the presentation.
   c. get them to like the buyers.
   d. tell them nothing about the buyers.

8. If you have an offer to present to a seller, and you are not the listing sales associate, you should
   a. excuse yourself after making the presentation, making sure the sellers have no further questions for you.
   b. require that the listing broker be present in case there is a problem during the presentation.
   c. not attend or present your offer but, instead, let the listing agent do so.
   d. first give the good-faith deposit to the listing agent for deposit, if the offer is accepted.

9. When buyers just want to "sleep on the decision," and you want them to make an offer on a home they love, the best way to help them make the decision is to
   a. tell them there are three other buyers interested, whether or not that's true.
   b. prepare the paperwork, then explain the sales agreement and the offer process.
   c. tell them you'll be out of town for the rest of the week.
   d. offer to pay their closing costs.

10. Principal and interest on a new loan is $1,564.90. Annual taxes are estimated to be $3,575, and insurance is estimated to be $1,289 annually. What is the monthly payment?
    a. $6,428.90
    b. $5,139.90
    c. $1,970.24
    d. $1,862.82

APPLY WHAT YOU'VE LEARNED!

The author suggests the following actions to reinforce the material in *Section III—Selling Real Property:*

- ❏ Preview at least five homes in your favorite price range. Try to see five each day for the next five days. Use a tape recorder to describe each home thoroughly, and try to match it with a prospective buyer or type of buyer.

- ❏ From your preview visits, list the best homes on the market. Pick your favorite home from that list.

- ❏ Describe every characteristic of *your* favorite home from your preview trips as if you were writing a book on the house. Try to remember colors, room sizes and arrangements, and garage size. Describe each room in as much detail as possible. If you can't do it, go back to the house again and make careful notes. Try to increase your observation powers every time you preview homes.

- ❏ When you visit a vacant home, thoroughly describe each room aloud as if your buyer were sight-impaired.

- ❏ Keep a tape recorder near your phone. The next time you answer a call from a prospective buyer, turn on the recorder. (You must observe the law, however; record only *your* side of the conversation.) When you have completed the call, listen to the tape. Make written notes about what you would change about your side of the conversation.

- ❏ Ride through a neighborhood you have not yet explored, describing into your tape recorder the details you see. Then do the same thing in the surrounding area to find shopping areas, libraries, car washes, schools, and churches.

- ❏ Write the features you think some close friends would like in a home. From memory, list the properties you would show them and give reasons for your decisions. Make a buyer's cost statement based on a 90 percent conventional loan.

- ❏ Call your friends and tell them about the previous exercise. Ask whether they will let you show them the homes you chose for them. How well did you judge their tastes?

FINANCING AND CLOSING REAL ESTATE TRANSACTIONS

Licensees often are asked for advice by buyers about the most appropriate type of loan for to secure. The advice licensees provide requires an understanding of the advantages and disadvantages of each mortgage type and the situations that make certain mortgages more suitable.

Sales associates must understand the loan application and underwriting process completely to effectively assist a buyer when dealing with lenders. This section will give licensees a better idea of the steps required to take a loan from application to closing.

The closing is often the most troublesome part of a real estate sale. This section is intended to give licensees information on how to reduce stress levels at closings and to make the licensees more efficient and professional. Many problems result from communication failures between cooperating brokers and sales associates. This section explores methods of tracking the necessary components of the closing to ensure that everything is completed on time.

Sales associates are expected to oversee closings and to review the closing documents, particularly the closing statement. A sales associate must understand each part of the statement. This section provides hands-on practice for the sales associate in preparing closing statements.

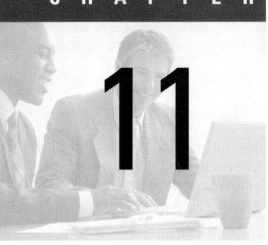

CHAPTER 11

EXPLORING MORTGAGE ALTERNATIVES

LEARNING OBJECTIVES

Upon completion of this chapter, you should be able to:

1. describe the components of the lender's required annual percentage rate (APR) disclosures;

2. calculate the effective interest rate on 30-year, fixed-rate loans and on loans for shorter periods;

3. calculate the PITI payment for a borrower;

4. compare the interest savings on a 15-year, fixed-rate mortgage versus a 30-year, fixed-rate mortgage;

5. discuss the pros and cons of an adjustable-rate mortgage (ARM);

6. explain the five components of an ARM;

7. calculate the interest rate adjustments on an ARM loan.

OVERVIEW

During the years 2003–2006, the United States experienced the biggest housing boom in its history, a boom that began to deflate in 2007, causing a meltdown in the credit markets. The fault belongs everywhere in the system, but perhaps the great engine of the catastrophe was Wall Street. Large banks, hedge funds, and investment firms had losses of a magnitude never imagined, eroding their capital bases and requiring large infusions of capital to avoid a systemic failure. The Federal Reserve worked to hold the system together to prevent catastrophic failure of the credit system.

In September 2008, Fannie Mae and Freddie Mac were placed under the conservatorship of the Federal Housing Finance Agency, one of the most sweeping government interventions in private financial markets in many years.

Lenders, Congress, the administration, and scholars have a lot to evaluate in making proposals to keep the system going, helping homeowners who are being foreclosed, and establishing regulations to prevent a future financial crisis.

Twenty years ago, commercial banks and savings associations originated more than 80 percent of home mortgages. That share has dropped sharply, and today mortgage companies are the dominant factor in the market, originating more than 50 percent of all home loans. Driven by market forces, lenders offer a wide variety of mortgage products tailored to the needs of consumers. Experts expect the changes in the mortgage industry to accelerate in the future.

A general knowledge of these changes can enhance the opportunities available to the real estate professional. Developing strong relationships with lenders who preapprove loans for prospective buyers saves licensees time and can significantly increase their income. ▪

STEPS BEFORE LOAN APPLICATION

Before buyers begin looking at houses, they should have a good understanding of their own financial capabilities and housing objectives. Licensees should explain both issues to their customers to help them understand the importance of getting preapproved. This is important because if a loan application is denied, the applicant may lose the opportunity to buy the home. In addition, some expense is involved in applying for a loan. Fees may range from $150 to $500, depending on the property and circumstances.

Mortgage Shopping

Licensees should advise buyers to look for competitive rates and a lender with a reputation for integrity and good service.

Surveys show that mortgage interest rates and closing costs vary in metropolitan markets for the same mortgage product. Comparing prices obviously is important, but it is not an easy task. Lenders charge a variety of fees a borrower may be asked to pay when he or she submits a loan application. Discount points, usually one of the largest fees lenders charge, also vary from lender to lender in the same market area. The points change the effective interest rate, and just two points more on a loan can mean significant additional expense to the borrower. The new GFE provides more information to a borrower who wants to evaluate whether to pay extra points to get a lower interest rate. There is also a worksheet for those borrowers who are shopping for a mortgage.

Licensees must learn which lenders can be trusted to act with speed and service to borrowers. Licensees should use and recommend only those that provide good service.

Seller-Paid Closing Costs

A buyer must have the necessary income and debt ratios to afford a mortgage payment. Coming up with enough cash to close is another big hurdle. The closing costs and prepayments on a typical mortgage loan for $120,000 can reach $5,000 in addition to the down payment. Many qualified buyers are forced to rent in order to accumulate the savings necessary to close. Licensees who know lender standards on seller-paid closing costs are able to sell to these buyers much sooner. The seller can pay part of the closing costs for conventional, FHA, and VA mortgage loans. Figure 11.1 shows the current allowed percentages.

A seller who could pay only 3 percent of the buyer's closing costs on a low down payment conventional loan for $120,000 would contribute $3,600. If a two-income family is saving $300 per month, the home purchase could be made 12 months sooner.

DISCUSSION EXERCISE 11.1

Do you think most licensees guide potential borrowers to lenders with which they have built relationships or to lenders that have the best mortgage rates on a given day?

F I G U R E 11.1 ■ **Maximum Seller-Paid Closing Costs That Can Be Applied to Buyer's Closing Costs, Prepaid Items, and Reserves, Expressed as a Percentage of the Purchase Price**

Type of Loan	Percent
Conventional	
Less than 10% down payment	3
19% or greater down payment	6
FHA	6
VA	6

Annual Percentage Rate (APR)

The Truth-in-Lending Act requires that mortgage lenders disclose their annual percentage rates to potential borrowers. The **annual percentage rate (APR)** is a standard expression of credit costs designed to give potential borrowers an easy method of comparing lenders' total finance charges. These financing costs include points and any other prepaid interest or fees charged to obtain the loan in addition to the contract interest cost. The APR must be, by law, the relationship of the total financing charge to the total amount financed, and it must be computed to the nearest one-eighth of 1 percent. Perhaps the best and most accurate definition of the APR is that it is the effective interest rate for a mortgage loan repaid over its full term.

The law allows a lender three days after loan application to inform the applicant of the APR. Effective July 30, 2009, the lender is required to notify the borrower within three days if the APR changes by more than $\frac{1}{8}$ of one percent.

Regulation Z of the Truth-in-Lending Act was amended by the Federal Reserve Board as a result of the losses sustained during the recent housing bubble. The rule, effective April 1, 2011, replaces the Housing Valuation Code of Conduct that had many similar provisions. The amendment:

- ■ requires that fee appraisers be paid reasonably and customary compensation,
- ■ prohibits coercion of appraisers for both permanent mortgages and home equity loans,
- ■ prohibits appraisers and appraisal management companies from having financial or other interests in the properties being appraised, and
- ■ requires creditors and closing agents that have information about appraiser misconduct to file reports to the appropriate state licensing authorities.

Another feature of this act is that it assumes that borrowers will keep their loans for the full number of years for which the loans are written. Records of mortgage lending, however, show that most borrowers either sell or refinance their homes in less than 12 years. The actual (effective) interest rate paid depends on the number of years a loan is kept.

F I G U R E 11.2 ■ **$100,000 30-Year Fixed-Rate Mortgage Comparison of Rates and Discount Points**

	A. Interest Rate	B. Discount Points	C. Principal and Interest Payment	D. Payment Difference from 5% Rate	E. Amount Paid in Discount Points	F. Months at Lower Rate for Points Payback (E ÷ D)
1.	5.000	0	$536.82	—	$ 0	0
2.	4.875	0.5	529.21	$7.61	500	65.70
3.	4.750	1.2	521.65	15.17	1,200	79.10
4.	4.625	1.7	514.14	22.68	1,700	74.96
5.	4.500	2.3	506.69	30.13	2,300	76.30

E X A M P L E : If the borrower expects to keep the loan for longer than 12 years, divide the points by 8 and add the result to the note interest rate. For example, if a lender has offered a first mortgage for 30 years at 5 percent and 3 points, the effective interest rate would be 5.375 percent, computed as follows:

$$\text{Note rate} + (\text{points} \div 8) = \text{Effective interest rate}$$
$$5\% + (.03 \div 8) = 5\% + .375\% = 5.375\%$$

When the lender gives a prospective borrower a rate quote, the borrower is often undecided about whether to pay discount points. Discount points can be considered prepaid interest that will reduce the interest rate on the note. In effect, a borrower has a "menu" of interest rates based on the amount paid as discount points. Figure 11.2 shows a sample market quote for a 30-year fixed-rate loan. Fluctuations in the market cause differences from day to day in the differential of discount points and yield.

From the example, it's obvious that a person who intends to occupy the property for three years should avoid paying points because it will take almost six years to break even. In some cases, a borrower should ask the lender to raise the interest rate not only to avoid discount points but also to avoid paying an origination fee.

If a person expects to remain in the property for the full 30-year period and will not be refinancing or making an early loan payoff, the savings could be worth paying points. At line 5, for instance, the borrower breaks even at 76 months. The difference in payments of $30.13 for the remaining 283 months would total $8,526.80, well worth paying the points.

Of course, the better way to analyze points is by considering the time value of money. Using the 4.5 percent rate on line 5, the borrower pays $2,300 in *today*'s dollars (that could be invested to return some interest) to get a savings sometime in the *future*. A financial calculator approach shows the payback period is longer (87 months versus 76.3 months).

Financial Calculator Keystrokes to Find Payback Period for $2,300 in Points with a 4.5 Percent Yield

%I	PMT	PV	FV	Solve for N
.3750	30.13	2,300	0	91 months

Where:
% = monthly market interest rate: 4.5% ÷ 12 months = .375
PMT = savings per monthly payment = $30.13
PV = Dollars paid in points = $2,300
FV = input zero for this problem = 0

Solve for: N = Number of months to pay back points

Solution is 91 months

DISCUSSION EXERCISE 11.2

John has been transferred to Miami and expects to be in the location for about three years before being transferred again. He needs to borrow $200,000 for his new home. With no points, he can get a 5 percent fixed-rate mortgage with principal and interest payments of $1,073.64. The lender offers him a 4.6 percent mortgage (payments of $1,025.29) with two points.

Should John take the lower interest rate mortgage?

Using simple math, how many months will it take John to break even by paying the points if he takes the lower interest rate?

PITI Payment

Customers often ask licensees to calculate the monthly mortgage payment for a possible purchase or sale. Most lenders require an amount each month that includes principal and interest plus escrow items—property taxes, homeowners' insurance, and possibly mortgage insurance or homeowners'/condominium association dues. This entire package of payments commonly is referred to as the **PITI payment.**

Principal and interest payments on the mortgage are the largest part of the monthly PITI payment. Using the mortgage payment factors shown in Table 11.1, multiply the loan amount by the appropriate factor to get the principal and interest portion of the payment.

For example, the payment factor for a 30-year mortgage at 5 percent is .0053682. To calculate the monthly principal and interest for a 30-year loan of $198,000 at 5 percent, use the following equation:

$$\$198,000 \times .0053682 = \$1,062.90$$

While the factor table has been included in this text so that all students can calculate the monthly payment, most real estate licensees use a financial calculator to obtain the monthly mortgage payment of principal and interest.

F I G U R E 11.3 ▇ PITI Worksheet

Mortgage amount $ _____

Interest rate   _____ %

Term of loan   _____ years

Mortgage payment factor _____

Principal and interest payment: $ _____

($ _____ × _____)

(mtg. amt.)   (factor)   _____

Property taxes: $ _____ ÷ 12   _____

Hazard insurance: $_____ ÷ 12   _____

Mortgage insurance:

$ _____ × _____ ÷ 12

(mtg. amt.)   (premium rate)

TOTAL MONTHLY MORTGAGE PAYMENT (PITI) $_____

Source: Adapted by permission from Thomas C. Steinmetz, *The Mortgage Kit,* 4th ed. (Chicago: Dearborn Financial Publishing, Inc.®, 1998), 163.

In the example on the previous page, the licensee with a financial calculator would solve the problem as shown below:

N	%I	PV	FV	Solve for: PMT
360	.4167	198,000	0	$1,062.90

Where: N = number of monthly periods in loan term

%I = interest rate (5% ÷ 12 months = .4167)

PV = loan amount

FV = input zero when solving for present value

Solve for: PMT = monthly mortgage payment

Note: Small difference in payment is due to rounding.

A PITI worksheet that licensees can use in helping their clients and customers calculate at the PITI amount for a potential loan is shown in Figure 11.3.

FIXED-RATE MORTGAGES

Any mortgage written to preclude change in the interest rate throughout the entire duration of the loan is a **fixed-rate mortgage.** The term includes the traditional 30-year mortgage, the 15-year mortgage, and the biweekly mortgage. The use of a due-on-sale clause in a fixed-rate mortgage reserves the lender's right to make an interest rate change if a transfer of ownership takes place. Practically all conventional mortgages issued since the early 1980s contain a due-on-sale clause.

Traditional 30-Year Mortgage

The fixed-rate, fully amortizing mortgage loan has been the standard of the real estate finance industry for the past 50 years. A 30-year term provides a reasonably low payment for the amount borrowed, while the interest rate, payment amount, and repayment schedule are set permanently at the beginning of the loan period. Fixed-rate loans often

T A B L E 11.1 ▥ Mortgage Payment Factors

Multiply the mortgage principal times the factor to solve for the mortgage payment.

	Term of Loan				
Interest Rate	**10 years**	**15 years**	**20 years**	**25 years**	**30 years**
5.00%	0.0106066	0.0079079	0.0065996	0.0058459	0.0053682
5.25%	0.0107292	0.0080388	0.0067384	0.0059925	0.0055220
5.50%	0.0108526	0.0081708	0.0068789	0.0061409	0.0056779
5.75%	0.0109769	0.0083041	0.0070208	0.0062911	0.0058357
6.00%	0.0111021	0.0084386	0.0071643	0.0064430	0.0059955
6.25%	0.0112280	0.0085742	0.0073093	0.0065967	0.0061572
6.50%	0.0113548	0.0087111	0.0074557	0.0067521	0.0063207
6.75%	0.0114824	0.0088491	0.0076036	0.0069091	0.0064860
7.00%	0.0116108	0.0089883	0.0077530	0.0070678	0.0066530
7.25%	0.0117401	0.0091286	0.0079038	0.0072281	0.0068218
7.50%	0.0118702	0.0092701	0.0080559	0.0073899	0.0069921
7.75%	0.0120011	0.0094128	0.0082095	0.0075533	0.0071641
8.00%	0.0121328	0.0095565	0.0083644	0.0077182	0.0073376
8.25%	0.0122653	0.0097014	0.0085207	0.0078845	0.0075127
8.50%	0.0123986	0.0098474	0.0086782	0.0080523	0.0076891
8.75%	0.0125327	0.0099945	0.0088371	0.0082214	0.0078670
9.00%	0.0126676	0.0101427	0.0089973	0.0083920	0.0080462
9.25%	0.0128033	0.0102919	0.0091587	0.0085638	0.0082268
9.50%	0.0129398	0.0104422	0.0093213	0.0087370	0.0084085
9.75%	0.0130770	0.0105936	0.0094852	0.0089114	0.0085915
10.00%	0.0132151	0.0107461	0.0096502	0.0090870	0.0087757
10.25%	0.0133539	0.0108995	0.0098164	0.0092638	0.0089610
10.50%	0.0134935	0.0110540	0.0099838	0.0094418	0.0091474
10.75%	0.0136339	0.0112095	0.0101523	0.0096209	0.0093348
11.00%	0.0137750	0.0113660	0.0103219	0.0098011	0.0095232
11.25%	0.0139169	0.0115234	0.0104926	0.0099824	0.0097126
11.50%	0.0140595	0.0116819	0.0106643	0.0101647	0.0099029
11.75%	0.0142029	0.0118413	0.0108371	0.0103480	0.0100941

1 are sold in the secondary market because they appeal to pension funds and other investors
2 searching for a relatively safe investment with a known interest rate and a long duration.

3 **Advantages of a 30-year mortgage.** Monthly payments on the loan are spread over 30
4 years, offering the borrower protection against future increases in interest rates and infla-
5 tion rates while providing for the orderly repayment of the amount borrowed. Household
6 budgets are easier to manage when the borrower does not have to plan for changing pay-
7 ment amounts or interest rates.

8 **Disadvantages of a 30-year mortgage.** If overall interest rates drop, as they did in years
9 2000–2001, the rate on a fixed-rate mortgage will not go down with them. To take

advantage of lower interest rates, the original loan must be **refinanced,** requiring the borrower to pay substantial closing costs on the new loan.

15-Year Mortgage

The 15-year fixed-rate mortgage has become popular with both lenders and borrowers in recent years. It is just like a traditional 30-year loan, except that its monthly payment is higher, its interest rate typically is slightly lower, and it is paid off in 15 years. The 15-year mortgage saves the borrower thousands of dollars in interest payments.

The popular press sometimes compares the two mortgage plans, showing dramatic savings from the 15-year plan. The gross savings, however, usually are overstated. The higher payments on the 15-year plan have an opportunity cost. If the difference were invested, the return on the investment would reduce the net cost of the 30-year mortgage. The tax savings from mortgage interest deductions also would reduce the savings.

For many borrowers, the 15-year mortgage may be the best way to finance a home because in addition to the overall savings in total cost, it forces a monthly saving in the form of extra equity and allows a person who needs it a sense of confidence that her home will be paid off in 15 years. This is true for those planning in advance for retirement. Also, many in the baby boomer generation are in their 40s, with a growing number eager to end their mortgage payments and own their homes free and clear.

Licensees should point out, however, that the 15-year mortgage robs the borrower of some flexibility. A 15-year mortgage cannot be extended to 30 years, but a 30-year mortgage can be paid off in 15 years if the borrower accelerates monthly payments to create a 15-year loan or remits a lump-sum payment on principal each year. The borrower retains the right to decide when, or if, he will make extra payments. Borrowers must evaluate the benefits of the 15-year mortgage based on their personal situations.

Advantages of a 15-year mortgage. Because lenders get their money back sooner than they do with traditional 30-year mortgages, they charge slightly lower rates for 15-year loans. Also, the loans are paid off faster, less money is borrowed for less time, and less total interest is paid over the lives of the loans—more than 50 percent less. As with a 30-year, fixed-rate loan, the interest rate on a 15-year mortgage does not change, and the monthly principal and interest payment does not go up. Finally, the higher monthly payment results in forced savings in the form of faster equity buildup.

Disadvantages of a 15-year mortgage. The monthly payment on a 15-year loan is higher, and the borrower forgoes investment opportunities voluntarily for the extra dollars paid on the loan each month. Some income tax advantages related to home mortgages and investment opportunities are lost. Flexibility of mortgage payment is sacrificed, and any future increase in income tax rates could increase the 15-year mortgage's net costs.

Biweekly Mortgage

The development of computer programs to service biweekly mortgages properly, the creation of a secondary market (Fannie Mae), increased familiarity with the product, and growing consumer demand all are combining to bring about a comeback for the biweekly mortgage. The **biweekly mortgage** alternative is a fixed-rate loan, amortized over a 30-year period, with payments made every two weeks instead of every month. Borrowers pay half the normal monthly payment every two weeks, which means a total of 26 payments each

TABLE 11.2 ■ **Comparison of Interest Costs for Various Mortgage Plans for a $100,000 Loan at 5% Interest**

Payment Pattern	Regular Payment Amount	Total Paid Each Year	Time Until Paid Off	Total Interest Paid
30-Year Mortgage	$536.82	$6,441.84	30 years	$93,255
Added $25/Month	561.82	6,742.00	27 yrs. + 2 mos.	83,153
Added $100/Month	636.82	7,642.00	21 yrs. + 4 mos.	63,026
Biweekly Mortgage	268.41	6,979.00	25 yrs. + 3 mos.	76,345
15-Year Mortgage	$790.79	$9,489.00	15 years	$42,342

year, or the equivalent of 13 monthly payments. The extra month's payment each year reduces the principal faster and results in considerable savings in interest, as well as a reduction in the duration of the loan to between 19 and 21 years.

Normally, interest rates for biweekly mortgages are comparable to the rates charged for traditional 30-year mortgages. Most biweekly loans are scheduled to mature in 30 years even though the actual number of years to maturity depends on the interest rate. The higher the interest rate, the larger the monthly payment, and the more that is applied to reducing mortgage principal. A biweekly mortgage with a 7 percent interest rate, for example, would be paid off in approximately 23 years, 9 months.

Consumer Reports Magazine analyzed several mortgage options and concluded that a $100,000 biweekly mortgage at 8 percent interest would save a borrower approximately $34,000 in interest, when compared with a traditional 30-year, fixed-rate mortgage at the same interest rate.

Table 11.2 compares the results of making scheduled payments on a traditional 30-year mortgage, of adding different amounts of additional principal payments each month, and of making scheduled payments on a biweekly mortgage amortized over 30 years.

Advantages of a biweekly mortgage. A biweekly mortgage combines the benefits of the 30-year loan and the 15-year loan without the increased payments of the 15-year loan. It offers borrowers the affordability of the 30-year loan because the two biweekly payments come within a few pennies of the one monthly payment on a 30-year loan.

Also, Fannie Mae requires that payments be deducted automatically from a borrower's checking or savings account every two weeks. Because more than half of the nation's workforce is paid on a biweekly basis, it is compatible with a large number of paychecks. Some lenders include a conversion clause that permits a borrower to change a biweekly mortgage to a traditional 30-year, fixed-rate, amortized mortgage at little or no cost with only 30 days' advance notice.

Disadvantages of a biweekly mortgage. The biweekly mortgage has the same disadvantages as other fixed-rate mortgages. In addition, the biweekly loan threatens those borrowers who do not maintain stable checking or savings account balances. The biweekly mortgage also locks borrowers into payment plans that they could set up themselves, at their own discretion, with a traditional 30-year loan. Some lenders also charge a set-up fee.

DISCUSSION EXERCISE 11.3

If the biweekly mortgage combines the good features of both the traditional 30-year, fixed-rate mortgage and the 15-year, fixed-rate mortgage, why is it so seldom used, comparatively speaking, to finance residential purchases?

ADJUSTABLE-RATE MORTGAGES

The **adjustable-rate mortgage (ARM)** is an alternative to the traditional 30-year, fixed-rate, level-payment mortgage. The popularity of ARMs increases when interest rates rise, and they lose favor when interest rates are low. An adjustable-rate mortgage is, as the term implies, a financing instrument that allows the lender to increase or decrease the interest rate based on the rise or fall of a specified index.

Components of Adjustable-Rate Mortgages

The primary elements in determining the acceptability of an ARM from the borrower's viewpoint are the index, the lender's margin, the calculated interest rate, the initial interest rate, and the interest rate caps.

Lending institutions are permitted legally to link the interest rate of a conventional ARM to any recognized **index** (indicator of cost or value) that is not controlled by the lender and is verifiable by the borrower. The **margin,** also called the *spread,* is a percentage added to the index. The margin usually remains constant over the life of the loan, while the selected index may move up or down with fluctuations in the nation's economy. The calculated (or actual) interest rate is calculated by adding the selected index to the lender's margin (index plus margin equals calculated interest rate). This calculated interest rate may be discounted during the initial payment period, but it is the rate to which all future adjustments and caps apply.

To be competitive, lenders sometimes reduce the first year's earnings by discounting the calculated interest rate, thus creating a lower initial interest rate. This helps to qualify potential buyers at artificially low interest rates, which may or may not be a service to the borrowers, and establishes the amount of the monthly loan payment during the first time period of the loan. Be aware that many lenders now use the second year's interest rate rather than the discounted rate as the qualifier. Both Fannie Mae and Freddie Mac require borrowers with less than a 20 percent down payment on one-year, adjustable-rate loans to be qualified at the initial interest rate plus 2 percent.

The main appeal of ARM loans is the lower-than-market initial interest rates offered as inducements (teasers). But without some type of protection from unacceptable increases in interest rates, borrowers would be in danger of being unable to make future mortgage payments. To prevent this, most lenders and all federal housing agencies have established standards calling for ceilings on increases. Three types of **caps** (ceilings) limit increases in the calculated interest rates of ARM loans:

1. Amount of increase that can be applied at the time of the first adjustment (for example, cap of 1 percent or 2 percent per adjustment period)

T A B L E 11.3 ■ **$100,000 Mortgage Loan, 30-Year Term, 8% Fixed-Rate Versus 5.5% Adjustable-Rate Mortgage (Annual Cap 2%, Lifetime Cap 6%)**

	Fixed Rate			Adjustable Rate			ARM Savings (Loss)	
Year	Payment	Rate		Payment	Rate		Monthly	Accumulated
1	$734	8%		$568	5.5%		$166	$1,992
2	734	8		699	7.5		35	2,412
3	734	8		841	9.5		(107)	1,128
4*	734	8		990	11.5		(256)	(1,944)

*ARM savings exhausted in fifth month of year 4.

2. Amount of increase that can be applied during any one adjustment interval (for example, no more than 2 percent during any one-year period)

3. Total amount the interest rate may be increased over the life of the loan (for example, no more than 6 percent)

Borrowers should be cautious when payments are capped and interest rates are not because of the probability that **negative amortization** will be involved in the loan. Negative amortization occurs when the monthly payment is not enough to pay the interest on the loan. The shortfall is added to the mortgage balance.

Lenders must provide potential borrowers with a worst-case example at loan application. This disclosure must show the maximum possible payment increases if conditions should warrant maximum interest rate increases at the earliest opportunities.

Conventional ARM

To help you better understand adjustable-rate versus fixed-rate mortgages, Table 11.3 compares two approaches to a $100,000 conventional mortgage using a worst-case scenario for interest rate increases.

In this example, all monthly payment amounts are for principal and interest, and the amounts are rounded to the nearest dollar. The upfront costs of points and fees will be discussed later.

ARM loans have lower initial rates than fixed-rate mortgages, primarily because lenders can avoid the risk of market interest changes for the full 30 years of the loan period. ARM loans reduce the risk, so lenders don't need as much cushion for contingencies. New ARM products are available that combine the ARM features of lower initial interest rate with a longer fixed-rate period between adjustments. For example, three-year, five-year, or ten-year ARMs are available at slightly higher initial rates than one-year ARMs, but at lower rates than 30-year fixed mortgages.

DISCUSSION EXERCISE 11.4

In your opinion, do the lower initial rates offered on ARM loans cause borrowers to take on more mortgage debt than they can afford? Why or why not?

Interest rates and recognized indexes. The index to which a conventional ARM is tied can increase or decrease the volatility of interest rate changes. There are four principal indexes used for residential mortgages:

1. The LIBOR (London Interbank Offered Rate) index is the base interest rate paid on deposits between banks in the Eurodollar market.
2. MTA—Monthly Treasury Bill Average—This stable, slow-moving index is a 12-month moving average of the U.S. One-Year Treasury Bill.
3. COFI—11th District Cost of Funds Index—Another stable, slow-moving index, consisting of the weighted average of deposits and borrowings between banks in the Federal Home Loan Bank District of San Francisco.
4. PRIME rate is the rate charged to most favored customers by major banks. This rate is commonly used for adjustments to home equity or second mortgages and can be quite volatile.

Lenders must provide consumers with details on conventional ARMs to assist them in comparison shopping. Potential borrowers must be informed of the index used, how often the loan will be adjusted, and the maximum amount of loan payment increase allowed.

When helping prospective borrowers sort through the many factors to be considered in selecting a conventional adjustable-rate loan, licensees should make sure the borrowers know:

- what rate will be used when interest rate caps are applied to an ARM loan;
- that the margin is one of the most important benchmarks in comparing lenders (most other ARM features are relatively similar, but the margins can vary considerably);
- to seek another lender if the one they are considering has policies that call for ARM increases exceeding the 2 percent annual cap or the 6 percent lifetime cap;
- not to consider loans that call for negative amortization;
- to compare upfront costs, such as underwriting fees, points, and origination fees, because some lenders offer lower interest rates but make up for it with inflated upfront costs; and
- not to stretch their borrowing to the limit, as they could with a fixed-rate loan, because the payments remain fixed and income should increase. Borrowing to the limit can become a disaster when an ARM is involved. Prospective borrowers should calculate their first-year payments at the initial interest rate plus 2 percent; otherwise, the first adjustment could hurt them financially.

Advantages of the ARM loan. The ARM's low initial interest rate and the borrower's ability to qualify for a larger mortgage top the list of advantages of adjustable-rate mortgages. ARMs are most appropriate for those who plan to hold the mortgage loans for no more than four years. Also, any time the interest rate gap between a fixed-rate loan and an adjustable-rate loan reaches 3 percent in favor of the ARM, an ARM loan with interest rate caps and a one-year Treasury bill constant maturity index should make sense to homebuyers. Many ARMs are now written with conversion privileges, allowing the mortgagors to convert to fixed-rate loans for a modest fee during a specified period. This enables borrowers to take advantage of falling interest rates if they desire to do so. One of the standard features of ARMs is no prepayment penalty.

Longer adjustment periods are available. Many borrowers prefer an ARM loan that won't adjust for several years. For example, the low initial rate may last for three, five, or seven years, then adjust once each year. Such loans would be called 3/1, 5/1, or 7/1 ARMs. Other options would be for loans that had an initial rate that lasted five years, then went to a fixed-rate loan at the prevailing rates available for the fifth year. This would be called a 5/25. There are 3/27s, 5/25s, 7/23s, or 10/30s. No one program is better for everyone, so each borrower must evaluate the possibilities based on his or her personal situation.

Disadvantages of the ARM loan. ARM borrowers bet against the lenders that interest rates will not rise to the extent that the maximum interest rate caps will be needed. The main disadvantages of the ARM loan are the uncertain amounts of future mortgage payments and the difficulty in calculating adjustments in interest rates as they occur. Lenders, of course, do the actual calculation of adjustments, but they have been known to make mistakes, and such mistakes can be expensive to the borrowers. Calculation details are spelled out in each loan document, but they are somewhat complicated and require the use of either a financial calculator or a handbook of ARM payment tables. For a borrower who wants to audit a lender's ARM adjustments without going to the trouble of research and math calculations, Loantech, Inc., a Gaithersburg, Maryland, mortgage consulting firm (1-800-888-6781), will do a complete individual ARM adjustment review for a fee, based on the terms of the loan document submitted.

FHA Adjustable-Rate Mortgage

Section 251 of the National Housing Act authorizes the Federal Housing Administration (FHA) to insure adjustable-rate mortgages on single-family properties. The interest rate is the sum of the index and the margin. The index changes, but the margin will remain the same over the life of the loan. The initial interest rate may be a result of combining the current one-year Treasury bill index with the margin at the time the loan is closed. This combination of components produces what is often called the **calculated interest rate.** Each FHA-approved lender is allowed to discount the calculated interest rate to a lower amount if local competition requires it, or the calculated interest rate may become the initial interest rate. The initial interest rate cannot be a rate higher than the current index plus margin.

Once the initial interest rate is set, annual adjustments to FHA ARMs must be calculated. The first interest rate adjustment may not occur sooner than 12 months from the due date of the first monthly payment or later than 18 months from that first designated payment date. In other words, the first adjustment must be made during a six-month period or it is forfeited. This time frame permits lenders to complete the collection or pooling of many mortgages for sale to secondary market institutions. Whatever date is designated as the initial interest rate adjustment date, all subsequent rate adjustments must be made on the anniversary of that first adjustment date.

Unlike the conventional ARM choice of index, all FHA ARMs must use the published "Constant Maturity of the One-Year Treasury Security" index, using the most recently available figure that applied exactly 30 calendar days before the designated change date. The new current index plus the constant margin rounded to the nearest one-eighth of one percentage point is the new calculated interest rate. It is then compared with the existing interest rate. If it is the same as the existing interest rate, no change is made to the existing rate. If it is up to 1 percent higher or lower than the existing interest rate, the new calculated interest rate becomes the new adjusted interest rate. If it is more than 1 percent higher or lower than the existing interest rate, the new adjusted interest rate is limited to a 1 percent increase or decrease of the existing interest rate.

The new adjusted interest rate becomes effective on the designated change date and is regarded as the existing interest rate until the next allowable change date. In no event may any future combination of interest rate adjustments exceed five percentage points higher or lower than the initial interest rate.

The FHA considers interest payable on the first day of the month following the month in which the interest accrued. Therefore, adjusted monthly mortgage payments resulting from the adjusted interest rate are not due until 30 days after the designated change date. No negative amortization is allowed with FHA ARMs. The FHA requires that payments be recalculated each year to provide for complete amortization of the outstanding principal balance over the remaining term of the loan at the new adjusted interest rate. Lenders must give borrowers at least 30 days' notice of any increase or decrease in the monthly mortgage payment amount. The adjustment notice must contain the date the adjustment notice is given, the ARM change date, the new existing interest rate, the amount of the new monthly mortgage payment, the current index used, the method of calculating the adjustment, and any other information that may be required to clarify the adjustment.

FHA required disclosure statement. All approved lenders making FHA adjustable-rate loans must provide each borrower with a mortgage loan information statement that includes a worst-case example form. The borrower must receive this statement and be given an opportunity to read the informative explanation before signing the borrower's certification on the loan application. Licensees are urged to obtain personal copies of the FHA adjustable-rate mortgage disclosure statement to use when counseling clients or advising customers.

Advantages of the FHA ARM. An FHA ARM has several advantages over a conventional ARM. Often, an FHA ARM bears a slightly lower interest rate because of the government insurance provided the lender. In addition, the FHA commonly uses more lenient qualification formulas. The down payment (required investment) also is lower in many cases, and the interest rate increase each year is limited to 1 percent, with an overall cap of 5 percent (conventional caps usually are 2 percent per year, with a 6 percent overall cap). FHA loans continue to be easier to assume than conventional loans, although the FHA has increased the requirements for assumption of FHA loans. The FHA now requires a review of the creditworthiness of each person seeking to assume an FHA-insured loan.

Disadvantages of the FHA ARM. The FHA imposes a maximum loan amount that differs from region to region, depending on the cost of living in each region. Also, the FHA requires an upfront mortgage insurance premium (UFMIP) of 1.5 percent, although this cost may be financed along with the mortgage. If FHA loans are repaid early, mortgagors may apply for partial refunds of the mortgage insurance premiums.

Bond Money for First-Time Homebuyers

States, counties, and cities can offer below-market mortgage financing by selling tax-free bonds. These loans are available to first-time homebuyers (who haven't owned a home for the previous three years). Sometimes divorced persons who want to buy their own home also qualify. These programs come and go, so check with local lenders for availability.

MORTGAGE INSURANCE

Conventional lenders usually require that the borrower pay for private mortgage insurance (PMI). PMI protects the lender if the borrower defaults on the loan. The *Homeowners Protection Act of 1998*, which became effective in 1999, established rules for automatic termination and borrower cancellation of PMI on home mortgages. These protections apply to certain home mortgages signed on or after July 29, 1999. These protections do not apply to government-insured FHA- or VA-guaranteed loans or to loans with lender-paid PMI.

For conventional home mortgages signed on or after July 29, 1999, PMI must, with certain exceptions, be terminated *automatically* when the borrower has achieved 22 percent equity in the home *based on the purchase price*, if the mortgage payments are current. PMI also can be canceled when the borrower *requests it*—with certain exceptions—when the borrower achieves 20 percent equity in the home based on the original property value, if the mortgage payments are current.

There are three exceptions for which the PMI may continue:

1. If the loan is "high-risk"
2. If the borrower has not been current on the payments within the year prior to the time for termination or cancellation
3. If the borrower has other liens on the property

The FHA Homebuyer Savings Plan has also reduced mortgage insurance premiums on loans originated after January 1, 2001, to 1.5 percent of the original loan amount from 2.25 percent. FHA has also eliminated the .5 percent premium for borrowers who have achieved 22 percent equity in their house, based on the lower of the purchase price or the appraisal.

WEB LINK

Fannie Mae Home Page: *www.fanniemae.com*

Freddie Mac Home Page: *www.freddiemac.com*

U.S. Department of Housing and Urban Development: FHA: *www.hud.gov/offices/hsg/fhahistory.cfm*

Federal Reserve Board: *www.federalreserve.gov*

U.S. Department of Veterans Affairs: *www.va.gov*

S U M M A R Y

Real estate licensees should assist their clients and customers in the initial two steps of prequalifying and shopping for a mortgage loan. Too often, the process begins instead with the loan application. Various proven tools and techniques exist for doing both before applying to a lender for a loan.

Fixed-rate mortgages remain popular. While the 30-year, fixed-rate mortgage is the most common, 15-year and biweekly mortgages are gaining in popularity. Adjustable-rate mortgages are less popular when interest rates are low. Conventional and FHA adjustable-rate mortgages are available. Each financing instrument has its own advantages and disadvantages, and licensees who understand the current and ever-changing mortgage market increase their chances for success in the business.

K E Y   T E R M S

adjustable-rate mortgage (ARM)	calculated interest rate	negative amortization
annual percentage rate (APR)	caps	PITI payment
biweekly mortgage	fixed-rate mortgage	refinance
	index	
	margin	

P R A C T I C E   E X A M

1. The FHA-required disclosure statement indicates the initial interest rate for an FHA ARM loan may remain in effect for up to how many months?
   a. 12
   b. 18
   c. 24
   d. 30

2. The primary elements a borrower uses to determine whether to accept an adjustable-rate mortgage are the index, the lender's margin, and the
   a. seller's income and credit history.
   b. housing expense ratio and total obligations ratio.
   c. calculated interest rate, initial interest rate, and interest rate caps.
   d. amount of the buydown and amount of negative amortization.

3. Of the recognized indexes used on ARM loans, which of the following is most volatile?
   a. Prime rate charged by money center banks
   b. One-year Treasury bill index
   c. LIBOR index
   d. Cost-of-funds index of the Federal Home Loan Bank, 11th District

4. Total interest rate increases on an FHA adjustable-rate loan may not exceed what percentage over the life of the loan?
   a. 5%
   b. 3%
   c. 2%
   d. 1%

5. On January 10, the one-year Treasury bill index was 4 percent. Southern Federal Savings Association used that index to write a new one-year adjustable-rate mortgage that included a 2 percent cap on annual interest rate increases. The margin was 2½ percent. What is the calculated interest rate contained in the new ARM loan above?
   a. 4%
   b. 6%
   c. 6½%
   d. 8%

6. Using the information in question 5, assume the index rose to 6½ percent in year two. What interest rate will be charged in year two?
   a. 8%
   b. 8½%
   c. 9%
   d. 9½%

7. A buyer takes out a $127,000, 30-year fixed-rate mortgage at 5½ percent. The mortgage payment factor is .0056779. Taxes for the year are $2,400, and insurance is $600. What will the buyer pay in monthly PITI payments?
   a. $721.09
   b. $771.09
   c. $921.09
   d. $971.09

8. The component of an adjustable-rate mortgage that does NOT usually change is the
   a. margin.
   b. index.
   c. points.
   d. calculated rate.

9. Jack purchased a new home at the FHA appraisal amount of $100,000 and financed it with an FHA mortgage loan. To what amount must he reduce the outstanding loan balance before he no longer has to pay the ½ percent annual mortgage insurance premium?
   a. $90,000
   b. $85,000
   c. $78,000
   d. $80,000

10. What is the index measuring the base interest rate paid on deposits between banks in the Eurodollar market that is used in many adjustable-rate mortgages?
    a. COFI
    b. MTA
    c. PRIME
    d. LIBOR

11. A borrower who is shopping for an acceptable ARM probably should reject a loan that has
    a. annual caps of more than 2%.
    b. a lifetime cap greater than 4%.
    c. a margin greater than 2%.
    d. annual caps of 2%.

12. What is the maximum amount of a buyer's closing costs that can be paid by the seller under conventional lending standards when the borrower is making a 5 percent down payment?
    a. 6% of the purchase price
    b. 4% of the loan amount
    c. 3% of the purchase price
    d. 3% of the loan amount

13. A woman is buying a new home and will make a 10 percent down payment. The beginning interest rate on her ARM loan is 7 percent. The buyer's sales associate prequalified the woman based on a payment from the factor table at 7 percent, plus escrow items (PITI). Which is correct?
    a. The sales associate should have qualified the buyer without the escrow items in the payment.
    b. The sales associate should have qualified the buyer at a 9 percent payment factor plus escrow items.
    c. The buyer can't get a 90 percent ARM loan; 80 percent is the maximum loan-to-value ratio.
    d. The sales associate should have qualified the buyer at a 9 percent payment factor without escrow items.

14. Marian is shopping for a new $150,000 mortgage. She expects to live in her new home for about four years. She can get a 30-year, 4.75 percent fixed-rate mortgage with principal and interest payments of $1,074.62 with no points. She can also get a 4.25 percent mortgage loan (payments of $1,023.26) with three points. How many months will it take Marian to break even on the points if she takes the lower interest rate loan, using simple arithmetic?
    a. 48.5
    b. 58.6
    c. 87.6
    d. 101

15. ARM loans are more popular
    a. than fixed-rate mortgages in most markets.
    b. when interest rates are low.
    c. for people who are risk-averse.
    d. when interest rates are high.

16. A man is shopping for a new loan and has narrowed the field to two choices. One is a 30-year, fixed-rate loan that has principal and interest payments of $940 per month. The other is a biweekly mortgage. What is the difference in the man's annual payments based on this information?
    a. $940
    b. No difference in payments but a big difference in interest saved
    c. No difference in payments and no difference in interest saved
    d. $470

17. When compared with a 30-year mortgage, a 15-year mortgage has
    a. more flexibility in repayment possibilities.
    b. slightly higher interest rates.
    c. slightly lower interest rates.
    d. lower monthly payments.

18. Popular literature shows dramatic interest savings from a 15-year loan versus a 30-year loan. What is true about most of these analyses?
    a. Amounts saved usually are less because income tax effects are not factored in.
    b. Amounts saved usually are less because opportunity costs of the additional payments required are not considered.
    c. They usually show that the amounts of interest saved are not substantial.
    d. Both a and b are true.

19. Disclosure of the annual percentage rate of interest need NOT
    a. be given to the borrower within three days of loan application.
    b. be computed to the nearest one-eighth of 1 percent.
    c. show the total financing cost in relation to the amount financed.
    d. be given to a prospective buyer of a single-family home who is paying all cash.

20. Which is true about a loan's effective interest rate?
    a. Each point equals a ½% increase in the lender's yield.
    b. Origination fees should be added to the points charged in making the calculation.
    c. Each point equals one-eighth of a 1% increase in the lender's yield, even if the loan is in force for less than five years.
    d. Origination fees should not be considered on an ARM based on index changes.

12

ACQUIRING FINANCING FOR THE PROPERTY

LEARNING OBJECTIVES

Upon completion of this chapter, you should be able to:

1. list three federal statutes that control the information a lender may obtain and consider when qualifying an applicant;

2. list the four basic loan processing procedures;

3. describe the characteristics of a nominee loan;

4. differentiate between qualifying the borrower and qualifying the property;

5. describe how lenders are using credit scoring to assist in the underwriting process;

6. itemize at least three sources of income that will be counted when qualifying a buyer;

7. list the components of a full title report;

8. describe the differences between an owner's title insurance policy and a lender's title insurance policy.

OVERVIEW

The regulatory overhaul following the financial crisis is resulting in big changes in how buyers get a mortgage. There are more protections against risky or complex mortgages. There are fewer choices of loans available, and the loans could be a little more expensive. Fewer borrowers will qualify. Lending standards are tighter today than at any time during the past 20 years.

The origination of a home mortgage is subject to a number of federal statutes, particularly the Equal Credit Opportunity Act (ECOA), the Consumer Credit Protection Act (Title I: Truth-in-Lending Act), and the Real Estate Settlement Procedures Act (RESPA). Together, these laws control the information a lender may obtain and consider in qualifying consumer mortgage loan applicants. They also dictate both the content and the form of information lenders must present to borrowers, the procedure for closing mortgage loan agreements, the documents to be used in closings, and the fees that may be charged.

Lenders are required by the Civil Rights Acts, and the amendments to them, not to discriminate against consumer mortgage loan applicants on the basis of race, color, national origin, religion, sex, age, or marital status. In addition, borrower rights have been better protected since passage of the Equal Credit Opportunity Act and the Federal Reserve Board of Governor's Regulation B, which implemented the act. The act requires fair consideration of consumer loan applications from women, minority races, part-time employees, and others who may have suffered prejudicial treatment in the past. Additionally, lenders may not discriminate based on the fact that all or part of the applicant's income comes from any public assistance program or on the fact that the applicant has exercised any right under any federal consumer credit protection law.

As a result of increasing concern about protection of consumer rights, most mortgage lenders have developed specific guidelines for loan underwriters to follow to ensure compliance with federal laws affecting consumer mortgage lending. Although the guidelines are protective of consumers' rights, they do not interfere with the analysis of an applicant's credit standing. The purpose of such guidelines is to prevent homebuyers from being victimized, not to guarantee that a loan will be approved. In the final analysis, good underwriting policies and practices by a lender combine compliance with the continual search for financial safety and streamlined processing. Licensees can serve themselves and their customers well by becoming knowledgeable about residential mortgage loan processing and closing.

To accomplish the above-stated goals of government agencies and originating lenders, the following four basic **loan processing procedures** have been developed:

1. Determining a borrower's ability to repay the loan
2. Estimating the value of the property being pledged as collateral to guarantee this repayment
3. Researching and analyzing the marketability of the collateral's title
4. Preparing the documents necessary to close the loan transaction

Most lenders follow loan processing procedures that reflect a combined concern for the borrower's credit ability and the collateral's value. Some loan transactions require an emphasis of one factor over the other, but generally both borrower credit and collateral value are essential determinants in the real estate finance loan processing equation.

Loan underwriting is the evaluation of the risks involved when issuing a new mortgage. This process involves qualifying the borrower and the property to determine whether they meet the minimum requirements established by the lender, investor, or secondary market in which the loan probably will be sold.

TRENDS IN THE MORTGAGE MARKET

Starting in 2010, lending standards became tight due to the financial crisis and plummeting housing values. New regulations require:

- lenders to retain at least 5 percent of the loans that are securitized, except for those fully documented fixed-rate loans that are considered "safe";

- stricter limits on prepayment penalties or fees that lenders charge when a loan is paid off early;

- borrowers to show they can pay the loan, and lenders will have to require much more documentation—self-employed borrowers may have more problems getting a loan also; and

- creation of management companies to facilitate the ordering of appraisals by lenders and also act as insulators from lender pressure in arriving at market value.

These changes were the result of loose regulation during the bubble years of real estate lending. Wall Street was responsible for many of the problems, with pressure to securitize more and more mortgages. The result was many fraudulent mortgages.

Mortgage Fraud

Florida had the dubious distinction in the years 2006 through 2009 of having more mortgage fraud cases than any other state. The Federal Bureau of Investigation (FBI) has made mortgage fraud one of its top priorities in the last five years because of the huge financial losses to banks and investors.

Mortgage brokers, appraisers, real estate licensees, sellers, buyers, builders, and others have been found guilty of financial fraud, identity theft, mail fraud, and other crimes, carrying sentences of up to 30 years in prison. The descriptions of all types of mortgage fraud may help new licensees recognize violations and take action to get out of such transactions.

FBI fraud cases include the following:

■ **Property flipping**—Property is purchased, improperly appraised at a higher value, then quickly sold. This practice involves fraudulent appraisals, doctored loan documentation, inflated buyer income, etc.

■ **Silent second mortgage**—The buyer borrows the down payment from a seller through the issuance of an undisclosed second mortgage. The lender on the first mortgage thinks the buyer has invested his own money in a down payment, when in fact, the funds are borrowed. This is also done sometimes by builders who have a large inventory of unsold homes. In other cases, a buyer agrees to pay a much-inflated price for property, with the difference in the inflated value and the fair value of the home in a "disappearing second" mortgage held by the mortgage broker. After the closing, the mortgage broker tears up the second mortgage papers, then sells the loan as a 75 percent loan-to-value ("safer") loan when the borrower truly paid nothing down.

■ **Nominee loans**—The identity of the borrower is concealed through the use of a nominee (also called a *straw buyer*) who allows the borrower to use the nominee's name and credit history to apply for the loan.

■ **Stolen identity**—The applicant's name, personal identifying information, and credit history is used without the true person's knowledge.

■ **Equity skimming**—An investor may use a straw buyer, false income documents, or false credit reports to obtain a mortgage in the straw buyer's name. After closing, the straw buyer signs over the property with a quit claim deed to an investor. The investor rents the property without making payments on the mortgage until foreclosure takes place several months later.

■ **Air loans**—This loan is totally false. The mortgage broker invents a property and a borrower. The broker sets up a bank of telephones for verifications and uses one phone number as the employer's, another as the appraiser's, another as the credit agency's, etc.

■ **Chunking**—A swindler holds a seminar promising to show investors how to get rich buying property with no money down. Using the investors' personal information, the swindler submits multiple mortgage applications, pocketing the loan proceeds.

The FBI has compiled a list of activities it believes could indicate mortgage fraud, and that includes:

■ **inflated appraisals**, usually involving the exclusive use of one appraiser;

■ **higher than customary commissions** and fees paid to brokers and appraisers;

■ **falsification of loan applications**, with mortgage brokers showing buyers how to falsify the application, or asking a borrower to sign a blank application;

- **fake supporting loan documentation**, with buyers being asked to sign blank employee or bank forms;
- **purchase loans disguised as refinance**, typically requiring less documentation by the lender.

To protect themselves from becoming a victim of mortgage fraud, consumers should do the following:

- **Get referrals** for real estate and mortgage professionals. Check the licenses of the industry professionals with state, county, or city regulatory agencies.
- **Be suspicious because if it sounds too good to be true, it probably is.** An outrageous promise of extraordinary profit in a short period of time signals a problem.
- **Be wary of strangers and unsolicited contacts**, as well as high-pressure sales techniques.
- **Look at written information** to include recent comparable sales in the area and other documents such as tax assessments to verify the value of the property.
- **Understand what they are signing** and agreeing to: If they do not understand, they should re-read the documents, or seek assistance from an attorney.
- **Make sure the name on the application matches** the name on your identification.
- **Review the title history** to determine if the property has been sold multiple times within a short period because that could mean that this property has been "flipped" and the value falsely inflated.
- **Know and understand the terms of the mortgage.** Check the information against the information in the loan documents to ensure they are accurate and complete.
- **Never sign any loan documents that contain blanks,** leaving the consumer vulnerable to fraud.

FLORIDA OFFICE OF FINANCIAL REGULATION

The Florida Office of Financial Regulation oversees loan originators and mortgage brokers under the provisions of Chapter 494, FS. As a result of the housing and financial crisis, Chapter 494 was changed in many areas to better protect Florida's consumers.

Effective January 1, 2010

Persons who engage in loan modification activities must be licensed under Chapter 494.

Loan originators working as employees of lenders are no longer exempt from licensing. Loan modification activities require the borrower's written consent. The modifier may charge fees only after performing all services under the agreement, and only if the modification results in material benefit to the borrower.

Effective September 1, 2010

All mortgage broker, mortgage brokerage business, correspondent mortgage lender, and mortgage lender licenses issued before October 1, 2010, expired on December 31, 2010. Persons with an active mortgage broker license issued before October 1, 2010, who applied for the new loan originator license between October 1, 2010, and December 31, 2010, may continue to operate until the Office of Financial Regulation either approves or denies the loan originator license. The office shall have 60 days to issue a deficiency letter and 180 days to approve or deny a completed application.

Effective October 1, 2010

Applicants and licensees must submit filings on uniform forms via the Nationwide Mortgage Licensing System and Registry (NMLS). The application review will include not only a criminal background check but also a review of the applicant's credit history. Applicants who have a bankruptcy or who have charge-offs must provide a satisfactory explanation.

License titles were changed as follows: Individual Mortgage Broker to Loan Originator and Mortgage Brokerage Business to Mortgage Broker. Mortgage Lender license is unchanged. The following license titles were repealed: Mortgage Business Schools, Correspondent Mortgage Lenders, and Savings Clause Mortgage Lenders.

A Mortgage Broker Guaranty Trust Fund, somewhat like the Real Estate Recovery Fund, was established, with payments into the fund by applicants and licensees. Payment from the fund in settlement of a claim against a licensee will result in revocation of the license.

All licenses issued under Chapter 494 must be renewed annually by December 31 via the NMLS. A criminal background check and a credit report are required for each renewal

The principal loan originator or branch manager must sign and date the mortgage broker agreement, and include the loan originator's unique NMLS identifier. Fees received by the business (mortgage broker) from a borrower must be identified as a loan origination fee, with the exception of application and third-party fees. Fees must be disclosed in dollar amounts.

The office may summarily suspend a license if there is reason to believe that a licensee poses an immediate, serious danger to the public's health, safety, or welfare, if the licensee has been arrested for any felony crime or any crime involving fraud, dishonesty, breach of trust, money laundering, or any other act of moral turpitude.

Mortgage lenders must meet specific net worth requirements, depending on the activities of the lender, and provide financial statements to the office.

The law added penalties for the following:

- Attempting to manipulate or influence an appraiser's evaluation of a property
- Being convicted of, or entering a plea of guilty or nolo contendere to, regardless of adjudication, any felony
- Having a loan originator, mortgage broker, or mortgage lender license, or the equivalent of such license, revoked in any jurisdiction
- Engaging in unfair, deceptive, or misleading advertising

Maximum fines for violations of Chapter 494 were increased to $25,000 for each count or separate offense. Persons who are guilty of unlicensed activity may be fined up to $1,000 per day to a maximum $25,000. The Office of Financial Regulation must report disciplinary actions to the NMLS.

Some penalties carry lifetime bans from licensure.

Changes to Florida's Appraisal Laws

In 2010, the Florida Legislature amended Chapter 475, Part II, to establish regulation over appraisal management companies. These companies retain appraisers to perform appraisal services for clients, or act as intermediaries between clients and appraisers to facilitate the clients' contracting with appraisers.

Appraisal management companies must be registered with the DBPR. Owners, directors, officers, or partners, depending on the type of entity, must be registered with the department and pass a criminal background check. All must sign a pledge to comply with the Uniform Standards of Professional Appraisal Practice (USPAP). These persons may not have had a registration or license to practice any profession denied or revoked.

For example, if Bayfront National Bank has taken a loan application, the bank may contact XYZ Appraisal Managers, Inc. to arrange for the required appraisal for the loan. XYZ will then assign one or more appraisers from its appraisal panel to prepare the appraisal report. XYZ would violate the law if it:

- instructs an appraiser to violate the USPAP;
- accepts an appraisal assignment if the fee is contingent on a predetermined result;
- contracts with an appraiser whose license has been suspended or revoked; or
- attempts to influence the appraisal by:
    - withholding payment or future business,
    - promising future business,
    - conditioning a request for service based on a preliminary estimate from the appraiser,
    - requesting a preliminary valuation from the appraiser,
    - providing to the appraiser a desired value for a subject property,
    - allowing the removal of an appraiser from an appraiser panel without prior written notice, or
    - paying for a second appraisal without cause.

In Practice

Refuse to get involved in questionable practices involving mortgage loans. State and federal authorities promise vigorous enforcement of the law.

QUALIFYING THE BORROWER

The framework for current real estate financing is the 30-year amortization schedule and regular monthly payments of principal and interest. In addition, mortgagees currently can lend up to 100 percent of a property's value. High loan-to-value ratios combined with long-term loan amortization payment schedules require that a lender look to the credit of the borrower as the primary protection.

Even though lenders using insured or guaranteed programs of real estate finance do not bear the risks of default directly, they still must follow the directions of their guaranteeing agencies and carefully screen loan applicants to derive some reasonable estimate of borrowers' ability to pay and their inclinations to meet their contractual obligations responsibly. Thus, a great effort is made to check and evaluate thoroughly a potential mortgagor's credit history and current financial status to predict her future economic stability.

Loan Application

Forms To Go

When a licensee works with a buyer, one of the services the licensee can offer is that of helping the buyer obtain financing. Before the buyer goes to the lender to make an application, the licensee should provide a list of items the buyer will need. A Mortgage Loan Application Checklist is shown in Forms To Go, Appendix B.

Data verification. The loan processor will verify the information included in the application by actually checking with the various references given, the banks where deposits are held, and the applicant's employer.

Deposits. The borrower must sign a separate deposit verification form for each bank account, authorizing the bank to reveal to the lender the current balance in the borrower's account. Under the Federal Right to Privacy Act, the bank cannot release such confidential information without a verification form. The knowledge that the loan processor can verify account amounts usually is enough incentive for the borrower to be truthful in reporting financial information. When the deposit balances are verified, the appropriate entries are made in the applicant's file.

Employment. The applicant also is required to sign an employment verification form authorizing the employer to reveal confidential information concerning the applicant's job status. Not only will the applicant's wages or salary and length of employment be verified but the employer also will be requested to offer an opinion of the applicant's job attitude and give a prognosis for continued employment and prospects for advancement. Employment may be checked again before closing.

Credit report. Simultaneously with the gathering of financial and employment information, the loan processor sends a formal request for the borrower's credit report to a local company offering this service. The credit report is a central part of the loan approval process, and the lender relies on it heavily. Of the two types of credit reports, consumer credit and mortgage credit, the discussion here centers on the latter.

A credit report is the result of the compilation of information accumulated from a thorough check of the creditors indicated on the loan application, as well as a check of the public records to discover whether any lawsuits are pending against the applicant. When completed, the credit search company sends the loan processor a confidential report of its findings.

This report usually states the applicant's (and co-applicant's) age, address, status as a tenant or owner, and length of residency at his or her current address and includes a brief employment history and credit profile, both past and present. The credit profile itemizes the status of current and past accounts, usually identified by industry, such as banks, department and specialty stores, and finance companies. In addition, it indicates the quality and dates of the payments made, and their regularity; delinquency, and any outstanding balances also are reported. This payment history is the most important part of the report because it indicates how well the applicant has managed debt over time. Underwriters view a person's past behavior as the best indicator of future attitude toward debt repayment. Research tends to reinforce these opinions, indicating that slow and erratic payers generally retain those attitudes when securing new loans and that prompt and steady payers also are consistent in meeting their future obligations. As a result, lenders pay careful attention to the last section of a credit report, which indicates an applicant's attitude toward debt and his or her payment pattern.

When a credit report is returned revealing a series of erratic and delinquent payments, the loan is usually denied at this point and the file closed. If an applicant is denied a loan because of adverse information in a credit report, the applicant has the right to inspect a summary of that report, to challenge inaccuracies, and to require corrections to be made (see the most current RESPA-required brochure, *Settlement Costs: A HUD Guide*). If one or two unusual entries stand out in a group of otherwise satisfactory transactions, the applicant will be asked to explain these deviations.

As with many standardized procedures, credit reporting has become computerized, dramatically shortening the time needed for completing a check. In exchange for time efficiency, however, credit-reporting bureaus risk sacrificing the borrower's confidentiality. The fraudulent use of credit reports is increasing now that information is so easily accessed. Credit reports should be used only by the persons or institutions requesting the information and only for the purposes stated. As a result of increased seller financing, credit bureaus are receiving more requests from agents and sellers to check the credit of potential purchasers. To protect a buyer's confidentiality, most credit agencies insist on receiving the buyer's written permission before issuing any information.

After the deposit and employment verifications are returned with acceptable information and a favorable credit report is obtained, the lending officer makes a thorough credit evaluation of the data collected before continuing with the loan process.

Evaluation of Credit Ability

Despite the standardization of the detailed guidelines used in the lending process, the one area allowing for the greatest amount of latitude in interpretation is the analysis and evaluation of a borrower's credit ability. A degree of subjective personal involvement may be introduced into an otherwise strongly objective and structured format by an evaluator's unintentional bias or by a loan company's changing policies.

In addition, credit standards are altered periodically to reflect a lender's changing monetary position. When money is scarce, standards are more stringent; when money is plentiful, standards are lowered. An applicant who qualifies for a loan at one time may not at another. Thus, although a credit analyst is governed by guidelines, rules, and regulations, the criteria fluctuate with the analyst's discretionary powers. In the long run, a lender's success is demonstrated by a low rate of default on approved loans and by the fact that no discrimination complaints have been filed.

Credit Scoring

One of the most significant changes in mortgage lending has been the use of credit scores to better evaluate a borrower's ability to repay.

Credit scoring uses statistical samples to predict how likely it is that a borrower will pay back a loan. To develop a model, the lender selects a large random sample of its borrowers, analyzing characteristics that relate to creditworthiness. Each of the characteristics is assigned a weight based on how strong a predictor it is. Credit scores treat each person objectively because the same standards apply to everyone. Credit scores are blind to demographic or cultural differences among people.

The most commonly used credit score today is known as a **FICO score,** named after the company that developed it, Fair, Isaac, & Co. FICO scores range from 300 to 850. The lower the score, the greater the risk of default.

Freddie Mac has found that borrowers with credit scores above 660 are more likely to repay the mortgage, and underwriters can do a basic review of the file for completeness. For applicants with scores between 620 and 660, the underwriter is required to do a comprehensive review. A very cautious review would be made for persons with credit scores below 620.

Is credit scoring valid? With credit scoring, lenders can evaluate millions of applicants consistently and impartially on many different characteristics. To be statistically valid, the system must be based on a big enough sample. When properly designed, the system promotes fast, impartial decisions.

Fair, Isaac has recently completed NextGen®, designed to more precisely define the risk of borrowers because it analyzes more criteria than the old model. Using the new model, lenders can evaluate credit profiles of high-risk borrowers in terms of degrees, rather than lumping them into the same category.

What information does credit scoring use? The scoring models use the following information when evaluating a score:

- Of the score, 35 percent is determined by payment history with higher weight for recent history. If late payments, collections, and/or bankruptcy appear in the credit report, they are subtracted from the score.

- Outstanding debt is very close in importance to payment history—30 percent of the total score. Many scoring models evaluate the amount of debt compared with the credit limits. If the amount owed is close to the credit limit, it affects the score negatively.

- Of the score, 15 percent is the result of credit history. A long history is better if payments are always on time.

- The score assigns 10 percent to very recent history and "inquiries" for new credit. If the applicant has applied for credit in many places recently, it will negatively affect the score. This problem occurs when a person goes car shopping. Sales associates at each car lot will ask for the consumer's Social Security number in order to pull a credit report (at "no charge"). The shopper has no idea that as more reports are ordered, the shopper's credit rating declines.

- Finally, 10 percent is based on the mix of credit, including car loans, credit cards, and mortgages. Too many credit cards will hurt a person's credit score. In some models, loans from finance companies or title loan companies will also hurt the score.

F I G U R E 12.1 ■ Results on FICO Score from Certain Financial Decisions

Assume that your current FICO score is 707 (very good).
This table shows the likely effect on your score based on the following actions:

Action	New FICO Range
You currently have a combined revolving balance of $2,230 and you pay down $750 on the balance	
Paying your bills on time is a substantial factor affecting your FICO score. Generally speaking, if you have no negative items on your file, your score will remain fairly stable as you continue to pay your bills on time.	
If you have some history of late payments, how recently they occurred is important. The more recently they happened, the more impact they will likely have on your score. As they age, their impact on your score will gradually lessen.	707 to 727
Max out your credit cards	
Carrying extremely high balances on all of your revolving accounts makes you look "maxed out" on your available credit. It is often considered a high-risk trait by lenders and the FICO score.	
In this simulation, the impact to your FICO score will depend on how high your current balances are on your revolving accounts. If you already carry high balances, the impact will probably be minimal. The impact will be more noticeable if you currently have a low or medium balance.	637 to 687
Apply for and receive a new credit card with a credit limit of $3,000	
Consumers seeking and obtaining new credit are generally riskier than consumers who are not. The impact on your FICO score will vary, depending on your current credit profile. The score takes into consideration the level of your existing credit history (recently opened files versus more mature files, for example), the amount of recently opened credit you currently have on file, and other factors.	
This simulation is based on your applying for and receiving a new credit card with a limit of at least $3,000.	697 to 717
Miss payments on all accounts with a payment due	
FICO scores evaluate late payment information in a variety of ways—in terms of the *frequency* of missed payments, the *recency* of the missed payments and the *level of delinquency* (how late the payment is).	
In this simulation, the impact on your score of missing a payment will depend on your current status and the level of the delinquency. For example, the impact will probably be more substantial if you miss a payment this month, and you currently have a spotless or relatively clean credit report. There will be less impact on the score if you currently have multiple negative items on your credit report.	582 to 632

SOURCE: Fair, Isaac & Co.

To improve the credit score, persons should pay bills on time, pay down outstanding balances, and not take on new debt. It may take a long time to improve the score significantly. See Figure 12.1 for examples of the effects on the FICO credit score caused by actions a potential borrower might take.

Getting a mortgage loan is more difficult for some people. During the years 2002 through 2006, the capital markets, particularly hedge funds, purchased from lenders what are called subprime mortgages. These were mortgages made to people who ordinarily would not have qualified for financing. In many cases, little or no documentation was required. Lending standards are now much stricter, and persons with poor credit find it almost impossible to get financing for a house purchase.

Because of the default rate, many lenders that made mortgage loans to self-employed persons have gone out of business. Lenders that still offer the loans have made it tough. The self-employed will need the following:

- **More documentation.** Now, small business owners will need more documentation, including two years of tax returns, profit-and-loss statements, bank statements, and proof that they've been in business for at least two years.

- **More money down.** They'll also need a bigger down payment. It may take 20 percent down to qualify.

- **Great credit.** A credit score lower than 700 probably will result in a turndown.

WEB LINK

HSH Associates, Financial Publishers: *www.hsh.com*
Fannie Mae Home Page: *www.fanniemae.com*
Freddie Mac Home Page: *www.freddiemac.com*
FHA Home Page: *www.hud.gov/fha/fhahome.html*
Federal Reserve Board: *www.federalreserve.gov*
U.S. Department of Veterans Affairs: *www.va.gov/*
Fair, Isaac & Co.: *www.fairisaac.com*

The quantity and quality of an applicant's income are the two major considerations in determining ability to support a family and make the required monthly loan payments. Analysts consider the **quantity of income**—the total income—when they review a loan application. Not only is the regular salary of a family's primary supporter basic to the analysis but also a spouse's full income usually is accepted. Extra sources of income also may be included in the analysis if circumstances warrant it.

Any bonuses will be accepted as income only if they are received on a regular basis. If commissions are a large part of an applicant's income base, the history of past earnings will be scrutinized to estimate the stability of this income as a regular source for an extended time period. Overtime wages are not included in the analysis unless they have been—and will be—earned consistently. Pensions, interest, and dividends are treated as full income, although it is recognized that interest and dividends fluctuate over time and could stop if an investment were cashed out.

A second job is accepted as part of the regular monthly income if it can be established that the job has existed for approximately two years and there is good reason to believe it will continue. Child support also can be included in the determination of monthly income, but only if it is the result of a court order and has a proven track record. Government entitlement funds must also be considered.

In addition to its total quantity, a loan analyst pays careful attention to the **quality of income.** An applicant's employer will be asked for an opinion of job stability and possible advancement. Length of time on the job no longer carries the importance it once did. Applicants whose employment records show frequent shifts in job situations that result in upward mobility each time will be given full consideration. Lenders will, however, be wary of an applicant who drifts from one job classification to another and cannot seem to become established in any specific type of work.

When the accumulated data strongly support a positive or negative decision, the loan underwriter's decision is easy, and minimal use of discretion is needed. However, numerous borderline cases make it difficult for a loan officer to form objective judgments. In such a case, the loan officer schedules an in-depth personal interview with the applicant during which questions regarding data appearing on the credit report are clarified or mistakes in bank balances can be explained. More often, however, the loan officer merely wishes to visit with the applicant to observe and probe her attitudes regarding the purchase of the property and the repayment of the prospective loan. Thus, although a person's credit history can be measured objectively, personal character is subject to interpretation.

After reviewing all of the information provided in the application as well as the other data collected, the loan officer decides either to approve or to disapprove the loan application. If the officer judges a loan application to be unacceptable, he or she states the reasons for the rejection, the parties to the loan are informed, and the file is closed.

QUALIFYING THE COLLATERAL

Despite the current trend toward emphasizing a borrower's financial ability as the loan-granting criterion, real estate lenders and guarantors are practical and fully understand that life is filled with events beyond one's control. Death is a possibility that can abruptly eliminate a family's wage earner. Economic conditions can exert devastating financial impact. Corporate downsizing and layoffs have resulted in hardship for many families. Honest mistakes in personal decisions can result in bankruptcies, often damaging or destroying credit.

To reduce the risk of loss, real estate lenders look to the value of the collateral (the real property) as the basic underlying assurance for recovery of their investments in a default situation. The recent drop in home values has made the valuation process more difficult. The old definition of market value that excluded comparables when the sale was under duress has been modified so that some foreclosed properties are used as comparable sales.

DISCUSSION EXERCISE 12.1

Which do you consider the more important factor in granting or denying a mortgage application: the borrower's ability to make the required payments or the value of the collateral? Why?

ANALYZING THE TITLE

The assurance of good title is as essential to a loan's completion as are the borrower's credit and the collateral's value. In anticipation of issuing a loan, the loan officer secures a title report on the collateral property. The components of a full title report are a survey, a physical inspection of the collateral, and a search of the records to determine all the interests in a property. Normally, property interests are perfected through the appropriate filing and recording of standard notices. A recorded deed notifies the world that a grantee has the legal fee simple title to the property. A recorded construction lien, for example, is notice of another's interest in the property.

In Florida, two methods have been used to obtain assurance of good title: (1) the abstract and attorney's opinion of title and (2) title insurance. Title insurance is preferred. If title is later found to be bad, and an attorney's opinion was used, the buyer or lender would have to sue the attorney to recover, but the attorney may not have the financial strength to reimburse for the loss. Lenders prefer title insurance, but whichever method is used, the title report should provide the loan officer and the lender's attorney with all available information relevant to the legal status of the subject property, as well as any interests revealed by constructive notice. This title search requirement represents another effort by the lender to protect the loan investment. Because title insurance is most lenders' and buyers' method of choice, it is discussed here.

Title Insurance

Title insurance companies combine the abstracting process with a program of insurance that guarantees the validity and accuracy of the title search. A purchaser of title insurance can rely on the insurance company's assets to back up its guarantee of a property's marketable title. This guarantee is evidenced by a policy of title insurance. Most financial institutions now require that a title policy be issued to them for the face amount of a loan. Insurance is defined simply as coverage against loss.

When a title insurance policy is issued to a lender, it is usually in the American Land Title Association (ALTA) form. While a standard title policy insures against losses overlooked in the search of the recorded chain of title, an ALTA policy expands this standard coverage to include many unusual risks, such as forgeries, incompetency of parties involved in issuing documents pertaining to the transfer of ownership, legal status of parties involved in the specific loan negotiations, surveying errors, and other possible off-record defects. Some additional risks can be and usually are covered by special endorsements to an insurance policy. These could include protection against any unrecorded easements or liens, rights of parties in possession of the subject property, mining claims, water rights, and additional negotiated special items pertinent to the property involved. Participants in the secondary mortgage market (Fannie Mae, Freddie Mac, and Ginnie Mae) generally require the expanded ALTA policy for the added protection it provides. Many lenders use the phrase "an ALTA policy" when describing an extended-coverage policy.

Surveys

Whether the abstract and opinion of title method or the title insurance policy method is used, a property's title is searched by an experienced abstractor who prepares a report of those recorded documents that clearly affect the quality of ownership. In addition, lenders usually require a survey of the collateral property as a condition for a new loan. Although many properties are part of subdivisions that have been engineered and described by licensed and registered surveyors and engineers, some owners might have enlarged their homes or made additions to the improvements since the original survey. These might not meet the various setback restrictions set forth in the local zoning laws. Some properties might have been resubdivided, while others now might have encroachment problems.

An ALTA survey is a boundary survey prepared in a way that meets minimum standards adopted by the American Land Title Association/American Congress on Surveying and Mapping (ALTA/ACSM). It's much more than just a boundary survey of the land with flags at the corners. An ALTA survey shows improvements, easements, rights-of-way, and other encumbrances that affect land ownership.

The surveyor must have a current title commitment. The title commitment includes the legal description of the property and legal descriptions of any easements and encumbrances. The surveyor works closely with the title insurance company, as they depend on the others' work. The surveyor must show any encroachments, including pertinent information. The certification language of the ALTA survey includes the names of the parties, including the buyer, seller, title company, and lender.

Defects

If a defect is found, sometimes called a *cloud on the title*, the loan process does not continue until this cloud is cleared to the lender's satisfaction. Such a cloud could be an unsatisfied construction lien, an income tax lien, a property tax lien, an easement infraction, an encroachment, or a zoning violation. Sometimes a borrower's name is not correct on the deed, an error exists in the legal description, or the deed has a faulty acknowledgment or lacks the appropriate signatures. Because of the many complexities in a real estate transaction, there are possibilities for defects to appear in a title search and property survey. It is the abstractor's responsibility to discover and report them.

In certain instances where clouds are difficult to remove by ordinary means, they must be cleared by filing suits to quiet title. After appropriate evidence is submitted, a judge removes or modifies an otherwise damaging defect in a title. The loan process can continue when a clear chain of title is shown on the public records.

S U M M A R Y

The housing and financial crisis has resulted in tighter loan processing guidelines. Appraisal management companies have become a very important factor in the mortgage lending process. Many mortgage brokers have gone out of business, and those that remain are more carefully regulated.

The process of obtaining a real estate loan includes four steps: qualifying a borrower, evaluating the collateral, analyzing the title, and closing the loan transaction.

Beginning with an application to obtain a loan, the borrower's credit, financial condition, and personal attitudes are analyzed to determine his or her ability and willingness to honor debts and repay the loan as agreed. Current assets and employment are verified, a credit rating is obtained, and often a private interview is held between the borrower and loan officer to estimate certain credit characteristics. Other basic criteria used to determine the applicant's creditworthiness include gross monthly earnings of approximately four times the required monthly mortgage payment (sometimes higher for large loans), stability of earnings, and a good prognosis for continued employment and advancement.

Once the loan applicant's credit is accepted, either a staff appraiser or an independent fee appraiser analyzes the value of the real estate to be pledged as collateral. A certified appraisal report offering the appraiser's opinion of the subject property's value is submitted to the loan officer.

After the borrower's credit and the collateral's value are verified, the legal status of the property's title is examined and analyzed carefully, usually by a trained abstractor. The abstract is delivered to the lender's attorney for an opinion of accuracy and validity. Because of the growing activity of this nation's secondary mortgage market and its concurrent necessity for added protection, lenders generally require title insurance to guarantee the title search.

Finally, after approval of the borrower's credit, the collateral's value, and the title's marketability, the loan processor prepares the documents necessary for closing. With the delivery of the funds to the seller and the recording of the necessary papers transferring title, the loan transaction is completed.

KEY TERMS

automated underwriting	FICO score	quality of income
automated valuation	loan processing procedures	quantity of income
computer valuation	loan underwriting	
credit scoring	paperless mortgage	

PRACTICE EXAM

1. Qualifying the buyer has to do with income and assets. Qualifying the property has to do with the
   a. income, credit report, and appraisal.
   b. appraisal, survey, and title report.
   c. appraisal, title report, and credit report.
   d. survey, title report, and income.

2. A lender, interested in evaluating an applicant's willingness to pay, reviews
   a. income.
   b. assets.
   c. the credit report.
   d. all of the above.

3. A federally related loan transaction is covered under RESPA guidelines if it involves
   a. a 100-acre tract of land.
   b. an apartment complex of 60 units.
   c. a one-family to four-family home.
   d. all of the above.

4. Rob has a FICO credit score of 725. He pays an additional $1,000 down on his installment debt. His FICO score will most likely
   a. decline because he has less debt.
   b. increase because he has less debt.
   c. decline because he has less credit.
   d. be unaffected unless he does this for at least three months running.

5. What is given greatest weight in calculating the FICO credit score?
   a. Outstanding debt
   b. Credit history
   c. Payment history, with higher weight for recent history
   d. Recent "inquiries" for new credit

6. What is the term given to a fraudulent mortgage in which the mortgage broker invents both a property and a borrower?
   a. Chunking
   b. Nominee loan
   c. Air loan
   d. Silent second

7. The maximum fine for each violation that can be levied against a Florida mortgage loan originator or mortgage broker under Chapter 494 was increased to
   a. $5,000.
   b. $10,000.
   c. $25,000.
   d. $75,000.

8. Joan earns $1,000 per week. Based on Fannie Mae's 28 percent housing expense ratio guidelines, what monthly payment would she qualify for?
   a. $1,213.33
   b. $1,120.00
   c. $1,000.00
   d. $867.33

9. Bonuses are acceptable as income on a loan application, provided that they
   a. are actually collected.
   b. are regular occurrences.
   c. exceed $2,000 per year.
   d. total less than $2,000 per year.

10. A second job will NOT be counted as a source of income on a loan application if it
    a. pays less than $2,000 per year.
    b. is likely to continue.
    c. has been held for at least two years.
    d. is temporary.

11. The guidelines for loan underwriting are tightly structured. The one facet that allows the most subjectivity on the part of the lender's evaluation is the
    a. credit ability.
    b. amount of debt.
    c. asset valuation.
    d. income quantity.

12. The primary assurance to the lender if the borrower defaults on the loan is the
    a. borrower's income.
    b. borrower's assets.
    c. borrower's net worth.
    d. property value.

13. A title policy offering coverage over and above the standard coverage is which of the following types of policies?
    a. Mortgagor's
    b. Fannie Mae
    c. Owner's
    d. ALTA

14. Because of the financial crisis, lender standards have become more
    a. lenient.
    b. strict.
    c. relaxed in the evaluation of credit.
    d. relaxed in the evaluation of income.

15. When a loan officer evaluates a credit report, the most important part of the report is the
    a. employment history.
    b. payment history.
    c. public records section.
    d. applicant's current address.

16. The employment verification is a NOT a check on the applicant's
    a. length of employment.
    b. salary.
    c. prognosis for continued employment.
    d. assets.

17. The components that together make a title report complete are a physical inspection of the collateral property, a search of the public records, and a(n)
    a. abstract of title.
    b. title insurance policy.
    c. satisfaction of previous mortgage document.
    d. survey of the property.

18. Which action will NOT negatively affect a FICO score?
    a. Applying for credit in several places
    b. Slow payment history
    c. High balances on credit cards
    d. Paying down debt

19. If a cloud on title exists that cannot be easily removed by ordinary means, a court case is often the result. The legal action is called a suit
    a. for certiori.
    b. to quiet title.
    c. for partition.
    d. for declaratory judgment.

20. The most common credit scoring used by lenders today was developed by
    a. Fanning and Investors Company.
    b. ING Investments.
    c. Fannie Mae.
    d. Fair, Isaac, & Co.

CLOSING REAL ESTATE TRANSACTIONS

LEARNING OBJECTIVES

Upon completion of this chapter, you should be able to:

1. name the steps that a sales associate must follow after writing a contract to ensure a timely closing;

2. list the things that a sales associate should do after a closing;

3. describe the reasons why a licensee might not want to personally order repairs on a property and what steps can be taken to protect the sales associate from liability;

4. list at least four objectives of a preclosing inspection;

5. describe the reasons a real estate sales associate should provide closing documents to the buyer and seller at least one day in advance of a closing;

6. describe the methods lenders use to set up an escrow account for prepaid taxes, hazard insurance, and private mortgage insurance;

7. calculate prepaid interest for a new loan;

8. calculate the expenses on the closing statement;

9. describe the most significant change to the HUD-1 Settlement Statement; and

10. prepare and review a HUD-1 Settlement Statement.

OVERVIEW

Once the real estate contract has been signed, the licensee's work has just begun. The parties to a transaction expect their sales associate personally to monitor and coordinate all the details of their closing. While the licensee may believe he has "passed the torch" to the next group of professionals (lenders and closing agents), the buyer and seller continue to look to their sales associate to coordinate all the details of the transaction.

A sales associate must be familiar with the documents that will be presented to the parties at the closing table. One of the most important documents, the HUD-1 Settlement Statement, relates to the financial side of the transaction. A closing statement is, in effect, the purchase and sales agreement reduced to numbers. The sales associate must understand each number in the statement and be able to explain it clearly to the buyer or seller. Chapter 13 is designed to make the process easier. ▪

FIGURE 13.1 ■ **The Road to Closing**

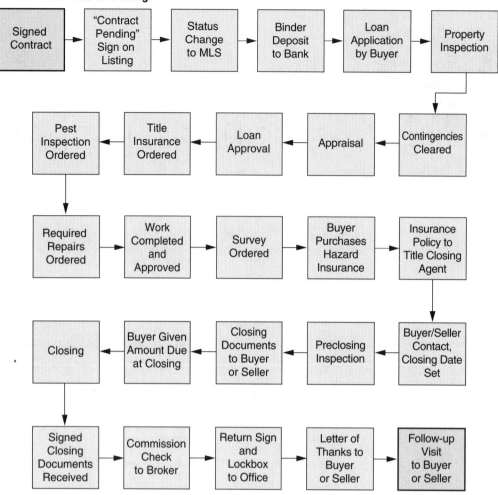

TEN STEPS TO A SUCCESSFUL CLOSING

Sales associates can avoid closing problems by following each of these ten steps:

1. Disclose everything to all parties that will affect their decisions before the buyer and seller sign the contract. Surprises after a contract is signed almost certainly will result in one party wanting to get out of the contract.

2. Write the contract carefully and properly explain it to the parties.

3. Recommend that buyers and sellers select lenders and title closing agents who are organized professionals able to meet deadlines.

4. Tell the loan officer and closing agent what the licensee expects in the way of communication and performance.

5. Prepare a Property Sale Information Sheet similar to the one in Forms To Go, Appendix B.

6. Give the closing agent a copy of the prior title insurance policy, if possible.

7. Provide a complete legal description of the property to the closing agent.

**Forms
To Go**

Forms To Go

8. Ask a lender and title agent to communicate by e-mail, speeding the process while also giving written documentation of the transaction.

9. Use a checklist of duties, such as the Closing Progress Chart provided in Forms To Go, Appendix B.

10. Ask the closing agent to close the buyer's and seller's sides separately to reduce confusion during the closing.

THE SALES INFORMATION SHEET

Forms To Go

To organize the work program, the sales associate needs to complete the Property Sale Information Sheet. (See Forms To Go, Appendix B.) It provides necessary data about the sale, the cooperating agent, the lender, the title company, and more. This form should be clipped inside the closing file and referred to as necessary when servicing the sale.

Establishing a Plan of Action

One of the first steps after both buyer and seller sign the contract is to set up a plan for closing. This step is even more important if another sales associate is involved because miscommunication often delays closings and causes unnecessary problems. Organization and attention to detail are keys to a successful closing.

THE CLOSING PROGRESS CHART

The Closing Progress Chart will help the licensee organize the details of the closing. If there is a cooperating licensee, the chart should be a joint effort so that licensees agree about which licensee will handle certain duties and when the tasks should be completed. Once agreement has been reached, each sales associate should place a copy of the chart in the closing file. Additionally, each date scheduled should be transferred to the sales associate's appointment book. As each task is completed, the sales associate should place a check mark in the appropriate row. An "X" in the chart indicates that comments have been made on the back of the form. A discussion of each item follows.

Preclosing Duties

"Sold" or "Sale Pending" sign on listed property. Placing a "Sold" or "Sale Pending" sign on the listed property is a function of the listing sales associate. Until recently, Florida Real Estate Commission (FREC) rules prohibited placing a "Sold" sign on property until the sale had been closed, but that rule was repealed, and licensees now have their choice of signs. Some sellers prefer a "Sold" sign so that prospective buyers are no longer escorted through the property, while others do not want to discourage activity until at least after the buyer's loan approval.

Notice of "under contract" to MLS. Most multiple-listing services (MLSs) require that all offices be notified of a listed property's status. Failure to change the status to "under contract" can result in agents from other offices appearing at the property with customers or clients. This wastes both the sales associate's and the prospective buyers' time, and reflects poorly on the listing office.

Binder deposited in bank. A sales associate must give the earnest money deposit to the broker no later than the end of the next business day. FREC rules require that the buyer's good-faith deposit be placed in a bank no later than three business days after receipt of the funds. The broker might deposit the funds immediately or wait until the seller accepts the contract (in no case, however, may the broker wait longer than three days). If a title-closing agent will hold the deposit, the broker must deliver the deposit to the title-closing agent within the same time frames allowed by FREC for depositing the funds in a broker-age account. The broker should get a receipt for the funds.

Get a receipt if the title closing agent is holding the deposit. If the buyer's deposit will be held by an attorney or title insurance company, you must indicate the name and address of the entity, and get a written receipt proving you delivered the deposit on time.

Additional binder received, if required. If the contract requires that the buyer put up addi-tional funds as a good-faith deposit, it is the sales associate's responsibility to ensure that the funds are received and deposited according to FREC requirements. The buyer's failure to comply with contract requirements is a default. The seller must be notified and the seller's instructions followed.

Loan application made by buyer. The FAR contract requires that the buyer make applica-tion for the loan by a certain date. The buyer's failure to comply with contract terms is a default, and the seller must be notified.

Contingencies cleared in writing. Sales associates must ensure that **contingencies** are satisfied as soon as possible. Some normal contingencies include a home inspection, a soil test, a roof inspection, and financing. If a problem arises with one of the contingencies, sales associates should do everything within their power to correct the problem, and all parties should be made aware of the situation.

Appraisal. The appraisal normally is ordered and paid for at the time of loan application. The sales associate wants to be certain that the appraiser selected by the financial institu-tion has complete cooperation, particularly with respect to access to the property. Failure to provide access wastes the appraiser's time and may delay the closing.

Loan approval. The FAR contract requires a loan commitment within a certain number of days from the contract's effective date. The licensee must monitor the lender's progress and provide to the lender without delay any information or documents requested. The lender's failure to provide the commitment within the required time may allow the buyer or the seller to void the contract.

Title insurance ordered. Many lenders permit the sales associate to select the title-closing agent, provided the company is on the lender's approved list. The seller or buyer also may have a preference in making the decision, based on who will pay for the policy. Many title companies prefer that the agent deliver the contract and financing information even before loan approval is obtained so that the title search can begin. Often little time is available from loan approval to closing, and the companies like a head start. If that is the case, the licensee must verify that the title company agrees to take the risk of a failed clos-ing and that it will not charge a fee if the sale does not close.

The licensee should give the title-closing agent the following items when a title insur-ance order is placed:

- A signed and dated sales contract
- A previous title insurance policy on the property, if available

- Enough information about the sellers, buyers, property, and lender to process and close the transaction, including:

   a. the sellers' and buyers' marital status;
   b. a complete legal description, for example, lot, block, subdivision name, phase or unit, recording information, and county;
   c. street address including ZIP code;
   d. terms of any purchase-money mortgage the title company must prepare;
   e. closing date and information about whether all parties will attend; and
   f. information on commission to broker and commission splits between brokers.

Wood-destroying organisms inspection ordered. As soon as possible after loan approval, the wood-destroying organisms (WDO) inspection should be ordered. When it is completed, copies of the report should be delivered to the buyer, lender, and title-closing agent. If treatment or repairs are required, agents working with the buyer and seller should communicate and agree on the details. If a structural inspection is required, a licensed contractor should be engaged to report on and estimate repair costs. Normally, the lender requires that treatment and repairs be completed satisfactorily before closing, so parties should act without delay in having the work performed.

Required repairs ordered. Many contracts require repairs other than those covered by termite damage. The appraisal could show the need for a new roof, or the buyer may have made the contract contingent on the seller's replacing a swimming pool vinyl liner, for example. As soon as loan approval is obtained, the work should be ordered.

Forms To Go

In Practice

Don't order repairs in your name. If the transaction doesn't close, you might have to pay for the repairs ordered. The seller or buyer, as appropriate, should contract for the work. You should limit your activities to getting estimates and putting the parties in touch. There's a sample form you can use in Forms To Go, Appendix B.

Required repairs completed and approved. When the work has been completed, the appropriate party should inspect the work to be sure that it has been done properly. A licensee who takes on this responsibility may be held responsible if deficiencies are discovered later.

Survey ordered. The lender or the title-closing agent often orders the survey after loan approval. A licensee who orders the survey without written approval may be liable for the fee if the sale does not close. In case of survey problems such as encroachments, the sales associate must act quickly to help clear up the problems.

Buyer purchases hazard insurance. The buyer should purchase the hazard insurance policy as soon as possible in the transaction, especially during Florida's hurricane season. If a hurricane or tropical storm develops anywhere within the "box," as shown in Figure 13.2, insurance companies stop writing insurance until the danger has passed. If there are several hurricanes at sea, the delay could be for a week or more, and could cause significant delay of a closing.

Contact buyer and seller for closing appointment. Soon after loan approval, the title-closing agent should be able to set a closing date and time. The sales associate should

F I G U R E 13.2 ■   Area of Tropical Storms and Hurricanes That Cause Insurance Delays

coordinate with the buyer and seller in setting a time agreeable to all. All parties should
be notified of the date, time, and place of the closing as far in advance as possible.

Preclosing inspection. The buyer should make a **preclosing walk-through inspection.**
The inspection is to ensure that

- the property is ready for occupancy;

- personal property the seller is required to leave remains on the property;

- all required repairs and maintenance have been completed; and

- the property has been maintained in the condition as it existed at the time of
  contract, ordinary wear and tear excepted.

The sales associate should not conduct such an inspection because of the liability
involved. When the inspection has been completed to the buyer's satisfaction, the sales
associate should ask the buyer to sign a preclosing clearance form, such as the one shown
in Forms To Go, Appendix B, Preclosing Walk-Through Inspection Results.

**Forms
To Go**

Closing papers reviewed with the buyer and seller one day before closing. A sales associate should attempt to work with lenders and title-closing agents who understand the sales
associate's need to provide the highest level of service to his customers. Those lenders and
title agents work diligently to provide all documents for the closing one day in advance.
The sales associate must monitor all phases of the closing, including a careful review of
the closing statements. Many buyers and sellers attend their closings—at which large sums
of money are disbursed—without having seen any of the documents beforehand. They
are expected to sign all documents after a cursory review at the closing table. This is not
fair to the participants, and it can lead to embarrassment for their sales associates. Often
a sales associate gets little more than the dollar amount that the buyer must bring in the
form of a certified or cashier's check. This is simply not satisfactory to the sales associate
who wishes to handle the closing professionally.

Upon receiving the documents, the sales associate should arrange an appointment to
visit the buyer or seller and deliver copies of all documents that the person will sign. The
sales associate should review the closing statement carefully to ensure that all items are
correct and should explain each item to the buyer or seller at the appointment. The sales

associate working with the buyer should compare the closing statement with the lender's good-faith estimate. The closing will go more quickly and pleasantly for the person who has reviewed all documents the evening before.

> **In Practice**
>
> As soon as you get the closing documents, compare the HUD-1 form with the Sellers' Net Proceeds statement you prepared for the sellers, or that the lender made for the buyers. If the figures are materially different (especially if they're higher than predicted) you need to track down the difference and get ready to explain it.
>
> Closing statements are covered later in this chapter.

Buyer given figure for certified check for closing. This settlement check figure should be provided to the buyer as soon as possible to allow him time to get a **certified check** for the proper amount from his bank.

Binder check prepared to take to closing. At least one day before closing, the sales associate should get the binder check from the broker and clip it to the file folder that will be taken to the closing. Also included in the folder will be the contract and other related material, as well as copies of the inspection reports.

THE CLOSING STATEMENT

Buyers and sellers expect their sales associates to coordinate and monitor every step of the closing process. The last step is the closing itself. A sales associate must be familiar with the documents that will be presented to the parties at the closing table. One of the most important documents, the HUD-1 Settlement Statement, relates to the financial side of the transaction.

A closing statement is, in effect, the purchase and sales agreement reduced to numbers. The sales associate must understand each number in the statement and be able to explain it clearly to the buyer or seller. The material in this chapter is designed to make the process easier.

PRORATIONS AND PREPAYMENTS

In every closing, property income and expenses should be prorated between the buyer and the seller. Usually, the 365-day method is used for prorations of annual expenses. The annual cost is divided by 365 days to get a daily rate. That rate is then multiplied by the number of days involved to get the amount due.

Proration calculations should be based on the last day of seller ownership. The day of closing is charged to the buyer, although it is possible that, by negotiation or custom in an area, the day of closing would be charged to the seller.

Property tax is the most common proration on a closing statement.

Prorating Property Taxes

The buyer normally pays property taxes in arrears, so they would be a debit to the seller and credit to the buyer. If the closing occurs in November or December, it is possible that the seller has paid the tax bill already, resulting in a credit to the seller and a debit to the buyer.

Closing date—April 15

Property taxes—$2,275

Beginning 1/1		**Closing date** 4/15		End 12/31
	Seller		Buyer	
	104 days		261 days	

Number of days from January 1 through April 15:

January	31
February	28
March	31
April	14
Total	104

Daily rate—$2,275 ÷ 365 days = $6.23288 per day

Proration—$6.23288 × 104 days = $648.22

- Debit the seller, credit the buyer.

PROPERTY TAX PRORATION EXERCISE 13.1

Do the following property tax prorations:

Closing Date	Taxes	Debit	Credit	Amount
September 12	$2,567.00			$
November 18	$4,260.00 (Paid 11/3)			$
April 24	$1,892.56			$

Prepayments for New Loan

When an institutional lender makes a new loan, and if the loan-to-value ratio is greater than 80 percent, the lender likely will require that an escrow fund for taxes, hazard insurance, and mortgage insurance be maintained. The borrower must deposit a sum into a lender's escrow account so that adequate funds will be available to make the payments when required. The amount of the specific charges varies with the time of the year at which the loan is closed. Once the escrow account is established, a monthly amount for taxes, insurance, and any required mortgage insurance is added to the monthly principal and interest payment. These funds, placed in a trust account, become the responsibility of the financial institution, which must pay such items when they are due. Some of those prepaid items are discussed below.

Prepaid Taxes

The lender normally collects taxes by adding the months of the year through closing, then adding two or three more months. For instance, if the closing is in April, the lender takes four months plus another three. In effect, the proration credit for three-plus months that the buyer receives from the seller offsets the effect of the lender's charge.

Closing date—April 15
Taxes—estimated at $2,275 for the year
Monthly taxes—$2,275 ÷ 12 = $189.58

The first payment will be on June 1. The lender will escrow seven months, so that when November comes the lender will have sufficient funds to pay the property tax bill.

$$\text{Monthly taxes } \$189.58 \times 7 \text{ months} = \$1,327.06$$

■ Debit the buyer for the amount of prepaid taxes.

The buyer has received a proration credit of $648.22 from the seller, so the net from the buyer to set up the account is $678.84.

PREPAID TAX CALCULATION EXERCISE 13.2

Assuming the lender wants three extra months, calculate the amount of taxes to be escrowed.

Closing Date	Taxes for the Year	Prepaid Amount
January 18	$2,400.00	$
July 3	$4,842.30	$
September 30	$1,453.89	$

Prepaid insurance. The buyer must pay the first year's policy in advance, plus two months. For example, if the insurance policy is $1,160, the monthly payment is $96.67 ($1,160 ÷ 12). Often the statement shows 14 months prepayment. In other cases, if the buyer has paid the premium outside closing (POC), the statement shows only two months.

■ Debit the buyer for one year plus two months prepaid insurance.

PREPAID INSURANCE CALCULATION EXERCISE 13.3

Calculate the amount of insurance to be escrowed in the following example. The lender wants it paid in advance plus two extra months.

Closing	Insurance for the Year	Prepaid Amount
January 18	$2,400	$
July 3	$900	$
September 30	$2,200 (POC)	$

Prepaid Interest

Because the first payment covers the interest for the previous month, interest is collected at closing for the days remaining in the closing month.

Closing date—April 15

First payment on the mortgage—June 1

The first payment covers May interest. Interest must be collected on the day of closing from April 15 through April 30 (16 days).

Closing date		1st Payment
4/15	5/1	6/1
	4/15–4/30 to be prepaid	1st pmt. pays interest for May

$112,500 × .09 = $10,125 per year

$10,125 per year ÷ 365 days per year = $27.73973 per day

$27.73973 per day × 16 days = $443.84

■ Debit the buyer $443.84 for prepaid interest.

PREPAID INTEREST CALCULATION EXERCISE 13.4

Calculate the interest prepayment for the new loans as follows:

Closing Date	Mortgage Loan Amount	Interest Rate	Prepaid Amount
September 12	$245,000	8.875%	$
January 17	$92,500	8.75%	$
December 29	$127,000	9.0%	$

Prepaid Mortgage Insurance

If mortgage insurance is required as part of an FHA or conventional mortgage loan, the borrower is charged for the coverage required.

The FHA requires homebuyers to pay two types of **mortgage insurance premiums (MIPs)**:

1. Up-front MIP (UFMIP), which is a percentage of the mortgage amount

2. Annual premium, which is calculated on the unpaid principal balance

The VA does not charge for guaranteeing a loan; however, it imposes a **funding fee** based on the mortgage amount. This funding fee may be included as part of the amount borrowed or paid in one lump sum at closing. A lender also may require an amount in cash adequate to open an escrow account, plus 1 percent of the loan amount as a maximum placement fee. Under VA loan rules, the closing costs and placement fees cannot be included in the loan amount.

Conventional lenders require **private mortgage insurance (PMI)** when a loan-to-value (LTV) ratio is more than 80 percent. Premiums fall into two general categories. In the first case, a single premium covers a lender's risk for a ten-year period. In the second case, a lender imposes a lower initial fee on the borrower and charges an insurance premium each year after that until the unpaid principal is reduced to a designated amount, normally 80 percent of appraised value. The first plan's one-time, single-premium charge or the second plan's lower initial cost is payable by the borrower at the time the loan closes. It should be noted that a PMI rate card must be used because of the different types of loans available and the different coverages required.

It is probably best *not* to make a large up-front payment but instead make a higher monthly payment. In case of an early loan payoff, the premium is not refunded.

DOCUMENTARY STAMP TAXES AND INTANGIBLE TAXES

Documentary stamp taxes are collected on the deed and the note. The seller normally pays for stamps on the deed, and the buyer pays for note stamps. The deed stamps are based on the sales price and are $.70 per $100 or fraction thereof. For example, if a property sells for $140,000, the documentary stamp taxes would be calculated as follows:

$$140,000 \div \$100 = 1,400 \text{ increments}$$
$$1,400 \times \$0.70 = \$980$$

DEED STAMPS TAX CALCULATION
EXERCISE 13.5

Calculate the documentary stamp taxes on the deed for the following sales prices:

Sales Price	Document Stamp Amount
$325,000	$
$127,415	$
$93,000	$

Documentary stamp taxes on the new note are based on the amount of the new or the assumed mortgage and are $.35 per $100 or fraction thereof. No stamps are charged on notes taken subject to the mortgage because the buyer has not assumed any of the debt obligations. For example, if the note amount on a new mortgage were $112,500, the documentary stamp tax would be calculated on the note amount as follows:

$$112,500 \div \$100 = 1,125 \text{ increments}$$
$$1,125 \times \$.35 = \$393.75$$

Intangible tax on the new mortgage is calculated by multiplying the mortgage amount by .002. No tax is charged on existing recorded mortgages. The buyer normally pays this charge. For example, the intangible taxes on a new mortgage of $112,500 would be calculated as follows:

$$112,500 \times .002 = \$225. \text{ There is no rounding.}$$

RESPA SETTLEMENT STATEMENT (HUD-1)

Forms To Go

The HUD-1 Settlement Statement provides an itemized listing of the funds payable at closing (See Figure 13.3). Closing agents must prepare the HUD-1 for the parties in a federally related mortgage loan. The HUD-1 is now used in nearly all residential closings, whether or not the form is legally required. Each item in the statement is assigned a separate number within a standardized numbering system. The totals at the bottom of page 1 of the HUD-1 statement show the seller's net proceeds and the amount due from the buyer at closing. A blank HUD-1 statement is included in Forms To Go, Appendix B.

Effective January 1, 2010, the HUD-1 statement has three pages. Page 1 shows the parties, the property description, the lender, the settlement agent, and a summary of the borrower's and seller's transactions. Page 2 (Section L) itemizes the settlement charges for each party, such as the broker's commission, loan closing costs, prepaid items, escrow account setup, title charges, and recording charges. The totals for each party on page 2 are transferred to the summary page on the front. When explaining the statement to the buyer and seller, the closing agents start at page 2, then go to page 1. The new page 3 compares the amounts on the HUD-1 statement to the lender's good faith estimate (GFE).

CLOSING STATEMENT EXAMPLE

Anita Wilson purchases a home from Wendy Stratton. Closing date is April 15, with the day of closing charged to the buyer. The price of the property is $125,000, and Anita is financing the purchase with a new 7.5 percent loan for 90 percent of the purchase price. She gives the broker a $5,000 binder check. The seller will pay off the existing first mortgage. The payoff amount, including interest, is $74,298.60. The seller has agreed to give the buyer a $2,000 allowance for new carpeting. The lender has approved the allowance. Annual property tax, estimated at $1,750, is the only item to be prorated.

The lender requires that a hazard insurance policy be purchased and the premium paid for one year ($545). An escrow account is collected at closing for three months of taxes, two months of hazard insurance, and two months of private mortgage insurance. The first payment on the mortgage is due on June 1.

The buyer paid for the appraisal ($300) at the time of loan application. Other expenses to be entered on each line item are discussed on the following pages.

F I G U R E 13.3 ■ HUD-1 Settlement Statement

OMB Approval No. 2502-0265

A. **Settlement Statement (HUD-1)**

B. Type of Loan					
1. ☐ FHA 2. ☐ RHS 3. ☐ Conv. Unins. 4. ☐ VA 5. ☐ Conv. Ins.		6. File Number:	7. Loan Number:	8. Mortgage Insurance Case Number:	

C. Note: This form is furnished to give you a statement of actual settlement costs. Amounts paid to and by the settlement agent are shown. Items marked "(p.o.c.)" were paid outside the closing; they are shown here for informational purposes and are not included in the totals.

D. Name & Address of Borrower:	E. Name & Address of Seller:	F. Name & Address of Lender:

G. Property Location:	H. Settlement Agent:	I. Settlement Date:
	Place of Settlement:	

J. Summary of Borrower's Transaction		K. Summary of Seller's Transaction	
100. Gross Amount Due from Borrower		**400. Gross Amount Due to Seller**	
101. Contract sales price		401. Contract sales price	
102. Personal property		402. Personal property	
103. Settlement charges to borrower (line 1400)		403.	
104.		404.	
105.		405.	
Adjustment for items paid by seller in advance		**Adjustment for items paid by seller in advance**	
106. City/town taxes to		406. City/town taxes to	
107. County taxes to		407. County taxes to	
108. Assessments to		408. Assessments to	
109.		409.	
110.		410.	
111.		411.	
112.		412.	
120. Gross Amount Due from Borrower		**420. Gross Amount Due to Seller**	
200. Amount Paid by or in Behalf of Borrower		**500. Reductions In Amount Due to seller**	
201. Deposit or earnest money		501. Excess deposit (see instructions)	
202. Principal amount of new loan(s)		502. Settlement charges to seller (line 1400)	
203. Existing loan(s) taken subject to		503. Existing loan(s) taken subject to	
204.		504. Payoff of first mortgage loan	
205.		505. Payoff of second mortgage loan	
206.		506.	
207.		507.	
208.		508.	
209.		509.	
Adjustments for items unpaid by seller		**Adjustments for items unpaid by seller**	
210. City/town taxes to		510. City/town taxes to	
211. County taxes to		511. County taxes to	
212. Assessments to		512. Assessments to	
213.		513.	
214.		514.	
215.		515.	
216.		516.	
217.		517.	
218.		518.	
219.		519.	
220. Total Paid by/for Borrower		**520. Total Reduction Amount Due Seller**	
300. Cash at Settlement from/to Borrower		**600. Cash at Settlement to/from Seller**	
301. Gross amount due from borrower (line 120)		601. Gross amount due to seller (line 420)	
302. Less amounts paid by/for borrower (line 220)	( )	602. Less reductions in amounts due seller (line 520)	( )
303. Cash ☐ From ☐ To Borrower		**603. Cash** ☐ To ☐ From Seller	

The Public Reporting Burden for this collection of information is estimated at 35 minutes per response for collecting, reviewing, and reporting the data. This agency may not collect this information, and you are not required to complete this form, unless it displays a currently valid OMB control number. No confidentiality is assured; this disclosure is mandatory. This is designed to provide the parties to a RESPA covered transaction with information during the settlement process.

F I G U R E 13.3 ■ HUD-1 Settlement Statement (continued)

L. Settlement Charges		Paid From Borrower's Funds at Settlement	Paid From Seller's Funds at Settlement
700. Total Real Estate Broker Fees			
Division of commission (line 700) as follows :			
701. $ to			
702. $ to			
703. Commission paid at settlement			
704.			
800. Items Payable in Connection with Loan			
801. Our origination charge	$ (from GFE #1)		
802. Your credit or charge (points) for the specific interest rate chosen	$ (from GFE #2)		
803. Your adjusted origination charges	(from GFE #A)		
804. Appraisal fee to	(from GFE #3)		
805. Credit report to	(from GFE #3)		
806. Tax service to	(from GFE #3)		
807. Flood certification to	(from GFE #3)		
808.			
809.			
810.			
811.			
900. Items Required by Lender to be Paid in Advance			
901. Daily interest charges from to @ $ /day	(from GFE #10)		
902. Mortgage insurance premium for months to	(from GFE #3)		
903. Homeowner's insurance for years to	(from GFE #11)		
904.			
1000. Reserves Deposited with Lender			
1001. Initial deposit for your escrow account	(from GFE #9)		
1002. Homeowner's insurance months @ $ per month $			
1003. Mortgage insurance months @ $ per month $			
1004. Property Taxes months @ $ per month $			
1005. months @ $ per month $			
1006. months @ $ per month $			
1007. Aggregate Adjustment -$			
1100. Title Charges			
1101. Title services and lender's title insurance	(from GFE #4)		
1102. Settlement or closing fee	$		
1103. Owner's title insurance	(from GFE #5)		
1104. Lender's title insurance	$		
1105. Lender's title policy limit $			
1106. Owner's title policy limit $			
1107. Agent's portion of the total title insurance premium to	$		
1108. Underwriter's portion of the total title insurance premium to	$		
1109.			
1110.			
1111.			
1200. Government Recording and Transfer Charges			
1201. Government recording charges	(from GFE #7)		
1202. Deed $ Mortgage $ Release $			
1203. Transfer taxes	(from GFE #8)		
1204. City/County tax/stamps Deed $ Mortgage $			
1205. State tax/stamps Deed $ Mortgage $			
1206.			
1300. Additional Settlement Charges			
1301. Required services that you can shop for	(from GFE #6)		
1302. $			
1303. $			
1304.			
1305.			
1400. Total Settlement Charges (enter on lines 103, Section J and 502, Section K)			

F I G U R E 13.3 ■ HUD-1 Settlement Statement (continued)

Comparison of Good Faith Estimate (GFE) and HUD-1 Charrges		Good Faith Estimate	HUD-1
Charges That Cannot Increase	**HUD-1 Line Number**		
Our origination charge	# 801		
Your credit or charge (points) for the specific interest rate chosen	# 802		
Your adjusted origination charges	# 803		
Transfer taxes	# 1203		

Charges That In Total Cannot Increase More Than 10%		Good Faith Estimate	HUD-1
Government recording charges	# 1201		
	#		
	#		
	#		
	#		
	#		
	#		
	#		
Total			
Increase between GFE and HUD-1 Charges		$ or	%

Charges That Can Change		Good Faith Estimate	HUD-1
Initial deposit for your escrow account	# 1001		
Daily interest charges $ /day	# 901		
Homeowner's insurance	# 903		
	#		
	#		
	#		

Loan Terms

Your initial loan amount is	$
Your loan term is	years
Your initial interest rate is	%
Your initial monthly amount owed for principal, interest, and any mortgage insurance is	$ includes ☐ Principal ☐ Interest ☐ Mortgage Insurance
Can your interest rate rise?	☐ No ☐ Yes, it can rise to a maximum of %. The first change will be on and can change again every after . Every change date, your interest rate can increase or decrease by %. Over the life of the loan, your interest rate is guaranteed to never be **lower** than % or **higher** than %.
Even if you make payments on time, can your loan balance rise?	☐ No ☐ Yes, it can rise to a maximum of $
Even if you make payments on time, can your monthly amount owed for principal, interest, and mortgage insurance rise?	☐ No ☐ Yes, the first increase can be on and the monthly amount owed can rise to $. The maximum it can ever rise to is $.
Does your loan have a prepayment penalty?	☐ No ☐ Yes, your maximum prepayment penalty is $
Does your loan have a balloon payment?	☐ No ☐ Yes, you have a balloon payment of $ due in years on .
Total monthly amount owed including escrow account payments	☐ You do not have a monthly escrow payment for items, such as property taxes and homeowner's insurance. You must pay these items directly yourself. ☐ You have an additional monthly escrow payment of $ that results in a total initial monthly amount owed of $. This includes principal, interest, any mortgage insurance and any items checked below: ☐ Property taxes ☐ Homeowner's insurance ☐ Flood insurance ☐ ☐ ☐

Note: If you have any questions about the Settlement Charges and Loan Terms listed on this form, please contact your lender.

The seller pays a commission of 7 percent, an attorney's fee of $225, documentary stamp taxes on the deed, and other items as discussed below.

Based on the following information, complete the blank HUD-1 statement in Figure 13.3. Start on page 2 with the buyer's side.

Page 2

PAID FROM BORROWER'S FUNDS AT SETTLEMENT

ITEMS PAYABLE IN CONNECTION WITH LOAN

801	Origination fee—1% of the loan amount	?

(Loan amount times the percentage: $112,500 × .01 = $?)

802	Loan discount—1 point	?

(Loan amount times points: $112,500 × .01 = $?)

804	Appraisal fee POC* $300.00 buyer	
805	Credit report fee	$55.00
806	Tax service fee	$59.00
808	Underwriting fee	$100.00
809	Document preparation fee	$75.00
810	Courier fee	$13.00

*POC on the statement means "paid outside closing."

ITEMS REQUIRED BY LENDER TO BE PAID IN ADVANCE

901	Daily interest from 4/15 to 4/30	?

(Loan amount times interest rate divided by 365 times number of days remaining in month of closing, counting the day of closing:

$112,500 × .075 = $8,437.48
$8,437.48 ÷ 365 = $23.1164 per day:
$23.1164 × 16 days = $?)

903	Homeowners' insurance premium for 12 months to State Farm	$545.00

RESERVES DEPOSITED WITH LENDER

1002	Hazard insurance 2 mo. @ $?/mo	?

(Annual insurance divided by 12 months times number of months required by lender: $545.00 ÷ 12 = $? per month; $? × 2 months = $?)

1003	Homeowners' insurance 2 months @ $?/mo.	?

($545 per yr. divided by 12 months = $? per month: $? per month × 2 months = $50.00)

1004	County property taxes ($1,750) 7 mo. @ $?/mo.	$1,020.81

(Annual taxes divided by 12 months times number of month's reserve required by lender: $1,750.00 ÷ 12 = $? per month; $? × 7 months = $?)

TITLE CHARGES

1101	Title insurance and lender's title insurance	$922.50
1102	Abstract or title search to Jones & Smith law firm	$100.00
1103	Owner's title insurance	$475.00

GOVERNMENT RECORDING AND TRANSFER CHARGES

1201	Government recording charges	$66.00
1202	Deed $6.00; Mortgage $60.00	
1205	Intangible taxes on mortgage	$225.00
	(Loan amount times .002)	
1204	Documentary stamp tax on note	?
	(Loan amount divided by 100, round up to next whole n umber, multiply by $.35)	
1302	Survey to All Corners Surveyor	$250.00
1303	Pest inspection to All Pest Control	$50.00
1400	Total settlement charges (total, then enter on page one, line 103)	?

PAID FROM SELLER'S FUNDS AT SETTLEMENT

701	Commission paid to Tillie Evans Realty	?
	(Sales price times commission rate of 7%) (Sales price moves to under 701)	
703	Carry total to this line	
1102	Attorney's fees to Jones & Smith law firm	?
1111	Courier fee for mortgage payoff to Jones & Smith law firm	$20.00
1202	Satisfaction (release) recording fee	$6.00
1204	Documentary stamp tax on deed	$875.00
	(Sales price divided by 100, rounded to next higher whole number, times $.70)	
1400	Total settlement charges (total, then enter on page one, line 502)	?

Page 1

SUMMARY OF BORROWER'S TRANSACTION

101	Purchase price	125,000.00
103	Settlement charges to borrower (from page two, line 1400)	?
120	Gross amount due from borrower	?
201	Deposit or earnest money	5,000.00
202	Principal amount of new loans	112,500.00
	(Price times loan-to-value ratio: $125,000 × .90 = $112,500)	

207	Carpet allowance to buyer	2,000.00
211, 511	Property taxes for the year (paid in arrears)—$1,750	?
	(Annual taxes divided by 365 days times number of seller days)	
220	TOTAL PAID BY/FOR BORROWER (Sum of lines 201–219)	?
301	GROSS AMOUNT DUE FROM BORROWER (Line 120)	?
302	LESS AMOUNTS PAID BY/FOR BORROWER (Line 220)	?
303	CASH FROM BORROWER	?

SUMMARY OF SELLER'S TRANSACTION

401	Purchase price	$125,000.00
420	GROSS AMOUNT DUE TO SELLER	?
502	Settlement charges to seller (from page 2, line 1400)	?
504	Payoff of existing first mortgage (given)	$74,298.60
507	Carpet allowance to buyer	$2,000.00
511	Property taxes for the year (paid in arrears)—$1,750	?
	(See calculation for line 211)	
520	TOTAL REDUCTION AMOUNT DUE SELLER (Sum of lines 501–519)	?
601	GROSS AMOUNT DUE TO SELLER (Line 420)	?
602	LESS REDUCTION AMOUNT DUE SELLER (Line 520)	?
603	CASH TO SELLER	?

AT THE CLOSING TABLE

The closing normally includes the buyers, the sellers, and their respective licensees, if any. Sometimes attorneys of the parties attend, and occasionally a lender's representative. The title-closing agent conducts the closing.

Separate Closings

Many licensees prefer that the buyers and sellers close separately, rather than at the same closing table. This reduces confusion, makes it more private, and allows the title-closing agent to focus completely on each party. It is appropriate if the parties have had a dispute over some issue. Sometimes separate closings occur when there is a mail-away closing package, or when the buyers or sellers live out of town.

Closing Disputes

The title closer is not an advocate for any of the parties. It is the title closer's job to close the transaction based on the contract and the lender's closing instructions. If there is a problem between the buyer and the lender, the closer gets them together on the phone. If there is a dispute between the buyer and the seller, the closer will often step out of the room until the dispute is settled and the parties are ready to close.

Truth-in-Lending Disclosure

If there is an institutional loan, the first document to be reviewed must be the Truth-in-Lending (TIL) disclosure. If the buyers were informed by the lender or the licensee when they applied for the loan that the annual percentage rate (APR) shown on the TIL would be higher than the interest rate on their note, this will not be a problem. If they were not informed, however, some buyers, upon seeing a 7.875 percent APR on the disclosure form say, "Wait a minute! I was supposed to be getting a 7½ percent loan!" The closer must explain that origination fees and discount points are included to calculate the APR, but the loan rate remains the same.

Loan Application

Usually the lender will want a typed loan application signed at closing, verifying the information given to the lender at the time of application.

Note

The closer presents the note for the buyer's signature. The note shows the principal balance, number of payments, and the dates and the amount of the payments. The amount will be for principal and interest only. The first payment date will normally be the first day of the second month after closing. The note is not witnessed or notarized. If a signature appears on the face of the note along with the borrower's signature, that person becomes a cosigner on the note.

Mortgage

The mortgage is the security for the note. It is the document that may require that the borrower pay 1/12 of the ad valorem taxes and the hazard insurance and mortgage insurance premiums, along with the principal and interest. It requires that payments be made on time, that taxes be paid, and that the property be covered by insurance and describes prepayment options. It also probably states that a transfer of the property will make the loan due immediately.

The Warranty Deed

The warranty deed is the most common deed, with the seller guaranteeing to the buyer that he has good title, without material defects or encumbrances, and will stand by the guarantee forever. Special attention should be given to the names and legal description and to any items in the "subject to" section, such as restrictive covenants and mortgages.

Other Documents

Some of the other documents the buyer may sign include an anticoercion statement that says the lender did not require that the buyer choose a certain insurance company. The lender and title insurance company will want a compliance agreement that the parties will do anything necessary to give the lender an acceptable loan package, such as signing new documents, if required. If the loan is above 80 percent of a home's value, the lender will want an affidavit that the buyer will occupy the property. The seller will be required to sign an affidavit that (1) she owns the property, (2) she has the right to convey it, and (3) it is not encumbered by any lien or right to a lien, such as a construction lien.

Disbursements at Closing

Everyone expects to be paid at closing. This is not always possible, and licensees should be prepared to explain the problem to the sellers. Perhaps an example using a broker's trust account is easier to understand. Many real estate brokers have hundreds of thousands of dollars in their escrow accounts. A broker who disburses from the escrow account before making a deposit into the account, even if the future deposit would be in certified funds, is guilty of a serious violation because the broker would be using funds that belong to others.

Title insurance companies are faced with a similar problem. Some title insurance companies agree to disburse the proceeds at closing if the certified checks will be deposited by the close of business that day. (A real estate broker may never do this.) Many title insurance companies will not disburse if the closing takes place too late to make a same-day deposit or if the lender is holding the loan proceeds check until the loan package is delivered.

Warehousing

Some companies are hesitant to insure title until the "gap" between the time of the title commitment and the time of recording is checked. Any documents filed against the property during the gap period may affect the title. A lot depends on whether the title insurance company has any reason to suspect problems.

After the closing, the title company makes all deposits, and the deeds and mortgages are copied for the lender's package before they are taken for recording. The closing package is prepared for the lender, awaiting only the recording information. The person who records the documents should ensure that the check amounts are correctly calculated, that the documents are put in the correct recording order (deed first, then mortgages), and that the "return to" address is properly entered. When the documents are recorded, the information, including the date and time and the book and page number, is entered into the final title insurance policy and the package is sent to the lender.

When the recorded instruments are returned, the closing agent will send the buyer the original deed with recording information, a copy of the mortgage (the lender gets the original), and the title insurance policy.

Signed closing papers received by sales associate. The sales associate should be careful that the office file is fully documented. This includes any walk-through clearance papers the buyer signs for the seller and the closing statements all parties must sign. If disbursement is made at closing, the commission check also is received at this time.

Postclosing Duties

The sales associate is also responsible for the postclosing duties discussed below.

Give commission check to broker. Upon returning to the office, the sales associate should give the closing file as well as the commission check to the broker.

Pick up sign and lockbox from property. The listing sales associate should ensure that the sign and lockbox are removed from the property and returned to the office. Often the sales associate does this just before closing. Many sales associates remove the lockbox for security reasons immediately after the contract has been signed.

Send letter of thanks to buyer or seller. The letter, which should include both the sales associate's and the broker's signatures, will be appreciated by the customer, will foster goodwill, and likely will result in future business. Many companies request that the buyer or seller complete a questionnaire about the level of service provided in the transaction.

Visit buyer or seller to follow up. The sales associate who calls on the customer after the closing demonstrates the careful attention needed to ensure that all details of the transaction have been completed satisfactorily.

Provide notice of closed sale to the MLS. Most MLS systems require that listing status changes be submitted as soon as possible. This provides brokers and sales associates in the area with the most current information about listing availability and comparable sales information.

S U M M A R Y

The sales associate's job really is just beginning when the parties sign the contract. Much work must be completed to ensure a successful closing. One of the first steps is to plan for each required task and enter it on a timeline. Each sales associate and broker involved should agree about who must do what, and when it must be done.

Licensees must complete tasks such as attaching a "contract pending" sign, notifying the MLS, making the binder deposit, helping the buyer with the loan application, and taking care of inspections and repairs. A major part of the sales associate's duties is reviewing the closing documents with the buyer or seller before closing.

K E Y   T E R M S

certified check	intangible tax	preclosing walk-through
contingencies	mortgage insurance	inspection
documentary stamp taxes	premium (MIP)	private mortgage insurance
funding fee		(PMI)

P R A C T I C E   E X A M

1. When sales associate Phyllis sells her listing, she places a sign on the property. In this situation, which statement is correct?
   a. Phyllis must put up a "contract pending" sign, by FREC rule.
   b. Phyllis must put up a "sale pending" sign, by FREC rule.
   c. Phyllis may not place the "sold" sign without the seller's approval.
   d. Phyllis may place the "sold" sign without the seller's approval.

2. The preclosing walk-through inspection is NOT intended to ensure that
   a. personal property the seller is required to leave remains on the property.
   b. all required repairs have been completed.
   c. the property has been maintained in the condition as it existed at the time of the contract, ordinary wear and tear excepted.
   d. the roof is structurally sound.

3. Sales associate Brian listed the Brantlys' home at 3217 Woodbrook Circle. Based on information the seller provided, Brian disclosed to the buyers, Jack and Helen Maxwell, that the pool liner was defective and needed replacement. The contract was written reflecting that the Maxwells would be responsible for the charges related to replacing the liner. After the sellers signed the contract, Brian contacted Pretty Pools Company and authorized the liner replacement at a cost of $1,750. The Maxwells were subsequently turned down for the required financing, and the sale did not close. Based on this information, Brian
   a. is not liable to the pool company; the Maxwells are.
   b. is not liable to the pool company; the Brantlys are.
   c. might have to pay for the pool liner.
   d. may sue the Maxwells, because they defaulted.

4. The best way for a buyer to determine that the seller has moved out and the property is ready for occupancy is by
   a. requiring a home inspection company to provide a report.
   b. reading a termite report.
   c. doing a preclosing walk-through inspection.
   d. asking the sales associate.

5. To expedite a closing, catch errors made in documents, and make the buyers feel more comfortable about documents they must sign, what should a sales associate do?
   a. Obtain a hold-harmless agreement from the title insurance company
   b. Limit the time for actually doing the closing
   c. Get the papers to the parties at least 24 hours in advance of the closing
   d. Have the lender sign an estoppel letter

6. When the title closing agent gave the buyer the Truth-in-Lending Disclosure showing the annual percentage rate was 7.62 percent, the buyer declared, "Wait, I was told the interest rate was going to be 7.25 percent. This is wrong!" What is the most likely reason for the discrepancy?
   a. Rates have gone up since the date of application.
   b. The lender is trying to make extra money, believing the borrower won't remember the original interest quote.
   c. While the note rate is probably 7.25 percent, the inclusion of lender fees such as discount points and origination fees has increased the annual percentage rate.
   d. The Federal Reserve Board mandates a 3/8 percent interest differential in mortgage loans.

7. A sales associate must give the earnest money deposit to the broker no later than the end of
   a. the next business day.
   b. the second business day.
   c. the third business day.
   d. 15 days.

8. Contract contingencies should be cleared
   a. within five days before closing.
   b. within five days after loan approval.
   c. within three days of contract.
   d. as soon as possible after the contract has been signed.

9. Jill listed a property for Sam, and he accepted an offer made on the property. The contract called for an additional binder to be deposited within ten days of the contract date. If the buyer failed to meet the contract's terms concerning the additional binder, the:
   a. contract is null and void.
   b. contract works like an option contract; the only remedy is the loss of the original binder.
   c. buyer has defaulted.
   d. contract should not have been accepted as written.

10. What would NOT be given to the title-closing agent when the order is given?
    a. A signed and dated listing agreement.
    b. The seller's and buyer's marital status.
    c. A complete legal description.
    d. Property address, including zip code.

PRACTICE HUD-1 CLOSING STATEMENT

Questions 11–15 relate to the following information.

You recently listed and sold a home. The closing is scheduled for May 15. You have just received the HUD-1 settlement statement from Jillian Winkle at Smith, Jones, and Adams, P.A. (See Figure 13.4.) Using the listing agreement, the sales contract, and the good-faith estimate of settlement costs given by the lender at the time of application, you begin the review. You intend to visit both the sellers and the buyers to go over the closing information before the closing.

As you review the sales contract, you trace certain items to the HUD-1 statement and check off each as you do so. Names of the buyers (Kyle and Kari Byers) are as listed on the contract. The sellers' legal names, John and Susan Sellars, were taken from their deed when you first took the listing. They are shown correctly. The property address on the contract is 1462 Lyme Drive. The contract sales price is $120,000. The Byers gave a $4,000 earnest money deposit. The new mortgage is for $108,000 at 7.5 percent interest.

You know the lender charges 1 percent for discount points and 1 percent for the loan origination fee. The Byers paid an appraisal fee of $300 at the time of loan application (POC). The good-faith estimate of settlement costs given by the lender at the time of application shows a $55 credit report fee, $25 for an amortization schedule, $1,070 for title insurance, and $20 for courier services. The estimate also shows recording fees of $10.50 for the deed and $42 for the mortgage, the documentary stamp tax on the note, and intangible tax on the mortgage. The survey was estimated at $250.

The Byers must prepay interest on the loan from May 15 through May 31 because the first payment on the new mortgage is not due until July 1. The Byers also need to buy a one-year hazard insurance policy. They have chosen a State Farm policy with an annual premium of $840.

The lender requires that an escrow account be set up with two months' advance hazard insurance deposit, two months' advance mortgage insurance ($540 annual premium), and eight months' advance property taxes based on an estimate of $2,100 annually.

The payoff letter for the existing first mortgage requires $45,452.65, including interest. The Sellars have agreed to pay for recording the satisfaction of mortgage, and the $10.50 charge looks about right. The $20 courier fee to send the payoff check also seems OK. They have agreed to pay a bill from Fix It All, Inc., for $245 for miscellaneous repairs to the property. You calculate the documentary stamps on the deed and check your figures against the closing agent's figures. The Sellars' hazard insurance policy will be canceled. You review the listing agreement to see that the commission is 7 percent. It is not to be split with any cooperating brokerage firm.

If you find any errors on the statement, circle them and replace them with the correct figures. Totals on the statement may need to be changed. Once you have completed the review, answer questions 11 through 15.

11. What incorrect entries, if any, are in the Byers' expenses in Section L?
    a. There are no incorrect entries.
    b. The title insurance charges are wrong.
    c. The discount points and origination fees are incorrect.
    d. The documentary stamp taxes on the note are wrong.

12. What incorrect entries, if any, are in the Sellars' expenses in Section L?
    a. There are no incorrect entries.
    b. The commission is calculated incorrectly.
    c. The documentary stamp taxes on the deed are calculated incorrectly.
    d. The total at the bottom of the page is wrong.

F I G U R E 13.4 ■ HUD-1 Settlement Statement

OMB Approval No. 2502-0265

A. **Settlement Statement (HUD-1)**

B. Type of Loan					
1. ☐ FHA 2. ☐ RHS 3. ☐ Conv. Unins. 4. ☐ VA 5. ☒ Conv. Ins.	6. File Number: EDODONNELL8LEM	7. Loan Number: 12345678		8. Mortgage Insurance Case Number:	

C. Note: This form is furnished to give you a statement of actual settlement costs. Amounts paid to and by the settlement agent are shown. Items marked "(p.o.c.)" were paid outside the closing; they are shown here for informational purposes and are not included in the totals.

D. Name & Address of Borrower:	E. Name & Address of Seller:	F. Name & Address of Lender:
KYLE BUYERS AND KARI BYERS 1460 LYME DRIVE TALLAHASSEE, FL 32301	JOHN SELLARS AND SUSAN SELLARS 2100 W ST AUGUSTINE ROAD JACKSONVILLE, FL 32217	FIRST SOUTH BANK, A FEDERAL SAVINGS BANK 3020 HARTLEY ROAD, SUITE 1 JACKSONVILLE, FL 32257

G. Property Location:	H. Settlement Agent:	I. Settlement Date:
1460 LYME DRIVE TALLAHASSEE, FLORIDA 32301 LOT 8, ORANGE PARK SUBDIVISION	SMITH, JONES, AND ADAMS, P.A. Place of Settlement: 7889 THOMASVILLE RD, TALLAHASSEE, FL	MAY 15, 2011

J. Summary of Borrower's Transaction		K. Summary of Seller's Transaction	
100. Gross Amount Due from Borrower		**400. Gross Amount Due to Seller**	
101. Contract sales price	$120,000.00	401. Contract sales price	$120,000.00
102. Personal property		402. Personal property	
103. Settlement charges to borrower (line 1400)	$7,288.76	403.	
104.		404.	
105.		405.	
Adjustment for items paid by seller in advance		**Adjustment for items paid by seller in advance**	
106. City/town taxes to		406. City/town taxes to	
107. County taxes 5/1/10 to 12/31/10	$1,329.04	407. County taxes 5/1/10 to 12/31/10	$1,329.04
108. Assessments to		408. Assessments to	
109.		409.	
110.		410.	
111.		411.	
112.		412.	
120. Gross Amount Due from Borrower	$128,642.80	**420. Gross Amount Due to Seller**	$121,329.04
200. Amount Paid by or in Behalf of Borrower		**500. Reductions In Amount Due to seller**	
201. Deposit or earnest money	$4,000.00	501. Excess deposit (see instructions)	
202. Principal amount of new loan(s)	$108,000.00	502. Settlement charges to seller (line 1400)	$9,315.50
203. Existing loan(s) taken subject to		503. Existing loan(s) taken subject to	
204.		504. Payoff of first mortgage loan	$45,452.65
205.		505. Payoff of second mortgage loan	
206.		506.	
207.		507.	
208.		508.	
209.		509.	
Adjustments for items unpaid by seller		**Adjustments for items unpaid by seller**	
210. City/town taxes to		510. City/town taxes to	
211. County taxes to		511. County taxes to	
212. Assessments to		512. Assessments to	
213.		513.	
214.		514.	
215.		515.	
216.		516.	
217.		517.	
218.		518.	
219.		519.	
220. Total Paid by/for Borrower	$112,000.00	**520. Total Reduction Amount Due Seller**	$54,768.15
300. Cash at Settlement from/to Borrower		**600. Cash at Settlement to/from Seller**	
301. Gross amount due from borrower (line 120)	$128,642.80	601. Gross amount due to seller (line 420)	$121,329.04
302. Less amounts paid by/for borrower (line 220)	($112,000.00)	602. Less reductions in amounts due seller (line 520)	($54,768.15)
303. Cash ☒ From ☐ To Borrower	$16,642.80	**603. Cash** ☒ To ☐ From Seller	$66,560.89

The Public Reporting Burden for this collection of information is estimated at 35 minutes per response for collecting, reviewing, and reporting the data. This agency may not collect this information, and you are not required to complete this form, unless it displays a currently valid OMB control number. No confidentiality is assured; this disclosure is mandatory. This is designed to provide the parties to a RESPA covered transaction with information during the settlement process.

FIGURE 13.4 ■ HUD-1 Settlement Statement (continued)

L. Settlement Charges

700. Total Real Estate Broker Fees $120,000 @ 7% = $8,400.00		Paid From Borrower's Funds at Settlement	Paid From Seller's Funds at Settlement
Division of commission (line 700) as follows :			
701. $ 8,400.00 to BIG BEND REALTY			
702. $ to			
703. Commission paid at settlement			$8,400.00
704.			

800. Items Payable in Connection with Loan			
801. Our origination charge 1.000% $ 1,200.00 (from GFE #1)			
802. Your credit or charge (points) for the specific interest rate chosen 1.000 % $ 1,200.00 (from GFE #2)			
803. Your adjusted origination charges (from GFE #A)		$2,400.00	
804. Appraisal fee to TALLAHASSEE APPRAISAL COMPANY (POC) $300.00 BUYER (from GFE #3)			
805. Credit report to CREDCO (from GFE #3)		$55.00	
806. Tax service to (from GFE #3)			
807. Flood certification to (from GFE #3)			
808.			
809.			
810.			
811.			

900. Items Required by Lender to be Paid in Advance			
901. Daily interest charges from 5/15/10 to 6/01/10 @ $ 22.19 /day (from GFE #10)		$377.26	
902. Mortgage insurance premium for months to (from GFE #3)			
903. Homeowner's insurance for 1 years to STATE FARM (from GFE #11)		$840.00	
904.			

1000. Reserves Deposited with Lender			
1001. Initial deposit for your escrow account (from GFE #9)		$1,630.00	
1002. Homeowner's insurance 2 months @ $ 70.00 per month $ 140.00			
1003. Mortgage insurance 2 months @ $ 45.00 per month $ 90.00			
1004. Property Taxes 8 months @ $ 175.00 per month $ 1,400.00			
1005. months @ $ per month $			
1006. months @ $ per month $			
1007. Aggregate Adjustment -$			

1100. Title Charges			
1101. Title services and lender's title insurance (from GFE #4)		$275.00	
1102. Settlement or closing fee SMITH, JONES, AND ADAMS, P.A. $ 100.00			
1103. Owner's title insurance SMITH, JONES, AND ADAMS, P.A. (from GFE #5)		$700.00	
1104. Lender's title insurance SMITH, JONES, AND ADAMS, P.A. $ 25.00			
1105. Lender's title policy limit $ 108,000.00			
1106. Owner's title policy limit $ 120,000.00			
1107. Agent's portion of the total title insurance premium to $			
1108. Underwriter's portion of the total title insurance premium to $			
1109. FL 9		$70.00	
1110. ALTA 8.1		$25.00	
1111. COURIER FEE		$20.00	$20.00

1200. Government Recording and Transfer Charges			
1201. Government recording charges (from GFE #7)		$52.50	
1202. Deed $ 10.50 Mortgage $ 42.00 Release $ 10.50			$10.50
1203. Transfer taxes (from GFE #8)		$594.00	
1204. City/County tax/stamps Deed $ 840.00 Mortgage $ 378.00			$840.00
1205. State tax/stamps Deed $ Mortgage $ 216.00			
1206.			

1300. Additional Settlement Charges			
1301. Required services that you can shop for (from GFE #6)			
1302. SURVEY TO ALL CORNERS SURVEYOR $ 250.00		$250.00	
1303. PEST INSPECTION (NO REQUIRED FEE PER CONTRACT) $			
1304. MISC REPAIRS TO FIX IT ALL, INC.			$245.00
1305.			

1400. Total Settlement Charges (enter on lines 103, Section J and 502, Section K)		$7,288.76	$9,515.50

FIGURE 13.4 ■ HUD-1 Settlement Statement (continued)

Comparison of Good Faith Estimate (GFE) and HUD-1 Charrges		Good Faith Estimate	HUD-1
Charges That Cannot Increase	**HUD-1 Line Number**		
Our origination charge	# 801	$1,200.00	$1,200.00
Your credit or charge (points) for the specific interest rate chosen	# 802	$1,200.00	$1,200.00
Your adjusted origination charges	# 803	$2,400.00	$2,400.00
Transfer taxes	# 1203	$594.00	$594.00

Charges That In Total Cannot Increase More Than 10%		Good Faith Estimate	HUD-1
Government recording charges	# 1201	$52.50	$52.50
Credit Report Fee	# 805	$55.00	$55.00
Amortization Schedule	# 808	$25.00	$0.00
Title Insurance	#	$1,070.00	$1,070.00
Courier Fee	# 1111	$20.00	$20.00
Recording Fee	# 1201	$52.50	$52.50
	#		
	#		
Total			
Increase between GFE and HUD-1 Charges		$ or %	

Charges That Can Change		Good Faith Estimate	HUD-1
Initial deposit for your escrow account	# 1001	$1,630.00	$1,630.00
Daily interest charges $ 22.19 /day	# 901	$665.70	$377.26
Homeowner's insurance	# 903	$975.00	$850.00
Survey Fee	# 1302	$250.00	$250.00
	#		
	#		

Loan Terms

Your initial loan amount is	$ 108,000.00
Your loan term is	30 years
Your initial interest rate is	7.5 %
Your initial monthly amount owed for principal, interest, and any mortgage insurance is	$ 800.15 includes [X] Principal [X] Interest [X] Mortgage Insurance
Can your interest rate rise?	[X] No [ ] Yes, it can rise to a maximum of %. The first change will be on and can change again every after . Every change date, your interest rate can increase or decrease by %. Over the life of the loan, your interest rate is guaranteed to never be **lower** than % or **higher** than %.
Even if you make payments on time, can your loan balance rise?	[X] No [ ] Yes, it can rise to a maximum of $
Even if you make payments on time, can your monthly amount owed for principal, interest, and mortgage insurance rise?	[X] No [ ] Yes, the first increase can be on and the monthly amount owed can rise to $. The maximum it can ever rise to is $.
Does your loan have a prepayment penalty?	[X] No [ ] Yes, your maximum prepayment penalty is $
Does your loan have a balloon payment?	[X] No [ ] Yes, you have a balloon payment of $ due in years on .
Total monthly amount owed including escrow account payments	[ ] You do not have a monthly escrow payment for items, such as property taxes and homeowner's insurance. You must pay these items directly yourself. [X] You have an additional monthly escrow payment of $ 245.00 that results in a total initial monthly amount owed of $ 1045.15 . This includes principal, interest, any mortgage insurance and any items checked below: [X] Property taxes [X] Homeowner's insurance [ ] Flood insurance [ ] [ ] [ ]

Note: If you have any questions about the Settlement Charges and Loan Terms listed on this form, please contact your lender.

13. What incorrect entries, if any, were made in the general information section of the statement?
    a. There are no incorrect entries.
    b. The Sellars' names are spelled incorrectly.
    c. The Byers' names are incorrectly spelled.
    d. The address is incorrect.

14. Is the tax proration correct?
    a. Yes, it is correct.
    b. No, line 107 should be $1,329.04 and line 407 should show the difference, $770.96.
    c. No, the amount shown on lines 107 and 407 should be calculated from 1/1/11 through 5/14/11 ($770.96).
    d. No, the amount shown on line 107 should be calculated form 1/1/11 through 5/14/11 ($770.96) and be transferred to line 211 and 511.

15. Are there any other problems on the statement?
    a. No problems exist on the statement.
    b. There are at least eight more mistakes.
    c. The expenses on line 502 are incorrect.
    d. The purchase price on line 101 is incorrect.

APPLY WHAT YOU'VE LEARNED!

The author suggests the following actions to reinforce the material in *Section IV—Financing and Closing Real Estate Transactions:*

❏ Select a three-bedroom home that is currently for sale that you would like to own. Calculate the PITI payment, assuming you pay the listed price and make a 10 percent down payment. Use current interest rates.

❏ Based on the previous action, divide the PITI payment by the mortgage amount. This will give you the mortgage payment factor *including taxes, insurance, and PMI*. It will probably be just under 1 percent.

❏ Ask a title-closing officer to show you the entire closing process (avoid doing this at the end of the month because that's a busy time). Ask to watch a title search to see what the title company looks for. Examine the closing officer's checklist for closings. See what an instruction package from the lender looks like. Watch as the closing officer enters information into the computer for the HUD-1 settlement statement.

❏ With your broker's approval, randomly select five file folders for closed transactions. Thoroughly review each file, and list every document in the file. Do some files seem more complete to you? Are there any that you believe are *not* complete? Note what documents you want in all *your* closed files.

❏ Start again at the first file folder. Inspect the contract, the good-faith buyer's estimate of settlement costs and payment amounts, and the HUD-1 form. Check to see whether the amount the sales associate estimated for the seller or buyer matched the actual amount on the HUD-1 form. Can you account for any material differences?

❏ Next, check every entry on the HUD-1 form for accuracy.

❏ If you have not yet had a closing, arrange with an associate to attend one of his closings. Remember, you should listen, not talk, at the closing.

SECTION FIVE

ANALYZING AND MANAGING INVESTMENT PROPERTY

CHAPTER 14 ANALYZING AND MANAGING INVESTMENT PROPERTY

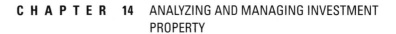

Many real estate professionals focus on the sale and management of investment property. This section discusses the advantages and disadvantages of investing in income property, how the general economy affects the performance of income property, the feasibility analysis involved in purchasing income properties, and the need for professional management.

A substantial part of our country's wealth has been generated by investments in real property. Chapter 14 shows the pros and cons of different property types, and methods of evaluating the investment.

Because of the substantial amounts of capital required for real estate investments, most owners want the property managed professionally. Chapter 14 describes the relationship between owners and property managers, the employment of resident managers, and the marketing and maintenance of property. ▪

CHAPTER 14

ANALYZING AND MANAGING INVESTMENT PROPERTY

LEARNING OBJECTIVES

Upon completion of this chapter, you should be able to:

1. categorize the three basic changes and trends in the economy;

2. itemize the four phases of an economic cycle;

3. list the major headings of an income property financial statement;

4. enumerate the four major property maintenance categories;

5. list at least three different advertising media that help to market rental property;

6. describe the uses and benefits of a show list;

7. specify at least five of the essential elements of a valid lease;

8. identify and explain the purpose of three of the financial reports an apartment building owner needs; and

9. describe those property managers who are exempt from the provisions of F.S. 475.

OVERVIEW

Real estate licensees who specialize in commercial and investment property are expected to understand the fundamentals of investment property. An investment study includes analysis of the national and local economies, specifically as they relate to real estate.

Investing in real estate has advantages and disadvantages, and each investor must evaluate the suitability of an investment. Chapter 14 focuses primarily on investment opportunities in smaller income properties such as raw land and residential, office, and commercial properties.

Investment ratios help buyers analyze properties to help reduce risk. Investors may use some of these ratios to determine the appropriate amount to offer for a property.

While federal income taxes are an important consideration when weighing an investment in real estate, the property's operating economics are more important.

Investors generally agree that professional property management is important in maximizing their returns. The professional property manager must have a comprehensive understanding of the economic forces at work in the real estate market. He must be able to evaluate the property in terms of operating income, forecast its potential for the future, and construct a management plan that reflects the owner's objectives. The property manager must become a specialist skilled in space marketing, tenant psychology, the legal aspects of the landlord-tenant relationship, maintenance procedures, and accounting. Chapter 14 examines these topics. ■

THE GENERAL BUSINESS ECONOMY

Timing is important in real estate investment. A good property purchased at the wrong time may result in substantial losses to the investor. Many investors also understand that a rapidly appreciating real estate market can make even marginal properties show accept-able returns, but they should carefully evaluate the market to avoid buying in a "bubble" market. Before deciding which type of real estate is right, the investor must try to under-stand the current economic trends.

Trends in the business economy may either originate from or result in changes in the real estate market. The condition of one directly affects the condition of the other. Changes and trends in the general economy fall into three basic categories: seasonal varia-tions, cyclic fluctuations, and random changes.

Seasonal Variations

Changes that recur at regular intervals at least once a year are called **seasonal varia-tions.** Such changes arise from both nature and custom. In the northern United States, for example, construction stops during the winter months; this seasonal change affects both the general economy and the real estate economy. Customs such as the nine-month school year have a seasonal effect on residential sales. Each year, retired persons fleeing cold weather swell Florida's winter population.

Cyclic Fluctuations

Business cycles, referred to as **cyclic fluctuations,** usually are defined as wavelike move-ments of increasing and decreasing economic prosperity. A **cycle** consists of four phases: expansion, recession, contraction, and recovery. (See Figure 14.1.)

Production increases during **expansion** periods. High employment levels, wages, and consumer purchasing power increase demand for goods and services. Prices rise because of greater demand, and credit is easy, making more money available for purchasing.

Recession normally is defined as two successive quarterly declines in the **gross domes-tic product (GDP).** GDP is the sum total of goods and services produced by the United States. The four major components of GDP are: consumption, investment, government purchases, and net exports.

Contraction begins immediately after recession. Confidence in the economy is shaken, and consumers reduce spending in anticipation of lower earnings.

Slower sales cause reduced production, worker layoffs, and unemployment. Prices are reduced to clear out inventories of unsold goods.

Recovery, defined as two successive quarterly increases in the GDP, begins when con-sumers, lured by lower prices, venture back into the market. As business activity increases, confidence begins to return. Slowly, production facilities gear up to meet the new consumer demand, capital begins to flow back into business enterprises, and additional employees are hired. Finally, as the gradual rise in employment generates more spendable income

FIGURE 14.1 ■ **General Business Cycle**

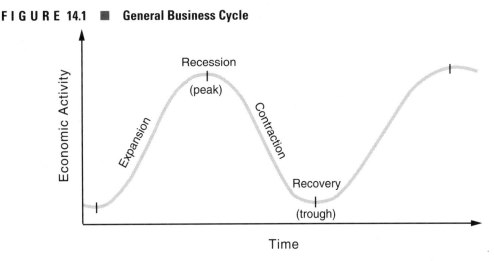

Source: Adapted by permission from Robert C. Kyle and Floyd M. Baird, *Property Management,* 6th edition (Dearborn™ Real Estate Education, 1997), 25.

1 and an increasing demand for more goods, the business cycle again enters the expansion
2 phase.

3   Although business cycles technically consist of the four phases defined above, most
4 discussions deal simply with expansion and contraction, measuring expansion from trough
5 to peak and contraction from peak to trough. Business cycles are recurrent, but not peri-
6 odic; that is, they vary in duration and timing. Economists have observed that a complete
7 cycle in the general economy may vary from 6 to 12 years.

Specific Cycles

9 **Specific cycles** are wavelike movements similar to business cycles. They occur in specific
10 sectors of the general economy, such as the real estate economy, and in individual sectors
11 of the real estate economy, such as housing starts and real estate sales. Specific cycles do
12 not always coincide with cycles of the general business economy, as the business cycle
13 actually is a weighted average of all specific cycles.

14   Regardless of the state of the national economy, certain areas boom in recessions and stag-
15 nate in prosperous times because local demand runs counter to current broad economic trends.
16 Northeastern manufacturing towns were in trouble in the early 1980s, for example, while an
17 influx of new residents and industries into central Florida kept that area building and growing.

Random Changes

19 **Random changes** are irregular fluctuations of the economy that may be caused by legisla-
20 tive and judicial decisions or by strikes, revolutions, wars, fires, storms, floods, and other
21 catastrophes. These changes, impossible to predict or analyze, may affect one or more
22 sectors of the aggregate economy. They may influence all industries in an area or one
23 industry nationwide. Real estate activity, especially construction, is very vulnerable to
24 labor strikes, political changes, and natural disasters. One example of a random change in
25 regard to real estate is a zoning ordinance change allowing undeveloped land to be used for
26 industrial purposes that would stimulate construction activity locally. Government policy

changes and changes in tax laws also can cause random changes in real estate activity on a nationwide scale. Investors must be aware of what is happening on both the national and local levels and have contingency plans to cope with events as they occur.

THE REAL ESTATE ECONOMY

The real estate economy is an important component of the general business economy, subject to the same four types of fluctuations. Specific cycles are the most pronounced and important trends that appear in the real estate sector. They can be observed in all phases of real estate: land development, building, sales, finance, investment, rental, and redevelopment.

Most sectors of the real estate economy are subject to both long and short cycles. Long-term cycles last from 15 to 22 years, and short-term cycles take about 3 years.

A controlling factor in the building cycle is the availability of money and credit in the mortgage and construction markets. During the years 2001 through 2006, the Federal Reserve made money very easy to get and fed the boom in real estate, all the way up to the bursting of the bubble. In general, when the economy is strong and prices are rising, the Federal Reserve tightens the money supply to control speculation. The resulting higher interest rates make real estate investment less attractive because builders must either pass the higher costs on to consumers or accept lower profits. Either situation slows the rate of construction. The Fed did not apply the brakes in time.

An extremely important indicator for forecasting the economy is the monthly report of Housing Starts, published by the Census Department between the 16th and the 20th of each month. Housing starts, along with auto sales, are the first to rise in an economic recovery and the first to drop in a recession. Not only does new housing have a direct effect on the market but housing-related purchases such as furniture and appliances also fuel a rebounding economy. In 2010, housing starts were at a 20-year low.

If investors believe that the general economic situation is beginning to turn around, it may be time to review the advantages and disadvantages of investment in real estate.

FLORIDA'S REAL ESTATE MARKET

During the years of 2003 through 2006, low interest rates fueled a real estate boom. At the same time, speculators entered into contracts to purchase real property with the intent of "flipping" the contract for a higher price even before they had to close on the purchase. Also, many subprime loans were granted that were unsound. Property appreciation rates were abnormally high resulting in high profits for owners and speculators who sold.

However, as the market cooled, many speculators failed to close on their purchases. This left developers and builders with large inventories of condominiums and houses. Coupled with high foreclosure rates on subprime mortgages and tightened credit standards, the seller's market turned into a buyer's market overnight in many areas of Florida. The imbalance may take many years to correct itself. In the meantime, smart money moving into the market is likely to find many bargains.

REAL ESTATE INVESTMENT ANALYSIS

Most of the wealthy people in this country amassed their great fortunes from real estate investments. The most significant asset of most families is the equity in their homes. Real estate may not be the right investment for everyone, however. Advantages and disadvantages exist, and should be evaluated by each individual.

Advantages of Investing in Real Estate

The advantages of investing in real estate include high leverage, good return, shelter from federal income taxes, and personal control of the asset.

Leverage. **Leverage** is the use of other people's money to increase the investor's return. Few other investments offer the high leverage real estate does. Stocks and bonds typically require at least a 50 percent down payment; mutual funds want 100 percent invested. Yet real estate investments can be made with 25 percent down payments, and less in many cases. The following example shows the benefits of leverage.

PRACTICE EXERCISE 14.1
LEVERAGE

Jack Gormley is considering the purchase of a duplex in an attractive neighborhood. He has reviewed the rental records for the previous four years that the property manager provided. The property's net income has increased about 4 percent annually. Property values have increased at about the same rate. The property value is $100,000, with a $20,000 down payment. Based on the new financing, Jack anticipates before-tax cash flows of about $1,500 per year. He wants to compare this investment with a mutual fund that has averaged a 10 percent return over the previous five years. Assuming a holding period of five years and an annual property appreciation of 4 percent, how does the simple arithmetic look?

Property value at a 4% annual compound rate	$121,665
Less mortgage balance at year five	$73,800
Equals increase in equity	$ 47,865
Plus $1,500 per year for five years	$7,500
Equals total cash from investment	$ 55,365

The final figure averages $11,073 for each year. Divided by the original investment of $20,000, the average annual return is about 55 percent. The return from annual cash flows was only 7.5 percent ($1,500 ÷ $20,000); the balance came from the increase in equity.

This type of analysis would be more accurate using the discounted cash flow approach, but the mutual fund returns would come in about the same pattern, making the comparison valid. Because of leverage, Jack's clear choice is the real estate.

Good returns. Many careful and astute investors achieve excellent returns, often exceeding 20 percent.

Income tax shelter. Most investment opportunities such as savings accounts, bonds, stocks, and mutual funds require that investors pay taxes on all current income (dividends). Real estate investments often provide tax-deferred cash flows, primarily because of cost recovery deductions (depreciation). This allows investors to avoid paying taxes on the cash flows until they sell the property.

Exchanging and installment basis reporting are other ways to defer paying taxes. These methods will be discussed later in this section.

More personal control. Many investors are uncomfortable with the notion of entrusting their assets to other persons or companies with little or no control over the use of those assets. The purchase of real estate gives an investor much more control over the investment's operation and management. This is true even if the investor employs a property manager, as the manager is under the investor's control.

Disadvantages of Investing in Real Estate

Disadvantages of investing in real estate include the following: management time, high capital requirements, poor liquidity, personal stress, and high risk.

Management time. Along with the advantage of personal control comes the disadvantage of the amount of time required to manage the property. Continuing review and management of an income property's operations is absolutely essential. A prudent investor takes an active role in overseeing management. The investor must seek a higher return on the investment to compensate for the time requirements.

High capital requirements. Real estate requires a substantial capital investment. Not only do the investors need funds to acquire the property, they also must have reserve funds available to make major renovations when required or to cover unexpected events. If vacancy rates are high, the investors will find it difficult to sell the property and may need to inject more money into the real estate to pay its operating costs and debt service to carry them through the hard times.

Poor liquidity. Investment real estate is a complicated purchase, even in the best markets. Land-use requirements, environmental audits, maintenance inspections, lease reviews, and new financing all take a substantial amount of time. A seller must understand that it could be a year or more after putting the property on the market before a sale is closed. In bad markets, however, it can be close to impossible to sell property at a fair price because so many other properties are available. This is a significant disadvantage of investment real estate.

Personal stress. Many first-time real estate investors suffer rude awakenings when they discover that property management isn't just about cash flow projections and planning, but it is also about personal interaction with tenants. Because an owner's first few properties usually are not large or profitable enough to justify hiring a manager, an owner is left with the task. When the mortgage payment is due, slow-paying tenants can become an irritation. Tenant complaints take time and interpersonal skills to resolve. Tenants sometimes leave a property in poor condition when they move, requiring a large contribution of time and money to restore the premises for the next tenant. Eviction is sometimes necessary and is usually distressing to both landlord and tenant.

High risk. It is said that the longer an asset is held, the greater the chance of catastrophe. Many examples exist of seemingly good real estate investments gone bad. Failure could result from overbuilding in the market, causing high competition and lower rents. Environmental laws also may require expensive retrofitting. Or a major employer may relocate to another area, causing widespread unemployment. Insurance does not cover this dynamic risk. To overcome dynamic risk, the investor must analyze a property carefully before purchasing, then manage it effectively.

Static risk is risk that can be insured. Examples include fire, windstorm, accident liability, floods, appliance contracts, and worker's compensation.

TYPES OF INVESTMENT PROPERTY

A wide range of property is available for investment, and the type of property suitable for an investor often depends on the investor's age, assets, and risk profile. Young investors usually are willing to take greater risks. This may be due partly to optimism that has not been dimmed by hard knocks and partly to higher energy levels. Older investors want to keep what they have because they don't have a lot of time to get it back if it is lost. They avoid high risk and are more likely to look for attractive current cash flows as opposed to speculative appreciation.

Persons with very few assets have little to lose and are often risk-takers in their efforts to strike it rich. Persons who are financially comfortable usually are more conservative in their investment decisions.

Risk-averse investors ordinarily are not comfortable with industrial property, speculative land, or new construction of income property. They are more likely to want established income property with a proven record of income.

Types of investment property discussed below are raw land, residential income properties, office buildings, commercial properties, and industrial properties.

Raw land. Investment in raw land can be extremely profitable if good research skills, good instincts, and good luck come together in one transaction. This type of property investment also can be extremely risky for the novice investor. Cities and counties in Florida, when trying to get a handle on growth guidelines, often change land uses in an area, which may have either wonderful or disastrous consequences for the investor. Income tax laws can change the feasibility of many projects. Raw land usually does not offer a cash flow to the investor and requires continuing infusions of funds to pay property taxes and interest on mortgages. Timing is important because the longer the property is held, the lower the rate of return tends to be.

The most important determinant of value for a vacant site is location. If land is planned for commercial use, it must have access and visibility from a major arterial road. Shopping centers should have easy access to expressways. Topography is important because it can affect building costs to correct for heavily sloping land.

Residential income properties. A single-family home usually is the investor's initial purchase. A single-family rental home provides the investor with a breakeven cash flow or a little income if the investor combines good management with good luck. It also has some limited tax advantages from depreciation. Because the margins are so slim, however, a vacancy for even a month can wipe out all the profit for the year.

As the investor's assets and borrowing power grow, the next investment may be a multifamily property. Larger properties benefit from the efficiencies of land use and management. Where single-family homes usually are breakeven propositions for the investors, larger properties can bring substantially higher yields. Because of the much larger invest-ment required, a buyer should make a complete and detailed investment analysis.

Office buildings. Small investors must analyze the office building market carefully before committing their funds. What is the competition? How many new buildings are permit-ted? What's happening in the area economy? It is not enough to look at the overall occu-pancy rate. An investor should segment the market by age, location, and amenities. It is possible that vacancies are high in the older downtown buildings, while newer suburban office parks are nearly full. Prestige office buildings can be unprofitable for the investor; they're really pretty but often have low yields.

When analyzing the rent rates for competitive properties, the investor should pay care-ful attention to the services and tenant improvements included. Many buildings pay for utilities and janitorial service and give each tenant an initial allowance for partitioning.

Many investors prefer office buildings to residential apartments because tenants tend to occupy the properties longer, tenant complaints usually are made during business hours, and fewer collection problems occur. Smaller office buildings tend to have somewhat higher tenant turnover than buildings rented by national tenants.

Commercial properties. Many opportunities exist for small investors as well as shop-ping center developers to invest in commercial properties. Small strip shopping centers, because of their rectangular shape, lend themselves well to a variety of uses. They can be converted from storefronts to offices to restaurants with relatively little expense. A typi-cal strip center consists of a 100' by 60' building with four 25' or five 20' wide bays. The market in many areas became very soft during the last economic downturn, making new construction loans difficult to obtain for some years. The market has improved in recent years, becoming attractive again to small investors.

Larger neighborhood shopping centers usually include a grocery store or a drugstore as the anchor, along with some personal service stores such as dry cleaners, laundromats, or restaurants.

Community shopping centers may include a Home Depot, K-Mart, or Stein Mart as the anchor, along with a supermarket and other retailers, restaurants, and service com-panies. Management should try to arrange the mix of tenants so that each complements the others in the center and the overall effect is to generate additional traffic. Lease terms in these centers run longer than in strip centers. Professional property managers usually manage centers of this kind.

Regional shopping centers usually have three or more major department stores as anchors. They generally are located near expressways to draw more distant shoppers to the sites. The centers often have large numbers of general merchandise retailers. A profes-sional manager is essential to enhance the value of this very large investment.

Industrial properties. Industrial properties usually are located near expressways, airports, seaports, or railroad lines. Investment in industrial property requires substantial research and carries significant risk. Most small investors should be wary about investment in this market. Many industrial properties serve special purposes and are subject to long periods of vacancy in market downturns. However, with a successful company as a tenant, an industrial property can achieve reasonable returns.

MARKET ANALYSIS

Once the investor is satisfied that the economy is sound and begins to target the type of property for investment, a market study is the next necessary step. A regional market analysis should include demographic and economic information such as population statistics and trends, a list of major employers in the area, and income and employment data. It should explore the economic base of the city and prospects for the future in that locale. A neighborhood market analysis should assess five major factors:

1. **Boundaries and land usage.** Rivers, lakes, railroad tracks, parks, or major highways may help define the neighborhood's boundaries.

2. **Transportation and utilities.** Transportation and utilities are crucial to the success of income property. The investor should analyze the effect of major traffic artery changes, as well as proposed or scheduled widening of streets, opening or closing of bridges, or new highway construction, all of which may enhance or hurt a location.

3. **Economy.** The investor also should review the neighborhood's economic health. Rental rates in the neighborhood are a sound indicator of the real estate market's economic strength. The investor can obtain the most reliable current rental rate information by shopping the competition.

4. **Supply and demand.** A high occupancy rate indicates a shortage of space and the possibility of rental increases. A low rate, as evidenced by many For Rent signs posted in the area, results in tenant demands for lower rents and other owner concessions.

5. **Neighborhood amenities and facilities.** The neighborhood's social, recreational, and cultural amenities can be important. Parks, theaters, restaurants, schools, and shopping centers attract potential tenants.

FINANCIAL ANALYSIS

After analyzing the market, the investor must examine the property's financial performance. This provides the basis for estimating the property's value, based on return criteria the investor establishes. Assembling the data is the most time-consuming part of the analysis process. The investor must review the property's financial history, as well as rent data, financial results, and amenities for competing properties. The first step after assembling the data is to prepare a one-year financial statement for the property.

Estimate potential gross income. By multiplying the amount of space in the building by the base rental rate for that type of space, the investor can estimate rental income for each type of space found in the building. For example, the residential investor multiplies the number of studio, one-bedroom, and two-bedroom apartments by the rent for each type. The total of the estimated rent amounts from each type of space is the **potential gross income (PGI)** for the entire property.

Estimate effective gross income. **Effective gross income (EGI)** is potential gross income minus vacancy and collection losses plus other income. Vacancy and collection losses are forecast from the experience of the subject property and of competing properties in the market, assuming typical, competent management. A good balance of supply and demand is a 95 percent occupancy rate. Occupancy rates change based on changing economic conditions, such as rising unemployment rates or overbuilding. Other income from sources such as vending machines and laundry areas is added to potential gross income after subtracting vacancy and collection losses.

Estimate operating expenses. The next step is to calculate the property's **operating expenses (OE).** Operating expenses are divided into three categories: fixed expenses, variable expenses, and reserves for replacement (see below). Ad valorem taxes and property insurance are examples of fixed operating expenses. Their amounts normally do not vary with the level of the property's operation. Variable expenses include such items as utilities, maintenance, trash removal, supplies, janitorial services, and management. These expenses move in direct relationship with the level of occupancy. Regional norms for these expenses are available through trade journals and professional property management associations.

Establish necessary reserves for replacement. If the level of expenses fluctuates widely from year to year, based on major maintenance and replacements of property components, it is difficult for the analyst to get a clear picture of typical expenses. To be meaningful, the expense figure must be stabilized. This is accomplished by establishing a **reserves for replacement** category of expenses. It is not a current cash outlay but an annual charge that should account for future expenses. The most accurate way to establish reserves is to divide the cost of each item and piece of equipment by its expected useful life in years.

Estimate net operating income. The **net operating income (NOI)** is obtained by deducting operating expenses (fixed, variable, and reserves) from effective gross income.

Determine before-tax cash flow. Income properties normally are purchased with mortgage financing, so owners must make mortgage payments from the NOI. When an annual mortgage payment is subtracted from NOI, the remaining amount is called **before-tax cash flow (BTCF),** sometimes called *cash throwoff.*

Constructing a Financial Statement for a Residential Investment

The following example describes the process of analyzing a residential investment. Sigrid Fleming is considering an investment in an apartment property located in southeast Tallahassee. The property, which is well-maintained and about seven years old, is located near some office buildings and shopping. Many of the tenants are employed in clerical and secretarial positions. The rental rates are very competitive in the area. Sigrid's broker has given her the bookkeeper's statements for the previous two years. Based on those statements and information from competing properties, she has constructed the operating statement shown in Figure 14.2.

The capitalization rate. Capitalizing net operating income is a basic approach to estimating value. While an appraiser uses a rate determined by verified sales in the marketplace, an investor sets the rate that provides an acceptable return using subjective criteria the investor establishes. The *capitalization rate* is the one-year before-tax operating return on a real property investment without considering debt service on the property. If an investor pays all cash for a $300,000 investment and the net operating income is $30,000, the rate of return is 10 percent. This is calculated by dividing the net operating income by the value ($30,000 ÷ $300,000).

DISCUSSION EXERCISE 14.1

What is the capitalization rate for the Tallahassee Villas Apartments?
If Sigrid desires a return of 14 percent, what will she pay for the property?

FIGURE 14.2 ■ **Operating Statement for Residential Property**

Tallahassee Villas Apartments
Operating Statement
Purchase Price: $1,000,000/Mortgage $800,000

Potential Gross Income	
25 units @ $425/mo.	$127,500
12 units @ $500/mo.	72,000
	$199,500
Less vacancy and collection losses @ 5%	9,975
Effective Gross Income	$189,525
Operating Expenses:	
Property taxes	$8,700
Garbage collection	2,800
Pest control	4,500
Insurance	3,500
Maintenance	9,600
Management @ 5%	9,476
Resident manager's apartment	4,200
Reserves for replacements	$30,000
Total Operating Expenses	$72,776
Net Operating Income	$116,749
Mortgage payment ($800,000 @ 10% for 25 years)	$87,235
Before-Tax Cash Flow (cash throw-off)	$29,514

Assume, however, that the investor would not purchase the property unless it yielded 12 percent. By dividing the net operating income by the rate desired ($30,000 ÷ .12), the investor would agree to pay only $250,000.

INTRODUCTION TO PROPERTY MANAGEMENT

A professional property manager may be an individual licensee, a member of a real estate firm specializing in property management, or a member of the property management department of a large full-service real estate company. She also may work within the trust department of a financial institution or within the real estate department of a large corporation or public institution. Regardless of their employment status, property managers pursue similar objectives and handle a wide variety of duties, including planning, merchandising, maintenance, and accounting. Although management duties vary according to the specific situation and particular property, a successful manager is competent in all of these areas.

The **Institute of Real Estate Management (IREM)** was created in 1933 by a group of property management firms as a subsidiary group of the National Association of REALTORS®. Currently, individuals wishing to join the institute must satisfy education and experience requirements, pass examinations given or approved by the institute, and adhere to a specific code of ethics. They are then awarded the prestigious designation **Certified Property Manager (CPM)** in recognition of their professional status as property managers.

CLASSIFICATION OF REAL PROPERTY

Real estate property managers manage four major classifications of real property: residential, commercial, industrial, and special-purpose. Each classification can be further subdivided and requires a different combination of property management knowledge and skills. This chapter introduces the field; it is not intended to be a complete discussion of property management. Residential property is emphasized in this introduction.

> ### DISCUSSION EXERCISE 14.2
>
> Relate a personal experience in renting or leasing residential property as a landlord or tenant.

Residential Property

Residential real estate is the largest source of demand for the services of professional property managers. Two principal categories of residential real estate exist: single-family homes and multifamily residences.

Single-family homes. Freestanding, single-family homes are the most popular form of housing in the United States. According to the Census Bureau, more than 60 percent of housing in this country is owner-occupied and does not require professional management. Although homes that are rented to other parties often are managed directly by the owners, there is a growing trend toward professional management of such properties, particularly condominiums and vacation homes. Many large corporations and their relocation companies hire property managers for homes vacated by employees who have been transferred.

Rising construction costs and a decrease in the availability of usable land have resulted in the growing popularity of town houses, condominiums, and cooperatives. Although each unit is a single-family residence, the individual owners of the units share certain responsibilities—such as maintenance of the roof, common walls, grounds, and common facilities—for the development as a whole. They usually employ professional managers to handle these jobs and maintain accounting records.

Multifamily residences. The economy of design and land usage inherent in multifamily housing allows for a lower per-family cost of construction. Thus, multifamily residences are a rapidly growing segment of the national residential real estate market.

Multifamily residences can be held under various forms of ownership. Small properties of two to six units often are owner-occupied and owner-managed, whereas most large highrise apartment communities are professionally managed for their owners. Cooperative and condominium apartments usually are owner-occupied buildings governed by boards of directors the owners elect. These boards generally hire professional managers for their properties.

Multifamily residences can be classified as garden apartments, walkup buildings, or highrise apartments. Each type is unique in its location, design, construction, services, and amenities.

OWNER-BROKER RELATIONSHIP

Three basic relationships can exist between the individual or corporate owner of a building and the property manager: owner-broker, employer-employee, and trustor-trustee. Property managers in all categories are considered professionals, and their responsibilities are very similar. Because this section focuses on residential property management, only the principal-agent relationship is covered here.

Usually, when an owner engages a broker to be the property manager, the broker acts as a single agent for the owner. The principal-agent relationship is created by a written contract signed by both parties that empowers the property manager, as agent, to act on behalf of the owner, or principal, in certain situations. Specifically, the agent acts for the principal to bring him or her into legal relations with third parties. Implicit in this fiduciary relationship are the legal and ethical considerations that any agent must accord her or his principal. The property manager has the duties of skill, care and diligence, obedience, loyalty, accounting, disclosure, and confidentiality.

THE MANAGEMENT CONTRACT

Once the property manager and the owner have agreed on principles, objectives, and a viable management plan, it is in both parties' best interests to formalize their accord. The manager and the owner must work out the structure of their relationship, their specific responsibilities and liabilities, the scope of the manager's authority, management fees, and the duration of the management agreement. In addition, the owner must turn over management records and other information to the manager to facilitate the property's operation.

Whether the property involved is a duplex or a highrise complex, the responsibilities the manager assumes are of enough importance to warrant a written statement of intent. An agreement signed by both the manager and the owner defines the relationship between the parties, serves as a guide for the property's operation, and helps prevent misunderstandings. The terms of management contracts are varied, but most share the following essential elements:

- Identification of the parties and the property
- The term of the contract
- Responsibilities of the manager
- Responsibilities of the owner
- Fees and leasing/sales commissions
- Signatures of the parties

PROPERTY MAINTENANCE

Maintenance is a continual process of balancing services and costs in an attempt to please the tenants, preserve the physical condition of the property, and improve the owner's long-term margin of profit. Efficient property maintenance demands careful assessment of the status of the building's condition. Staffing and scheduling requirements vary with the type, size, and regional location of the property, so owner and manager usually agree in advance on maintenance objectives for the property. In some cases, the owner instructs the manager to reduce rental rates and expenditures for services and maintenance. Under this shortsighted policy, the manager may encounter management problems and the manager's reputation may be affected adversely. Properties can command premium rental rates if they are kept in top condition and operated with all possible tenant services.

Types of Maintenance

The successful property manager must be able to function effectively at four different levels of maintenance operations:

1. Preventive maintenance

2. Corrective maintenance

3. Routine maintenance

4. New construction maintenance

Preventive maintenance is aimed at preserving the physical integrity of the premises and eliminating corrective maintenance costs. Regular maintenance activities and routine inspections of the building and its equipment disclose structural and mechanical problems before major repairs become necessary.

Corrective maintenance involves the actual repairs that keep the building's equipment, utilities, and amenities functioning as contracted for by the tenants. Fixing a leaky faucet and replacing a broken air-conditioning unit are corrective maintenance activities.

Routine maintenance is the most frequently recurring type of maintenance activity. Common areas and grounds must be cleaned and patrolled daily. Also, cleaning and housekeeping chores should be scheduled and controlled carefully because such costs easily can become excessive.

New construction maintenance, linked closely with leasing and tenant relations, is designed to increase the property's marketability. This may be as elementary as new wallpaper, light fixtures, and carpeting. If the new construction is extensive, it might include new entryways, the addition of a swimming pool, conversion of space to a meeting room, or renovation of a previously occupied space. New construction often is performed at a tenant's request and expense. Sometimes a landlord redecorates or rehabilitates a space for a tenant as a condition of lease renewal.

Deferred maintenance is necessary maintenance that cannot or will not be performed. Deferred maintenance results in physical deterioration, unhappy tenants, and reduced rent collections.

On-Site Maintenance Staff

The manager's hiring policy for on-site maintenance personnel usually is based on the cost differential between maintaining a permanent building staff and contracting for the needed services. For example, the amount of construction activity stemming from alterations that tenants require determines the hiring policy. It makes sense to hire outside contractors for major construction jobs or for small buildings that cannot support permanent staffs.

The Building Owners and Managers Institute (BOMI) sponsors instruction that leads to professional designations for maintenance personnel and supervisors. These courses are particularly instructive for on-site maintenance personnel. Property managers who wish to learn more about the technical and mechanical aspects of their properties will find these courses a good source of information.

Contract Services

Services performed by outside persons on a regular basis for specified fees are known as **contract services.** For the protection of both the manager and the owner, a service contract always should be in writing and contain a termination provision. The latter stipulation becomes important if service is not satisfactory or if the property is sold.

Before entering into any service contract, managers should solicit competitive bids on the job from several local contractors. They can then compare the cost of contracting with the expense of using on-site personnel. The management agreement terms often set a ceiling on the service contracts that managers can execute without owner approval. Window cleaning, refuse removal, pest control, and security are services that usually can be performed more efficiently and inexpensively by outside contractors. Managers should check a contracting firm's references and work history before they employ them. Managers should determine whether the firm's employees are bonded and whether it has the necessary licenses or permits.

RESIDENT MANAGER—PROPERTY MANAGER RELATIONSHIP

Most properties of 20 units or more have a manager on the premises at all times. This **resident manager** is a salaried employee who usually coordinates rent collection, tenant relations, and maintenance work on the property. Obviously, these responsibilities increase with the building's size. The resident manager reports to the property manager. With this system, a single property manager can stay current with the operations of several large apartment properties without becoming consumed by the details. In addition to reviewing the reports submitted by resident managers, the property manager should visit each building regularly to gather information on necessary maintenance and repairs. Periodic inspections show the property manager how occupancy rates may be increased, indicate where operating costs can be cut, help improve tenant relations, and provide training and feedback reviews to the on-site manager.

In the past, building superintendents not only collected rents but also served as the maintenance staff. As the property management field grows more sophisticated and building equipment becomes more complicated, managers who perform all four maintenance functions have become the exception rather than the rule. Property managers are expected to recognize when maintenance is necessary and know where to turn for help with specific maintenance problems. While a property manager need not be a jack-of-all-trades, she should understand the basic operation of mechanical and electrical systems well enough to make intelligent decisions about their care and operation. The manager also must understand the economics, staffing, and scheduling involved in the smooth performance of maintenance tasks.

The hiring and firing of employees should be under the control of the property manager, not the resident manager. When screening a potential employee or making a decision to terminate an employee, the property manager should ask for the resident manager's opinion of the person's integrity, industry, and skills.

MARKETING THE SPACE

Two basic principles of marketing are "Know your product" and "Your best source of new business is your present customer base." Thorough preparation is required to give a suitable presentation of the premises as well as to determine such items as rental rates and advertising methods necessary to attract tenants. Maximum use of referrals from satisfied tenants is the best and least expensive method of renting property and is essential to any marketing effort.

It is the property manager's responsibility to generate the maximum beautification and functional utility per dollar spent. Items such as an attractive lobby, well-landscaped grounds, and the use of pleasant colors inside and outside the building may not create greater functional utility, but they may increase marketability and profitability.

Rental space is a consumer good that can be marketed with promotional techniques like those used to sell cars or homes. Because most apartment renter prospects come to the property as a result of a neighborhood search, attractive signage and strong curb appeal are essential. Each residential property should display a tasteful sign on the premises identifying the community, the management firm, the type of apartment, the person to call for further information, and a telephone number. However, walk-ins alone will not supply all the prospects needed. Other types of advertising also are necessary to attract qualified tenants.

Advertising and Display

Even if the property is priced at the appropriate market level, the premises are clean and attractive, and the property has a good location, the building still may experience an unacceptable vacancy rate if prospective tenants are not attracted to inspect the premises. The most common advertising is newspaper classified and display ads and apartment guides. The Florida Real Estate Commission (FREC) mandates that a broker's advertising must describe the property fairly and must not mislead. It also requires that the brokerage name appear in all advertising. Other agencies also impose restrictions on ads, particularly with respect to fair housing laws.

Classified ads. Newspaper classified advertising is the most important advertising medium for renting apartments. The property manager must keep the prospective tenant's needs in mind when composing the ad. For example, in a neighborhood where three-bedroom apartments are difficult to rent, an ad may appeal to a broader segment of the market if it offers a two-bedroom apartment with den. The classified advertisement should include the amount of rent, apartment size, property address, and manager's phone number. A brief summary of the property's major amenities also is very effective.

Display ads. More prestigious residential projects, especially when newly built, find it advantageous to use display advertisements. These larger ads attract immediate attention, appeal to potential tenants' desire for attractive living space, and demonstrate the many amenities a building offers. The specific rental rates often are omitted, with reference to a general range.

> ### DISCUSSION EXERCISE 14.3
>
> Bring to class a copy of the entire classified ad section of your local newspaper. Examine the sections dealing with display ads for large residential properties and compare various ads' effectiveness. Also, examine the help wanted sections for property and resident managers.

Apartment guides. Just as homes magazines are one of the most effective ways to market residential homes for sale, apartment guides appeal to potential tenants. Color photos make the property's presentation attractive and interesting. Many management firms report that the excellent response to ads in the guides is beginning to rival the effectiveness of newspaper classified advertising.

Broker Cooperation

While all selling activities have as their ultimate objective the closing of a sale or lease with the ultimate user, the property manager will want to take advantage of all opportunities for reaching customers. This means that sales efforts should be directed not only toward prospective buyers and tenants but also toward brokers and agents who can reach rental prospects.

Broker cooperation can be especially helpful when renting or leasing a new or very large development. Managers secure that cooperation by sending to key brokers brochures or newsletters describing available properties. Compensation usually is a split commission or referral fee. A manager also can make brokers aware of a property by making a personal presentation or by sponsoring an open house.

Rental Rate Strategy

Even when the space itself is clean, attractively decorated, and in good condition, market conditions may be such that some units cannot be leased. An alert manager quickly realizes which units are renting rapidly or are not moving fast enough and either adjusts the price or changes the method of advertising and display.

The goal in establishing a rental fee schedule is to realize the maximum market price for each unit. If each apartment type is priced correctly, all types will have the same rate of demand; that is, demand for studio, one-bedroom, and two-bedroom units will be equal, and the manager will be able to achieve a balanced occupancy rate for all three types. However, this level of demand is the exception in the real market. More often than not, the manager will have to raise the base rent on the unit types that are fully occupied and decrease the rate for those units less in demand. An optimal price structure assures the manager of a 95 percent occupancy level for all units. For this strategy to be economically sound, the revenue from the new 95 percent schedule must exceed the income that was collected when some types of units were fully occupied and others had tenant levels of less than 95 percent. The optimum rental rates in a local market are best determined by market analysis.

Show List

To establish a reasonable rental price schedule, the manager must follow certain organizational procedures, such as compiling a **show list.** This show list should designate a few specific apartments in the building that are available currently for inspection by prospects. No more than three apartments of each type and size should be on the list at any one time; when a unit is rented, it should be replaced by another vacated apartment that is ready for rental.

The manager should use the show list both as a control guide for the marketing program and as a source of feedback on its success or failure. The features of particular units are itemized on the list so that the manager can do a better and more informed selling job. The maintenance staff will have no problem keeping a small number of vacant units on the list in top-notch condition. The limited number of show units also suggests that space is at a premium and that the prospective tenant must make her decision quickly.

The show list and traffic count should be reviewed weekly to determine which units are not moving. Particular units may not rent even after several showings to prospects. The manager then should inspect these units personally to find out why they are hard to rent. All curable flaws (for example, worn carpeting or obsolete fixtures) should be corrected. If poor curb appeal is the problem, painting or cleaning up entranceways, planting new landscaping, cutting grass, and trimming shrubs often works wonders.

It is important that fair housing laws be observed carefully. The limited show list must never be used as a method of illegal steering within the property.

Selling the Customer

The best advertising programs, landscaping, decorating, and maintenance may be wasted if the rental agent is unresponsive or unprofessional or does not properly show the property. Probably the most important ingredient of achieving occupancy targets is well-trained rental staff members who are personable, enthusiastic, and professional. Many large management organizations spend substantial time and money to ensure that rental agents have the technical knowledge and sales skills to best represent the property owner. The property manager should maintain records carefully, including guest books to record visitors' names. The rental agent should describe the result of each visit and record subsequent follow-up calls.

LEASES AND TENANT RELATIONS

Potential conflicts between property managers and tenants usually can be avoided when sound property management practices are employed. Sound management begins with negotiation between the property manager and the prospective tenant, the results of which should be in written form (the lease).

Essentials of a Valid Lease

The general requirements for a valid lease are similar to those for any legally enforceable contract:

1. Complete and legal names of both parties (lessor and lessee)
2. Legal description of the property

3. Contractual capacity of the parties and legal purpose of the agreement

4. Consideration or amount of rent

5. Term of occupancy

6. Use of the premises

7. Rights and obligations of the lessor and lessee

8. In writing and signed (if for more than one year)

Licensees may fill in the blanks on only the lease forms specifically approved by the Florida Supreme Court. Changing or adding to the terms of the approved forms or completing the blanks on any other lease form is considered unauthorized practice of law. Currently, there are two leases approved by the Florida Supreme Court: the Residential Lease for Single-Family Home and Duplex, and a form developed by the Florida Bar.

The manager should explain the key points in the lease agreement. Rent collection policies should be covered. Tenants will usually pay rent promptly if the collection policy is efficient, effective, and reasonable. The manager should itemize other regulations that control the property and discuss the methods of enforcing them. The manager must be certain that the tenant understands maintenance policies and how responsibilities are divided between landlord and tenant. These policies and procedures are often outlined in a tenant brochure.

Most tenant-management problems center on maintenance service requests. When such a request is made, the tenant should be told immediately whether it will be granted. The tenant is the customer, not an adversary, and the staff should be reminded of that fact continually. Happy tenants remain in residence, eliminate expensive turnover, protect the owner's property (which lowers maintenance costs), and promote the property's reputation (which reduces vacancy losses and promotional expenses).

A tenant request for service should be entered on a standardized request form. The top copy and a copy to be left in the unit on completion of the work are assigned to the maintenance person answering the request. The manager keeps the third copy until the job is completed. An estimated completion date should be entered on the manager's copy for follow-up. The resident manager should contact the tenant to ensure that the work was completed properly.

Landlord and Tenant Act

Chapter 83, F.S., the Florida Residential Landlord and Tenant Act, outlines the rights and duties of landlords and tenants, as well as the legal remedies available to both parties in case of noncompliance with lease terms. The law's intent was to create a reasonable balance between the two parties in their legal relationship. The law includes, among its many requirements, very specific rules for handling security deposits and advance rent. Florida licensees acting as residential managers must comply with the act. Those real estate licensees desiring to know more about this subject should obtain a current copy of this Florida law.

OPERATING REPORTS

Owners of residential rental apartments need current operating reports to measure the profitability of their investments. The annual operating budget, cash flow statement, and profit and loss statement give an owner the data necessary to evaluate his property and its management.

Operating Budget

The property manager must prepare a meaningful annual operating budget that includes all anticipated income and expense items for the property. The starting point for this year's budget most often is based on the actual data from the previous year. The annual budget is helpful as a guide for overall profitability. It must, however, be broken down into monthly budgets if it is to be useful for controlling operations. There, the manager should produce monthly statements that compare actual and budgeted amounts and should be able to explain any significant variations.

Cash Flow Statement

**Forms
To Go**

Probably the most important operating record is the manager's monthly **cash flow report** on receipts and disbursements. This report includes all operating income, such as the income from parking, washing machines, dryers, and vending machines, and all operating expenses as well as debt service. The reports show the owner how the property is doing on a cash basis. The report also can include the annual budget as well as the previous year's results, providing a budgetary control as well as a cash control. A sample cash flow statement is shown in Forms To Go, Appendix B.

Profit and Loss Statement

A **profit and loss statement** is a financial report of a property's actual net profit, which may differ from the cash flow. The full mortgage payment is not shown; only the interest payment is an expense. The manager usually prepares a profit and loss statement quarterly, semiannually, and yearly. Monthly income and expense reports provide the raw data for these statements. The more detail provided in the report, the better the opportunities for meaningful analysis.

Additional Reports

Managers must be completely familiar with all phases of a property's operation. Other reports, such as vacancy ratios, bad-debt ratios, showings-to-rent ratios, and changes in tenant profiles, illustrate important trends that may require corrective action. Scrutiny of the budgets and actual expenditures per account from month to month and year to year can indicate the relative performance of management personnel.

LICENSING REQUIREMENTS IN FLORIDA

Property managers must be certain that the requirements of Chapter 475 of the Florida Statutes are followed carefully. The law requires that any person who rents or leases real property for another party for compensation have a current, active license. The following two exemptions exist:

1. Salaried employees of an owner, or of a registered broker working for an owner or for the properly licensed property manager of an apartment complex, who work in an on-site rental office of the apartment community in a leasing capacity

2. Salaried persons employed as managers of condominiums or cooperative apartment complexes who rent individual units, if the rentals arranged by the employees are for periods not exceeding one year

These exemptions are granted under the law to unlicensed, salaried employees. They may not be paid a commission or any form of compensation on a transactional basis.

Community Association Management

Property managers of certain community associations must obtain community association manager licenses from the Department of Business and Professional Regulation. This law does not affect apartment properties and commercial property.

S U M M A R Y

Real estate licensees are quite active in marketing investment properties. Most small investors concentrate initially on small residential properties but later may investigate the opportunities in the office and commercial markets.

An understanding of the general business economy is helpful in timing investment decisions. If the market is at the top of the cycle, buyers should be wary, but sellers might wish to market their properties aggressively. Specific cycles are the most important cycles that affect the real estate market. Low interest rates are a critical component to a strong real estate market.

Real estate investing offers many advantages, such as leverage, good returns, tax shelters, and personal control. However, those advantages are tempered by problems with stress, management time, risk, and poor liquidity.

Licensees have an opportunity to help their customers take one of the most important steps of their lives—beginning a program of real estate investment. When an owner hires a manager, the parties enter into one of three relationships: principal-agent, employer-employee, or trustor-trustee. Most management contracts share six basic characteristics and specify the duties and details of management operations that must be decided before responsibility for the property is transferred to the manager.

To handle the property's maintenance demands, the manager must know the building's needs and the number and type of personnel required to perform the maintenance functions. Staff and scheduling requirements vary with a property's type, size, and regional location.

Four types of maintenance operations exist: preventive maintenance, corrective maintenance, routine housekeeping, and new construction. Deferred maintenance is the term applied to accumulated postponed maintenance.

The hiring policy for on-site maintenance staff depends on the cost differential between maintaining a permanent building staff and contracting for needed services. A particular property's circumstances dictate which alternative is more efficient and economical.

Multifamily dwellings differ from one another in size, structure, location, and number of amenities provided. These differences exert a direct influence on the advertising techniques used to market each type of space. A show list of units available for inspection also is important to a property manager's marketing program, as is newspaper advertising, the most widely used medium for renting space because it reaches a large audience.

In addition to leasing, supervising the resident manager, and inspecting the maintenance of the premises, the property manager must provide the owner with regular financial reports. Various financial statements provide the owner with the data necessary to evaluate the performance of the manager and the property itself.

Property managers in Florida must meet the requirements of Chapters 83 and 475 of the Florida Statutes, unless specifically exempted.

KEY TERMS

before-tax cash flow
  (BTCF)
cash flow report
Certified Property Manager
  (CPM)
contraction
cycle
cyclic fluctuations
contract service
corrective maintenance
deferred maintenance
dynamic risk
effective gross income
  (EGI)

expansion
gross domestic product
  (GDP)
Institute of Real Estate
  Management (IREM)
leverage
net operating income (NOI)
new construction
  maintenance
operating expenses (OE)
potential gross income
  (PGI)
preclosing walk-through
  inspection

preventive maintenance
private mortgage insurance
  (PMI)
profit and loss statement
random changes
recession
recovery
reserves for replacement
resident manager
routine maintenance
seasonal variations
show list
specific cycles
static risk

PRACTICE EXAM

1. A salaried, unlicensed manager of a resort condominium in Florida legally may rent individual condominium units if the rental periods do NOT exceed
   a. 1 month.
   b. 90 days.
   c. 6 months.
   d. 1 year.

2. A person who provides services that require licensing under the Community Association Management Act must be licensed by the
   a. Florida Real Estate Commission.
   b. Department of Administration.
   c. Department of Business and Professional Regulation.
   d. Department of Community Affairs.

3. Maintenance on a building that cannot or will not be performed when necessary is which type of maintenance?
   a. Elective
   b. Deferred
   c. Corrective
   d. Routine

4. Funds set aside to prepare for the eventual replacement of worn-out appliances, carpeting, and drapes are called
   a. contingency funds.
   b. reserves for expenses.
   c. reserves for replacements.
   d. operating expenses.

5. Changes and trends in the general business economy fall into three categories—seasonal, random, and
   a. expansion.
   b. recovery.
   c. periodic.
   d. cyclic.

6. Wavelike movements of increasing and decreasing economic prosperity in the general economy usually are called
   a. random changes.
   b. cyclic fluctuations.
   c. seasonal variations.
   d. long-term movements.

7. Apartments that are vacant and available for immediate rental are placed on the
   a. floor list.
   b. up list.
   c. show list.
   d. cleared list.

8. According to the text, most tenant-management problems are related to
   a. late or unpaid rent.
   b. maintenance service requests.
   c. conduct of tenants and their guests.
   d. handling of security deposits and advance rent.

9. Another term used for *before-tax cash flow* is
   a. capitalization.
   b. effective gross income.
   c. cash throw-off.
   d. equity dividend rate.

10. Which is NOT a category of property maintenance?
    a. Elective
    b. Preventive
    c. Routine
    d. Corrective

11. You are the property manager for a new, 60-unit garden apartment complex. The annual potential gross income is $291,000, other income is $480 per month, and vacancy and collection losses are 5 percent. What is the property's effective gross income?
    a. $276,450
    b. $276,930
    c. $281,922
    d. $282,210

12. What is NOT a requirement for a valid lease?
    a. Contractual capacity of the parties
    b. Amount of leasing commissions
    c. Term of occupancy
    d. Consideration

13. An apartment property has potential gross income of $155,000, effective gross income of $150,000, operating expenses of $58,000, including reserves for replacement of $2,400, and debt service of $40,800. What is the property's net operating income?
    a. $48,800
    b. $51,200
    c. $92,000
    d. $94,600

14. Howard is an employee of a property management firm. He shows prospective tenants many of the duplexes the company manages around the city and writes up leases on the court-approved forms. Howard is paid $700 per month plus $50 per signed lease. Howard
    a. must have a community association manager's license.
    b. must have a community association manager's license *and* a real estate license.
    c. must have a real estate license.
    d. need not be licensed because he is not paid a commission.

15. Total operating expenses include variable expenses, fixed expenses, and
    a. debt-service expenses.
    b. management expenses.
    c. reserves for replacement.
    d. property taxes.

16. A problem many investors have with industrial properties is that
    a. land boundaries are unstable.
    b. many properties serve special purposes and are difficult to rent once they are vacant.
    c. they rarely need proximity to airports.
    d. rates of return are always low.

17. Changes that recur annually are called
    a. familiar changes.
    b. long-term cyclic changes.
    c. random changes.
    d. seasonal variations.

18. The type of maintenance aimed at preserving the physical integrity of the premises is
    a. deferred.
    b. preventive.
    c. corrective.
    d. routine.

19. How many apartments should be on the show list?
    a. At least five of each type
    b. No more than one
    c. No more than three of each type
    d. All available units

20. An investor obtains the best and most reliable information about rental rates in a neighborhood by checking
    a. the Bureau of Labor Statistics' survey of sample cities.
    b. competing properties.
    c. classified ads in local newspapers that cover the past 18 to 24 months.
    d. current classified ads in local newspapers for advertisements of comparable space.

APPLY WHAT YOU'VE LEARNED!

The author suggests the following actions to reinforce the material in *Section V—Analyzing and Managing Investment Property:*

- ❏ Select an apartment property in your area that has at least 30 units and learn the rental rate. Find out the typical vacancy rates in the area, then prepare a financial statement. Use an operating expense ratio of 40 percent.

- ❏ When you have completed the financial statement, capitalize the income at 10 percent to estimate a "ride-by" opinion of value.

- ❏ Travel on a thoroughfare and visit at least three vacant commercial buildings. Make notes on the structures and try to decide the highest and best uses. List three potential tenants for each site. Call the listing agent and get information on each property.

- ❏ Assume a potential buyer from out of town asks you to describe the local economy and estimate about what it will do in the next three years. Write your response as completely as possible. Get information from the local chamber of commerce and compare your description with your classmates' descriptions.

- ❏ If you work in residential real estate, you often may encounter potential commercial customers. Ask your broker which commercial broker he recommends for referrals. Check with a licensee in that firm to see whether the referrals could go in both directions, with you getting her residential referrals.

- ❏ Visit several apartment properties in your area. List the ones you would recommend to a friend looking for an apartment.

RESOURCES

The following sources are selective and not exhaustive. Each is listed by section in the book and in the order recommended by the author for further study. Numerous other available resources exist, including books, journals (e.g., FAR's Florida REALTOR® magazine), periodicals, newsletters, articles, legal cases, research studies, video programs, and seminars. Consult your broker, instructor, or local board of REALTORS® librarian for further assistance.

SECTION I. LAYING THE FOUNDATION FOR A SUCCESSFUL CAREER

1. Reilly, John W. *Agency Relationships in Real Estate*. 2nd edition. Chicago: Dearborn Real Estate Education®, 1994.

2. Crawford, Linda L., and Edward J. O'Donnell. *Florida Real Estate Broker's Guide*. 3rd edition. Chicago: Dearborn Real Estate Education®, 2008.

3. Gaines, George, Jr., David S. Coleman, and Linda Crawford. *Florida Real Estate Principles, Practices & Law*. 33rd edition. Chicago: Dearborn Real Estate Education®. 2010.

4. Lyons, Gail G., and Donald L. Harlan. *Buyer Agency Today*. 4th edition. Chicago: Dearborn Real Estate Education®, 2005.

5. O'Donnell, Edward J. *Continuing Education for Florida Real Estate Professionals*. 11th edition. Chicago: Dearborn Real Estate Education®, 2010.

6. O'Donnell, Edward J. *30-Day Track to Success*. Tallahassee: O'Donnell Publishing, 2010.

7. Zeller, Dirk. *Your 1st Year in Real Estate*. New York: Three Rivers Press, 2001.

8. Ferry, Mike. *How to Develop a Six Figure Income in Real Estate*. Chicago: Dearborn Real Estate Education®, 1993.

SECTION II. OBTAINING LISTINGS THAT SELL

1. Keller, Gary. *The Millionaire Real Estate Agent*. New York: McGraw-Hill, 2004.

2. Lyons, Gail G. *Real Estate Sales Handbook*. Chicago: Dearborn Real Estate Education®, 1994.

3. Davis, Darryl. *How to Become a Power Agent in Real Estate*. New York: McGraw-Hill, 2003.

4. Edwards, Kenneth W. *Your Successful Real Estate Career*. 4th edition. New York: Amacom, 2003.

SECTION III. SELLING REAL PROPERTY

1. Galaty, Fillmore W., et al. *Modern Real Estate Practice*. 17th edition. Chicago: Dearborn Real Estate Education®, 2006.

2. Reilly, John W. *The Language of Real Estate*. 6th edition. Chicago: Dearborn Real Estate Education®, 2006.

3. Karp, James, et al. *Real Estate Law*. 6th edition. Chicago: Dearborn Real Estate Education®, 2006.

4. Ventolo, William L., Jr., and Martha R. Williams. *Fundamentals of Real Estate Appraisal*. 10th edition. Chicago: Dearborn Real Estate Education®, 2008.

5. Crawford, Linda L., and Edward J. O'Donnell. *Florida Real Estate Broker's Guide*. 3rd edition. Chicago: Dearborn Real Estate Education®, 2008.

SECTION IV. FINANCING AND CLOSING REAL ESTATE TRANSACTIONS

1. Sirota, David. *Essentials of Real Estate Finance*. 11th edition. Chicago: Dearborn Real Estate Education®, 2006.

2. Crawford, Linda L., and Edward J. O'Donnell. *Florida Real Estate Broker's Guide*. 3rd edition. Chicago: Dearborn Real Estate Education®, 2008.

3. Steinmetz, Thomas C. *The Mortgage Kit*. 4th edition. Chicago: Dearborn Real Estate Education®, 1998.

4. Mettling, Stephen R., and Gerald R. Cortesi. *Modern Residential Financing Methods*. 2nd edition. Chicago: Dearborn Real Estate Education®, 1993.

5. Gaines, George, Jr., David S. Coleman, and Linda Crawford. *Florida Real Estate Principles, Practices & Law*. 33rd edition. Chicago: Dearborn Real Estate Education®, 2010.

6. O'Donnell, Edward J. *Continuing Education for Florida Real Estate Professionals*. 11th edition. Chicago: Dearborn Real Estate Education®, 2010.

7. Koogler, Karen E. *Closing Concepts—A Title Training Manual for Settlement Escrow Professionals*. 3rd edition. Largo, FL: The Koogler Group, 1996.

SECTION V. ANALYZING AND MANAGING INVESTMENT PROPERTY

1. Sirota, David. *Essentials of Real Estate Investment*. 8th edition. Chicago: Dearborn Real Estate Education®, 2008.

2. Kyle, Robert C., and Floyd M. Baird. *Property Management*. 7th edition. Chicago: Dearborn Real Estate Education®, 2007.

3. Crawford, Linda L., and Edward J. O'Donnell. *Florida Real Estate Broker's Guide*. 3rd edition. Chicago: Dearborn Real Estate Education®, 2008.

4. Downs, James C., Jr. *Principles of Real Estate Management*. 12th edition. Chicago: Institute of Real Estate Management, 1980.

FORMS TO GO

Appendix B is intended as a resource for real estate professionals. The forms included here have been carefully prepared and may be freely copied and used in your practice. While we believe the forms to be complete and accurate, we make no representations as to their legality. Before using these forms, licensees are cautioned to seek legal and other professional advice.

No Brokerage Relationship Notice

NO BROKERAGE RELATIONSHIP NOTICE

FLORIDA LAW REQUIRES THAT REAL ESTATE LICENSEES WHO HAVE NO BROKERAGE RELATIONSHIP WITH A POTENTIAL SELLER OR BUYER DISCLOSE THEIR DUTIES TO SELLERS AND BUYERS.

As a real estate licensee who has no brokerage relationship with you, _____ *(insert name of real estate entity)* and its Associates owe to you the following duties:

1. Dealing honestly and fairly.
2. Disclosing all known facts that materially affect the value of residential real property which are not readily observable to the buyer.
3. Accounting for all funds entrusted to the licensee.

_____   _____

Date   Signature

_____   _____

Date   Signature

Single Agent Notice

SINGLE AGENT NOTICE

FLORIDA LAW REQUIRES THAT REAL ESTATE LICENSEES OPERATING
AS SINGLE AGENTS DISCLOSE TO BUYERS AND SELLERS THEIR DUTIES.

As a single agent, _____ *(insert name of real estate entity)* and its
Associates owe to you the following duties:

1. Dealing honestly and fairly;
2. Loyalty;
3. Confidentiality;
4. Obedience;
5. Full disclosure;
6. Accounting for all funds;
7. Skill, care, and diligence in the transaction;
8. Presenting all offers and counteroffers in a timely manner, unless a party has previously directed the licensee otherwise in writing; and
9. Disclosing all known facts that materially affect the value of residential real property and are not readily observable.

_____

Date

_____

Date

_____

Signature

_____

Signature

Consent to Transition to Transaction Broker Notice

CONSENT TO TRANSITION TO TRANSACTION BROKER

FLORIDA LAW ALLOWS REAL ESTATE LICENSEES WHO REPRESENT A BUYER OR SELLER AS A SINGLE AGENT TO CHANGE FROM A SINGLE AGENT RELATIONSHIP TO A TRANSACTION BROKERAGE RELATIONSHIP IN ORDER FOR THE LICENSEE TO ASSIST BOTH PARTIES IN A REAL ESTATE TRANSACTION BY PROVIDING A LIMITED FORM OF REPRESENTATION TO BOTH THE BUYER AND THE SELLER. THIS CHANGE IN RELATIONSHIP CANNOT OCCUR WITHOUT YOUR PRIOR WRITTEN CONSENT.

As a transaction broker,_____ *(insert name of real estate entity)* and its Associates provide to you a limited form of representation that includes the following duties:

1. Dealing honestly and fairly;
2. Accounting for all funds;
3. Using skill, care and diligence in the transaction;
4. Disclosing all known facts that materially affect the value of residential real property and are not readily observable to the buyer;
5. Presenting all offers and counteroffers in a timely manner, unless a party has previously directed the licensee otherwise in writing;
6. Limited confidentiality, unless waived in writing by a party. This limited confidentiality will prevent disclosure that the seller will accept a price less than the asking or listed price, that the buyer will pay a price greater than the price submitted in a written offer, of the motivation of any party for selling or buying property, that a seller or buyer will agree to financing terms other than those offered, or of any other information requested by a party to remain confidential; and
7. Any additional duties that are entered into by this or by separate written agreement.

Limited representation means that a buyer or seller is not responsible for the acts of the licensee. Additionally, parties are giving up their rights to the undivided loyalty of the licensee. This aspect of limited representation allows a licensee to facilitate a real estate transaction by assisting both the buyer and the seller, but a licensee will not work to represent one party to the detriment of the other party when acting as a transaction broker to both parties. I agree that my agent may assume the role and duties of a transaction broker.
[Must be initialed or signed]

_____   _____
Date   Signature

_____   _____
Date   Signature

Designated Sales Associate Notice

DESIGNATED SALES ASSOCIATE

I have assets of one million dollars or more. I request that _____ use the

(Name of broker)

designated sales associate form or representation.

Signature:_____ (circle one) Seller / Buyer

SINGLE AGENT NOTICE

FLORIDA LAW REQUIRES THAT REAL ESTATE LICENSEES OPERATING AS
SINGLE AGENTS DISCLOSE TO BUYERS AND SELLERS THEIR DUTIES

As a single agent, _____ *(insert name of real estate entity)*
and its Associates owe to you the following duties:

1. Dealing honestly and fairly;
2. Loyalty;
3. Confidentiality;
4. Obedience;
5. Full disclosure;
6. Accounting for all funds;
7. Skill, care, and diligence in the transaction;
8. Presenting all offers and counteroffers in a timely manner, unless a party has previously directed the licensee otherwise in writing; and
9. Disclosing all known facts that materially affect the value of residential real property and are not readily observable.

_____   _____   _____

Date   Signature   Signature

_____

Designated Sales Associate Notice

Florida law prohibits a designated sales associate from disclosing, except to the broker or persons specified by the broker, information made confidential by request or at the instruction of the customer the designated sales associate is representing. However, Florida law allows a designated sales associate to disclose information allowed to be disclosed or required to be disclosed by law and also allows a designated sales associate to disclose to his or her broker, or persons specified by the broker, confidential information of a customer for the purpose of seeking advice or assistance for the benefit of the customer in regard to a transaction. Florida law requires that the broker must hold this information confidential and may not use such information to the detriment of the other party.

_____   _____   _____

Date   Signature optional   Signature optional

Goals Worksheet

GOALS WORKSHEET

1. During the next 12 months, I want to earn $ _____

2. That works out to be monthly earnings of $ _____
   (Line 1 ÷ 12)

3. Approximately 60% of my earnings should come from listings sold $ _____
   (Line 2 × .60)

4. Approximately 40% of my earnings should come from sales made $ _____
   (Line 2 × .40)

Achieving my listing income:

5. In my market area, the average listing commission amount is $ _____
   (Get this amount from your broker.)

6. So I must have the following number of listings sold   _____
   (Line 3 ÷ Line 5)

7. If only 75% of my listings sell, I have to get this many listings: _____
   (Line 6 ÷ .75)

8. It may take this many listing appointments to get a listing: _____
   (Get this number from your broker.)

9. So I need to go on this many listing appointments   _____
   (Line 7 × Line 8)

10. It may take this many calls to get an appointment   _____
    (Get this number from your broker.)

11. So I have to make this many calls per month: _____
    (Line 9 × Line 10)

12. Which means this many calls per week   _____
    (Line 11 ÷ 4.3 weeks per month)

Achieving my sales income:

13. In my market area, the average sales commission is $ _____
    (Get this amount from your broker.)

14. So I've got to make this many sales per month: _____
    (Line 4 ÷ Line 13)

15. It takes about this many showings to make a sale: _____
    (Get this number from your broker.)

16. So I must show this many properties per month: _____
    (Line 14 × Line 15)

Seller's Real Property Disclosure Statement

Seller's Real Property Disclosure Statement
FLORIDA ASSOCIATION OF REALTORS®

NAME: _____

SELLER HAS ❑ HAS NOT ❑ OCCUPIED THE PROPERTY.

DATE SELLER PURCHASED PROPERTY?_____

IS THE PROPERTY CURRENTLY LEASED? NO ❑ YES ❑ TERMINATION DATE OF LEASE:_____

DOES THE PROPERTY CURRENTLY HAVE HOMESTEAD EXEMPTION? NO ❑ YES ❑; YEAR _____

GENERAL INFORMATION ABOUT PROPERTY:

PROPERTY ADDRESS: _____

LEGAL DESCRIPTION:_____

NOTICE TO BUYER AND SELLER:

In Florida, a Seller is obligated to disclose to a Buyer all known facts that materially affect the value of the property being sold and that are not readily observable. This disclosure statement is designed to assist Seller in complying with the disclosure requirements under Florida law and to assist the Buyer in evaluating the property being considered. This disclosure statement concerns the condition of the real property located at above address. It is not a warranty of any kind by the Seller or any Licensee in this transaction. It is not a substitute for any inspections or warranties the parties may wish to obtain. It is based only upon Seller's knowledge of the property condition. This disclosure is not intended to be a part of any contract for sale and purchase. All parties may refer to this information when they evaluate, market, or present Seller's property to prospective Buyers.

The following representations are made by the Seller(s) and are not the representations of any real estate licensees.

1. CLAIMS & ASSESSMENTS

   a. Are you aware of existing, pending, or proposed legal actions, claims, special assessments, municipal service taxing or benefit unit charges or unpaid assessments (including homeowners' association maintenance fees or proposed increases in assessments and/or maintenance fees) affecting the property? NO ❑ YES ❑ If yes, explain: ____
   _____

   b. Have any local, state, or federal authorities notified you that repairs, alterations or corrections of the property are required? NO ❑ YES ❑ If yes, explain:_____
   _____

2. DEED/HOMEOWNERS' ASSOCIATION RESTRICTIONS

   Are You Aware:

   a. of any deed or homeowner restrictions? NO ❑ YES ❑

   b. of any proposed changes to any of the restrictions? NO ❑ YES ❑

   c. of any resale restrictions? NO ❑ YES ❑

   d. of any restrictions on leasing the property? NO ❑ YES ❑

   e. If any answer to questions 2a-2e is yes, please explain:
   _____
   _____
   _____

   f. Are access roads private ❑ public ❑? If private, describe the terms and conditions of the maintenance agreement: _____

   g. If there is a homeowner association, is membership mandatory? NO ❑ YES ❑, and are fees charged by the homeowner association? NO ❑ YES ❑ If yes, explain: _____

3. PROPERTY-RELATED ITEMS

   Are You Aware:

   a. if you have ever had the property surveyed? NO ❑ YES ❑ Date: _____

   b. if the property was surveyed, did you receive an elevation certificate? NO ❑ YES ❑ Date: _____

   c. of any walls, driveways, fences or other features shared in common with adjoining landowners or any encroachments, boundary line disputes, setback violations, or easements affecting the property? NO ❑ YES ❑

   d. of any portion of the property that is fenced? NO ❑ YES ❑

   If any answer to questions 3a-3d is yes, please explain:_____
   _____
   _____
   _____

Buyer (_____) (_____) and **Seller** (_____) (_____) acknowledge receipt of a copy of this page, which is Page 1 of 5 Pages.

SRPD-3x   Rev. 10/06   © 2006   Florida Association of REALTORS®   All Rights Reserved

Seller's Real Property Disclosure Statement (continued)

4. **THE LAND:**

    Are You Aware:

    a. of any past or present settling, soil movement, or sinkhole problems on the property or on adjacent properties? NO ❑ YES ❑

        i. of any sinkhole insurance claim that has been made on subject property? NO ❑ YES ❑

        ii. if claim made, was claim paid? NO ❑ YES ❑

        iii. was the full amount of the insurance proceeds used to repair the sinkhole damage? NO ❑ YES ❑

    b. of any past or present drainage or flood problems affecting the property or adjacent properties? NO ❑ YES ❑

    c. of any past or present problems with driveways, walkways, patios, seawalls, or retaining walls on the property or adjacent properties due to drainage, flooding, or soil movements? NO ❑ YES ❑

    If any answer to questions 4a-4c is yes, please explain: _____

    _____

    _____

    _____

5. **ENVIRONMENT:**

    Was the property built before 1978? NO ❑ YES ❑

    Are You Aware:

    a. of any substances, materials, or products which may be an environmental hazard, such as, but not limited to, asbestos, urea formaldehyde, radon gas, mold, lead-based paint, fuel, propane or chemical storage tanks (active or abandoned), or contaminated soil or water on the property? NO ❑ YES ❑ If yes, explain: _____

    _____

        i. of any damage to the structures located on the property due to any of the substances, materials or products listed in subsection (a) above? NO ❑ YES ❑ If yes, explain: _____

    _____

        ii. of any clean up, repairs, or remediation of the property due to any of the substances, materials or products listed in subsection (a) above? NO ❑ YES ❑ If yes, explain: _____

    _____

    _____

    b. of any condition or proposed change in the vicinity of the property that does or will materially affect the value of the property, such as, but not limited to, proposed development or proposed roadways? NO ❑ YES ❑

    c. of wetlands, mangroves, archeological sites, or other environmentally sensitive areas located on the property? NO ❑ YES ❑

    If any answer to questions 5a-5c is yes, please explain: _____

    _____

    _____

    _____

6. **ZONING:**

    Are You Aware:

    a. of the zoning classification of the property? NO ❑ YES ❑ If yes, identify the zoning classification _____

    b. of any zoning violations or nonconforming uses? NO ❑ YES ❑

    c. if the property is zoned for its current use? NO ❑ YES ❑

    d. of any zoning restrictions affecting additions, improvements or replacement of the property? NO ❑ YES ❑

    e. if there are any zoning, land use or administrative regulations which are in conflict with the existing or intended use of the property? NO ❑ YES ❑

    f. of any restrictions other than association and flood area requirements affecting improvements or replacement of the property? NO ❑ YES ❑

    If any answer to questions 6a-6f is yes, please explain: _____

    _____

    _____

    _____

Buyer (_____) (_____) and **Seller (_____) (_____)** acknowledge receipt of a copy of this page, which is Page 2 of 5 Pages.

SRPD-3x   Rev. 10/06   © 2006   Florida Association of REALTORS®   All Rights Reserved

Seller's Real Property Disclosure Statement (continued)

7. FLOOD:

Are You Aware:

a. if any portion of the property is in a special flood hazard area? NO ❑ YES ❑

b. does the property require flood insurance? NO ❑ YES ❑

c. whether any improvements including additions, are located below the base flood elevation? NO ❑ YES ❑

d. whether such improvements have been constructed in violation of applicable local flood guidelines? NO ❑ YES ❑

e. if any portion of the property is seaward of the coastal construction control line? NO ❑ YES ❑

If any answer to questions 7a-7e is yes, please explain: _____
_____
_____
_____

8. TERMITES, DRY ROT, PESTS, WOOD DESTROYING ORGANISMS:

a. Do you have any knowledge of termites, dry rot, pests or wood destroying organisms on or affecting any improvements located on the property or any structural damage to the property by them? NO ❑ YES ❑ If yes, explain: _____
_____

b. Have you ever had the property inspected for termites, dry rot, pest or wood destroying organism? NO ❑ YES ❑ Date of inspection_____If so, what was the outcome of the inspection? _____
_____

c. Has the property been treated for termites, dry rot, pest or wood destroying organisms? NO ❑ YES ❑ Date and type of treatment_____
_____,Company name:_____
_____

9. STRUCTURE-RELATED ITEMS:

Are You Aware:

a. of any structural damage which may have resulted from events including, but not limited to, fire, wind, flood, hail, landslide, or blasting, and which materially affect the value of the property? NO ❑ YES ❑

b. of any structural condition or, in the case of a homeowner association, any condition in the common elements that materially affects the value of the property? NO ❑ YES ❑

c. of any improvements or additions to the property, whether by you or by others, that have been constructed in violation of building codes or without necessary permits? NO ❑ YES ❑

d. of any active permits on the property which have not been closed by a final inspection? NO ❑ YES ❑

If any answer to questions 9a-9d is yes, please explain: _____
_____
_____
_____

10. ROOF-RELATED ITEMS:

Are You Aware:

a. of any roof or overhang defects? NO ❑ YES ❑

b. if the roof has leaked since you owned the property? NO ❑ YES ❑

c. if anything was done to correct the leaks? NO ❑ YES ❑

d. if the roof has been replaced? NO ❑ YES ❑ If yes, when:_____

e. If there is a warranty on the roof? NO ❑ YES ❑ If yes, is it transferable? NO ❑ YES ❑

f. If the roof been inspected within the last twelve months? NO ❑ YES ❑

If any answer to questions 10a-10f is yes, please explain: _____
_____
_____
_____

Buyer (_____) (_____) and **Seller** (_____) (_____) acknowledge receipt of a copy of this page, which is Page 3 of 5 Pages.

Seller's Real Property Disclosure Statement (continued)

11. PLUMBING-RELATED ITEMS:
    a. What is your drinking water source? Public ❑ Private Well ❑ Other Source ❑. If your drinking water is from a well or other source, when was your water last checked for safety and what was the result of the test?_____
    _____
    b. Do you have a water conditioning system? NO ❑ YES ❑ If yes, type:_____Owned ❑ Leased ❑ c. What is the balance owed on the system? $_____
    d. Do you have a sewer ❑ or septic system ❑? If septic system describe the location of each system:_____
    _____
    e. Are you aware of any septic tanks or wells on the property which are not currently being used?
    NO ❑ YES ❑ If yes, explain: _____
    f. Are you aware of any plumbing leaks since you have owned the property? NO ❑ YES ❑ If yes, explain: _____
    _____
    _____
    g. Are you aware of any conditions that materially affect the value of the property relating to the septic tank/drain field, sewer lines, or any other plumbing related items? NO ❑ YES ❑ If yes, explain: _____
    _____
    _____

12. POOLS/HOT TUBS/SPAS:
    a. Does the property have a swimming pool? NO ❑ YES ❑ Hot tub? NO ❑ YES ❑ Spa? NO ❑ YES ❑
    b. If you answered yes to any part of 12a, was the certificate of completion received after Oct. 1, 2000 for the pool? NO ❑ YES ❑ For the spa? NO ❑ YES ❑ For the hot tub? NO ❑ YES ❑
    c. Check the pool safety features (as defined by Section 515.27, Florida Statutes) your swimming pool, hot tub or spa has: Enclosure that meets the pool barrier requirements ❑ Approved safety pool cover ❑
            Required door and window exit alarms ❑ Required door locks ❑ none ❑
    d. Are you aware of any conditions regarding these items that materially affect the value of the property?
    NO ❑ YES ❑ If yes, explain:_____
    _____
    _____

13. MAJOR APPLIANCES:
    Indicate existing equipment:
    Range ❑ Oven ❑ Microwave ❑ Dishwasher ❑ Garbage Disposal ❑ Trash Compactor ❑ Refrigerator ❑
    Freezer ❑ Washer ❑ Dryer ❑
    Are any of these appliances leased? NO ❑ YES ❑ Are any of these gas appliances? NO ❑ YES ❑
    Is the water heater: owned ❑ leased ❑; Is the water heater: electric ❑ gas ❑
    Are you aware of any problems with these appliances, including whether any of the appliances have leaked or over-flowed, since you have owned the property? NO ❑ YES ❑ If yes, explain:_____
    _____
    _____

14. ELECTRICAL SYSTEM:
    Are You Aware:
    a. of any damaged or malfunctioning switches, receptacles, or wiring? NO ❑ YES ❑
    b. of any conditions that materially affect the value or operating capacity of the electrical system? NO ❑ YES ❑
    If answers to questions 14a or 14b is yes, please explain: _____
    _____
    _____

15. HEATING AND AIR CONDITIONING:
    Indicate existing equipment:
    Air conditioning: **Heating:**
      Central ❑ Window/Wall ❑ Number of units_____   Electric ❑ Fuel Oil ❑ Gas ❑ Other ❑
    Solar Heating:
      Owned ❑ Leased ❑
    Wood-burning stove: NO ❑ YES ❑
    Fireplace: NO ❑ YES ❑ Describe fireplace equipment: _____
    Are you aware of any defects, malfunctioning or condensation problems regarding these items, since you have owned the property? NO ❑ YES ❑ If yes, explain:_____
    _____

Buyer (____) (____) and **Seller** (____) (____) acknowledge receipt of a copy of this page, which is Page 4 of 5 Pages.

Seller's Real Property Disclosure Statement (continued)

16. OTHER EQUIPMENT:
 Indicate existing equipment:
  Security System: NO ❑ YES ❑ Leased ❑ Owned ❑ Connected to Central Monitor ❑ Monthly Fee $_____
  Smoke Detectors: NO ❑ YES ❑, Number of smoke detectors?_____
  Lawn Sprinkler System: NO ❑ YES ❑ Sprinkler water source:_____If well is source, is there an
  iron filter? NO ❑ YES ❑ Is there a timer? NO ❑ YES ❑ Is the timer automatic? NO ❑ YES ❑
  Garage door openers? NO ❑ YES ❑, Number of transmitters?_____, Humidistat? NO ❑ YES ❑ Humidifier?
  NO ❑ YES ❑ Electric air filters? NO ❑ YES ❑ Vent fans? NO ❑ YES ❑
  Paddle fans? NO ❑ YES ❑, Number of paddle fans?_____

17. OTHER MATTERS:
 Is there anything else that materially affects the value of the property? NO ❑ YES ❑
 If yes, explain: _____
 _____
 _____
 _____

ACKNOWLEDGEMENT OF SELLER

The undersigned Seller represents that the information set forth in the above disclosure statement is accurate and complete to the best of the Seller's knowledge on the date signed below. Seller does not intend for this disclosure statement to be a warranty or guaranty of any kind. Seller hereby authorizes disclosure of the information contained in this disclosure statement to prospective Buyers of the property. Seller understands and agrees that Seller will notify the Buyer in writing within five business days after Seller becomes aware that any information set forth in this disclosure statement has become inaccurate or incorrect in any way during the term of the pending purchase by the Buyer.

Seller:_____ / _____ Date:_____
                (signature)   (print)
Seller:_____ / _____ Date:_____
                (signature)   (print)

RECEIPT AND ACKNOWLEDGMENT OF BUYER

Seller is using this form to disclose Seller's knowledge of the condition of the real property and improvements located on the property as of the date signed by Seller. This disclosure form is not a warranty of any kind. The information contained in the disclosure is limited to information to which the seller has knowledge. It is not intended to be a substitute for any inspections or professional advice the Buyer may wish to obtain. An independent professional inspection is encouraged and may be helpful to verify the condition of the property and to determine the cost of repairs, if any. Buyer understands these representations are not made by any real estate licensee.

Buyer hereby acknowledges having received a copy of this disclosure statement.

Buyer:_____ / _____ Date:_____
                (signature)   (print)
Buyer:_____ / _____ Date:_____
                (signature)   (print)

Buyer (____) (____) and **Seller** (____) (____) acknowledge receipt of a copy of this page, which is Page 5 of 5 Pages.

SRPD-3x   Rev. 10/06   © 2006   Florida Association of REALTORS®   All Rights Reserved

Lead-based Paint Warning Statement

Lead-based Paint Warning Statement
FLORIDA ASSOCIATION OF REALTORS®

(Use this form with contracts for the sale of residential property built in 1977 or earlier. This disclosure must be made beginning September 6, 1996, if Seller owns more than 4 dwelling units and beginning December 6, 1996, if Seller owns 1 - 4 dwelling units. Seller and licensees must keep a copy of this completed form for 3 years from the date of closing.)

Sale and Purchase Contract: This clause is incorporated into the Contract between
_____ **(Seller)** and _____ **(Buyer)**
concerning the residential Property built before 1978 and located at _____
_____.

"Every purchaser of any interest in residential real property on which a residential dwelling was built prior to 1978 is notified that such property may present exposure to lead from lead-based paint that may place young children at risk of developing lead poisoning. Lead poisoning in young children may produce permanent neurological damage, including learning disabilities, reduced intelligence quotient, behavioral problems, and impaired memory. Lead poisoning also poses a particular risk to pregnant women. The seller of any interest in residential real property is required to provide the buyer with any information on lead-based paint hazards from risk assessments or inspection in the seller's possession and notify the buyer of any known lead-based paint hazards. A risk assessment or inspection for possible lead-based paint hazards is recommended prior to purchase." For purposes of this addendum, lead-based paint will be referred to as "LBP" and lead-based paint hazards will be referred to as "LBPH."

    (1) LBP/LBPH in Housing: Seller has no knowledge of LBP/LBPH in the housing and no available LBP/LBPH records or reports, except as indicated: (describe all known LBP/LBPH information and list all available documents pertaining to LBP/LBPH and provide documents to **Buyer** before accepting **Buyer's** offer) _____
_____
_____
_____
_____
_____
_____
_____
_____
_____

    (2) Lead-based Paint Hazards Inspection: Buyer waives the opportunity to conduct a risk assessment or inspection for the presence of LBP/LBPH **unless** this box is checked (❑ **Buyer** may conduct a risk assessment or inspection for the presence of LBP/LBPH in accordance with the inspection, notice, repair and repair limits of paragraph 8(a) or H of the FAR Residential Sale and Purchase Contract or standard N of the FAR/BAR Contract for Sale and Purchase, as amended and as applicable).

    (3) Certification of Accuracy: Buyer has received the pamphlet "entitled "Protect Your Family From Lead in Your Home" and all of the information specified in paragraph (A) above. Licensee has notified **Seller** of **Seller's** obligations to provide and disclose information regarding lead-based paint and lead-based paint hazards in the property as required by federal law (42 U.S.C. 4852d) and is aware of his or her obligation to ensure compliance with federal lead-based paint law. **Buyer, Seller** and each licensee has reviewed the information above and certifies, to the best of his or her knowledge, that the information he or she has provided is true and accurate.

_____   _____   _____   _____
Buyer   Date   **Seller**   Date

_____   _____   _____   _____
Buyer   Date   **Seller**   Date

_____   _____   _____   _____
Selling Licensee   Date   **Listing Licensee**   Date

Buyer (____) (____) **Seller** (____) (____) **Listing Licensee** (____) (____) **Selling Licensee** (____) (____) acknowledge receipt of a copy of this page, which is Page 1 of 2 Pages.

LBPS-2x   Rev. 10/06   © 2006   Florida Association of REALTORS®   All Rights Reserved

Lead-based Paint Warning Statement (continued)

Notice from Real Estate Licensee to Seller/Landlord Regarding Responsibilities Under Federal Lead-Based Paint Law

I am notifying you of your responsibilities under the Lead-Based Paint Hazard Reduction Act of 1992 and its implementing regulations. As the owner of a residential dwelling unit built in 1977 or earlier, you have the following disclosure and other requirements (for purposes of this document, "LBP" will mean lead-based paint and "LBPH" will mean lead-based paint hazards, which are conditions that cause exposure to lead from lead-contaminated dust, soil or paint that is deteriorated or present in accessible surfaces or surfaces that rub together, like doors and windows):

1. Before You Sign a Contract/Lease. Before a buyer or tenant becomes obligated by contract to buy or lease your housing, you must complete the activities listed in A-D below. If you receive an offer before you provide the required information, you cannot accept the offer until after the information is given. This may be accomplished by making a counter offer that allows the buyer or tenant an opportunity to review the information and amend the offer if he or she so chooses. You must:

> **A. Disclose** to each licensee or other agent (for purposes of this law, anyone who enters into a contract with you or your representative for the purpose of selling your home, except for buyer's agents who are paid solely by the buyer and not by you or your representative, is considered an "agent") involved in the transaction:
>> **(1)** the presence of any LBP/LBPH about which you know;
>> **(2)** any additional information available concerning the LBP/LBPH, including the basis for determining that LBP/LBPH exists, the location of the LBP/LBPH and the condition of the painted surfaces; and
>> **(3)** the existence of any available records or reports pertaining to LBP/LBPH.
>
> **B. Provide** the buyer or tenant with:
>> **(1)** an EPA-approved lead hazard information pamphlet. This means either the EPA document entitled "Protect Your Family From Lead in Your Home" or an equivalent pamphlet approved by the EPA for use in Florida; and
>> **(2)** any records or reports available to you concerning LBP/LBPH in the unit, including records and reports regarding any common areas. If the unit is in multifamily housing that you own and you had an evaluation or reduction of LBP/LBPH in the housing as a whole, you must provide available records and reports regarding other residential dwellings in that housing.
>
> **C. Disclose** to the buyer or tenant:
>> **(1)** the presence of any known LBP/LBPH in the unit; and
>> **(2)** any additional information available concerning the LBP/LBPH, such as the basis for determining that LBP/LBPH exists, the location of the LBP/LBPH and the condition of the painted surfaces.
>
> **D. Allow** the buyer time to conduct a risk assessment or inspection for the presence of LBP/LBPH. You must give the buyer a 10 day period unless you agree with the buyer, in writing, to another period of time (such as within the time allowed for property inspections) or unless the buyer indicates in writing that he or she waives the right to conduct the risk assessment or inspection. This inspection requirement does not apply to tenants.

2. Sales Contract Requirements. You must ensure that the sales contract has an attachment having the following elements:

> **A.** The following Lead Warning Statement: "Every purchaser of any interest in residential real property on which a residential dwelling was built prior to 1978 is notified that such property may present exposure to lead from lead-based paint that may place young children at risk of developing lead poisoning. Lead poisoning in young children may produce permanent neurological damage, including learning disabilities, reduced intelligence quotient, behavioral problems, and impaired memory. Lead poisoning also poses a particular risk to pregnant women. The seller of any interest in residential real property is required to provide the buyer with any information on lead-based paint hazards from risk assessments or inspection in the seller's possession and notify the buyer of any known lead-based paint hazards. A risk assessment or inspection for possible lead-based paint hazards is recommended prior to purchase."
>
> **B.** A statement by you disclosing the presence of known LBP/LBPH in the home and any additional information available concerning the LBP/LBPH, such as the basis for determining that it exists, its location and the condition of the painted surfaces; OR indicating that you have no knowledge of the presence of LBP/LBPH in the home.
>
> **C.** A list of any records or reports described in 1.B.(2) above that are available to you and that you have provided to the buyer; OR a statement that no such records or reports are available to you.
>
> **D.** A statement by the buyer:
>> **(1)** affirming receipt of the information in 2.B and C above;
>> **(2)** affirming receipt of the lead hazard information pamphlet noted in 1.B.(1) above; and
>> **(3)** that he or she has either had the opportunity to conduct the risk assessment or inspection required as noted in 1.D. above or waived the opportunity.
>
> **E.** A statement by each real estate licensee/agent involved in the transaction that:
>> **(1)** the licensee/agent has informed you of your legal obligations; and
>> **(2)** the licensee/agent is aware of his or her duty to ensure compliance with the law.
>
> **F.** Signatures of you, the licensees/agents and the buyers certifying to the accuracy of their statements to the best of their knowledge, and the dates of the signatures.

3. Lease Requirements. As the owner of property being rented, you must ensure that every lease for the unit contains language within the lease itself or as an attachment having the following elements:

> **A.** The following Lead Warning Statement: "Housing built before 1978 may contain lead-based paint. Lead from paint, paint chips, and dust can pose health hazards if not managed properly. Lead exposure is especially harmful to young children and pregnant women. Before renting pre-1978 housing, lessors must disclose the presence of lead-based paint and/or lead-based paint hazards in the dwelling. Lessees must also receive a federally approved pamphlet on lead poisoning prevention."
>
> **B.** A statement by you disclosing the presence of known LBP/LBPH in the unit being leased and any additional information available concerning the LBP/LBPH, including the basis for determining that it exists, its location and the condition of the painted surfaces; OR indicating that you have no knowledge of the presence of LBP/LBPH.
>
> **C.** A list of any records or reports described in 1.B.(2) above available to you and that you have provided to the tenant, OR a statement that no such records or reports are available to you.
>
> **D.** A statement by the tenant:
>> **(1)** affirming receipt of the information paragraph 3.B. and C. above; and
>> **(2)** affirming receipt of the lead hazard information pamphlet noted in 1.B.(1) above.
>
> **E.** A statement by each real estate licensee/agent involved in the transaction that:
>> **(1)** the licensee/agent has informed you of your legal obligations; and
>> **(2)** the licensee/agent is aware of his or her duty to ensure compliance with the law.
>
> **F.** Signatures of you, the licensees/agents and the tenants certifying to the accuracy of their statements to the best of their knowledge, and the dates of the signatures.

4. Record Retention Requirements. Sellers and the licensees/agents involved in the sales transaction must keep a copy of the completed attachment described in paragraph 2 above for no less than 3 years from the date of closing. Landlords and the licensees/agents involved in the lease transaction must keep a copy of the completed attachment or lease form described in paragraph 3 above for no less than 3 years from the first day of the leasing period.

5. Impact of Law and Disclosures. Nothing in the law or regulations requires a seller or landlord to conduct any evaluation or reduction activities. However, the parties may voluntarily insert such a requirement in the contract. Neither you nor the licensees involved in the sale or lease transaction will be responsible for the failure of a buyer's or tenant's legal representative (such as an attorney or broker who receives all compensation from the buyer or tenant) to transmit disclosure materials to the buyer or tenant, provided that all required persons have completed and signed the necessary certification and acknowledgement language described under paragraphs 2 and 3 above.

This information sheet was provided by _____

(licensee) to Seller/Landlord on the _____ day of _____, _____ .

Buyer (_____)(_____) Seller (_____)(_____) Listing Licensee (_____)(_____) Selling Licensee (_____)(_____) acknowledge receipt of a copy of this page, which is Page 2 of 2 Pages.

Comparative Market Analysis

Comparative Market Analysis

Prepared by: _____

Date: _____

Prepared for: _____
Property Address: _____
Features: _____

Properties sold within the previous 12 months

Property Address	Sales Price	List Price	Days on Mkt.	Living Area	Features	Estimated Adjustment	Adjusted Sales Price	Comments

Percent sales price/list price _____ %   Median $ _____

Properties currently on the market

Property Address	List Price	Days on Mkt.	Living Area	Features	Estimated Adjustment	As Adjusted	Comments

Median $ _____

Properties which were listed but failed to sell during the previous 12 months

Property Address	List Price	Days on Mkt.	Living Area	Features	Estimated Adjustment	As Adjusted	Comments

Median $ _____

The suggested marketing range is $ _____ to $ _____

This information is believed to be accurate, but is not warranted.
This is an opinion of value and should not be considered an appraisal.

Mortgage Loan Application Checklist

Place personal and company information/logo here	Mortgage Lender: _____ Address: _____ Loan Officer: _____ Phone: _____ Date of Application: _____ Time: _____

Thanks for using our real estate firm to find your home. To assist you in making your mortgage loan application, we have prepared the list of items that may be needed by the lender. Additional information may be requested.

The Transaction:
❏ Copy of the signed purchase contract.
❏ If you have sold your present home, a copy of the HUD-1 closing statement. If the sale is not complete, a copy of the signed purchase contract.

Your Income:
❏ Original pay stubs for the latest 30-day period.
❏ Original W-2 forms for the previous two years.
❏ If you are self-employed or have commission income: a year-to-date profit and loss statement and balance sheet; copies of your last two years' personal and business signed federal tax returns.
❏ If you are using child support payments to qualify for mortgage: proof of receipt.

Your Assets:
❏ Original bank statements for all checking and savings accounts for the past three months. You should be able to explain all deposits not from payroll.
❏ Original statements from investment or brokerage firms for the last three months (if applicable).
❏ Original IRA or 401(k) statements (if applicable).
❏ List of real estate owned: address, market value, mortgage balance, name and address of mortgage company.
❏ List of life insurance policies with company name, face value, beneficiaries, and cash surrender value.
❏ List of automobiles, with make, model, value, amount owed, lender name, address and account number.
❏ Estimate of replacement value of household furniture and appliances.
❏ Value of other assets (collections, art, etc.).
❏ If you have sold a home in the past two years, a copy of the closing statement and a copy of the deed given.

Your Liabilities:
❏ Credit cards: name, address, account number, monthly payment; and present balance.
❏ Other liabilities: name, address, account number, monthly payment and present balance.

Payments for Housing:
❏ List of addresses for previous two years, along with names, addresses and phone numbers of landlords and/or mortgage companies where housing payments were made.
❏ Last 12 month's cancelled checks for housing payments (landlord or mortgage company).

If you are divorced:
❏ Copies of all divorce decrees, including any modifications or stipulations.
❏ Child support or alimony payments: amount, duration, and proof of payment for 12 months.

If you are applying for an FHA loan:
❏ Photocopy of driver's license or other acceptable photo ID.
❏ Photocopy of Social Security Card.

If you are applying for a VA loan:
❏ VA Certificate of Eligibilty.
❏ Form DD-214.

For in-service veterans or those discharged within the past two years.
❏ Statement of Service.
❏ Most recent Leave and Earnings Statement.

Other items:
❏ If you have graduated from high school or college within the previous two years, a copy of your diploma or transcripts.
❏ If you have a gap in employment for 30 days or more, include a letter explaining the reason.
❏ If part of your down payment is a gift, the lender will give you a gift letter for signature when you apply.
❏ If you have filed bankruptcy in the last seven years, give a letter explaining the reasons, a copy of the Petition Decree, a Schedule of Creditors, and the Discharge document.
❏ If you have rental property, a copy of the current lease and two year's signed income tax returns.

Your Check:
❏ Your check for the appraisal and application fee.

Authorization for Sales Associate to Order Work and Customer's Agreement to Pay

Re: Property Address: _____

Responsible Person: _____ as ❏ Owner ❏ Buyer
Address: _____
Phone Number: _____
I hereby authorize _____ of _____ to
order on my behalf the item specified below and agree to pay for said item upon demand as required by
supplier regardless of the outcome of this property transaction. I understand that these arrangements are
being made by the sales associate as a courtesy to me. I shall look to the supplier only for performance
and workmanship and absolve sales associate and the brokerage firm for the performance and workmanship of the supplier.

Item to be ordered by sales associate:

_____

_____

Supplier: _____   Price Quoted: _____

Signature: _____   Date: _____

SUPPLIER AGREEMENT TO PROVIDE SERVICE AND
TO LOOK ONLY TO RESPONSIBLE PARTY FOR PAYMENT

Re: Property Address: _____
    City: _____

Supplier: _____
Phone Number: _____

I agree to provide the item/service specified below and agree to seek compensation from "responsible
party" shown above. I understand that these arrangements are being made by the sales associate in this
transaction as a courtesy to me. I agree to look to the "responsible party" only for compensation and
absolve sales associate and brokerage firm for the cost of the item/service.

Item to be ordered by sales associate:

_____

_____

Supplier: _____   Price Quoted: _____

Signature: _____   Date: _____

Sample Letter to a For-Sale-By-Owner

Dear Mr. Hendricks:

I heard recently that you were hoping to sell your house. Obviously, you have made the decision not to be assisted by a brokerage firm, and I understand and respect your decision. During the time you are working to sell your house, I hope you won't be offended if I "touch base" with you from time to time. I have enclosed some materials that may be helpful in your efforts:

- A sample sales contract;
- A buyers' statement that may show you what some of the buyers' costs may be; and
- Information on some currently available financing programs for your buyer.

I'll be happy to visit with you and perhaps suggest some ideas for the transaction specifically tailored to your situation.

I've assisted many sellers in this way, and have retained their confidence because I do not pressure them to "list." Often, sellers become weary of trying to sell on their own and have asked me to help. I only ask that if you change your plans that you consider me. In the meantime, if you have any questions, please don't hesitate to call.

Sincerely,

Alice Newby
Sales Associate

Preclosing Walk-Through Inspection Results

Property Address: _____ Date of Inspection: _____

Seller: _____ Buyer: _____

I have made a walk-through inspection of the property. I acknowledge that the sales associate has accompanied me to the property to make it available, and not to conduct the inspection. I take complete responsibility for the inspection and agree to hold harmless the sales associate and the brokerage firm from any liability in connection with the inspection.

My inspection shows that:

1. personal property items required by the contract to
   be left are present in the property   ❏ Yes   ❏ No

2. required repairs, if any, have been completed   ❏ Yes   ❏ No

3. the property has been maintained in the condition as it
   existed at the time of the contract, reasonable wear and
   tear excepted.   ❏ Yes   ❏ No

Comments _____

_____

I accept the property as inspected and release the sellers, sales associates, and brokers in this transaction of any further responsibility for warranting the property. I have been notified of the benefits of having the property covered by a homeowner's warranty. If the seller has not provided such a warranty, I ❏ accept   ❏ decline to purchase coverage at a cost of $ _____.

Buyer: _____ Date: _____

Buyer: _____ Date: _____

Property Sale Information Sheet

Property Address: _____

Seller: _____   Buyer: _____

Contract Date: _____   Closing Date (Est.): _____

Seller	Buyer

Seller

Listing Broker: _____

Phone: _____ Fax: _____

Listing sales associate: _____

Home Ph.: _____ Office Ph.: _____

Mobile Ph.: _____

Buyer

Selling Broker: _____

Phone: _____ Fax: _____

Selling sales associate: _____

Home Ph.: _____ Office Ph.: _____

Mobile Ph.: _____

Seller: _____

Old address: _____

New address: _____

City, State, Zip _____

Current Home Ph.: _____ Ofc.: _____

Buyer: _____

Present address: _____

City, State, Zip _____

Current Home Ph.: _____ Ofc.: _____

Will buyer occupy new home? _____

Existing mortgage for Payoff (P)

Assumption (A)

1st Mortgage holder: _____

2nd Mortgage holder: _____

New Mortgage Lender: _____

Type (Fixed; ARM: FHA, VA, Conv.): _____

LTV Ratio: _____ %   Interest Rate: _____%   Yrs: _____

Seller's Attorney: _____

Ph.: _____

Buyer's Attorney: _____

Ph.: _____

Lender: _____

Title Company: _____

Appraiser: _____

Date Scheduled to Close: _____

Loan Officer: _____

Closing Agent: _____

Service Providers:

  Pest inspection: _____

  Home inspection: _____

  Roof inspection: _____

  Contractor: _____

  Surveyor: _____

Ph.: _____

Ph.: _____

Ph.: _____

Ph.: _____

Ph.: _____

Buyer's Insurance Company: _____

Agent: _____   Phone: _____

Property status: ❑ Occupied by seller   ❑ Occupied by tenant   ❑ Vacant

Key to property for inspection: ❑ At listing office   ❑ In lockbox at property   ❑ Call seller for appointment

Closing Progress Chart								
Listing Sales Associate				**Closing Progress Chart**	**Selling Sales Associate**			
#	Sched Date	Actual Date	X	Closing Duties	Done	X	Sched Date	Actual Date
1				"Sale pending" sign on listing				
2				Notice of under contract to MLS				
3				Binder deposited in bank $_____				
4				Additional binder received, if required. $ _____				
5				Loan application made by buyer				
6				Contingencies cleared in writing:				
7				Home inspection by: _____				
8				Soil test from: _____				
9				Roof inspection by: _____				
10				Other (describe): _____				
11				Appraisal by: _____				
12				Loan approval from: _____				
13				Title insurance ordered from: _____				
14				Pest inspection ordered (after loan approval) from:				
15				Report received and delivered to buyer				
16				Report received and delivered to lender				
17				Treatment ordered, if required				
18				Structure inspection ordered, if necessary				
19				Work completed and approved				
20				Required repairs ordered				
21				Required repairs completed				
22				Survey ordered (After loan approval)				
23				Survey completed. Results. . .				
24				Encroachments, survey problems cleared				
25				Buyer to get hazard insurance				
26				Insurance policy to title closing agent				
27				Buyer/seller contacted for closing appointment				
28				Pre-closing inspection				
29				Closing papers reviewed with buyer/seller 1 day prior				
30				Buyer given figure for certified check for closing				
31				Binder check prepared to take to closing				
32				Closing date				
33				Signed closing papers received by sales associate				
34				Post-closing duties:				
35				Commission check to broker				
36				Sign/lockbox picked up from property				
37				Buyer/seller letter of thanks				
38				Follow-up visit to buyer/seller				
39				Notice of closed sale to MLS				

Residential Sale and Purchase Contract

Residential Sale and Purchase Contract
FLORIDA ASSOCIATION OF REALTORS®

1* **1. SALE AND PURCHASE:** _____ ("Seller")
2* and _____ ("Buyer")
3 agree to sell and buy on the terms and conditions specified below the property described as:
4* Address: _____
5* _____ County: _____
6* Legal Description: _____
7* _____ Tax ID No: _____
8 together with all existing improvements and attached items, including fixtures, built-in furnishings, major appliances (including
9* but not limited to range(s), refrigerator(s), dishwasher(s), washer(s), and dryer(s), ____ (#) ceiling fans (if left blank, all ceiling fans),
10 light fixtures, attached wall-to-wall carpeting, rods, draperies and other window treatments as of Effective Date. The only other
11* items included in the purchase are: _____
12* _____
13* _____
14* The following attached items are excluded from the purchase: _____
15* _____
16 The real and personal property described above as included in the purchase is referred to as the "Property." Personal property listed
17 in this Contract is included in the purchase price, has no contributory value and is being left for **Seller's** convenience.

18   PRICE AND FINANCING
19* **2. PURCHASE PRICE:** $_____ payable by **Buyer** in U.S. currency as follows:
20*   **(a)** $_____   Deposit received (checks are subject to clearance) on _____, _____ by
21*   _____ for delivery to _____ ("Escrow Agent")
22   _Signature_   _Name of Company_
23*   (Address of Escrow Agent) _____
24*   (Phone # of Escrow Agent) _____
25*   **(b)** $_____   Additional deposit to be delivered to Escrow Agent by _____,
26*   _____ or _____ days from Effective Date. (10 days if left blank)
27*   **(c)** _____   Total financing (see Paragraph **3** below) (express as a dollar amount or percentage)
28*   **(d)** $_____   Other: _____
29*   **(e)** $_____   Balance to close (not including **Buyer's** closing costs, prepaid items and prorations). All funds paid
30   at closing must be paid by locally drawn cashier's check, official bank check, or wired funds.

31* **3. FINANCING:** (Check as applicable) ❑ **(a) Buyer** will pay cash for the Property with no financing contingency.
32*   ❑ **(b) Buyer** will apply for new ❑ conventional ❑ FHA ❑ VA financing specified in paragraph 2(c) at the prevailing interest rate and
33* loan costs based on **Buyer's** creditworthiness (the "Financing") within _____ days from Effective Date (5 days if left blank) and
34 provide **Seller** with either a written Financing commitment or approval letter ("Commitment") or written notice that **Buyer** is unable to
35* obtain a Commitment within _____ days from Effective Date (the earlier of 30 days after the Effective Date or 5 days prior to Closing
36 Date if left blank) ("Commitment Period"). **Buyer** will keep **Seller** and Broker fully informed about loan application status, progress
37 and Commitment issues and authorizes the mortgage broker and lender to disclose all such information to **Seller** and **Broker**. If,
38 after using diligence and good faith, **Buyer** is unable to provide the Commitment and provides **Seller** with written notice that **Buyer** is
39 unable to obtain a Commitment within the Commitment Period, either party may cancel this Contract and **Buyer's** deposit will be
40 refunded. **Buyer's** failure to provide **Seller** with written notice that **Buyer** is unable to obtain a Commitment within the Commitment
41 Period will result in forfeiture of **Buyer's** deposit(s). Once **Buyer** provides the Commitment to **Seller**, the financing contingency is
42 waived and **Seller** will be entitled to retain the deposits if the transaction does not close by the Closing Date unless (1) the Property
43 appraises below the purchase price and either the parties cannot agree on a new purchase price or **Buyer** elects not to proceed, (2)
44 the property related conditions of the Commitment have not been met (except when such conditions are waived by other provisions
45 of this Contract), or (3) another provision of this Contract provides for cancellation.

46   CLOSING
47 **4. CLOSING DATE; OCCUPANCY:** Unless the Closing Date is specifically extended by the **Buyer** and **Seller** or by any other provision in
48 this Contract, the Closing Date shall prevail over all other time periods including, but not limited to, inspection and financing periods. This
49* Contract will be closed on _____, _____ ("Closing Date") at the time established by the closing agent, by which time **Seller**
50 will (a) have removed all personal items and trash from the Property and swept the Property clean and (b) deliver the deed, occupancy
51 and possession, along with all keys, garage door openers and access codes, to **Buyer**. If on Closing Date insurance underwriting is
52 suspended, **Buyer** may postpone closing up to 5 days after the insurance suspension is lifted. If this transaction does not close for any
53 reason, **Buyer** will immediately return all **Seller**-provided title evidence, surveys, association documents and other items.

54* **Buyer** (____) (____) and **Seller** (____) (____) acknowledge receipt of a copy of this page, which is Page 1 of 8 Pages.
FAR-9 4/07   © 2007 Florida Association of REALTORS®   All Rights Reserved

Residential Sale and Purchase Contract (continued)

55 **5. CLOSING PROCEDURE; COSTS:** Closing will take place in the county where the Property is located and may be conducted by
56 mail or electronic means. If title insurance insures **Buyer** for title defects arising between the title binder effective date and recording
57 of **Buyer's** deed, closing agent will disburse at closing the net sale proceeds to **Seller** and brokerage fees to Broker as per
58 Paragraph **19**. In addition to other expenses provided in this Contract, **Seller** and **Buyer** will pay the costs indicated below.
59   **(a) Seller Costs:**
60   Taxes and surtaxes on the deed
61   Recording fees for documents needed to cure title
62*   Other: _____
63*   **Seller** will pay up to $_____ or _____% (1.5% if left blank) of the purchase price for repairs to warranted items (**"Repair**
64* **Limit"**); and up to $_____ or _____% (1.5% if left blank) of the purchase price for wood-destroying organism treatment
65* and repairs (**"WDO Repair Limit"**); and up to $_____ or _____% (1.5% if left blank) of the purchase price for costs
66 associated with closing out open permits and obtaining required permits for unpermitted existing improvements (**"Permit Limit"**).
67   **(b) Buyer Costs:**
68   Taxes and recording fees on notes and mortgages
69   Recording fees on the deed and financing statements
70   Loan expenses
71   Lender's title policy
72   Inspections
73   Survey
74   Flood insurance, homeowner insurance, hazard insurance
75*   Other: _____
76   **(c) Title Evidence and Insurance: Check (1) or (2):**
77*   ❏ **(1)** The title evidence will be a Paragraph 10(a)(1) owner's title insurance commitment. ❏ **Seller** will select the title agent
78*   and will pay for the owner's title policy, search, examination and related charges or ❏ **Buyer** will select the title agent and pay
79*   for the owner's title policy, search, examination and related charges or ❏ **Buyer** will select the title agent and **Seller** will pay
80   for the owner's title policy, search, examination and related charges.
81*   ❏ **(2) Seller** will provide an abstract as specified in Paragraph 10(a)(2) as title evidence. ❏ **Seller** ❏ **Buyer** will pay for the
82   owner's title policy and select the title agent. **Seller** will pay fees for title searches prior to closing, including tax search and
83   lien search fees, and **Buyer** will pay fees for title searches after closing (if any), title examination fees and closing fees.
84   **(d) Prorations:** The following items will be made current (if applicable) and prorated as of the day before Closing Date: real
85 estate taxes, interest, bonds, assessments, association fees, insurance, rents and other current expenses and revenues of the
86 Property. If taxes and assessments for the current year cannot be determined, taxes shall be prorated on the basis of taxes for
87 the preceding year as of the day before Closing Date and shall be computed and readjusted when the current taxes are
88 determined with adjustment for exemptions and improvements. If there are completed improvements on the Property by
89 January 1 of the year of the Closing Date, which improvements were not in existence on January 1 of the prior year, taxes shall
90 be prorated based on the prior year's millage and at an equitable assessment to be agreed upon by the parties prior to Closing
91 Date, failing which, request will be made to the County Property Appraiser for an informal assessment taking into consideration
92 available exemptions. If the County Property Appraiser is unable or unwilling to perform an informal assessment prior to Closing
93 Date, **Buyer** and **Seller** will split the cost of a private appraiser to perform an assessment prior to Closing Date. Nothing in this
94 paragraph shall act to extend the Closing Date. This provision shall survive closing.
95   **(e) Special Assessment by Public Body:** Regarding special assessments imposed by a public body, **Seller** will pay (i) the full
96 amount of liens that are certified, confirmed and ratified before closing and (ii) the amount of the last estimate of the assessment
97 if an improvement is substantially completed as of Effective Date but has not resulted in a lien before closing, and **Buyer** will pay
98* all other amounts. If special assessments may be paid in installments ❏ **Buyer** ❏ **Seller** (if left blank, **Buyer**) shall pay
99 installments due after closing. If **Seller** is checked, **Seller** will pay the assessment in full prior to or at the time of closing. Public
100 body does not include a Homeowner Association or Condominium Association.
101   **(f) Tax Withholding: Buyer** and **Seller** will comply with the Foreign Investment in Real Property Tax Act, which may require
102 **Seller** to provide additional cash at closing if **Seller** is a "foreign person" as defined by federal law.
103*   **(g) Home Warranty:** ❏ **Buyer** ❏ **Seller** ❏ **N/A** will pay for a home warranty plan issued by _____ at a
104* cost not to exceed $_____. A home warranty plan provides for repair or replacement of many of a home's mechanical
105 systems and major built-in appliances in the event of breakdown due to normal wear and tear during the agreement period.

106 **PROPERTY CONDITION**
107* **6. INSPECTION PERIODS: Buyer** will complete the inspections referenced in Paragraphs **7** and **8(a)(2)** by _____,
108* _____ (the earlier of 10 days after the Effective Date or 5 days prior to Closing Date if left blank) ("Inspection Period");
109* the wood-destroying organism inspection by _____, _____ (at least 5 days prior to closing, if left
110 blank); and the walk-through inspection on the day before Closing Date or any other time agreeable to the parties; and the
111* survey referenced in Paragraph 10(c) by _____, _____ (at least 5 days prior to closing if left blank).

112* **Buyer** (_____) (_____) and **Seller** (_____) (_____) acknowledge receipt of a copy of this page, which is Page 2 of 8 Pages.
FAR-9   4/07   © 2007   Florida Association of REALTORS®   All Rights Reserved

Residential Sale and Purchase Contract (continued)

113 **7. REAL PROPERTY DISCLOSURES: Seller** represents that **Seller** does not know of any facts that materially affect the value
114 of the Property, including but not limited to violations of governmental laws, rules and regulations, other than those that **Buyer**
115 can readily observe or that are known by or have been disclosed to **Buyer.**

116 **(a) Energy Efficiency: Buyer** acknowledges receipt of the energy-efficiency information brochure required by Section 553.996,
117 *Florida Statutes.*

118 **(b) Radon Gas:** Radon is a naturally occurring radioactive gas that, when it has accumulated in a building in sufficient
119 quantities, may present health risks to persons who are exposed to it over time. Levels of radon that exceed federal and
120 state guidelines have been found in buildings in Florida. Additional information regarding radon and radon testing may be
121 obtained from your county public health unit. **Buyer** may, within the Inspection Period, have an appropriately licensed person
122 test the Property for radon. If the radon level exceeds acceptable EPA standards, **Seller** may choose to reduce the radon
123 level to an acceptable EPA level, failing which either party may cancel this Contract.

124 **(c) Flood Zone: Buyer** is advised to verify by survey, with the lender and with appropriate government agencies which flood
125 zone the Property is in, whether flood insurance is required and what restrictions apply to improving the Property and rebuilding
126 in the event of casualty. If the Property is in a Special Flood Hazard Area or Coastal High Hazard Area **and** the buildings are built
127 below the minimum flood elevation, **Buyer** may cancel this Contract by delivering written notice to **Seller** within 20 days from
128 Effective Date, failing which **Buyer** accepts the existing elevation of the buildings and zone designation of the Property.

129 **(d) Homeowners' Association:** If membership in a homeowners' association is mandatory, an association disclosure
130 summary is attached and incorporated into this Contract. **BUYER SHOULD NOT SIGN THIS CONTRACT UNTIL**
131 **BUYER HAS RECEIVED AND READ THE DISCLOSURE SUMMARY.**

132 **(e) PROPERTY TAX DISCLOSURE SUMMARY: BUYER** SHOULD NOT RELY ON THE **SELLER'S** CURRENT PROPERTY
133 TAXES AS THE AMOUNT OF PROPERTY TAXES THAT **BUYER** MAY BE OBLIGATED TO PAY IN THE YEAR SUBSEQUENT
134 TO PURCHASE. A CHANGE OF OWNERSHIP OR PROPERTY IMPROVEMENTS TRIGGERS REASSESSMENTS OF THE
135 PROPERTY THAT COULD RESULT IN HIGHER PROPERTY TAXES. IF YOU HAVE ANY QUESTIONS CONCERNING
136 VALUATION, CONTACT THE COUNTY PROPERTY APPRAISER'S OFFICE FOR FURTHER INFORMATION.

137 **(f) Mold:** Mold is part of the natural environment that, when accumulated in sufficient quantities, may present health risks to
138 susceptible persons. For more information, contact the county indoor air quality specialist or other appropriate professional.

139 **(g) Coastal Construction Control Line:** If any part of the Property lies seaward of the coastal construction control line as
140 defined in Section 161.053 of the Florida Statutes, **Seller** shall provide **Buyer** with an affidavit or survey as required by law
141 delineating the line's location on the Property, unless **Buyer** waives this requirement in writing. The Property being purchased
142 may be subject to coastal erosion and to federal, state, or local regulations that govern coastal property, including delineation
143 of the coastal construction control line, rigid coastal protection structures, beach nourishment, and the protection of marine
144 turtles. Additional information can be obtained from the Florida Department of Environmental Protection, including whether
145 there are significant erosion conditions associated with the shoreline of the Property being purchased.
146* ❏ **Buyer** waives the right to receive a CCCL affidavit or survey.

147 **8. MAINTENANCE, INSPECTIONS AND REPAIR: Seller** will keep the Property in the same condition from Effective Date until
148 closing, except for normal wear and tear ("Maintenance Requirement") and repairs required by this Contract. **Seller** will provide
149 access and utilities for **Buyer's** inspections. **Buyer** will repair all damages to the Property resulting from the inspections,
150 return the Property to its pre-inspection condition and provide **Seller** with paid receipts for all work done on Property upon its
151 completion. If **Seller** is unable to complete required repairs or treatments or meet the Maintenance Requirement prior to
152 closing, **Seller** will give **Buyer** a credit at closing for the cost of the repairs and maintenance **Seller** was obligated to perform. At
153 closing, **Seller** will assign all assignable repair and treatment contracts to **Buyer** and provide **Buyer** with paid receipts for all
154 work done on the Property pursuant to the terms of this Contract. At closing, **Seller** will provide **Buyer** with any written
155 documentation that all open permits have been closed out and that **Seller** has obtained required permits for improvements to
156 the Property.

157 **(a) Warranty, Inspections and Repair:**

158 **(1) Warranty: Seller** warrants that non-leased major appliances and heating, cooling, mechanical, electrical, security,
159 sprinkler, septic and plumbing systems, seawall, dock and pool equipment, if any, are and will be maintained in working
160 condition until closing; that the structures (including roofs, doors and windows) and pool, if any, are structurally sound
161 and watertight; and that torn or missing screens and missing roof tiles will be repaired or replaced. **Seller** warrants that
162 all open permits will be closed out and that **Seller** will obtain any required permits for improvements to the Property
163 prior to Closing Date. **Seller** does not warrant and is not required to repair cosmetic conditions, unless the cosmetic
164 condition resulted from a defect in a warranted item. **Seller** is not obligated to bring any item into compliance with
165 existing building code regulations unless necessary to repair a warranted item. "Working condition" means operating in
166 the manner in which the item was designed to operate and "cosmetic conditions" means aesthetic imperfections that
167 do not affect the working condition of the item, including pitted marcite; tears, worn spots and discoloration of floor
168 coverings/wallpapers/window treatments; nail holes, scratches, dents, scrapes, chips and caulking in bathroom
169 ceiling/walls/flooring/tile/fixtures/mirrors; cracked roof tiles; curling or worn shingles; and minor cracks in floor
170 tiles/windows/driveways/sidewalks/pool decks/garage and patio floors.

171 **(2) Professional Inspection: Buyer** may, at **Buyer's** expense, have warranted items inspected by a person who
172 specializes in and holds an occupational license (if required by law) to conduct home inspections or who holds a Florida
173 license to repair and maintain the items inspected ("professional inspector"). **Buyer** must, within 5 days from the end of the
174 Inspection Period, deliver written notice of any items that are not in the condition warranted and a copy of the portion of

175* **Buyer** (_____) (_____) and **Seller** (_____) (_____) acknowledge receipt of a copy of this page, which is Page 3 of 8 Pages.

Residential Sale and Purchase Contract (continued)

176   inspector's written report dealing with such items to **Seller**. If **Buyer** fails to deliver timely written notice, **Buyer** waives
177   **Seller's** warranty and accepts the items listed in subparagraph (a) in their "as is" conditions, except that **Seller** must meet
178   the maintenance requirement.

179   **(3) Repair: Seller** will obtain repair estimates and is obligated only to make repairs necessary to bring warranted items
180   into the condition warranted, up to the Repair Limit. **Seller** may, within 5 days from receipt of **Buyer's** notice of items
181   that are not in the condition warranted, have a second inspection made by a professional inspector and will report
182   repair estimates to **Buyer.** If the first and second inspection reports differ and the parties cannot resolve the differences,
183   **Buyer** and **Seller** together will choose, and equally split the cost of, a third inspector, whose written report will be
184   binding on the parties. If the cost to repair warranted items equals or is less than the Repair Limit, **Seller** will have the
185   repairs made in a workmanlike manner by an appropriately licensed person. If the cost to repair warranted items
186   exceeds the Repair Limit, either party may cancel this Contract unless either party pays the excess or **Buyer**
187   designates which repairs to make at a total cost to **Seller** not exceeding the Repair Limit and accepts the balance of
188   the Property in its "as is" condition.

189   **(4) Permits: Seller** shall close out any open permits and remedy any violation of any governmental entity, including
190   but not limited to, obtaining any required permits for improvements to the Property, up to the Permit Limit, and with final
191   inspections completed no later than 5 days prior to Closing Date. If final inspections cannot be performed due to delays
192   by the governmental entity, Closing Date shall be extended for up to 10 days to complete such final inspections, failing
193   which, either party may cancel this Contract and **Buyer's** deposit shall be refunded. If the cost to close out open
194   permits or to remedy any violation of any governmental entity exceeds the Permit Limit, either party may cancel the
195   Contract unless either party pays the excess or **Buyer** accepts the Property in its "as is" condition and **Seller** credits
196   **Buyer** at closing the amount of the Permit Limit.

197   **(b) Wood-Destroying Organisms:** "Wood-destroying organism" means arthropod or plant life, including termites, powder-post
198   beetles, oldhouse borers and wood-decaying fungi, that damages or infests seasoned wood in a structure, excluding fences.
199   **Buyer** may, at **Buyer's** expense, have the Property inspected by a Florida-licensed pest control business to determine the
200   existence of past or present wood-destroying organism infestation and damage caused by infestation. If the inspector finds
201   evidence of infestation or damage, **Buyer** will deliver a copy of the inspector's written report to **Seller** within 5 days from the date
202   of the inspection. If **Seller** previously treated the Property for the type of wood-destroying organisms found, **Seller** does not have
203   to treat the Property again if (i) there is no visible live infestation, and (ii) **Seller** transfers to **Buyer** at closing a current full treatment
204   warranty for the type of wood-destroying organisms found. Otherwise, **Seller** will have 5 days from receipt of the inspector's
205   report to have reported damage estimated by a licensed building or general contractor and corrective treatment estimated by a
206   licensed pest control business. **Seller** will have treatments and repairs made by an appropriately licensed person at **Seller's**
207   expense up to the WDO Repair Limit. If the cost to treat and repair the Property exceeds the WDO Repair Limit, either party may
208   pay the excess, failing which either party may cancel this Contract by written notice to the other. If **Buyer** fails to timely deliver the
209   inspector's written report, **Buyer** accepts the Property "as is" with regard to wood-destroying organism infestation and damage,
210   subject to the maintenance requirement.

211   **(c) Walk-through Inspection/Reinspection: Buyer**, and/or **Buyer's** representative, may walk through the Property solely
212   to verify that **Seller** has made repairs required by this Contract, has met the Maintenance Requirement and has met
213   contractual obligations. If **Buyer**, and/or **Buyer's** representative, fails to conduct this inspection, **Seller's** repair obligations
214   and Maintenance Requirement will be deemed fulfilled.

215   **9. RISK OF LOSS:** If any portion of the Property is damaged by fire or other casualty before closing and can be restored by the
216   Closing Date or within 45 days after the Closing Date to substantially the same condition as it was on Effective Date, **Seller**,
217   will, at **Seller's** expense, restore the Property and deliver written notice to **Buyer** that **Seller** has completed the restoration, and
218   the parties will close the transaction on the later of: (1) Closing Date; or, (2) 10 days after **Buyer's** receipt of **Seller's** notice.
219   **Seller** will not be obligated to replace trees. If the restoration cannot be completed in time, **Buyer** may cancel this Contract
220   and **Buyer's** deposit shall be refunded, or **Buyer** may accept the Property "as is", and **Seller** will credit the deductible and
221   assign the insurance proceeds, if any, to **Buyer** at closing in such amounts as are (i) attributable to the Property and (ii) not yet
222   expended in restoring the Property to the same condition as it was on Effective Date.

223   **TITLE**
224   **10. TITLE: Seller** will convey marketable title to the Property by statutory warranty deed or trustee, personal representative or
225   guardian deed as appropriate to **Seller's** status.

226   **(a) Title Evidence:** Title evidence will show legal access to the Property and marketable title of record in **Seller** in accordance with
227   current title standards adopted by the Florida Bar, subject only to the following title exceptions, none of which prevent residential
228   use of the Property: covenants, easements and restrictions of record; matters of plat; existing zoning and government regulations;
229   oil, gas and mineral rights of record if there is no right of entry; current taxes; mortgages that **Buyer** will assume; and
230   encumbrances that **Seller** will discharge at or before closing. **Seller** will, at least 2 days prior to closing, deliver to **Buyer Seller's**
231   choice of one of the following types of title evidence, which must be generally accepted in the county where the Property is located
232   (specify in Paragraph **5(c)** the selected type). **Seller** will use option (1) in Palm Beach County and option (2) in Miami-Dade County.

233   **(1) A title insurance commitment** issued by a Florida-licensed title insurer in the amount of the purchase price and
234   subject only to title exceptions set forth in this Contract.

235   **(2) An existing abstract of title** from a reputable and existing abstract firm (if firm is not existing, then abstract must be
236   certified as correct by an existing firm) purporting to be an accurate synopsis of the instruments affecting title to the

237   **Buyer** (_____) (_____) and **Seller** (_____) (_____) acknowledge receipt of a copy of this page, which is Page 4 of 8 Pages.

Residential Sale and Purchase Contract (continued)

238 Property recorded in the public records of the county where the Property is located and certified to Effective Date.
239 However, if such an abstract is not available to **Seller,** then a **prior owner's title policy** acceptable to the proposed
240 insurer as a base for reissuance of coverage. **Seller** will pay for copies of all policy exceptions and an update in a format
241 acceptable to **Buyer's** closing agent from the policy effective date and certified to **Buyer** or **Buyer's** closing agent,
242 together with copies of all documents recited in the prior policy and in the update. If a prior policy is not available to
243 **Seller** then (1) above will be the title evidence. Title evidence will be delivered no later than 10 days before Closing Date.
244 **(b) Title Examination: Buyer** will examine the title evidence and deliver written notice to **Seller,** within 5 days from receipt of
245 title evidence but no later than Closing Date, of any defects that make the title unmarketable. **Seller** will have 30 days from
246 receipt of **Buyer's** notice of defects ("Curative Period") to cure the defects at **Seller's** expense. If **Seller** cures the defects
247 within the Curative Period, **Seller** will deliver written notice to **Buyer** and the parties will close the transaction on Closing
248 Date or within 10 days from **Buyer's** receipt of **Seller's** notice if Closing Date has passed. If **Seller** is unable to cure the
249 defects within the Curative Period, **Seller** will deliver written notice to **Buyer** and **Buyer** will, within 10 days from receipt of
250 **Seller's** notice, either cancel this Contract or accept title with existing defects and close the transaction.
251 **(c) Survey: Buyer** may, at **Buyer's** expense, have the Property surveyed and deliver written notice to **Seller,** within 5 days from
252 receipt of survey but no later than closing, of any encroachments on the Property, encroachments by the Property's improvements
253 on other lands or deed restriction or zoning violations. Any such encroachment or violation will be treated in the same manner as a
254 title defect and **Buyer's** and **Seller's** obligations will be determined in accordance with subparagraph **(b)** above.

255   MISCELLANEOUS
256 **11. EFFECTIVE DATE; TIME; FORCE MAJEURE:**
257 **(a) Effective Date:** The "Effective Date" of this Contract is the date on which the last of the parties initials or signs and
258 delivers the final offer or counteroffer. **Time is of the essence for all provisions of this Contract.**
259 **(b) Time:** All time periods will be computed in business days (a "business day" is every calendar day except Saturday, Sunday
260 and national legal holidays). If any deadline falls on a Saturday, Sunday or national legal holiday, performance will be due the
261 next business day. All time periods will end at 5:00 p.m. local time (meaning in the county where the Property is
262 located) of the appropriate day.
263 **(c) Force Majeure: Buyer** or **Seller** shall not be required to perform any obligation under this Contract or be liable to
264 each other for damages so long as the performance or non-performance of the obligation is delayed, caused or prevented
265 by an act of God or force majeure. An "act of God" or "force majeure" is defined as hurricanes, earthquakes, floods, fire,
266 unusual transportation delays, wars, insurrections and any other cause not reasonably within the control of the **Buyer** or
267 **Seller** and which by the exercise of due diligence the non-performing party is unable in whole or in part to prevent or
268 overcome. All time periods, including Closing Date, will be extended (not to exceed 30 days) for the period that the force
269 majeure or act of God is in place. In the event that such "act of God" or "force majeure" event continues beyond the 30
270 days in this sub-paragraph, either party may cancel the Contract by delivering written notice to the other and Buyer's
271 deposit shall be refunded.

272 **12. NOTICES:** All notices shall be in writing and will be delivered to the parties and Broker by mail, personal delivery or electronic
273 media. Except for the notices required by Paragraph 3 of this Contract, Buyer's failure to deliver timely written notice to
274 **Seller,** when such notice is required by this Contract, regarding any contingencies will render that contingency null and
275 void and the Contract will be construed as if the contingency did not exist. Any notice, document or item delivered to
276 or received by an attorney or licensee (including a transaction broker) representing a party will be as effective as if
277 delivered to or by that party.

278 **13. COMPLETE AGREEMENT:** This Contract is the entire agreement between **Buyer** and **Seller. Except** for brokerage
279 agreements, no prior or present agreements will bind Buyer, Seller or Broker unless incorporated into this Contract.
280 Modifications of this Contract will not be binding unless in writing, signed or initialed and delivered by the party to be bound.
281 Signatures, initials, documents referenced in this Contract, counterparts and written modifications communicated electronically
282 or on paper will be acceptable for all purposes, including delivery, and will be binding. Handwritten or typewritten terms
283 inserted in or attached to this Contract prevail over preprinted terms. If any provision of this Contract is or becomes invalid or
284 unenforceable, all remaining provisions will continue to be fully effective. **Buyer** and **Seller** will use diligence and good faith in
285 performing all obligations under this Contract. This Contract will not be recorded in any public records.

286 **14. ASSIGNABILITY; PERSONS BOUND: Buyer** may **not** assign this Contract without **Seller's** written consent. The terms
287 "**Buyer,**" "**Seller,**" and "**Broker**" may be singular or plural. This Contract is binding on the heirs, administrators, executors,
288 personal representatives and assigns (if permitted) of **Buyer, Seller** and Broker.

289   DEFAULT AND DISPUTE RESOLUTION
290 **15. DEFAULT: (a) Seller Default:** If for any reason other than failure of **Seller** to make **Seller's** title marketable after diligent effort, **Seller**
291 fails, refuses or neglects to perform this Contract, **Buyer** may choose to receive a return of **Buyer's** deposit without waiving the right to
292 seek damages or to seek specific performance as per Paragraph 16. **Seller** will also be liable to Broker for the full amount of the
293 brokerage fee. **(b) Buyer Default:** If **Buyer** fails to perform this Contract within the time specified, including timely payment of all deposits,
294 **Seller** may choose to retain and collect all deposits paid and agreed to be paid as liquidated damages or to seek specific performance as

295* **Buyer** (_____) (_____) and **Seller** (_____) (_____) acknowledge receipt of a copy of this page, which is Page 5 of 8 Pages.
FAR-9   4/07   © 2007   Florida Association of REALTORS®   All Rights Reserved

296   per Paragraph **16**; and Broker will, upon demand, receive 50% of all deposits paid and agreed to be paid (to be split equally among
297   Broker) up to the full amount of the brokerage fee.

298   **16. DISPUTE RESOLUTION:** This Contract will be construed under Florida law. All controversies, claims and other matters in
299   question arising out of or relating to this transaction or this Contract or its breach will be settled as follows:
300   **(a) Disputes concerning entitlement to deposits made and agreed to be made: Buyer** and **Seller** will have 30 days from the
301   date conflicting demands are made to attempt to resolve the dispute through **mediation**. If that fails, Escrow Agent will
302   submit the dispute, if so required by Florida law, to Escrow Agent's choice of arbitration, a Florida court or the Florida Real
303   Estate Commission ("FREC"). **Buyer** and **Seller** will be bound by any resulting award, judgment or order. A broker's
304   obligation under Chapter 475, FS and the FREC rules to timely notify the FREC of an escrow dispute and timely resolve the
305   escrow dispute through mediation, arbitration, interpleader or an escrow disbursement order, if the broker so chooses,
306   applies to brokers only and does not apply to title companies, attorneys or other escrow companies.
307   **(b) All other disputes: Buyer** and **Seller** will have 30 days from the date a dispute arises between them to attempt to
308   resolve the matter through mediation, failing which the parties will resolve the dispute through neutral binding **arbitration**
309   in the county where the Property is located. The arbitrator may not alter the Contract terms or award any remedy not
310   provided for in this Contract. The award will be based on the greater weight of the evidence and will state findings of fact
311   and the contractual authority on which it is based. If the parties agree to use discovery, it will be in accordance with the
312   Florida Rules of Civil Procedure and the arbitrator will resolve all discovery-related disputes. Any disputes with a real
313   estate licensee or firm named in Paragraph **19** will be submitted to arbitration only if the licensee's broker consents in
314   writing to become a party to the proceeding. This clause will survive closing.
315   **(c) Mediation and Arbitration; Expenses:** "Mediation" is a process in which parties attempt to resolve a dispute by
316   submitting it to an impartial mediator who facilitates the resolution of the dispute but who is not empowered to impose a
317   settlement on the parties. Mediation will be in accordance with the rules of the American Arbitration Association ("AAA") or
318   other mediator agreed on by the parties. The parties will equally divide the mediation fee, if any. "Arbitration" is a process in
319   which the parties resolve a dispute by a hearing before a neutral person who decides the matter and whose decision is
320   binding on the parties. Arbitration will be in accordance with the rules of the AAA or other arbitrator agreed on by the
321   parties. Each party to any arbitration will pay its own fees, costs and expenses, including attorneys' fees, and will equally
322   split the arbitrators' fees and administrative fees of arbitration.

323   **ESCROW AGENT AND BROKER**
324   **17. ESCROW AGENT: Buyer** and **Seller** authorize Escrow Agent to receive, deposit and hold funds and other items in escrow and,
325   subject to clearance, disburse them upon proper authorization and in accordance with Florida law and the terms of this Contract,
326   including disbursing brokerage fees. The parties agree that Escrow Agent will not be liable to any person for misdelivery of escrowed
327   items to **Buyer** or **Seller**, unless the misdelivery is due to Escrow Agent's willful breach of this Contract or gross negligence. If Escrow
328   Agent interpleads the subject matter of the escrow, Escrow Agent will pay the filing fees and costs from the deposit and will recover
329   reasonable attorneys' fees and costs to be paid from the escrowed funds or equivalent and charged and awarded as court costs in
330   favor of the prevailing party. All claims against Escrow Agent will be arbitrated, so long as Escrow Agent consents to arbitrate.

331   **18. PROFESSIONAL ADVICE; BROKER LIABILITY:** Broker advises **Buyer** and **Seller** to verify all facts and representations that are
332   important to them and to consult an appropriate professional for legal advice (for example, interpreting contracts, determining the
333   effect of laws on the Property and transaction, status of title, foreign investor reporting requirements, the effect of property lying
334   partially or totally seaward of the coastal construction control line, etc.) and for tax, property condition, environmental and other
335   specialized advice. **Buyer** acknowledges that Broker does not reside in the Property and that all representations (oral, written or
336   otherwise) by Broker are based on **Seller** representations or public records. **Buyer** agrees to rely solely on Seller, professional
337   **inspectors and governmental agencies for verification of the Property condition, square footage and facts that materially affect**
338   **Property value. Buyer** and **Seller** respectively will pay all costs and expenses, including reasonable attorneys' fees at all levels,
339   incurred by Broker and Broker's officers, directors, agents and employees in connection with or arising from **Buyer's** or **Seller's**
340   misstatement or failure to perform contractual obligations. **Buyer** and **Seller** hold harmless and release Broker and Broker's officers,
341   directors, agents and employees from all liability for loss or damage based on **(1) Buyer's** or **Seller's** misstatement or failure to
342   perform contractual obligations; **(2)** Broker's performance, at **Buyer's** and/or **Seller's** request, of any task beyond the scope of
343   services regulated by Chapter 475, F.S., as amended, including Broker's referral, recommendation or retention of any vendor; **(3)**
344   products or services provided by any vendor; and **(4)** expenses incurred by any vendor. **Buyer** and **Seller** each assume full
345   responsibility for selecting and compensating their respective vendors. This paragraph will not relieve Broker of statutory obligations.
346   For purposes of this paragraph, Broker will be treated as a party to this Contract. This paragraph will survive closing.

347   **19. BROKERS:** The licensee(s) and brokerage(s) named below are collectively referred to as "Broker." **Instruction to Closing**
348   **Agent: Seller** and **Buyer** direct closing agent to disburse at closing the full amount of the brokerage fees as specified in separate
349   brokerage agreements with the parties and cooperative agreements between the brokers, except to the extent Broker has
350   retained such fees from the escrowed funds. In the absence of such brokerage agreements, closing agent will disburse
351   brokerage fees as indicated below. This paragraph will not be used to modify any MLS or other offer of compensation made by
352   **Seller** or listing broker to cooperating brokers.

353* **Buyer** (_____) (_____) and **Seller** (_____) (_____) acknowledge receipt of a copy of this page, which is Page 6 of 8 Pages.
FAR-9   4/07   © 2007   Florida Association of REALTORS®   All Rights Reserved

Residential Sale and Purchase Contract (continued)

354* _____   _____
355 *Selling Sales Associate/License No.*   *Selling Firm/Brokerage Fee: ($ or % of Purchase Price)*

356* _____   _____
357 *Listing Sales Associate/License No.*   *Listing Firm/Brokerage fee: ($ or % of Purchase Price)*

358   ADDENDA AND ADDITIONAL TERMS

359 **20. ADDENDA:** The following additional terms are included in the attached addenda and incorporated into this Contract (check if
360 applicable):

361* ❑ A. Condo. Assn.   ❑ H. As Is w/Right to Inspect   ❑ O. Interest-Bearing Account   ❑ V. Prop. Disclosure Stmt.
362* ❑ B. Homeowners' Assn.   ❑ I. Inspections   ❑ P. Back-up Contract   ❑ W. FIRPTA
363* ❑ C. Seller Financing   ❑ J. Insulation Disclosure   ❑ Q. Broker - Pers. Int. in Prop. ❑ X. 1031 Exchange
364* ❑ D. Mort. Assumption   ❑ K. Pre-1978 Housing Stmt. (LBP) ❑ R. Rentals   ❑ Y. Additional Clauses
365* ❑ E. FHA Financing   ❑ L. Insurance   ❑ S. Sale/Lease of Buyer's Property
366* ❑ F. VA Financing   ❑ M. Housing Older Persons   ❑ T. Rezoning   ❑ Other_____
367* ❑ G. New Mort. Rates   ❑ N. Lease purchase/Lease option ❑ U. Assignment   ❑ Other_____

368* **21. ADDITIONAL TERMS:**
369* _____
370* _____
371* _____
372* _____
373* _____
374* _____
375* _____
376* _____
377* _____
378* _____
379* _____
380* _____
381* _____
382* _____
383* _____
384* _____
385* _____
386* _____
387* _____
388* _____
389* _____
390* _____
391* _____
392* _____
393* _____
394* _____
395* _____
396* _____
397* _____
398* _____
399* _____
400* _____
401* _____
402* _____
403* _____
404* _____
405* _____
406* _____
407* _____
408* _____
409* _____

410* **Buyer** (_____) (_____) and **Seller** (_____) (_____) acknowledge receipt of a copy of this page, which is Page 7 of 8 Pages.

FAR-9   4/07   © 2007   Florida Association of REALTORS®   All Rights Reserved

Residential Sale and Purchase Contract (continued)

411   This is intended to be a legally binding contract. If not fully understood, seek the advice of an attorney prior to signing.

412   OFFER AND ACCEPTANCE
413* (Check if applicable: ❏ **Buyer** received a written real property disclosure statement from **Seller** before making this Offer.)
414 **Buyer** offers to purchase the Property on the above terms and conditions. Unless this Contract is signed by **Seller** and a copy
415* delivered to **Buyer** no later than _____ ❏ a.m.❏ p.m. on _____, _____, this offer will be revoked
416 and **Buyer's** deposit refunded subject to clearance of funds.

417   COUNTER OFFER/REJECTION
418* ❏ **Seller** counters **Buyer's** offer (to accept the counter offer, **Buyer** must sign or initial the counter offered terms and deliver a copy
419 of the acceptance to **Seller**. Unless otherwise stated, the time for acceptance of any counteroffers shall be 2 days from the
420* date the counter is delivered. ❏ **Seller** rejects **Buyer's** offer.

421* Date: _____   Buyer: _____
422*   Print name: _____

423* Date: _____   Buyer: _____
424* Phone: _____   Print name: _____
425* Fax: _____   Address: _____
426* E-mail: _____

427* Date: _____   Seller: _____
428*   Print name: _____

429* Date: _____   Seller: _____
430* Phone: _____   Print name: _____
431* Fax: _____   Address: _____
432* E-mail: _____

433* | Effective Date: _____ (The date on which the last party signed or initialed and delivered the final offer or counteroffer.) |

434* **Buyer** (_____) (_____) and **Seller** (_____) (_____) acknowledge receipt of a copy of this page, which is Page 8 of 8 Pages.

Counter Offer

Counter Offer
FLORIDA ASSOCIATION OF REALTORS®

1. **REJECTION OF OFFER:** ❏ **Seller** ❏ **Buyer** rejects the offer to purchase/sell dated the _____ day of _____, _____ ("**Offer**") for the property described as follows (legal description):

2. **TERMS:** This counter offer consists of all terms of the **Offer** with modifications to particular clauses as follows:

Clause   Counter Offer Term

3. **ACCEPTANCE AND EXPIRATION OF COUNTER OFFER:** This counter offer must be signed **and** delivered back to ❏ **Seller** or **Seller's** licensee   ❏ **Buyer** or **Buyer's** licensee within _____ hours from (time) _____ ❏ a.m. ❏ p.m. the _____ day of _____, _____ or it will expire.

4. **RIGHT TO WITHDRAW COUNTER OFFER:** The party making this counter offer reserves the right to withdraw the counter offer at any time prior to acceptance by the other party.

CO-2 Revised 10/97   ©1997 Florida Association of REALTORS®   All Rights Reserved

Counter Offer (continued)

Signatures of Parties Making Counter Offer:

_____   _____
                                                         Date

_____   _____
                                                         Date

Signatures of Parties Accepting Counter Offer:

_____   _____
                                                         Date

_____   _____
                                                         Date

Acceptance Received by (initial): _____ Date: _____ Time: _____ ❑ a.m. ❑ p.m.

CO-2 Revised 10/97   ©1997 Florida Association of REALTORS®   All Rights Reserved

Property Management Cash Flow Statement

Your firm logo here

PROPERTY CASH FLOW STATEMENT

Owner: _____   Report period: _____

Property location: _____   Prepared by: _____

Item	%	Actual	Budget	Comments
Cash Receipts				
Gross rents collected				
Other:				
Other:				
Total cash collected		$	$	
Cash Disbursements				
Accounting & Legal				
Advertising				
Insurance				
Management fee				
Payroll				
Property taxes				
Repairs and maintenance				

Services: janitorial
                  lawn
                  pest control
                  trash				

Supplies				

Utilities: electric
                 gas & oil
                 water & sewer				

Other:				
Other:				
Other:				
Other:				
Monthly mortgage payment				
Total cash disbursements		$	$	
Cash flow (deficit)		$	$	

DBPR 0080-1-Request for Address or Name Change

DBPR 0080-1 – Request for Address or Name Change

**STATE OF FLORIDA
DEPARTMENT OF BUSINESS AND
PROFESSIONAL REGULATION**

SELECT TRANSACTION TYPE
Transaction Type:

❑ Name Change (individual)   ❑ Change Contact Information (phone and/or e-mail)
❑ Name Change (business)
❑ Change Mailing Address   ❑ Change Physical Address

LICENSEE INFORMATION
License Number
Licensee Name (previous)
Licensee Name (new)

NEW MAILING ADDRESS
Street Address or P.O. Box

City	State	Zip Code (+4 optional)
County (if Florida address)	Country	

NEW CONTACT INFORMATION	
Primary Phone Number	Primary E-Mail Address

NEW PHYSICAL ADDRESS (IF DIFFERENT THAN MAILING ADDRESS)
Street Address

City	State	Zip Code (+4 optional)
County (if Florida address)	Country	

NEW ADDITIONAL CONTACT INFORMATION (OPTIONAL)	
Alternate Phone Number	Fax Number
Alternate E-Mail Address	

I affirm that I have provided the above information completely and truthfully to the best of my knowledge.

Licensee Sign Here:_____Date: _____

DBPR RE-2050—Request for Change of Status

DBPR RE-2050 – Request for Change of Status

**STATE OF FLORIDA
DEPARTMENT OF BUSINESS AND PROFESSIONAL REGULATION**
1940 North Monroe Street
Tallahassee, FL 32399-0783
Customer Contact Center: 850.487.1395
FAX: 850.488.8040
www.MyFloridaLicense.com

CHECK ACTION(S) REQUESTED
Transaction Type:
❑ Become Active – no charge
❑ Become Inactive – no charge
❑ Add/Delete Trade Name – no charge
❑ Become Sole Proprietor – no charge (Forms 2050 & 0080 required)
❑ Change Broker/Owner Employer – no charge
❑ Terminate Employee – no charge
❑ Add/Delete PA or LLC - $30.00 fee required – see F.S. 475.161
❑ Request for Multiple License - $95.00
❑ Renew license
❑ Qualifying Broker (CQ package required)
❑ Owner/Developer (Forms 2050 & 0080 required)

ASSOCIATE INFORMATION	
License Number	Licensee Name
Contact Information (telephone number or E-Mail address)	

BROKER OR ORGANIZATION INFORMATION	
Broker License Number	Organization License Number
Broker/Owner Name	
Organization Name	
Trade Name (if applicable)	Contact Info. (telephone number or E-Mail address)
Are you now or with the issuance of this license, an officer, director, member, or partner of any corporation, partnership, or L.L.C. which acts as a broker? Yes ❑ No ❑	
If yes, please list name of entity	

ATTEST STATEMENT
REQUIRES SIGNATURE OF BROKER AND ASSOCIATE*
(EXCEPT FOR ADD/DELETE PA OR LLC - WHICH MAY BE SIGNED BY THE LICENSEE)
I affirm that I have provided the above information completely and truthfully to the best of my knowledge.
Broker/Owner Sign Here: _____ Date: _____
*Bk Signature not req. for Assoc. inactive status or add/delete PA –LLC
Print Broker/Owner Name: _____
Associate Sign Here: _____ Date: _____
*All Associate requested changes require signature

Revised 6/2007

PRACTICE FINAL EXAM

Before you take the end-of-course examination, test your readiness by completing this 100-question, multiple-choice practice exam that is similar to the course exam. The questions are drawn from the 14 chapters in this book; they are of the same type and in the same form with a similar degree of difficulty to the end-of-course exam questions. If you score 75 or higher without using any reference material (in other words, if you simulate exam conditions), you are in a strong position to pass the course exam. Circle or otherwise mark your answers; your instructor can discuss the correct answers to each question. Be certain to review those subject areas you miss.

1. A sales associate who has been licensed for eight years did not renew his license last March 31 as required. What is his status?
   a. Void
   b. Suspended
   c. Voluntary inactive
   d. Involuntary inactive

2. When selling his property, a sales associate failed to disclose the fact that a person died in the home last year. The sales associate
   a. and his broker are legally liable to the buyer for damages.
   b. and his broker are subject to disciplinary action by the FREC.
   c. and his broker can have the court dismiss the suit.
   d. is liable; the broker is not.

3. Which duty is owed by the broker to a principal in a single-agency relationship that is NOT owed to a customer in a transaction broker relationship?
   a. Skill, care, and diligence
   b. Dealing honestly and fairly
   c. Loyalty
   d. Accounting for all funds

4. A broker who works with a seller is legally presumed to be a(n)
   a. disclosed dual agent.
   b. transaction broker.
   c. single agent.
   d. attorney-in-fact.

5. A broker was a transaction broker in the sale and purchase of an office building. The broker felt an obligation to tell the buyer about the seller's need to sell quickly. As a balance, the broker helped the seller get a better price from the buyer because of some comments the buyer made during the property inspection. What is correct?
   a. Because the disclosures were balanced and both buyer and seller were treated fairly, no violation has occurred.
   b. Disclosure of such information violates Chapter 475.
   c. While an ethical violation has occurred, no statutory violation has taken place.
   d. While allowed to disclose motivation information, the broker may not discuss specifically what price a seller might accept or the buyer might pay.

6. A person who authorizes another person (the agent) to represent her in a real estate transaction is the
   a. customer.
   b. prospect.
   c. principal.
   d. third party.

7. If a single-agent residential seller's broker wishes to provide limited representation to a buyer, what must the broker do?
   a. Have the seller sign the Consent to Transition to Transaction Broker Notice and have the buyer sign the Transaction Broker Notice.
   b. Have the buyer sign the Consent to Transition to Transaction Broker Notice and have both parties sign the Transaction Broker Notice.
   c. Have both the seller and buyer sign the Transaction Broker Notice.
   d. Become a single agent for the buyer also.

8. John and Bill are sales associates working for Southland Commercial brokers. Their broker allows John to act as a single agent for the buyer and Bill to act as a single agent for the seller. Both the buyer and seller have assets of more than $1 million and each agrees to this form of representation. The situation describes a
   a. transaction broker relationship.
   b. single agency.
   c. dual agency.
   d. designated sales associate.

9. A person wishing to avoid liability under the Comprehensive Environmental Response, Compensation, and Liability Act of 1980, claiming innocent purchaser status, must
   a. pay for an insurance bond issued by the Department of Environmental Regulation.
   b. require that the seller obtain an insurance bond issued by the Department of Environmental Regulation.
   c. exercise due diligence by investigating the property, usually in the form of an environmental audit.
   d. obtain certifications from the local planning commission that the property never has been used as a gas station or dry-cleaning establishment.

10. A property is sold by a married couple who file jointly and who have owned and occupied their personal residence for three years. Which statement is true about their tax liability?
    a. They must pay taxes at a 20 percent rate on the amount that the property's adjusted sales price exceeds the property's new price.
    b. They may exclude up to $600,000 of any gain before becoming liable for taxes.
    c. They may exclude up to $500,000 of any gain before becoming liable for taxes.
    d. Their maximum capital gains rate is reduced to 10 percent because it was a personal residence.

11. John sells an investment property he has owned for three years and has a capital gain of $125,000. His ordinary income tax rate is 28 percent. Long-term capital gains are taxed at a maximum of 15 percent. Using just this information, how much will his taxes be for this transaction?
    a.   He may exclude up to $500,000 of the gain before calculating taxes.
    b.   He will pay $12,500 in taxes.
    c.   His taxes will be $18,750.
    d.   His tax payment will be $35,000.

12. Under Florida's Growth Management Act
    a.   it is more difficult to subdivide parcels inside the urban services area.
    b.   concurrency means that schools must provide evidence of being in the upper quartile of performance before new construction can commence.
    c.   a county may not designate a land-use plan without a referendum.
    d.   it is more difficult to subdivide parcels outside the urban services area.

13. Patti, a licensed sales associate, has an unlicensed personal assistant who is salaried. The personal assistant hands out brochures at an open house but does not do any selling, nor does she write contracts. Which is correct?
    a.   Patti and her assistant have both committed a violation of Chapter 475.
    b.   This behavior is allowed under the rules of the Commission.
    c.   If the sales associate collects a commission, this is illegal.
    d.   The broker, Patti, and her assistant have all committed a violation of Chapter 475.

14. A sales associate hires a licensed personal assistant. The personal assistant's contract requires a salary of $1,000 per month and 15 percent of the sales associate's share of commissions. Which is correct?
    a.   The broker must pay both the salary and the commission to the personal assistant.
    b.   The sales associate may pay both the salary and the commission to the personal assistant.
    c.   The salary may be paid by either the sales associate or the broker. The broker must pay the commission.
    d.   Sharing commissions with a licensed personal assistant is a violation of Florida license law.

15. A lead-based paint hazard disclosure must be made if the house being sold was built before
    a.   1998.
    b.   1978.
    c.   1975.
    d.   1963.

16. The best way to acquire product knowledge is to
    a.   be in the marketplace.
    b.   read the many books available through NAR.
    c.   give on-the-job training classes.
    d.   attend a class at the community college.

17. Joining Toastmasters is one of the most effective ways to improve which type skills?
    a. Written communication
    b. Oral communication
    c. Nonverbal communication
    d. Product knowledge

18. Unlicensed personal assistants
    a. may not be present at an open house or hand out brochures to visitors.
    b. cannot be classified an independent contractors, and must pay withholding taxes.
    c. may be classified as independent contractors if they are able to determine working hours, even if the employer directs how they are to do their job.
    d. are usually not a worthwhile expense for sales associates, according to major real estate associations.

19. The most probable price a property should bring in an arm's-length transaction in a competitive and open market is called the
    a. market price.
    b. market value.
    c. exchange value.
    d. sales price.

20. A sales associate should normally avoid spending time on a FSBO prospect who
    a. does not need to sell.
    b. is moving to another city.
    c. is realistic about pricing.
    d. tells the agent he does not want to list right now.

21. Shady Acres neighborhood has had 103 homes sold last month out of a total of 560 homes in the area. Sunny Hills neighborhood has had 87 homes sold with 400 total homes. Windy Woods neighborhood has had 150 homes sold with 800 total homes. Still Waters neighborhood has had 145 homes sold with 625 total homes. All are in the same general price range in well-kept areas of the city. Which neighborhood would be the best farm area based on likely reward-to-effort ratios?
    a. Shady Acres
    b. Sunny Hills
    c. Windy Woods
    d. Still Waters

22. Most listings expire because they are
    a. not easy to show because of uncooperative owners or tenants.
    b. poorly maintained by the owners and don't show well.
    c. overpriced for the market.
    d. listed by sales associates who fail to properly market the property.

23. Writing ads for a new listing would be considered what type activity in the daily activity log?
    a. Direct $
    b. Office and administrative
    c. Wasted time
    d. Personal

24. Sam works an average of 9 hours each day. Last year, he worked for 260 days and made gross income of $102,000. What was his hourly rate?
    a. $18.40
    b. $22.94
    c. $43.59
    d. $392.31

25. Which FSBO activity is more likely to generate a listing?
    a. Mailing a letter
    b. Telephoning
    c. Visiting
    d. Advertising

26. John, an FSBO, has a home worth $240,000 with a mortgage balance of approximately $199,000. The sales associate assures him that a 6 percent commission should be acceptable. The commission as a percent of John's equity is
    a. 6.
    b. 14.
    c. 24.
    d. 35.

27. Sensitivity to the thoughts and feelings of others is
    a. feelings.
    b. courtesy.
    c. empathy.
    d. sympathy.

28. Which is correct about the National Do Not Call Registry?
    a. Licensees may call FSBOs and past customers, even if they're on the list.
    b. Licensees may not call either FSBOs or past customers, even if they are on the list.
    c. Licensees may call FSBOs but not past customers.
    d. Licensees may not call FSBOs, but they may call past customers for up to 18 months, even if they are on the list.

29. High interest rates usually result in
    a. more properties in listing inventory and a buyers' market.
    b. fewer properties in listing inventory and a sellers' market.
    c. higher home prices.
    d. lower total mortgage payments.

30. Which is the LEAST likely to help a sales associate obtain a listing?
    a. Persuasiveness
    b. Sympathy
    c. Persistence
    d. Empathy

31. Targeted strangers in your database should be contacted at least
    a. six times monthly.
    b. every other month.
    c. twice a month.
    d. twice each year.

32. To ensure maximum future value of the properties, subdivision restrictions rely on the principle of
    a. contribution.
    b. substitution.
    c. conformity.
    d. competition.

33. A comparative market analysis (CMA) with adjustments assumes that
    a. the subject property sold recently in the same neighborhood.
    b. adjustments for differences have been made to the subject property.
    c. adjustments for differences have been made to the comparable property.
    d. the sales associate knows construction costs for this type property.

34. A person who sends a fax
    a. need not allow the recipient to "opt-out" of getting more faxes.
    b. may have received the recipients number from a fax-spamming company.
    c. may send the fax only between 9 AM and 5 PM.
    d. must have an established business relationship with the recipient.

35. The principle of value that says improvement to a property is worth only what it adds to the property's market value, regardless of actual cost, is called the principle of
    a. substitution.
    b. conformity.
    c. contribution.
    d. competition.

36. A basic principle of value stating that a property's maximum value tends to be set by the cost of acquiring an equally desirable property is known as the principle of
    a. anticipation.
    b. conformity.
    c. increasing returns.
    d. substitution.

This information is to be used for questions 37–39:

When doing a CMA, you find a comparable property that sold two months ago for $138,000. It has four bedrooms (the subject property has three) and is 160 square feet larger as a result. You decide that the additional room/space makes an $8,000 difference. The subject is newer and in slightly better condition, so you estimate a difference of $5,000.

37. Due to the difference in square footage and bedrooms, you make a
    a. plus $8,000 adjustment to the comparable.
    b. plus $8,000 adjustment to the subject.
    c. minus $8,000 adjustment to the subject.
    d. minus $8,000 adjustment to the comparable.

38. The resulting net adjustment for size and physical condition is
    a. plus $3,000.
    b. minus $3,000.
    c. plus $5,000.
    d. minus $5,000.

39. The adjusted sales price of the comparable property is
    a. $143,000.
    b. $138,000.
    c. $135,000.
    d. $130,000.

40. Trees, landscaping, driveways, fences, pools, and other improvements of a home should be valued by the listing sales associate at
    a. their original cost.
    b. their original cost, less their physical depreciation.
    c. their contribution to value.
    d. the seller's best representation of their value.

41. Properties that should be rejected as comparables for determining a subject property's value include all properties EXCEPT those
    a. sold within the previous six months.
    b. that differ in quality of construction.
    c. that are much different in size.
    d. in which the buyers and sellers were relatives.

42. The licensee's goal when making adjustments to sold properties in a CMA is to find the
    a. monetary difference in features between the subject property and the comparable property.
    b. subject property's characteristics.
    c. price the subject property should sell for.
    d. current market influences.

43. After completing a review of the CMA, a sales associate and seller agree on a list price of $240,000. Sellers' expenses, including brokerage fee, are estimated at $17,600, and prorations for taxes and interest paid in arrears are estimated at $6,700. The mortgage payoff is expected to be $196,500. What is the seller's equity?
    a. $43,500
    b. $32,600
    c. $25,900
    d. $19,200

44. Using the information from the previous question, what is the estimated net proceeds to the seller?
    a. $43,500
    b. $32,600
    c. $25,900
    d. $19,200

45. The best location at which to make a listing presentation to prospective sellers is the
    a. sofa in the prospects' living room.
    b. kitchen or dining table.
    c. hood of your car.
    d. lunch counter at a busy restaurant.

46. What is the most persuasive argument to help get a for-sale-by-owner to list her house?
    a. The buyer needs to get financing.
    b. Writing a contract may be difficult.
    c. She is unlikely to "save" the commission.
    d. Handling the closing details are too time-consuming.

47. The first step when meeting the sellers for a listing appointment is to
    a. break the ice.
    b. shown them the sellers' net statement.
    c. go over the listing agreement.
    d. recommend the right price to sell the property.

48. A property is likely to sell fastest if it is priced at the
    a. "expired" section of the CMA.
    b. "sold" section of the CMA.
    c. "currently listed" section of the CMA.
    d. median value from all sections of the CMA.

49. What is NOT correct about listing agreements in Florida?
    a. Listing contracts for less than one year are covered by the statute of frauds.
    b. All written listings must have definite expiration dates.
    c. Oral listing contracts are enforceable.
    d. Listings are personal service contracts.

50. An agreement between a seller of real property and a real estate broker that authorizes the broker to sell the property on specified terms in return for a sales commission if the broker is successful is a(n)
    a. single agency contract.
    b. sales contract.
    c. option contract.
    d. listing contract.

51. A real estate contract given to one broker as sole agent for the sale of an owner's property, with a commission going to that broker regardless of who actually sells the property during the contract period, is a(n)
    a. unilateral agreement.
    b. exclusive-representation agreement.
    c. exclusive-agency listing.
    d. exclusive-right-to-sell listing.

52. At the time a listing agreement is negotiated, the listing broker should discuss with the seller all of the following subjects EXCEPT the
    a. pros and cons of subagency.
    b. seller's religious preference.
    c. use of the local MLS.
    d. seller's attitude toward the broker sharing the sales commission with a cooperating broker.

53. Given a choice, sales associates should spend most time working with buyers who have
    a. to move into the area in 60 days from out of town.
    b. a lease expiring in six months.
    c. not been on the job for at least two years.
    d. their house listed with a good friend.

54. If a buyer raises an objection to a property, the associate should first
    a. ridicule the objection to ensure the buyer is serious.
    b. refute the objection.
    c. confirm and isolate the objection.
    d. ask the customer whether he wants to continue their business relationship.

55. The strongest position for a single agent sales associate to have when presenting an offer to the sellers is representing a buyer who has
    a. met the sellers.
    b. been prequalified by a lender.
    c. been preapproved by a lender.
    d. given a good-faith deposit of $1,000.

56. Callers who are asking about property they saw from a sign usually ask for the
    a. address.
    b. price.
    c. square footage.
    d. owners' names.

57. Where the agreement of the parties is contrary to any of the provisions or standards in a preprinted sales contract, it is best to
    a. line out the particular provision or standard affected.
    b. insert one or more special clauses in an addendum to the contract.
    c. renegotiate the contrary item(s) with the parties to the contract.
    d. prepare a nonstandard contract.

58. Yesterday, broker Bono concluded a 90-day listing contract with a seller. The contract contains a self-renewing provision extending the agreement an additional 60 days after expiration unless either party cancels in writing. The listing contract is
    a. void.
    b. unconscionable.
    c. valid.
    d. implied.

59. Which is NOT allowed under the CAN-SPAM Act?
    a. E-mailing sellers about marketing efforts on their homes
    b. Failing to include an opt-out method in commercial advertisements
    c. E-mailing a newsletter without advertising
    d. Text-messaging information

60. Sales tax must be collected on personal property sold as part of a real estate transaction when it is
    a. depreciated for income tax purposes.
    b. itemized and valued in the sales contract.
    c. mentioned in the contract.
    d. used to determine the broker's compensation.

61. The law requiring that certain types of contracts be written to be enforceable is
    a. Chapter 455, F.S.
    b. the statute of frauds.
    c. the statute of limitations.
    d. the "Little FTC Act."

62. What is most important in a sales contract?
    a. Seller's marital status
    b. Serial number on each major appliance
    c. Buyer's maiden name
    d. Subject property's legal description

63. What is a contract that may be terminated at the option of one of the parties?
    a. Voidable
    b. Implied
    c. Option
    d. Dual representation

64. Which is NOT correct about fair housing?
    a. A real estate agent may not limit a home search to certain neighborhoods based on the customer's race.
    b. An apartment building owner may assign families with children to one particular building if older people live in the other buildings.
    c. A loan officer may turn down a Hispanic applicant because of the applicant's lack of steady income.
    d. An apartment building owner may turn down an applicant because of the applicant's poor housekeeping habits.

65. A bilateral agreement spelling out the complete terms between a buyer and a seller for the transfer of a parcel of real property is a(n)
    a. representation agreement.
    b. sales contract.
    c. option contract.
    d. wraparound mortgage.

66. An agreement to hold open for a set time period an offer to sell or lease real property is a(n)
    a. contract for deed.
    b. option contract.
    c. installment contract.
    d. agreement for deed.

67. Under which contract does the seller warrant appliances to be in working order?
    a. Quasi
    b. Executory
    c. FAR
    d. Implied

68. The FAR contract requires that the seller warrant appliances, heating and cooling systems, and plumbing systems to be in working order
    a. at closing.
    b. on the date of contract.
    c. as of ten days before closing.
    d. as of three days before closing.

69. The FAR Contract for Sale and Purchase is NOT suitable for
    a. contracts for deed.
    b. single-family dwellings.
    c. unimproved properties.
    d. condominium units.

70. In the FAR contract, if a survey shows an encroachment, the
    a. encroachment will be treated as a title defect.
    b. encroachment will be a breach of contract on the seller's part.
    c. seller must pay damages to the buyer for any delays due to the problem.
    d. buyer is responsible for any expenses associated with curing the problem.

71. In an adjustable-rate mortgage, the component that does not change from year to year is the
    a. margin.
    b. index.
    c. calculated rate.
    d. rate charged.

72. Most conventional residential mortgage lenders have adopted the Fannie Mae suggested housing expense ratio and the total long-term obligations ratio calculated from gross income amounts for underwriting loans. The Fannie Mae ratios for housing expense (HER) and total obligations (TOR) currently range from
    a. 3 to 1 (HER) and 4 to 1 (TOR).
    b. 28% (HER) and 36% (TOR).
    c. 30% (HER) and 30% (TOR).
    d. 40% (HER) and 40% (TOR).

73. The ratio of monthly housing expenses to monthly income is the
    a. housing expense.
    b. income and expense.
    c. total obligations.
    d. total consumer credit.

74. Richard expects to live in his new home for about five years. He is shopping for a new $100,000 mortgage. With no points, he can get a 30-year 8 percent fixed rate mortgage with principal and interest payments of $733.76. Another lender has a 7.75 percent mortgage (payments of $716.41) with one point. How many months will it take Richard to break even on the points if he takes the lower interest loan, using simple arithmetic?
    a. 48.5
    b. 57.6
    c. 68.6
    d. 69.2

75. The entire process of evaluating the risks involved in issuing a new real estate mortgage is commonly called
    a. buyer/borrower qualification.
    b. loan risk evaluation.
    c. buyer/borrower prequalification.
    d. loan underwriting.

76. A mortgage note normally shows the amount required to pay monthly
    a. principal and interest only.
    b. principal, interest, and one-twelfth of annual property taxes.
    c. principal, interest, and one-twelfth of annual hazard insurance.
    d. principal, interest, and one-twelfth of annual taxes and insurance.

77. The three components of a full property title report are a physical inspection of the property, a search of the public records, and a(n)
    a. survey.
    b. legal description.
    c. valid conveyance from all previous owners.
    d. abstract or opinion of title.

78. What is NOT a good reason to make a preclosing walk-through inspection?
    a. To determine that no encroachments exist
    b. To determine that the property has been maintained in the same condition it existed in when the contract was written, reasonable wear and tear excepted
    c. To ensure that all required repairs have been made
    d. To determine that all items of personal property are on the real property

79. A licensee should work hard to clear contract contingencies
    a. within five days before closing.
    b. within five days after loan approval.
    c. within three days of contract.
    d. as soon as possible after the contract has been signed.

80. How does the appraisal cost usually appear in the HUD-1 settlement statement when a new institutional mortgage has been used for the purchase?
    a. Debit to the seller
    b. Credit to the buyer
    c. Debit to the buyer
    d. POC

81. The Fair Housing Law applies to
    a. a religious organization that limit rentals of its properties to members of its religion.
    b. private clubs that limit rentals to its own members in noncommercial lodgings.
    c. a for-sale-by-owner selling his personal house (his only real property).
    d. an owner who lists his personal house (his only real property) with a broker.

Use the following information to answer questions 82 through 88.

Susan lists her home with Broker William for $90,000 on March 16. On August 1, Henry makes an offer of $85,000, accompanied by a binder deposit of $5,000, and asks the seller to pay points on a new loan of $80,000. Susan counters at a price of $87,500 and agrees to pay four points on a loan of $82,500. Henry accepts.

Henry qualifies for the loan at an interest rate of 9 percent and agrees to pay a 1 percent origination fee. The monthly payment for principal and interest is $663.81. Henry also will be charged for prepaid interest for the balance of the month of closing. The closing date is September 15, and Henry is charged for the day of closing.

Henry will purchase an insurance policy for $720. City and county taxes are $760. Susan agreed to pay her own attorney's fees of $125. Hart must pay $130 for attorney's fees, $56 to record the mortgage, $6 to record the deed, and $640 for title insurance.

The payoff on Susan's existing mortgage will be $64,455.16 on the day of closing. Broker William's fee is 6 percent. Doc stamps and intangible taxes are paid according to custom. Use the 365-day method for prorations.

82. How are the points to be handled on the closing statement?
    a. Credit Henry $3,500.
    b. Debit Susan $3,500.
    c. Debit Susan $3,300; credit Henry $3,300.
    d. Debit Susan $3,300.

83. If the lender wants a three-month tax escrow plus the number of months through the day of closing, what is the amount of prepaid taxes the lender collects at closing?
    a. $190.00
    b. $696.67
    c. $760.00
    d. $773.33

84. What is the proration of taxes between the seller and the buyer?
    a. Debit Henry; credit Susan $535.12.
    b. Debit Henry; credit Susan $224.88.
    c. Debit Susan; credit Henry $535.12.
    d. Debit Susan; credit Henry $224.88.

85. What is the amount of documentary stamp taxes on the note?
    a. $288.75
    b. $306.25
    c. $577.50
    d. $612.50

86. Using the 365-day method and the exact number of days in the month, how will prepaid interest be handled on the closing statement?
    a. Henry must pay $325.48 in prepaid interest at closing.
    b. Susan must pay $325.48 in prepaid interest at closing.
    c. Henry must pay $330.00 in prepaid interest at closing.
    d. Henry must pay $535.12 in prepaid interest at closing.

87. How are the documentary stamp taxes on the deed handled on the closing statement?
    a. Credit Henry $612.50.
    b. Debit Susan $612.50.
    c. Debit Henry $306.25.
    d. Debit Susan $306.25.

88. Assuming the mortgage insurance premium is $50.18 per month, what is the total monthly payment (PITI) on the mortgage?
    a. $663.81
    b. $725.89
    c. $787.14
    d. $837.32

89. The point where the business cycle, at its highest point, levels off and begins to fall is called
    a. expansion.
    b. recession.
    c. contraction.
    d. recovery.

90. When calculating a property's net operating income, such items as depreciation, income taxes, and property financing costs are
    a. included in variable operating costs.
    b. included in fixed operating costs.
    c. considered as funds reserved for operations or replacements.
    d. excluded from consideration.

91. When annual debt service is subtracted from net operating income, the resulting amount is the
    a. after-tax cash flow.
    b. before-tax cash flow.
    c. cash flow.
    d. net spendable income.

92. The relationship between a property's net operating income and its present value is the
    a. cash throwoff.
    b. debt service.
    c. capitalization rate.
    d. return on investment.

93. Which is NOT a type of operating expense?
    a. Fixed expenses
    b. Reserves for replacements
    c. Depreciation
    d. Variable expenses

94. Which illegal statement would most likely be termed *steering?*
    a. "I can list your house and get it sold before any more minorities move into this neighborhood."
    b. "I'm sorry, we won't be able to make the loan in that Hispanic neighborhood."
    c. "Are you certain you'll be comfortable in this predominantly white neighborhood?
    d. "I'm sorry, we don't rent to non-Christians here."

95. The optimum rental price for standard space in a local area is determined by
    a. market analysis.
    b. property analysis.
    c. neighborhood analysis.
    d. surveys of past, current, and projected tenant population figures.

96. The Monthly Housing Starts report is
    a. an extremely important economic indicator.
    b. a lagging economic indicator.
    c. not able to be forecast by the previous month's building permit data.
    d. prepared by the Department of Veterans Affairs.

97. What is the difference between effective gross income and net operating income?
    a. Before-tax cash flow
    b. Vacancy
    c. Operating expenses
    d. Cash throwoff

98. The relationship between supply and demand for a particular type of multifamily property at its current rental level is reflected by the
    a. rental market's equilibrium.
    b. turnover of tenants whose leases expire.
    c. area's location quotient.
    d. occupancy rate for that type of property.

99. The best and least expensive method of renting or leasing residential properties is the use of
    a. referrals from satisfied tenants.
    b. newspaper classified ads.
    c. radio ads of 30 seconds or less.
    d. short, relatively inexpensive television commercials.

100. Marilyn is searching for a new apartment. When she drives through the entrance of The Fountains, she gets a wonderful impression and decides to rent if the price is right. Marilyn's first impression is called
    a. market value.
    b. eye invitation.
    c. curb appeal.
    d. comparative market analysis.

GLOSSARY

A

abstract. A history of a property shown by the public records used to give an opinion of title. Less frequently used today than title insurance.

adjustable-rate mortgage (ARM). A loan that allows the borrower's interest rate to fluctuate based on some external index beyond the control of the lender.

adjustments. The method used by brokers and appraisers to account for differences in comparable properties. If a subject property is superior, the appraiser makes a dollar adjustment increasing the sale price of the comparable. If the subject property is inferior to the comparable property, a negative adjustment is made.

after-tax cash flow. The amount remaining to an owner of income property after all expenses, debt service, and income taxes have been paid.

agency. The relationship of agents and their principals.

agent. A person who represents another person in a fiduciary relationship.

ambiguity. A statement that is unclear or may have several meanings.

annual percentage rate (APR). An expression of credit costs over the life of a loan, taking into account the contract interest rate plus lender fees for originating, processing, and closing a mortgage loan.

antitrust. Federal law that prohibits monopolistic practices such as price fixing.

appraisal. An unbiased estimate of a property's market value.

appraising. The process of estimating the market value of property.

arm's-length transaction. A business transaction in which the parties are dealing in their own self-interest, not being under the control of the other party. One of the requirements before a comparable sale should be used in an appraisal.

assets. Things of value owned by a person or organization.

automated underwriting. The evaluation of a mortgage loan application using predetermined formulas and credit scores. Fannie Mae's *Desktop Underwriter* performs automated underwriting.

automated valuation. The use of computers and linear regression formulas to calculate the market value of property based on large numbers of comparable sales.

B

before-tax cash flow (BTCF). The amount of spendable income from an income property after paying operating expenses and debt service, but before the effect of income taxes. Sometimes called *cash throw-off*.

bilateral contract. A contract that requires both parties to perform, such as a sales contract.

biweekly mortgage. A mortgage that requires that the borrower make payments every two weeks (26 payments per year). The payment is calculated by dividing the monthly mortgage payment by two. The effective result is that the borrower makes 13 monthly payments per year.

blockbusting. The illegal act of a licensee who frightens homeowners into selling by raising fears that minority homeowners are moving into a neighborhood.

body language. Nonverbal communication expressed by the position of the body, hands, arms, legs, or facial expressions.

browser. A software program that makes access to Web pages possible. Firefox and Internet Explorer are examples.

buyer agency. The fiduciary relationship between a buyer and the buyer's single-agent broker.

buyer brokerage agreement. An agreement between a buyer and a broker for the broker to provide services to a buyer for compensation. The broker may be acting as a single agent, a transaction broker, or a nonrepresentative.

C

calculated interest rate. The interest rate in an adjustable-rate mortgage that is calculated by adding the margin to the index.

canvassing. Prospecting for buyers or sellers by telephoning or walking door-to-door.

cap. The maximum amount that an interest rate can increase per year, or during the life of a loan.

capitalization rate. The net operating income divided by the property value. A percentage representing the return on the investment, assuming the property was purchased for cash.

cash flow report. A property manager's monthly report to the owner, showing cash receipts and cash disbursements of an income property.

certified check. A check issued by a bank guaranteeing payment. The buyer is usually required to bring a certified check to closing by most title closing agents to speed disbursement at closing.

Certified Property Manager (CPM). A professional designation awarded by the Institute of Real Estate Management (IREM) to a property manager who has successfully completed required education and experience.

closing statement. A detailed accounting of charges and credits for the buyer and the seller in a real estate transaction.

Coastal Construction Control Line (CCCL). An imaginary line established by Florida counties a specified distance from the mean high water mark of the Atlantic Ocean or the Gulf of Mexico that prohibits construction seaward from the line.

collateral. Something of value given as security for a debt. In real estate, the mortgage pledges the property as collateral for the repayment of the loan.

commission. Compensation for professional services that is usually calculated as a percentage of the property's sales price.

community association manager. An individual licensed by the Department of Business and Professional Regulation who is paid to perform certain functions for a residential homeowners' association.

comparable property. A similar property in the same market area that may be used to help estimate the value of the property being appraised.

comparative market analysis (CMA). Similar to the comparable sales approach used by appraisers but usually less detailed. Used by brokers and sales associates to estimate the most likely selling price of properties they are listing or selling.

computer valuation. The use of computers and linear regression formulas to estimate the market value of property based on large numbers of comparable sales.

concurrency. A state law requiring that infrastructure such as roads, sewers, schools, etc., be in place as development occurs.

Consent to Transition to Transaction Broker Notice. A disclosure form that allows a single agent to become a transaction broker. The notice must be signed by the principal before the broker can make the change.

contingency. A condition in a contract that, unless satisfied, may make the contract voidable by one of the parties.

contract. An agreement between two or more parties to do or not do a specific act.

contraction. The phase of a business cycle that begins after a recession when economic conditions worsen.

contract service. A property maintenance service that is done by an individual or company not in the employ of the property manager.

cooperative sale. Sale of a property by a broker who is not the listing broker. Normally, commissions are split between the two brokerage firms.

corrective maintenance. The repairs to a building's structure and equipment following breakdown.

counteroffer. A substitution for the original offer made by the offeree who changes the price or terms offered, sending it back to the offeror. The original offer is terminated. The original offeree becomes the offeror.

credit scoring. A method of credit reporting using a numeric score. A higher score reflects a person with better credit history.

cross-defaulting clause. A mortgage clause that results in a default of a junior mortgage in case a senior mortgage becomes delinquent.

curb appeal. The impression, good or bad, that is made when a person first looks at a house from the street.

customer. A person who works with a sales associate or a broker. While the person could be a principal, the usual definition is that the broker is either a transaction broker or has no brokerage relationship with the person.

cycle. Periodic fluctuations of the overall economy, or any part of the economy, between good times and bad. The four parts of a general cycle are expansion, recession, contraction, and recovery.

cyclic fluctuation. Part of an economic cycle.

D

deferred maintenance. Maintenance that needs to be done, but has not been done for some reason, usually economic.

designated sales associate. A sales associate who is appointed by a broker to be a single agent for a buyer or seller in a nonresidential transaction when another sales associate in the firm has been appointed to be the single agent for the other party in the transaction. Both buyer and seller must have assets of at least $1 million and agree to the arrangement.

disclosure. The revelation of information important to a transaction.

documentary stamp taxes. A tax on a real estate transaction that may be levied on the sales price of a property or on the amount of a mortgage note.

dual agent. An illegal arrangement whereby the broker tries to represent both the buyer and the seller in the same transaction.

E

effective gross income (EGI). The amount of rent and other income actually collected by the owner. When preparing an income statement, vacancy and collection losses are deducted from potential gross income, and other income such as vending machine collections is added.

equity. The amount of the owner's portion of the property value after deducting mortgages and other liens.

ethical. The right thing to do. Usually a higher standard than legality.

exclusive-agency listing. A listing that requires that the owner pay the listing broker if the property is sold by any broker but allows the owner to personally sell the property without being liable for a commission.

exclusive-right-of-sale listing. A listing that requires that the owner pay the listing broker no matter who sells the property. The broker is automatically the procuring cause of the sale.

executed contract. A contract in which nothing else remains to be done. All requirements have been performed by the parties.

executory contract. A contract in which part of the agreement remains to be done. It has not yet "closed."

exercised. Used in connection with an option contract. An option contract is a unilateral contract until the optionee agrees to purchase and is then said to have "exercised" the option.

expansion. The phase of a business cycle that begins after a recovery when economic conditions improve.

express contract. An oral or written agreement where the words specifically describe the intent of the parties.

F

fact of execution. The acceptance of an offer. The offeree or his licensee must communicate the fact of execution to the offeror in order to make a valid contract.

Fair Housing Act. The federal law that prohibits discrimination in housing based on race, color, religion, sex, national origin, familial status, and handicap.

fallback list. A list of properties similar to the property being advertised that can be used by the licensee if the

advertised property does not appeal to the person responding to the ad.

false or misleading statement. In real estate, a statement made by a licensee or party in a real estate transaction that is not factual.

FAR Residential Sale and Purchase Contract. The most widely used real estate sales contract in Florida, prepared and updated regularly by the Florida Association of REALTORS®.

farm. A geographic area selected for special prospecting attention by a real estate licensee.

federally related transaction. A real estate transaction financed by a lender insured by the federal government or a loan insured or guaranteed by the federal government that requires the services of an appraiser.

fee. Compensation, either as a fixed dollar amount or a percentage of the sale price.

FICO score. A proprietary numeric credit score used to evaluate a prospective borrower, developed by Fair, Isaacs, & Co.

fiduciary relationship. A relationship of trust and confidence between an agent and principal.

fixed-rate mortgage. A loan secured by real estate that has the same rate of interest for the life of the loan.

for-rent-by-owner (FRBO). An owner who attempts to rent his or her own property without using a broker.

for-sale-by-owner (FSBO). An owner who attempts to sell his or her own property without using a broker.

funding fee. A charge levied by the Department of Veteran's Affairs to veterans who use VA loans.

G

gross domestic product (GDP). The sum total of goods and services produced by the United States. The four major components of GDP are consumption, investment, government purchases, and net exports.

I

implied contract. An agreement not spelled out in words, where the agreement of the parties is demonstrated by their acts and conduct.

index. An indicator beyond the control of a lender to which the interest rate on an adjustable-rate mortgage is tied.

innocent purchaser status. An amendment to the Comprehensive Environmental Response, Compensation, and Liability Act (CERCLA) that exempts from liability landowners who made reasonable inquiries about hazardous substances before purchasing the property.

intangible tax. A tax of 2 mills (.002) levied on the amount of new mortgage indebtedness.

J

jargon. A word or expression related to a specific vocation or profession that a layperson may not understand.

K

keysafe. A lockbox holding the key to the home, usually attached to a door handle allowing licensees who are members of the MLS easy access to the property.

L

latent defects addenda. A disclosure by the seller that informs the seller of a duty to disclose known property defects and to hold the licensee harmless for the seller's failure to disclose.

leverage. The use of borrowed money with the intent to increase the investor's return on the cash invested. If the return on the investment is greater than the interest rate paid by the borrower, the owner has positive leverage.

liabilities. Amounts owed by a person.

listing agreement. An agreement between a seller and a broker whereby the seller agrees to pay the broker a commission if the broker is successful in selling the property.

loan processing procedures. Steps taken by a lender to ensure that underwriting and documentation of a mortgage loan are done in a manner that reduces the lender's exposure to loss.

loan underwriting. The evaluation of risk when a lender makes a mortgage loan to reduce the lender's exposure to loss.

lockbox. A secure box holding the key to the home, usually attached to a door handle allowing licensees who are members of the MLS easy access to the property by using a special access key to the box.

M

margin. The additional percentage added to the index on an adjustable-rate mortgage, resulting in the calculated interest rate.

marketing knowledge. A licensee's knowledge of the sales process, including the psychology of selling, advertising, personal marketing, and prospecting.

material fact. An important fact that may affect a buyer's decision to buy or a seller's decision to sell. Licensees must disclose facts that materially affect the value of residential property.

misrepresentation. A false or misleading statement made intentionally or unintentionally, or the failure to disclose a material fact.

mortgage insurance premium (MIP). The amount paid by a borrower for insurance that protects the lender against loss in case of the borrower's default. FHA mortgage insurance is called *MIP*.

mutual recognition. An agreement between states to recognize a licensee's education obtained in another state. Florida has mutual recognition agreements with several states that exempt licensees in those states from taking a Florida pre license course if the licensee can pass a 40-question test on Florida real estate law.

N

negative amortization. A situation occurring, usually under a graduated payment mortgage, where the payment on the loan is less than the amount required to pay the accrued interest. The unpaid interest is added to the principal balance of the loan, and the loan balance gradually increases.

net operating income (NOI). The income from an investment property remaining after operating expenses have been paid from the effective gross income.

net worth. The amount remaining when liabilities are subtracted from assets.

new construction maintenance. Work done on an income property designed to enhance the property's appeal to tenants. Includes adding new wallpaper, carpeting, and light fixtures.

No Brokerage Relationship Notice. A disclosure that must be given by a licensee who does not represent a buyer or seller before entering into an agreement or showing a property.

nonverbal communication. Unspoken communication expressed by the position of the body, hands, arms, legs, or facial expressions, commonly called *body language*.

O

open listing. A nonexclusive agreement in which a seller agrees to pay a broker if the broker sells the property. The broker is not paid if the seller or another broker sells the property.

operating expenses (OE). Costs of operating an income property. Includes property taxes, maintenance, insurance, payrolls, and reserves for replacements.

opinion of value. A broker's price opinion, usually based on a comparative market analysis.

option contract. An agreement that allows one party to buy, sell, or lease real property for specified terms within a specified time limit.

oral communications skills. The ability to speak effectively one-on-one or in a group presentation.

P

paperless mortgage. A mortgage that is "signed" electronically, using digital signatures.

passive prospecting. A method of prospecting that does not include direct face-to-face or telephone conversations. Advertising and direct mail are examples of passive prospecting.

performance. The completion of a contract's requirements.

PITI payment. The payment required of a borrower that includes principal, interest, taxes, and insurance.

point. A lender's charge to the borrower that increases the lender's yield. One point is equal to 1 percent of the loan amount.

potential gross income (PGI). The total annual income a property would produce if it were 100 percent occupied, with no vacancy or collection loss.

power prospecting. A type of prospecting that seeks to make contact with many more buyers and sellers and that results in much higher income levels.

preclosing walk-through inspection. An inspection of the house by the buyer, done sometime before the sale closes, to determine that the property is in the same condition as it was when the contract was signed and to ensure that all required repairs have been completed.

prequalification. The preliminary process during which a prospective lender evaluates the buyer's ability to obtain a mortgage loan. Most licensees want a buyer to be prequalified or preapproved before showing properties.

preventive maintenance. A work program designed to preserve the physical integrity of the premises and eliminate the more costly corrective maintenance.

previewing properties. The activity a licensee uses to stay abreast of the market and to find specific properties to show to a prospective buyer.

principal. (1) The person who enters into a fiduciary relationship with a single-agent licensee. (2) The amount of money remaining due on a mortgage loan.

prioritize. To set up a list of activities in an order based on their importance.

private mortgage insurance (PMI). The amount paid by a borrower for insurance that protects the lender against loss in case of the borrower's default. Conventional lenders use the term *private mortgage insurance;* FHA mortgage insurance is called *MIP.*

product knowledge. A licensee's familiarity with the real estate market and specific properties available for sale.

professional ethics. A body of accepted codes of behavior for a specific industry.

profit and loss statement. A detailed report of the income and expenses of an investment property over a stated period of time.

property characteristics. The features of a property that are used as a basis of comparison in an appraisal or comparative market analysis.

property condition disclosure. A form designed for disclosure to a buyer of any property defects. The form is normally signed by the seller, and the buyer signs a receipt that the buyer has received the disclosure.

Q

qualifying. The process used by a licensee to determine whether to spend time working with a buyer or seller. For example, a buyer would first be qualified financially, then based on motivation to buy.

quality of income. A lender's analysis of factors that reveal the likelihood of the borrower's income continuing over a long period of time.

quantity of income. The total amount of a borrower's income from all sources.

quasi-contract. A contract that is imposed by law to prevent unjust enrichment. For example, if a person's bank made an error in the person's favor, the quasi-contract invented by the courts would require that the person repay the bank.

R

radon gas. A colorless, odorless gas occurring from the natural breakdown of uranium in the soil. Many experts believe radon gas to be the second leading cause of lung cancer.

random changes. Irregular fluctuations of the economy that may be caused by legislative and judicial decisions, wars, weather, etc.

Real Estate Settlement Procedures Act (RESPA). A federal law requiring disclosure of loan closing costs in certain real estate financial transactions.

recession. Two successive quarterly declines in the gross domestic product (GDP). This is the point at which economic activity has peaked and will be followed by a contraction.

reconciliation. The final step in the appraisal process before the report is prepared. The correlation of property values derived from each of the three appraisal approaches into a single estimate of value.

recovery. Two successive quarterly increases in the gross domestic product (GDP). This is the point at which economic activity has bottomed and will be followed by expansion.

redlining. A lender's refusal to loan money in an area based on illegal discrimination.

refinancing. Placing a new mortgage on a property to replace another mortgage.

Regulation Z. The part of the Truth-in-Lending Act that requires that lenders calculate and disclose the effective annual percentage rate to the consumer.

reserves for replacements. A portion of an investment property's income that is set aside to pay the cost of replacing major building components when necessary.

resident manager. A salaried individual employed for specific management functions for a single investment property.

rider. An attachment to a contract.

routine maintenance. The most common maintenance performed on an investment property, such as grounds care and housekeeping.

S

sales contract (contract for sale and purchase). A bilateral agreement in which a buyer agrees to purchase a seller's property at a specified price and terms.

seasonal variation. Changes in the economy (for example, winter tourism in Florida) that recur at regular intervals at least once a year.

seller agency. The relationship of a single agent and his principal, the seller.

Seller's Net Proceeds Form. A form used to show the seller's equity, expenses, and prorations, as well as the net amount the seller is estimated to receive as proceeds from the sale of the property.

servicing the listing. The actions of a licensee who stays in touch with a seller regularly, getting feedback from licensees who have shown the property, sending the seller copies of advertisements, and generally keeping the seller informed of the marketing efforts.

show list. A selected inventory of apartments that are available for inspection by prospective tenants.

single agent. A broker who represents either the seller or the buyer in a real estate transaction, but not both.

Single-Agent Notice. A disclosure form informing the principal of the duties of his single agent.

specific cycles. Wavelike movements similar to business cycles that occur in specific sectors of the general economy, such as the real estate market.

static risk. Risk that is quantifiable and insurable. For example, the risk of fire is a static risk. Fire insurance will transfer the risk from the owner to the insurance company.

statute of frauds. A body of law that requires certain contracts, such as those for the sale of real property, to be written.

steering. The illegal, discriminatory act of a sales associate who brings buyers into an area based on the racial or ethnic makeup of the neighborhood.

subject property. The property being appraised.

T

targeted strangers. Persons not known to a licensee who are qualified as prospects by income, occupation, or residence address.

technical knowledge. The knowledge needed by licensees to properly conduct their business that relates to filling out contracts, preparing seller's proceeds estimates, doing comparative market analyses, etc.

time is of the essence. A contract clause that requires strict compliance with all dates and times specified in the contract. If a party fails to perform some act by the time specified, the person may be in default.

time management. The organization of a person's day to maximize efficiency. It includes planning, scheduling, and prioritizing.

title insurance. A guarantee to reimburse a loss arising from defects in title or liens against real property.

to-do list. A daily list, usually designed in priority order, of tasks to be completed that day.

transactional characteristics. The factors related to a real estate transaction itself, such as time of sale, and financing terms.

transaction broker. A licensee who has limited representation to the buyer and/or the seller in a transaction. Instead of being an advocate for the buyer or the seller, the licensee is working for the contract.

Truth-in-Lending Act. A federal law that requires that lenders inform consumers of exact credit costs before they make their purchases.

U

Uniform Standards of Professional Appraisal Practice (USPAP). Strict requirements for appraisers interpreted and amended by the Appraisal Standards Board. Florida appraisers and brokers who prepare appraisals must follow the guidelines.

unilateral contract. A contract in which only one of the parties is required to perform, such as an option contract. The optionor must sell if the optionee exercises the option, but the optionee is not required to buy.

W

warranty of owner. A hold harmless clause in a listing agreement whereby the seller warrants that all information given to the broker is correct.

written communication skills. The ability to communicate effectively in letters, e-mails, and other documents.

INDEX

POST-LICENSING EDUCATION FOR FLORIDA REAL ESTATE SALES ASSOCIATES
STUDENT FEEDBACK SURVEY

Thank you for using this text to complete your post-licensing education requirement. We would appreciate your taking time to help make this a better course. We will use your comments to make this text current, relevant, and useful.

Date: _____

A. At what school did you take this course? _____

B. When did you complete the course? Month: _____ Year: _____

C. Overall, I found the textbook to be ❑ excellent ❑ good ❑ fair ❑ poor

D. What new subject areas do you think should be added to future editions of the book?

_____

E. Is your license active or inactive? ❑ active ❑ inactive

F. Other comments concerning this text:

_____

_____

Thank you for your comments.

We will give them careful consideration when planning the next edition.

Post-Licensing Education for Florida Real Estate Sales Associates
Eighth Edition

NOTE: This page, when folded over and taped, becomes a postage-free envelope that has been approved by the United States Postal Service. It has been provided for your convenience.

Important—Please Fold Over and Tape Before Mailing

- -

Important—Please Fold Over and Tape Before Mailing

- -

Return Address:

_____

_____

_____

BUSINESS REPLY MAIL

FIRST CLASS MAIL   PERMIT NO. 38   LA CROSSE, WI

POSTAGE WILL BE PAID BY ADDRESSEE:

Dearborn™
Real Estate Education
332 FRONT ST S FL 5
LA CROSSE WI 54601-9817

Attn: Editorial Department

Notes